Rural County, Urban Borough

Rural County, Urban Borough

A History of Queens

JEFFREY A. KROESSLER

Rutgers University Press
New Brunswick, Camden, and Newark, New Jersey
London and Oxford

Rutgers University Press is a department of Rutgers, The State University of New Jersey, one of the leading public research universities in the nation. By publishing worldwide, it furthers the University's mission of dedication to excellence in teaching, scholarship, research, and clinical care.

Library of Congress Cataloging-in-Publication Data

Names: Kroessler, Jeffrey A., author.
Title: Rural county, urban borough : a history of Queens / Jeffrey A. Kroessler.
Description: New Brunswick, New Jesey : Rutgers University Press, 2025. |
   Includes bibliographical references and index.
Identifiers: LCCN 2024044623 | ISBN 9781978837812 (hardcover) |
   ISBN 9781978837829 (epub) | ISBN 9781978837836 (pdf)
Subjects: LCSH: Queens (New York, N.Y.)—History. | New York (N.Y.)—History.
Classification: LCC F128.68.Q4 K76 2025 | DDC 974.7/243—dc23/eng/20250207
LC record available at https://lccn.loc.gov/2024044623

A British Cataloging-in-Publication record for this book is available from the British Library.

Copyright © 2025 by Jeffrey A. Kroessler
All rights reserved

No part of this book may be reproduced or utilized in any form or by any means, electronic or mechanical, or by any information storage and retrieval system, without written permission from the publisher. Please contact Rutgers University Press, 106 Somerset Street, New Brunswick, NJ 08901. The only exception to this prohibition is "fair use" as defined by U.S. copyright law.

References to internet websites (URLs) were accurate at the time of writing. Neither the author nor Rutgers University Press is responsible for URLs that may have expired or changed since the manuscript was prepared.

♾ The paper used in this publication meets the requirements of the American National Standard for Information Sciences—Permanence of Paper for Printed Library Materials, ANSI Z39.48-1992.

rutgersuniversitypress.org

Dedicated to the memory of
Vincent Seyfried, Barry Lewis, and Richard C. Wade.
Each in his own way taught me to appreciate Queens.

Contents

	Preface	ix
	Introduction	1
	Part I Rural County	
1	Queens under the Dutch and the English	19
2	The Rural Landscape	45
3	The Railroad and Long Island	63
4	The Verdant Suburbs	101
5	The Noxious Industries	119
6	The Leisure Landscape	133
	Part II Urban Borough	
7	The Politics of Consolidation	163
8	The Queensboro Bridge	189
9	The Booming Borough	217
10	The Crisis of the Great Depression	241

11	Building the World of Tomorrow: Robert Moses and the New Deal Landscape	261
12	Prosperity and Stability in Postwar Queens	281
13	The Most Diverse Place on the Planet	311

Acknowledgments 331
Notes 335
Bibliography 367
Index 389

Preface

This book represents the culmination of years of dedicated research and extensive New York City preservation experience. Jeffrey Kroessler was the foremost expert on the history and preservation of his beloved Queens. He was working on the final edits for this manuscript the day he unexpectedly passed in early February 2023. As his wife, my role became to complete the final touches and coordinate for publication with the editor and staff at Rutgers University Press, who generously encouraged posthumous publication. I will contribute a general background to the book and its author.

Jeffrey studied under Richard C. Wade, the soul of urban liberalism, at the City University of New York (CUNY) Graduate School where his 1991 PhD dissertation was "Building Queens: The Urbanization of New York's Largest Borough." While a graduate student researching Queens, he became involved with local historical societies and preservation groups. His interest in Queens and its preservation has been unswerving and evolving since the 1980s. In 1987, he was already championing the importance of Queens and was quoted in an article published in the *New York Times* titled "Queens Cultivates Its Heritage" by David Dunlap. Jeffrey stated, "The historic heritage of Queens is denigrated because it doesn't have H. H. Richardson and Louis Sullivan. What it has are builders, ... This is a borough of homes and factories. There's nothing glamorous about that. But there's something historic. And unique."

Jeffrey realized early on the importance of Queens to the history and development of the City of New York as well as its relationship to Long

Island. He embraced this unique urban history often overlooked by scholars. His research led him to work to protect this history through writing, lecturing, and preservation. In 1990, he coauthored the first guide to preserving Queens's landmarks and neighborhoods. He cofounded the Queensborough Preservation League in 1995, participated in the successful effort to landmark the New York Architectural Terra Cotta Works Building in Long Island City, and spearheaded the successful campaign to designate the Sunnyside Gardens Historic District. Jeffrey was a trailblazer and a tireless advocate for Queens, its history, and its buildings.

Jeffrey's early studies and preservation work was complemented by his experience living in Queens—first in Forest Hills, then Astoria, and finally in historic Sunnyside Gardens. This background gave him the ideal tools to approach this final comprehensive history of the borough, which at its core owes much to his dissertation. But this history extends the timeline farther back and moves it past 1945 forward into the present, creating a four-hundred-year spread covering typically overlooked material. Beginning in the colonial era with "Queens under the Dutch and the English" and ending in the present with "The Most Diverse Place on the Planet," he successfully charts the history of Queens as uniquely positioned between Manhattan and Long Island. Of course, there are many additional sources for specific topics mentioned in this comprehensive manuscript. If readers have interest in time prior to the colonial era, Robert Grumet's *The Lenapes (Indians of North America)* would provide insight into the Native Americans of the region. For more detailed discussion of the conditions of slaves in New York, see *Root and Branch: African Americans in New York and East Jersey, 1613–1863* by Graham Hodges. For more specific local data, see the online searchable Northeast Slavery Records Index, which is part of the CUNY Academic Commons. *Rural County, Urban Borough* creates the overall historical narrative, providing avenues for further research on many specific topics.

From the outset, thanks go to the manuscript readers, Joshua B. Freeman and Stephen Petrus. Each gave the original manuscript a thorough and fair reading and each has offered insightful and worthy criticisms and suggestions. Interestingly, Joshua encouraged Jeffrey to begin the history earlier, and thus it starts with the colonial era, and Stephen recommended it extend to the present. Jeffrey readily embraced these suggestions. The result is, as Joshua stated, "the first, full-length, modern, scholarly study of the borough." Peter Mickulas, editor at Rutgers University Press, enthusiastically encouraged publication, which was inspiring, and his patience is much appreciated.

Jeffrey would want this book to be popular and easy to read with compelling images in an effort to share his appreciation of Queens with a wide audience.

"It is very sad that Jeffrey Kroessler did not live to see the publication of *Rural County, Urban Borough*," Joshua observed. "It is a major scholarly contribution and, in its own way, a love letter to the place where he long resided." But Jeffrey knew his life's work would enrich the resources available to all those who want to further delve into the remarkable, and previously understated, history of Queens.

Laura Heim

Rural County, Urban Borough

Introduction

Queens today is a crowded cityscape of dense urban neighborhoods and suburban sprawl served by commuter railroads and mass transit lines, congested highways, and international airports. With a population of about 2.4 million, it would rank as the nation's fourth-largest metropolis. Queens also possesses the most culturally, ethnically, linguistically, and religiously diverse population in the nation, and probably the world. In 1993, for example, three thousand adults registered for free English-language classes at the Queens Borough Public Library, representing eighty-two countries and speaking fifty-one languages. Students at Newtown High School in Elmhurst represented a hundred nationalities and spoke forty different languages. That is what teachers and administrators grapple with in the present, and that surely is the future of the United States itself.[1]

It is not possible to speak of the history of Queens in isolation, for its story is the story of New York City and the story of Long Island. The physical boundaries of what defines Queens uniquely evolved over time, originally including areas at the western edge of current Long Island, to become a defined borough of New York City. Queens is integral to the history of both, but too often it is only mentioned in passing. Long Island, the island where Queens is physically located, must be approached as a geographic whole, as opposed to political pieces, and that puts Queens in the center of the story. In the same way, the economic, cultural, and political power of Manhattan has always influenced Queens, even prior to being incorporated as a borough, and to a large extent determined patterns of growth and change. And yet, Queens is different in so many ways.

The largest of the five boroughs in area, Queens today is certainly a multicultural mosaic, but that is just the most recent chapter in a very long and very rich story. Queens has a history reaching back two and a half centuries before it became part of Greater New York in 1898. The land was settled soon after the founding of New Amsterdam, and its political, social, cultural, and economic destiny has always been closely tied to the growing city. At the same time, it is not possible to understand the city's past without incorporating Queens into the narrative. For most historians, urbanists, and political scientists, however, the history of Queens before consolidation is of scant significance. It is almost as if the borough emerged full grown from the head of Andrew Haswell Green, the "Father of Greater New York," for only from that point forward does Queens enter the main narrative of the city's history, and even then almost exclusively from the perspective of the expanding metropolis.

The Shape of the Land

Geography shaped the course of Long Island's history long before the first humans happened across its irregular topography. Today, whether a site was once swamp or prairie, whether it is located on the outwash plain or on the hilly North Shore, is less important than the quality of the built environment and the market value of the block and lot in question. The natural features that once determined the patterns of societal development and economic vitality have become largely irrelevant. The indigenous peoples who inhabited Long Island lived in communities adapted to the abundance of the land and sea. When the Dutch arrived in the seventeenth century, topography dictated the thrust of settlement.

Daniel Denton visited Jamaica, Long Island, in the seventeenth century and published the earliest and most glowing description of Queens. Denton noted that Long Island was covered with fine timber of many varieties, and "sends forth such a fragrant smell that it may be perceived at Sea before they can make the Land." He declared that its greatest blessing, "that which adds happiness to all the rest, is the Healthfulness of the place, where many people in twenty years time never know what sickness is."[2]

Running through the center of Long Island from the East River to the north fork is the terminal moraine, the southern limit of the glacier that covered North America in the last Ice Age. When the mile-high wall of ice melted, geological debris deposited as it retreated and formed the moraine, and the water rushed over the southern portion of the island creating the outwash plain, a uniformly level surface gradually sloping to the sea. Samuel L. Mitchill was one of the renowned men of science in New York and a member of the city's intellectual elite. In his 1807 guidebook, *The Picture of New-York; or The Traveller's Guide, through the Commercial Metropolis of the United States, by a Gentleman Residing in This City*, he provided a naturalist's description of the moraine:

> The face of the country, on the one side of this elevation, which may be called the Spine of the Island, is exceedingly different from that on the other. On the north side it is variegated, uneven, and very much diversified with hills and dales; while on the south, little else is discovered by the traveller than a flat surface, sloping gradually away toward the ocean. Stones and rocks are very frequent on the side next to the continent; but on the Atlantic side of the hills, a carriage may be driven many miles without the least impediment from them. Indeed, that tract which lies northward of the ridge, not only resembles the adjoining parts of the main land in its face and general appearance, but also in its fossils and mineral productions. It appears to have been separated from the continent, during the lapse of ages, by the encroachments of the salt water.[3]

The moraine marked the historic boundary between the towns of Flushing and Jamaica, and from the crest of the moraine one has an unrivaled view of the communities stretching southward to Jamaica Bay. These features determined that the population of southern Queens would look to Brooklyn for markets and as the gateway to Manhattan. Flushing, on the other hand, always sought direct communication with New York by water, bypassing the cumbersome overland route through Jamaica to the Brooklyn ferries.

Newtown Creek, a three-and a half mile waterway flowing into the East River, marks the boundary between Kings and Queens. From the head of that short waterway, the boundary headed southeast in a straight line. Where exactly to set the line was not finally settled until January 1769, when representatives of the towns of Newtown and Bushwick agreed to mark it by a great glacial boulder that came to be known as Arbitration Rock. The line was more clearly defined through surveys over the years, and the historic rock was forgotten. In 2000, a boulder that may or may not be Arbitration Rock was unearthed beneath Flushing Avenue in Ridgewood and relocated

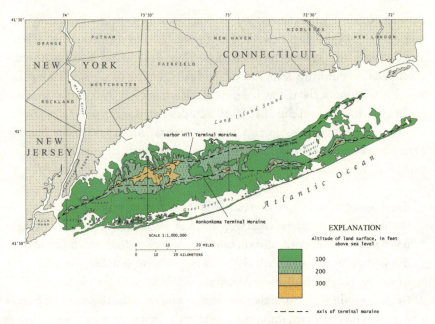

Terminal Moraines, Figure 62. (Courtesy of the U.S. Geological Survey.)

to the grounds of the adjacent Onderdonk House. While Kings and Queens remained rural, the straight line caused no problems, but the imposition of a street grid meant that the border cut diagonally through blocks, and even through rooms in a great many dwellings. The boundary was finally aligned with the grid in 1925.

On the North Shore, the retreating glacier cut several bays deep inland—Flushing Bay, Little Neck Bay, Manhasset Bay, Hempstead Harbor, and Oyster Bay—and these would shelter ships plying the coastal trade. In 1675, Little Neck Bay was set as the boundary between the towns of Flushing and Hempstead. Flushing Creek flowed north to the East River from the terminal moraine, a place called Head of the Fly, from the Dutch *vleigh* meaning "salt meadow." The expansive wetlands spread over thousands of acres and marked the historic boundary between the towns of Newtown and Flushing. This once navigable stream has all but vanished, its vestigial remains confined to concrete-lined channels in Flushing Meadows-Corona Park, the site of the 1939–1940 and 1964–1965 World's Fairs. Head of the Fly today is called Meadow Lake. In the early twentieth century, the pressures of urbanization transformed Flushing Meadows into the Corona Dumps, immortalized by F. Scott Fitzgerald in *The Great Gatsby* as the "valley of ashes."[4]

For travel on land, however, Flushing Creek proved an almost impenetrable barrier. There were no roads through the marsh until William Prince founded the first bridge company in 1800. Before then, according to a nineteenth-century historian, the only way across was in small rowboats powered by "two colored men."[5] Not surprisingly, most travelers from Flushing to New York went by boat down the East River rather than overland. A late-eighteenth-century advertisement for a grist mill in Flushing noted its location "on a fine creek, where a boat may be brought up to the side of the mill," adding that the site was "within the run of one tide from New York," an important consideration before the age of steam. Regular passage boat service had been initiated in the mid-eighteenth century, and the first steamer went into service in 1822.[6]

The South Shore is protected by a line of barrier islands stretching almost the entire length of Long Island. While the islands appear solid on the map, they are always changing. From the earliest European accounts down to the present, witnesses recorded how storms cut through the islands to create new channels into the bays, including Jones Inlet, Fire Island Inlet, and Shinnecock Inlet. The sweep of the ocean pushes sand from east to west, and as a result the Rockaway Peninsula has grown by about a mile westward.[7]

The predominant natural feature of southern Queens is Jamaica Bay, protected from the Atlantic by the Rockaway Peninsula. Streams flow south from the terminal moraine, yielding a landscape well suited to farming. The bay teemed with fish and shellfish; it attracted migratory waterfowl in spring and fall, and it yielded ample salt hay, prized for feeding livestock. The towns bordering Jamaica Bay—Jamaica and Hempstead in Queens and Flatlands in Kings County—had a proprietary interest in its resources and were always alert to ward off intruders. In 1763, the Jamaica town meeting resolved that "whereas divers persons, without any right or license so to do, have of late, with sloops, boats and other craft, presumed to come into Jamaica Bay and taken, destroyed and carried away quantities of clams, mussels and other fish, to the great damage of said town, this is to give warning to all persons who have no right or liberty that they do forbear to commit any such trespass in the bay for the future; otherwise they will be prosecuted at law." From the beginning, the town allotted farmers strips of marshland on islands in the bay to harvest the salt hay for their own use or for sale in the city. Even the barren strip of the Rockaway Peninsula was divided among the citizenry, the sand itself being a commodity valued in urban markets for cleaning floors and cooking utensils and for setting bricks and paving stones.[8]

By the late seventeenth century, dams had been erected along the streams feeding into Jamaica Bay to power sawmills and gristmills. In 1670, the Town of Jamaica agreed to build a "good dam for a mill, to be erected by Benj. Coe. He to grind the town's corn for the 12th [part of the total] (in preference to strangers), and they are to bring it such days as he may appoint." Today the path of one mill stream is directly under and along the Laurelton Parkway, one of the highways built with federal money during the New Deal.[9]

One road ran around Jamaica Bay leading to the beach, and already in 1791 "a light stage-wagon" pulled by "two good genteel horses with a careful driver" provided regularly scheduled service from Brooklyn ferry through to Rockaway, with a stop for refreshments in Jamaica. By 1800, Jeremiah Vanderbilt Jr. was advertising his hospitality at the Rockaway shore: "His house in a pleasant and healthy situation, is one hundred feet in front, with apartments for separate lodgings, and an airy dining room twenty by thirty-six feet, with six large windows. He has laid in a good stock of liquors of the first quality."[10]

The reputation of the area so advanced that Samuel L. Mitchill recommended Rockaway among his "Tours in the Neighborhood of New-York":

> There is a great scope for exercise on foot, on horseback, or in carriages; as the country is very level, and free from stones. There is as fine bathing in the surf, as is found in any place upon earth. And there are several houses of shelter, on the sea-side, for the accommodation of ladies and valetudinarians. At low-water, the surf-side of the beach is an excellent bottom to ride upon, and is equal to a turnpike road.
>
> The prospect of the unruffled ocean, is superb. All the vessels going in and out of New-York harbour, pass in sight. The lighthouse at Sandy-Hook, and the Neversunk hills are full in view. And the roaring and impetuosity of the waves, is sometimes truly sublime. In the adjoining bay, plenty of king-fish, sheep's head, and black-fish are to be taken, both in the seine and with the hook. And the variety of snipes, ducks, and plover, affords high gratification to shooting marksmen.[11]

Over the course of the nineteenth century, the Rockaway Peninsula remained a popular and relatively exclusive resort area, with grand hotels and large homes. The coming of the railroad in the late nineteenth century opened the beaches to day visitors, and the pace of change intensified.

The Hempstead Plain

The most unusual feature of the Queens landscape was the Hempstead Plains, a unique prairie extending over sixty thousand acres from the Town of Jamaica eastward, almost to Suffolk County. It was the only true, tall-grass prairie east of the Appalachians. The "Great Plains" stretched across what is now Nassau County, but there was also an area known as "Little Plains" in Jamaica. When the English took New Netherland from the Dutch in 1664, one of their earliest acts was to set a racecourse there, the beginnings of an enduring connection between Long Island and horse racing. Daniel Denton provided one of the first descriptions of this extraordinary landscape: "Towards the middle of Long-Island lyeth a plain sixteen miles long and four broad, upon which plain grows very fine grass, that makes exceedingly good Hay, and is very good pasture for sheep and other Cattel; where you shall find neither stick nor stone to hinder the Horse heels, or endanger them in their Races. There are two or three other small plains of about a mile square, which are no small benefit to those Towns which enjoy them."[12] Few Europeans had ever seen a landscape like it. An eighteenth-century writer noted, "There grows not a tree on it, and (it seems) never did; so that this is a singular curiosity in America, which strangers passing near are always shewn."[13]

Walt Whitman, a Long Island native, described that pastoral vista as he recalled it from his youth in about 1840:

> More in the middle of the island were the spreading Hempstead plains, then quite prairie-like, open, uninhabited, rather sterile, cover'd with killcalf and huckleberry bushes, yet plenty of fair pasture for the cattle, mostly milch-cows, who fed there by hundreds, even thousands, and at evening, (the plains too

Map of Hempstead Plains, Long Island, recently purchased by Mr. A.T. Stewart [1869], map on newsprint, Map No. L.I.-[1869].F1 (Map Collection, Brooklyn Public Library, Center for Brooklyn History.)

were own'd by the towns, and this was the use of them in common,) might be seen taking their way home, branching off regularly in the right places. I have often been out on the edges of these plains toward sundown, and can yet recall in fancy the interminable cow-processions, and hear the music of the tin or copper bells clanking far or near, and breathe the cool of the sweet and slightly aromatic evening air, and note the sunset.[14]

The poetic landscape Whitman gazed upon, however, was not the same landscape Denton observed. The plains had changed substantially over time, for generations of farmers let their livestock graze on the prairie, and the grasses, which had reached as high as six feet, were now close-cropped. Again, Mitchill offers an accurate description of this transformation: "It was naturally, or, at least, when the Europeans arrived, bare of trees, but covered with shrubbery and long grass. These have chiefly disappeared, except some andromedas, and plants of a smaller growth, on account of the vast herds of cattle and flocks of sheep with which it is pastured. The animals eat the plants very close, and give to this fine and neglected land a barren appearance." The ecology itself had changed, and many plant species, such as the bird's foot violet, which had once thrived in abundance were driven to the edges of the prairie, if not to extinction.[15]

Believing that "this great tract of land could never be cultivated" and that "nothing would grow upon it but the tall coarse grass which seems a native of the region," farmers had esteemed the plains as having "no value except to graze cattle, and feed half-wild Turkeys, (which last, by the way, are the best of the turkey kind which our country affords)." Thomas Gordon's 1836 *Gazetteer of the State of New York* notes that the "agricultural skill and means" of the first settlers "were inadequate to render it productive. Of late, experience has taught, that this is indeed a rich soil; treated with spent ashes, it produces crops of grain and grass scarce inferior to any in the Union." This revelation in the first decades of the 1800s "led to the taking in and enclosing of whole farms, the people regarding it as a kind of wasteland in which no one had so good a title as he who took possession and cultivated it." Looking ahead from midcentury, one observer envisioned "this extensive region of barren land, which was so long considered one of the wonders of the North American Continent," occupied by "highly cultivated fields and beautiful grass meadows." In 1845, the residents of the Town of Hempstead held in common only seventeen thousand acres of unenclosed land; by 1911 the prairie had shrunk to twelve thousand acres, and to barely six hundred by the 1960s. In 1988, the Nature Conservancy saved the last remnant, a nineteen-acre parcel squeezed between heavily traveled roads, and Nassau County later launched a modest effort to recover the prairie in Eisenhower Park around the edges of three golf courses, where ecologists are attempting to bring back the native grasses and remove the weed trees and shrubs that have established themselves.[16]

The memoirs of Frank Gray Griswold, a sportsman of renown among the fox-hunting set, provide additional evidence of this transformation in the last quarter of the nineteenth century. Referring to the Hempstead Plains, he praised the lay of the land as ideal for riding with the hounds, but also noted that "it was no child's play hunting hounds in Queens County, as the fences in those days were very big and strong, and there were many of them." With more than a touch of snobbery, Griswold mentioned that he "never has any trouble with the farmers. You can avoid those who object, and they were few in number. I found that if damages were promptly paid and broken fences mended, the American farmer, notwithstanding that he owns his land, seldom objects to hunting." An English visitor riding with the Queens County Hounds in 1892 described the plains at a moment early in the history of suburbanization: "The greater part of [Long Island's] interior is farming land and grassy plain—the former divided everywhere into fields of ten to twenty acres, or thereabouts, by means of strong timber-fences; the latter dotted here and there with villas, or boxes (as we might term them in the Old Country), belonging to the opulent citizens of New-York, who thus in their leisure hours attain country air and some country pursuits." The writer did not exaggerate the challenge of riding on the plain, as one newspaper account shows: "Another foxhunter sustained severe injuries in one of the meets of the Meadowbrook Hunt Club, his horse being thrown by its hoof catching the top rail of a high fence. The animal turned a complete somersault, falling upon its rider who suffered internal injuries."[17]

The Hempstead Plains shrank under agricultural pressures, as farmers appropriated the land for private use (hence the fences described by the huntsmen), but the prairie finally all but disappeared under the pressures of suburbanization, beginning in the 1870s with A. T. Stewart's planned community, Garden City—the "boxes" observed by the Englishman—and culminating in the archetypal postwar suburb, Levittown, which replaced the acres of potato fields that had displaced the native grasses.

Themes in the History of Queens

With the consent of the Dutch authorities in New Amsterdam, a group of Englishmen established the first settlement in what became Queens in 1642. While the Puritans in New England are presumed to be the standard-bearers of religious freedom, it was in the English villages of New Netherland where the principles of religious toleration and freedom of conscience were affirmed. William Penn founded the Quaker colony of Pennsylvania, but his Quaker friends established themselves in Flushing decades before the city of Philadelphia was laid out. Surely this story of religious freedom holds great relevance in the twenty-first century for such a religiously diverse borough.[18]

In 1683, almost twenty years after taking New Netherland from the Dutch, the English divided the province of New York into ten counties, with Queens, Kings, and Suffolk on Long Island. Queens stretched for twenty-six miles eastward from the East River to Suffolk County. The county contained five townships: Newtown, Flushing, Jamaica, Hempstead, and Oyster Bay. Each had a small village center serving the surrounding farmlands. Patriots in the northern part of Hempstead had declared their separation from that Loyalist-dominated town in 1775, and that break was formalized with the creation of North Hempstead in 1784.[19]

Beginning with the earliest Dutch settlements, the economy of Queens was integrated into New York's. At the same time, the inhabitants embraced a distinct identity as Long Islanders. With some of the richest farmland in the region, Queens became the city's breadbasket. The island's agricultural development responded directly to Manhattan's needs and was knit into the national and international markets beyond. With the opening of the Erie Canal in 1825, farmers turned from staples like wheat and corn to truck gardens. As late as 1900, Queens had the greatest agricultural output of any county in the nation. Even as the productive soil generated the county's wealth, as early as the 1850s manufacturers looked to Queens for new industrial sites. Many of these enterprises needed room to expand, but others were forced out of the central cities for being too dangerous, as was the case with oil refineries and storage facilities, or nuisances, such as distilleries, breweries, fertilizer plants, and chemical companies. Furthermore, regulation and political interference were negligible in Queens, and waste could flow directly into the waterways.

Each historical moment, each transformation stands out in such strong relief that Queens represents a textbook case of urbanization. The most intriguing question, however, is why this county, situated directly across the East River from Manhattan, urbanized so late, especially when compared with Brooklyn. Middle-class Victorian suburbs developed along the Long Island Railroad, but this suburban growth proceeded so haltingly that the incremental rise in the number of commuters could not ensure the railroad's profitability.

While the middle class invested in suburban Long Island, isolated from endemic urban ills, the city's working class found in Queens a playground. Residents of the city's congested immigrant neighborhoods fostered the growth of a leisure landscape in the county. Each Sunday thousands of city dwellers flocked to ball fields, racetracks, picnic grounds, amusement parks, beaches, and cemeteries. Over time, many of those visitors, or their children, became residents.

The history of Queens breaks neatly into two periods. Before joining Greater New York, the county grew slowly, with scattered suburban enclaves and industrial villages. After consolidation, urbanization advanced at a dizzying pace as the city invested in essential infrastructure—roads, sewers and water, schools, and the like. Queens was one of the fastest-growing counties in the nation in the first three decades of the twentieth century. In 1900, the borough's population stood at only 153,000. During the 1920s, the borough grew by more than 600,000, a number surpassing the total population of Baltimore, Pittsburgh, Buffalo, and most other American cities. In 1930, the population exceeded a million, and the borough ranked among the top fifteen manufacturing places in the nation.[20]

In effect, New York built a new city in Queens. Productive farmland rapidly disappeared under the dual pressures of real estate development and rising taxes. In large part, Manhattan's tax base financed the construction of new streets, sewers and water mains, schools, police precincts and fire stations. Today, we can scarcely imagine building the urban infrastructure for so many people in so short a time.

Outlying districts in Brooklyn, the Bronx, and Upper Manhattan also grew at a fantastic pace, becoming home to hundreds of thousands of New Yorkers while lowering the population density in the older tenement districts. The resulting low-density metropolis represents a marked contrast with the familiar urban patterns in Manhattan and Brooklyn and finally alleviated the endemic urban ills that had been the object of reformers since the mid-nineteenth century.

As the outer boroughs grew in the first half of the twentieth century, Manhattan gained its distinctive skyline. Most discussions of that transformation

View of Steinway Street, 1923. (Courtesy of the Queens Borough Public Library, Archives, Eugene L. Armbruster Photographs.)

focus on the origins of the skyscraper and its architectural evolution, and the rationale behind the 1916 zoning resolution and its effects. That iconic skyline came to define the city, but it was precisely as those skyscrapers were rising that mile after mile of low-density, low-rise row houses and single-family homes were built in Queens, Brooklyn, and the Bronx. Indeed, the common experience for many New Yorkers during that period was the suburban home, the thousands of one- and two-family, wood-frame and brick row houses built in new neighborhoods across the boroughs. The story of the development of Queens illuminates the question of metropolitan, as opposed to strictly urban, expansion.

In the late 1920s, the feverish economic boom began to cool, and the impact of the Great Depression was as severe in Queens as in any other place. The relatively high level of homeownership in the borough meant that thousands of families saw their dreams foreclosed. When Franklin Roosevelt opened the federal treasury for a massive public works program, New York City reaped the benefits of the New Deal's largess, and few places benefited more than Queens. New Deal agencies financed construction of the borough's twentieth-century infrastructure: highways, bridges and tunnels, an airport, public housing, and parks. The 1939 World's Fair, "Building the World of Tomorrow," brought together the country's largest corporations and government agencies to present a glowing vision of the nation's future. The Fair rose atop the infamous Corona Dumps, the city's largest landfill. Parks Commissioner Robert Moses had promised a metamorphosis "from dump to glory," and he delivered with the final piece of the New Deal landscape.

The development of Queens in the first half of the twentieth century looked as much toward the suburban future as it did toward the historic patterns of urban growth exemplified by the older tenement districts and rowhouse neighborhoods built during the nineteenth century in Manhattan and Brooklyn. It is this break with the historic patterns of New York's growth that makes the urbanization of Queens so crucial to any interpretation of the metropolis in the twentieth century. By all measures—population density, homeownership, families per household, age of housing—the emerging borough of Queens differed from Manhattan, Brooklyn, and the Bronx, even at moments of simultaneous growth.

After 1945, Queens resumed its impressive growth as the last remaining agricultural acres began sprouting new homes. Today the only remnant of the county's rich agriculture heritage is the Queens County Farm Museum close to the Nassau County line.[21] As mass transit spurred development in earlier decades, widespread automobile ownership fostered this new growth spurt. Queens added a quarter million residents in the 1940s, and another quarter million in the 1950s. In no small measure, this growth was made possible by the infrastructure completed under Robert Moses in the 1930s to accommodate the automobile. Together with his parks, including the opening of public golf courses and the rehabilitation of beaches and boardwalks, Moses had well prepared the ground for the county's middle-class destiny.

During the 1950s and 1960s, thousands of single-family homes, row houses, garden apartments, and massive apartment buildings went up. The population was also evolving. The wave of European immigration ended in the 1920s, and their children were now moving out to the suburbs and beyond. While ethnic neighborhoods maintained their character, the main thrust of change was assimilation rather than a reinforcement of ethnic identities.

The postwar decades also brought an evolving racial landscape. Blacks, both slave and free, had been resident in Queens almost from the beginning, but the Great Migration brought many thousands of newcomers from the rural South to the urban North. Just as whites moved up from crowded tenements in Manhattan and Brooklyn to suburban Queens, so too did

Blacks aspire to this American dream. The suburban enclave of Addisleigh Park in the southeast corner of the borough attracted an African American aristocracy. Many jazz musicians called the neighborhood home, Lena Horne, Ella Fitzgerald, and Count Basie among them. Louis Armstrong and his wife, meanwhile, lived in a modest home in Corona. It is now a museum, kept as it was when they lived there.[22] Still, the housing options for most African Americans were rather limited, as many of the attractive new developments like Fresh Meadows and Lefrak City excluded Blacks.

The advent of new federally funded public housing ushered in a new form of segregation. New housing projects in Astoria, Flushing, and the Rockaways were not intended to warehouse minorities, but by the 1980s they were predominately home to African Americans, segregated by income no less than race. At the same time, ascendant urban liberalism sought to transcend the racial dilemma. In 1963, Rochdale Village opened on the site of the old Jamaica Racetrack. With 5,800 apartments, it was the largest cooperative apartment complex in the world. More than that, however, it had been built as a model of racial integration.[23] For a moment, that dream was realized, but high ideals could not counter the inevitable movement of the white middle class to the suburbs. Crime in the surrounding neighborhood also doomed this experiment in integrated living. Just a few years later, a proposal for a large public housing project in Forest Hills met with obstinate resistance.

The 1960s and 1970s were decades of turmoil, as American cities experienced social, cultural, and economic crises. Queens was not immune, as evidenced by the "lovable bigot" Archie Bunker of *All in the Family*, a situation comedy that went on the air in 1971.[24] All America recognized Archie as representative of blue-collar Queens, an ordinary family man attempting to cope with a world changing around him. His city was beset by racial conflict, rising crime, deteriorating infrastructure, and declining municipal services. Many New Yorkers fled, but the Bunkers stayed. And in truth, New York was in decline. Jamaica Avenue, once the borough's most vibrant shopping and entertainment hub, lost business to new shopping malls, and many whites, alarmed at the area's changing complexion, avoided the place entirely. The 1970s saw an unprecedented decline in the city's population, a drop of over eight hundred thousand; even Queens lost a hundred thousand residents. At the time, it was not unreasonable to view that decline not as an aberration, but as New York's permanent and irreversible condition.

But unlike other cities, New York did not continue on its downward spiral. The city recovered more rapidly and more spectacularly than critics, policy makers, and academics could have imagined. Queens did not decline as sections of Brooklyn and the Bronx did, and escaped the widespread housing abandonment that consumed some neighborhoods there. Two main factors protected Queens from decay. First, Queens was characterized by a high degree of homeownership in all neighborhoods, and property owners have a particular interest in keeping their neighborhoods viable.

The second factor was the Immigration and Nationality Act of 1965, also known as the Hart-Cellar Act. An unheralded aspect of Lyndon Johnson's Great Society when enacted, this bill saved Queens—and all of New York City. When *All in the Family* went on the air, the borough's white population comprised 85 percent of the total, and Blacks numbered 13 percent. Asians and Hispanics together made up a scant 2 percent of the residents. Half a century later, the (albeit flawed) 2020 U.S. census revealed a county of unrivaled diversity. The non-Hispanic white population had contracted to less than a quarter of the total, and Blacks comprised 17 percent; by contrast, the Asian population had jumped to 27 percent and Hispanics 28 percent. Such crude racial categorization masks the diversity of places from which the new residents originated, and those percentages are further muddied by the tens of thousands of people identifying as "mixed-race," a new kind of assimilation.[25] What revitalized Queens was not diversity in and of itself; it was the investment of these newcomers in homes and businesses and their commitment to their new home.

This brief summary of the growth of Queens touches upon many of the major themes in the nation's history: agriculture, industrialization, immigration, transportation, suburbanization, urban planning, the changing role of the federal government, and the rise and decline of urban liberalism. In its details, the history of Queens illuminates these issues while also enhancing and filling out the story of New York City. The question is how

Liberty Avenue, Jamaica, 2018. (Laura Heim Architect.)

to integrate the story of Queens into the story of the metropolis. It is scarcely possible to write a history of the city without acknowledging that the farms of Queens fed the city's populace and that the city's street sweepings—manure—fertilized those farms; that Brooklyn found its water supply in the ponds and streams of southern Queens; that working-class families found in Queens leisure spots denied them in Manhattan and Brooklyn; that the city's manufacturers found vacant land removed from complaints about obnoxious pollutants; that housing reformers found a field to put their ideas into practice; that Queens boasts the best examples of the New Deal's public works programs and pointed toward the city's transformation by the automobile; that the urban decay that characterized urban America in the 1960s, 1970s, and 1980s was arrested by the arrival of hundreds of thousands of new immigrants. In sum, Queens reveals the great arc of American urban history.

Rural Country, Urban Borough is primarily a history of place, of the transformation of the Queens landscape. While I analyze population growth over the centuries, I have not attempted to compile an in-depth demographic history, documenting the ethnic and racial changes over the decades and describing the resulting tensions and achievements. That would be a book in itself. Nor is this a political history, an analysis of voting patterns, parties, and elected officials. In the main, I have endeavored to chronicle how Queens has been used, and abused, by those seeking homes, work, and wealth; and how its relationship with the city has evolved.

Queens today is thriving, welcoming families from all parts of the world who seek the American Dream. How can the borough absorb an even larger influx of newcomers and maintain its character? Given its unparalleled diversity, does Queens even have a defining character? Or will it undergo another as yet unimagined transformation? These are the questions for the decades to come.

Part 1

Rural County

1

Queens under the Dutch and the English

After many years of trading voyages and seasonal encampments along the Hudson River, the Dutch founded the permanent settlement of New Amsterdam in 1626. A venture of the Dutch West India Company, the purpose was purely economic. The pattern of growth in New Netherland stood in sharp contrast with the story of New England. In the two decades after the landing of the Pilgrims in 1620, thousands of English arrived, a great many of them Puritans and other religious dissenters. They saw the opportunity for wealth through their stout efforts, but the motivation for many of them was distinctly religious.

From the beginning New Netherland was different. It was avowedly commercial in nature, and while all of the original inhabitants were Protestants, religion was at best a secondary consideration. Further, while the inhabitants of New England were almost entirely of English stock, New Netherland was diverse and worldly. Writing in 1646, three years after his rescue from cruel captivity among the Mohawks, Father Isaac Jogues, a French Jesuit, wrote that in and around Manhattan "there may well be four or five hundred men of different sects and nations" speaking eighteen different languages. "No religion is publicly exercised but the Calvinist,

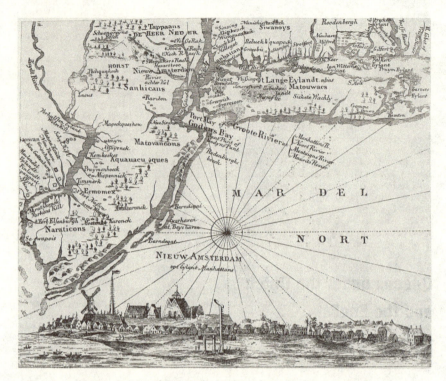

Adriaen van der Donck, *Map of New Netherlands, with a view of New Amsterdam, (now New-York) A.D. 1656.* (The New York Public Library Digital Collections, The Miriam and Ira D. Wallach Division of Art, Prints and Photographs: Picture Collection.)

and orders are to admit none but Calvinists, but this is not observed, for there are, besides Calvinists, in the colony Catholics, English Puritans, Lutherans, Anabaptists, here called Muistes &c." Unlike New England, which rapidly grew in population, New Amsterdam struggled to attract migrants, and the Dutch, while the majority, were part of a polyglot community.

A decade after the founding of New Amsterdam, the Dutch established a presence on Long Island. When they first explored the place, they followed the Native American trails and found the fertile land densely cultivated with fields of corn across what is now Kings County. Individuals purchased tracts along Wallabout Bay, Gowanus, Flatlands (originally Amersfoort), Flatbush (Mitwout), and what is now downtown Brooklyn (Breukelen).[1] Not until the 1640s were villages established in Queens, and almost all of the newcomers were English, not Dutch.

English Towns in New Netherland

In 1642, with the consent of the Dutch authorities in New Amsterdam, Reverend Francis Doughty and his Presbyterian congregation from Massachusetts established the first settlement in what became Queens at the head of Newtown Creek, a place the indigenous inhabitants called Mespat (today's Maspeth). The fledgling settlement was abandoned the next year when war erupted between the Dutch and the Native Americans, but settlement proceeded swiftly after the end of hostilities. Other Englishmen, many arriving from New England, received charters for Hempstead in 1644, Vlissingen (Flushing) in 1645, and Rustdorp (Jamaica) in 1656.

The population of New Amsterdam was predominantly Dutch, but on Long Island, the towns in what became Queens, though part of New Netherland, were largely English; the towns in what became Kings had more Dutch inhabitants. The Dutch never controlled the east end, which was settled by New Englanders.

Freedom of Conscience

The 1640 charter for the Dutch colony decreed that "no other Religion shall be publicly admitted in New Netherland except the Reformed, as it is at present preached and practiced by public authority in the United Netherlands; and for this purpose the [Dutch West India] Company shall provide and maintain good and suitable preachers, schoolmasters, and comforters of the sick." This followed the law in the Netherlands, which established the Reformed Church as the state religion. Still, religious toleration was greater there than in any other place in Europe. Adherents of dissident sects were permitted freedom of conscience, but their public worship was officially banned. Enforcement was generally soft, however, and many were able to do so. Those who arrived in New Netherland expected the same degree of toleration, but it was not so.[2]

Peter Stuyvesant replaced Willem Kieft as director general of New Netherland in 1647. A seasoned military veteran and a strict Calvinist, Stuyvesant was intent upon restoring order in the unruly colony. A key part of his campaign was to uphold the official status of the Reformed Church and suppress all religious dissent. His first test came in 1654, when the first Jews arrived, refugees from the Dutch colony in Brazil, which had fallen to the Portuguese.

Dominie Johannes Megapolensis wrote to the authorities in Amsterdam, noting the intolerable religious diversity in the province and requesting that the Jews be denied the right to settle. "We have here Papists, Mennonites and Lutherans among the Dutch," he explained, "also many Puritans or Independents, and many Atheists and various other servants of Baal among the English under this Government, who conceal themselves under the name of Christians; it would create still further confusion, if the obstinate and immovable Jews came to live here." While directors reiterated the primacy of the established church, the West India Company was also concerned with the economic viability of the province. They replied that as much as it may have been wished that the Jews had not arrived, banning them "would be somewhat unreasonable and unfair, especially because of the considerable loss sustained by this nation, with others, in the taking of Brazil, as also because of the large amount of capital which they still have invested in the shares of this company." They were permitted to stay on the same grounds as other minorities—free to practice in private, but denied the right to public worship.[3]

In early 1656, Stuyvesant issued a proclamation reinforcing the status of the official church by prohibiting preachers "not having been called thereto by ecclesiastical or temporal authority," so as to "promote the glory of God, the increase of the Reformed religion, and the peace and harmony of the country." Unlicensed preachers and those who attended their services would be subject to fines. The director general's proclamation contained a significant exception, however, disclaiming "any prejudice to any patent heretofore given, and lording over any conscience, or any prohibition of the reading of God's holy word, and the domestic praying and worship of each one in his family."[4]

The edict was specifically aimed at the small Lutheran congregation, and they were not slow in protesting to the West India Company. In June, the authorities in Amsterdam wrote to Stuyvesant that they preferred not to have heard these complaints, "because it has always been our intention to let them enjoy all calmness and tranquility." They admonished Stuyvesant and directed that he should "not hereafter publish any similar placards without our previous consent, but to allow all the free exercise of their religion within their own house." Disregarding this order, he persisted in harassing the Lutherans, so that in July 1657 the Reverend Johannes Gutwasser went into hiding, where he remained for two years until illness forced him out. He was soon deported.[5]

The issue of freedom of conscience came to a head with the English towns on Long Island. While the Jews and Lutherans were few in number, the

English were the majority in those towns and efforts to prohibit their public worship were met with resistance. The arrival of a new dissident sect in 1657 and their welcome among the English brought the issue to the fore.

The ship *Woodhouse* arrived on August 1 that year with eleven Quakers on board. Six continued on to Rhode Island, where they found safety, and Puritan New England, where they faced condemnation, torture, and death. Two days later Mary Weatherhead and Dorothy Waugh "went into the streets and publicly exhorted the people." A Reformed minister described the events in a letter to the Classis of Amsterdam:

> A ship came from the sea to this place, having no flag flying from the topmast, nor from any other part of the ship. . . . They fired no salute before the fort. When the master of the ship came on shore and appeared before the Director-General, he rendered him no respect, but stood with his hat firm on his head as if a goat. At last information was gained that it was a ship with Quakers on board. We suppose they went to Rhode Island for that is the receptacle of all sorts of riff raff people and is nothing else than the sewer of New England. They left behind two strong young women. As soon as the ship had departed they began to quake and go into a frenzy, and cry out loudly in the middle of the street that men should repent, for the day of judgment was at hand. Our people not knowing what was the matter ran to and fro while one cried fire and another something else. The Fiscal seized them both by the head and led them to prison.

For eight days the women continued their rantings, then they were led from their "separate noisome dungeons" with hands tied and deported to Rhode Island.[6]

The others, Robert Hodgson, Richard Doudney, and Sarah Gibbons, visited the English towns of Gravesend, Rustdorp (now Jamaica), and Hempstead. At Hempstead, Hodgson made known that he would hold a meeting in a nearby orchard on the ninth of August. While pacing among the trees to gather his thoughts, he was arrested by the local magistrate and confined in the man's house. Hodgson later wrote that when the magistrate "went to his worship many staid and heard the truth declared," for he preached from a window in the room where he was confined. This impromptu gathering was later recognized as the first meeting of the Society of Friends in New Netherland.

Stuyvesant sent an armed company to drag Hodgson to New Amsterdam. He was thrown into a small room in the Stadt Hus, a dungeon "full of vermin . . . so odious, for wet and dirt, as I never saw." Sentenced to a fine of 600 guilders or two years chained to a wheelbarrow working alongside a

Black slave, he refused to submit. Denied food, he was hung by his hands with weights on his feet and severely beaten. Only intervention by Stuyvesant's sister ended Hodgson's five-week ordeal, and like the others, he was deported to Rhode Island.[7]

Wishing to eliminate the sect from the province, Stuyvesant proclaimed that anyone who sheltered Quakers even for one night would be fined 50 florins, with half to go to the informer, and ordered the seizure of any ship carrying Quakers into New Amsterdam. The English residents of Flushing, most of them recent arrivals from New England, defied the edict. Encompassing about sixteen thousand acres, the town of Vlissingen, or Flushing, received its patent in 1645. The original patentees belonged to no single denomination, and their charter guaranteed them the right "to have and enjoy liberty of conscience, according to the custom and manner of Holland, without molestation or disturbance from any magistrate that may pretend jurisdiction over them."[8]

At a town meeting in the home of Michael Milner on December 27, 1657, Edward Hart, the town clerk, prepared a remonstrance to be presented to Stuyvesant. Few if any of the men who signed their names were members of the Society of Friends, though several had signed the original patent twelve years before. Tobias Feake, the town sheriff, journeyed to New Amsterdam to deliver the statement.[9]

The document offered two arguments justifying their opposition. First, the order to reject the Quakers conflicted with their faith. They could not "condemn them in this case, neither can we stretch out our hands against them, for out of Christ God is a consuming fire, and it is a fearful thing to fall into the hands of the living God. Wee [sic] desire therefore in this case not to judge least we be judged, neither to condemn least we be condemned, but rather let every man stand or fall to his own Master." Where the laws of the state conflict with the demands of faith, they asserted their obligation to follow their conscience. Secondly, they pointed to the guarantee of religious liberty in their original patent. The document concluded: "Therefore if any of these said persons come in love unto us, we cannot in conscience lay violent hands upon them, but give them free egresse and regresse unto our Town, and houses, as God shall persuade our consciences, for we are bounde by the law of God and man to doe good unto all men and evil to noe man. And this is according to the patent and charter of our Towne, given unto us in the name of the States General, which we are not willing to infringe, and violate, but shall houlde to our patent and shall remaine, your humble subjects, the inhabitants of Vlishing."

Stuyvesant was enraged. He arrested Feake and ordered the arrest of two town magistrates, William Noble and Edward Farrington. Feake was fined 200 guilders as the leader of the group who signed "the seditious and detestable" document and for defending "that heretical and abominable sect called Quakers." The men defended their act, but at the same time pledged "to offend no more in that kind." Hart stated that this was not the opinion of any one individual, but reflected "the general votes of the inhabitants." He languished in jail for three weeks before his neighbors secured his release. He penned an apology, but bid Stuyvesant "for your mercy, not your judgment." The director general then attempted to alter the town's charter and demanded that all residents be taxed twelve stuivers to support a clergyman, presumably not a Quaker.[10]

The Flushing Remonstrance

Right Honorable

You have been pleased to send unto us a certain prohibition or command that we should not receive or entertain any of those people called Quakers because they are supposed to be, by some, seducers of the people. For our part we cannot condemn them in this case, neither can we stretch out our hands against them, for out of Christ God is a consuming fire, and it is a fearful thing to fall into the hands of the living God.

Wee desire therefore in this case not to judge least we be judged, neither to condemn least we be condemned, but rather let every man stand or fall to his own Master. Wee are bounde by the law to do good unto all men, especially to those of the household of faith. And though for the present we seem to be unsensible for the law and the Law giver, yet when death and the Law assault us, if wee have our advocate to seeke, who shall plead for us in this case of conscience betwixt God and our own souls; the powers of this world can neither attach us, neither excuse us, for if God justifye who can condemn and if God condemn there is none can justifye.

And for those jealousies and suspicions which some have of them, that they are destructive unto Magistracy and Ministerye, that cannot bee, for the Magistrate hath his sword in his hand and the Minister hath the sword in his hand, as witnesse those two great examples, which all Magistrates and Ministers are to follow, Moses and Christ, whom God raised up maintained and defended against all enemies both of flesh and spirit; and therefore that of God will stand, and that which is of man will come to nothing. And as the Lord hath taught Moses or the civil power to give an outward liberty in the state, by the law written in his heart designed for the good of all, and can truly judge who is good, who is evil, who is true and who is false, and can pass definitive sentence of life or death against that man which arises up against the fundamental law of the States General; soe he hath made his ministers a savor of life unto life and a savor of death unto death.

The law of love, peace and liberty in the states extending to Jews, Turks and Egyptians, as they are considered sons of Adam, which is the glory of the outward state of Holland, soe love, peace and liberty, extending to all in Christ Jesus, condemns hatred, war and bondage. And because our Saviour sayeth it is impossible but that offences will come, but woe unto him by whom they cometh, our desire is not to offend one of his little ones, in whatsoever form, name or title hee appears in, whether Presbyterian, Independent, Baptist or Quaker, but shall be glad to see anything of God in any of them, desiring to doe unto all men as we desire all men should doe unto us, which is the true law both of Church and State; for our Saviour sayeth this is the law and the prophets.

Therefore if any of these said persons come in love unto us, we cannot in conscience lay violent hands upon them, but give them free egresse and regresse unto our Town, and houses, as God shall persuade our consciences, for we are bounde by the law of God and man to doe good unto all men and evil to noe man. And this is according to the patent and charter of our Towne, given unto us in the name of the States General, which we are not willing to infringe, and violate, but shall houlde to our patent and shall remaine, your humble subjects, the inhabitants of Vlishing.

Written this 27th of December in the year 1657, by mee.
Edward Hart, Clericus

The Remonstrance was not the end. In early 1658, Dutch Reformed ministers wrote to the Classis in Amsterdam informing them of the situation. "The raving Quakers have not settled down," they complained, "but continue to disturb the people of this province by their wanderings and outcries." Undoubtedly, the commercial-minded citizens of New Amsterdam did not relish such interruptions, preferring to be left alone in their pursuit of gain. Continuing, the ministers explained, "For although our government has issued orders against these fanatics, nevertheless they do not fail to pour forth their venom. There is but one place in New England where they are tolerated and that is Rhode Island which is the *caaca latrina* [sewer] of New England."[11]

Though the director general issued further edicts against the Quakers, the English towns remained obstinate. In 1661, the ministers learned that Henry Townsend had permitted meetings in his home in Rustdorp; he was twice fined before being arrested and sentenced to banishment. Stuyvesant then appointed the informers—Richard Everett, Nathaniel Denton, and Andrew Messenger—as town magistrates. They pledged "that if any meeting or conventicles of Quakers shall be in this town of Rustdorp that we know of, then we will give information to the authority set up in this place by the governor, and also assist the authority of the town against any such person or persons called Quakers as needs shall require." Twelve of their neighbors signed, but six men refused and soldiers were then quartered in their homes. The following year, the magistrate reported that the majority of the town's inhabitants were Quakers, and, according to one sympathetic history, "the absurd order was sent to the constable to arrest all such persons."[12]

John Bowne, "a plain, strong-minded English farmer," built his home in Flushing in 1661, and his arrest the following year brought this simmering conflict to a climax. Bowne's wife had been one of the first adherents of the sect in the province, and Bowne permitted the Quakers to use his home for their meetings. The authorities in Rustdorp informed Stuyvesant, as they had pledged, and on September 14 Bowne was fined 25 Flemish pounds and threatened with banishment. He refused to pay and was imprisoned in the fort. For emphasis, Stuyvesant issued a new edict banning the public exercise of any religion but the Dutch Reformed "in houses, barns, ships, woods, or fields." Penalties started at a fine of 50 guilders, which doubled and quadrupled for subsequent offenses, and permitted "arbitrary correction."[13]

Bowne remained obdurate. At one point, Stuyvesant permitted him to visit his family for three days, fully expecting him to flee. But Bowne returned. Finally, "for the welfare of the community, and to crush as far as possible that abominable sect who treat with contempt both the political magistrates and the ministers of God's holy word, and endeavor to undermine the police and the religion," the council ordered Bowne, "if he continues obstinate," to be deported "in the first ship ready to sail, for an example to others." In January 1663, he was put aboard the *Gilded Fox* with only the clothes on his back.[14]

Put ashore at the first port in England, Bowne made his way to Amsterdam, where he brought his case before the directors of the Dutch West India Company. He argued, "For which of you, being taken by force from your wife and family (without just cause), would be bound from returning to them, unless upon terms to act contrary to your conscience and deny your

John Bowne House, 1923. (Courtesy of the Queens Borough Public Library, Archives, Eugene L. Armbruster Photographs.)

faith and religion, yet this (in effect) do you require of me and not less." Holding to his conscience was "the very cause for which I rather chose freely to suffer want of the company of my dear wife and children, imprisonment of my person, the ruin of my estate in my absence there, and the loss of my goods here, than to yield or consent unto such an unreasonable act as you would hereby enjoin me unto. For which I am persuaded you will not only be judged in the sight of God, but by good and godly men."[15]

In a remarkably short time after Bowne presented his case, the West India Company rendered a decision. They vindicated Bowne and in a dispatch dated April 16 so informed Stuyvesant. While acknowledging the commercial nature of their enterprise, the company emphasized the great principle at stake:

> Although it is our anxious desire that similar and other sectarians not be found among you, yet we *doubt* extremely the policy of adopting rigorous measures against them. In the youth of your existence, you ought rather to encourage than check the population of the colony. The *conscience* of men ought to be *free* and *unshackled* so long as they continue moderate, peaceable,

inoffensive, and not hostile to the government. Such have been the maxim of prudence and toleration by which the magistrates of this city [Amsterdam] have been governed; and the consequences have been that the oppressed and *persecuted* from every country have found among us an *Asylum* from distress. *Follow the same steps, and you will be blessed.*[16]

Two years after his deportation, Bowne finally returned home, arriving after the English had taken New Amsterdam and renamed it New York. Peter Stuyvesant remained in the city even after surrendering the colony—he owned considerable property, after all—and Bowne encountered him on the street. By all accounts the former director general was contrite and admitted that his treatment of the Quakers had been unjust and that they had proved to be contributing members of the community. Significantly, when the English took the city, the articles of capitulation guaranteed that "the Dutch here shall enjoy the liberty of their Consciences in Divine Worship and Church discipline."[17]

As for Bowne, he remained a leader of the community. In 1672 he welcomed George Fox, the founder of the Society of Friends, to Flushing. Fox preached to a crowd of hundreds near the Bowne House under what became known as the Fox Oaks. The oaks are gone, but a stone marker identifies the spot. Bowne later hosted William Penn in his home, and led his neighbors in building the Quaker Meeting House nearby. Completed in 1694, the wooden structure continues to serve an active Quaker meeting place. Bowne's descendants continued to live in the house into the twentieth century, when it became a museum.[18]

Lessons drawn from the experience of the Flushing Quakers over the centuries have reflected their times, from a moment in the line of resistance to arbitrary authority culminating in the Revolution to the imperious individual threatening the rights of free men to a parable of the evils of totalitarianism in the aftermath of World War II and the era of the Cold War. In each iteration, the story was held up as an expression of the values that made America.

An 1843 volume claimed that "individuals entertaining the opinions of the Quakers ... became victims of that odious intolerance so disgraceful to any government, and which, beyond all question, had a principal agency in bringing about the overthrow of the Dutch power in 1664." (Actually, it was an English fleet.) Continuing, the author stated that "these revolting scenes, in which it was basely attempted to circumscribe the exercise of religious liberty, by public authority, took place between the years 1650 and 1664, when the arbitrary disposition could no longer be indulged." Another

Flushing Meeting House as enlarged in 1717; view from Northern Boulevard ca. 1895. (Ann Gidley Lowry, *The Story of the Flushing Meeting House* [1939], Jeffrey Kroessler Archive.)

mid-nineteenth-century historian described the events as "a gross violation of the rights of conscience." By contrast, a history of New Netherland published in 1978 justified the banishment of John Bowne as a "reasonable solution," at least when considering the tortures endured by Quakers in Puritan New England.[19]

The Pageant of Flushing Town, a preachy amateur theatrical staged in 1937 to mark the centennial of the founding of the village, celebrated how their forefathers defied tyranny: "The Sword of the Spirit—their only weapon from the spiritual armory. They gather now to read before him their Remonstrance 'gainst their peoples wrongs." The playwright declared, "Justice is not settled by legislators and laws—it is in the Soul."[20]

The tercentenary of the founding of Flushing offered an opportunity for a reinterpretation of its history in 1945. The Bowne House Historical Society purchased the house from the sisters Anna and Bertha Parsons, direct descendants of John Bowne. In 1945, the home was dedicated as a "National Shrine of Religious Freedom," and Mayor Fiorello LaGuardia delivered a radio address from the parlor. "This is a shrine, he said." "It belongs to our city, because it made so much history here, of endurance and fortitude. It belongs to our country because it is typical of America, and it belongs to the world because it is a symbol of what the world is looking for today." After Edward R. Murrow's broadcasts describing Buchenwald and the publication of photographs of the concentration camps, no one hearing LaGuardia could doubt the meaning of his words. One of the first visitors to the house was a German teenager, a refugee, who heard of the Bowne House while a prisoner and vowed to visit if ever he was released. In 1948, Judge Charles S. Colden, who led the campaign to acquire and preserve the house, installed a plaque above the hearth: "In this room an oppressed people found sanctuary.... Here was born religious freedom in the American way of life."[21]

In the 1950s, the Remonstrance was recognized as a cornerstone of the nation's legacy of opposition to tyranny, and the marking of the three-hundredth anniversary of the Remonstrance in 1957 re-established the message of tolerance at a time when American values were being tested at home and challenged abroad. A legislative committee declared that the document was "the first public petition by a free people for religious freedom for men and women" and that it "established as a permanent part of our theory of government that the right of the people to worship in the manner of their choosing shall not be denied by the Government." The committee drew a direct line from "the courageous expression" contained in the Remonstrance to the Bill of Rights.[22] The document went on display in City Hall (dramatically delivered from Albany in an armored car), and on December 27, the actual date of the signing, the Postal Service issued a commemorative stamp honoring "Religious Freedom in America" (ironically depicting a hat representing the Puritans, who viciously persecuted Quakers).

The ceremony on October 10, 1957, was a national event (the date marked the anniversary of the original town patent in 1645), attended by more than three thousand. Memories of the war against totalitarianism and the horrors of the Holocaust were painfully fresh, and the immediacy of the Cold War bolstered this interpretation. Only the year before, Russian tanks had crushed the revolt in Hungary. Queens Borough President James A. Lundy declared it a day when the borough's residents "should pause in the pursuit of their daily occupations to honor the memory of those men who took so brave a stand in the face of tyranny," adding in a boosterish touch that they should "thank Almighty God that in the Borough of Queens there lived men so unselfish and so courageous."[23]

President Eisenhower sent a message stating that the document expressed "a basic premise in the American way of life—our freedom of religion. The individual liberties of our people begin with the free conscience of each citizen." Governor Averell Harriman drew a parallel between the event in the seventeenth century and the recent ugliness in Little Rock, Arkansas, when Governor Orval Faubus sent troops to block the integration of a public high school. Harriman remarked pointedly that "the fight for equality and against discrimination in other forms has not been finally won." Senator Jacob Javits added, "It proves that all minorities must fight for the rights of all other minorities if they're to survive." Mayor Robert Wagner eloquently praised his city's tradition of tolerance, declaring that in New York "there live work and worship in peace and harmony the largest aggregation of peoples of mixed origin—racial, religious and cultural—of any city on the face of the globe. It is a pattern not simply of tolerance but of mutual respect. And it is for its courageous part in the creation of this pattern that the Remonstrance and its thrilling history has for me its richest meaning."

An editorial in the *Long Island Star-Journal* reminded readers that this heritage "seems doubly precious in these troubled days when the torch of liberty and religious freedom can barely be seen through the ... bigotry that covers some sections of the country."[24] All recognized a direct connection between the struggle for racial justice and the struggle for freedom of conscience three hundred years before. Surely the story of the Flushing Remonstrance and the stance of John Bowne will find new meaning in the extraordinarily diverse Borough of Queens in the twenty-first century.

The English County

As the contest over religious toleration in New Netherland played out in the seventeenth century, larger geopolitical forces were emerging. Both England and the Netherlands may have been Protestant states, but they were also imperialist rivals. In a gesture of elegant generosity, King Charles II gave the Dutch possession to his brother James, the Duke of York. It was for the duke to take possession.

Under the authority of the Duke of York, Captain John Scott visited the English towns on Long Island in January 1664. He marched on the Dutch towns with 150 men but was not well received in Breukelen. On January 14, Stuyvesant sent a commission to Jamaica to resolve this situation and, he hoped, reassert his authority. Scott informed the Dutch of King Charles's intention, and Stuyvesant had few options. Many of the English inhabitants welcomed the pending change, and Stuyvesant lacked the capacity to force the issue. In February, he recognized that the situation was untenable and relinquished his authority over Westchester, the Connecticut River Valley, and almost all of Long Island.

Anticipating further English demands, Stuyvesant called the provincial assembly to meet in New Amsterdam. Before the representatives from

Rensselaerwyck, Fort Orange, Breukelen, Midwout, Amersfoort, New Utrecht, Boswyck, New Haarlem, Wiltwyck, Bergen, and Staten Island, as well as the leading citizens of New Amsterdam, Stuyvesant appealed for funds and supplies to check the English threat, but the practical citizens refused.

In late August, four British warships—the *Guinea*, the *Elias*, the *Martin*, and the *William and Nicholas*—carrying five hundred soldiers anchored in the Narrows. Colonel Richard Nicolls quickly occupied Staten Island without encountering resistance, and he demanded that Stuyvesant surrender the province. When the fleet anchored directly opposite the fort and landed troops near Breukelen, prominent citizens urged Stuyvesant to surrender peaceably. In a letter to the Classis in Amsterdam, Reverend Samuel Drisius related the turn of events:

> We have been brought under the government of the King of England. On the 26th of August, there arrived . . . near Staten Island, four great men-of-war . . . well manned with sailors and soldiers. They were provided with a patent or commission . . . to demand and take possession of this province, in the name of His Majesty. If this could not be done in an amicable way, they were to attack the place, and everything was to be thrown open for the English soldiers to plunder. We were not a little troubled by the arrival of these frigates. . . .
>
> Our Honorable rulers of the Company and the municipal authorities of the city were inclined to defend the place, but found that it was impossible, for the city was not in a defensible condition. . . . Therefore upon the earnest request of our citizens . . . our authorities found themselves compelled to come to terms, for the sake of avoiding bloodshed and pillage.[25]

Stuyvesant yielded and signed the Articles of Capitulation, and significantly, religious freedom was upheld.

Cornelis van Ruyven wrote to friends in Boswyck (Bushwick), describing how Richard Nicolls, "with two companies of men, marched into the Fort, accompanied by the Burgomasters of the city, who inducted the Governor and gave him a welcome reception. Governor Nicolls has altered the name of the city of Nieuw Amsterdam, and named the same New York, and the Fort, 'Fort James.'"[26]

For the Long Island towns, the transition to English control did not dampen their determination for self-government. In late February 1665, thirty-four delegates from Long Island and Westchester met at Hempstead and adopted the Duke of York's laws, modeled after New England law, but without demands for religious conformity. The next year, however, when

Governor Nicolls tried to impose new taxes, the townsmen resisted to the point of assaulting his agents. Nicolls offered a compromise, permitting the towns to pay their own bills directly instead of going through his administration, thereby preserving their tradition of self-imposed taxation.

Thomas Dognan took office as the fifth governor of the Province of New York on August 28, 1683, with a message from the Duke of York assuring the inhabitants that the "General Assembly shall have free liberty to consult and debate among themselves all matters as shall be apprehended proper to be established for laws for the good government of said colony of New York and its dependencies, and that if such laws be propounded as shall appear to me to be for the manifest good of the country in general, and not prejudicial to me, I will assent and confirm them."[27] The General Assembly met in October and adopted a new "Charter of Liberties and Privileges Granted by His Royal Highnesse to the Inhabitants of New Yorke, and its Dependencies." The charter granted freedom of religion to all Christian churches, and stated that no taxes or duties would be imposed without the consent of the assembly. Further, all Christian inhabitants were naturalized, as would those arriving after, upon taking an oath of allegiance.[28]

The document also divided the Province of New York into twelve counties: Queens, Kings, Suffolk, New York, Richmond, Westchester, Ulster, Dutchess, Orange, and Albany (two others were later dropped). Queens stretched for twenty-six miles from the East River to Suffolk County. Newtown Creek, a three-and-a-half-mile estuary, marked the boundary with Kings, and the line then ran southeast to Jamaica Bay. The new county contained five townships: Newtown, Flushing, Jamaica, Hempstead, and Oyster Bay. Each had a small village center serving the surrounding farmlands.[29]

The occasion of the tricentennial (1983) of the county's founding popularized the idea that Queens had been named in honor of Catherine of Braganza, the wife of Charles II. The daughter of the king of Portugal, Catherine was given in an arranged marriage in what amounted to an alliance and a property transaction. Her dowry included trading privileges in Tangier and Bombay, then Portuguese possessions. It may have seemed likely that Queens had been named for her, but there is no documentary evidence to substantiate that claim.[30]

Regardless, in the late 1980s a Portuguese trade association formed "Friends of Queen Catherine" for the purpose of erecting a statue of the queen. In 1992, sculptor Audrey Flack designed a thirty-six-foot statue that would stand atop a fifteen-foot base to be sited on the waterfront in Hunters Point across from the United Nations headquarters. The political establishment fell

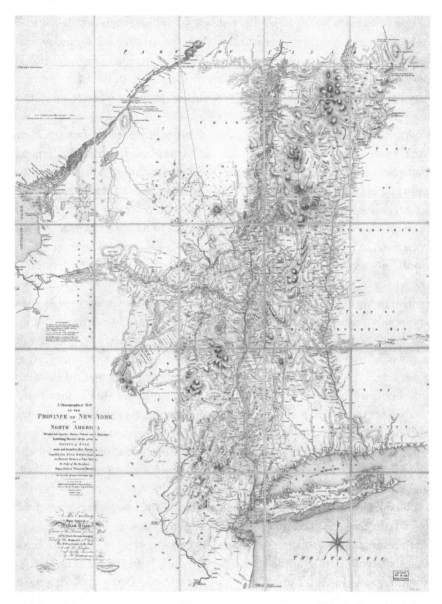

Claude Joseph Sauthier, *A chorographical map of the province of New York in North America: divided into counties, manors, patents, and townships: exhibiting likewise all the private grants of land made and located in that province* (Albany, NY, 1849). (Library of Congress, Geography and Map Division.)

in line behind the idea, Borough President Claire Shulman taking the lead in acquiring a site in the Port Authority's proposed Queens West development. Presented as a public amenity, all decisions were made behind closed doors. There would be no review by the Art Commission, the local community board, or any other agency. Port Authority property was not subject to any public review, let alone control.[31]

As the massive bronze figure was being crafted in a forge at Beacon, New York, voices of opposition finally made themselves heard. A historian argued that the orb in the hand of the queen represented imperialism, surely an unhappy juxtaposition with the United Nations. Second, the statue represented fealty to a royal house, scarcely a message reflecting our republican heritage. Further, while the statue was intended to honor a woman, she had been given in an arranged marriage. Finally, both the Portuguese and English royal houses profited from the slave trade. In sum, the statue would honor the wrong history.[32]

The rhetoric escalated. Betty Dobson declared that Catherine's "hands are bloody with the murder of millions of Africans. Do we really need a statue of a slave mistress?" Tom Donnelly stated, "The Irish are just one of many cultures victimized by royal tyranny, before, during, and after Catherine's reign. Although the Irish are still the 'favorite doormat' of Britain's iron boot, we are about to pull the mat out from under this bronze Brit." Catherine, of course, had no power at court to oppress the Irish or anyone else. And David Gold wrote letters to local Queens papers and the *New York Times* reminding readers of the role of the Portuguese monarchy in the Inquisition. "She, like other members of her family who sat on the Portuguese throne before and after, countenanced the murder of Jews for the simple reason that they were Jews."[33] It was a perfect New York trifecta— Jews, Irish, and African Americans united in opposition.

In response, the supporters offered a bewildering array of justifications— that she was an immigrant in a strange land; she was an abused, if loyal wife; and there were too few statues of women in the city. Audrey Flack described her work, not as homage to the county's namesake, but as "a personification which rises above an individual person from a particular country. My intent was for her to represent every woman. I struggled for six years to develop a face that would have multiracial features, a face that could speak to everyone. Black, white, Latino, Native American, etc." As for the glass sphere in her outstretched hand, it represents "a clean slate, a new vision for the new millennium."[34] Her reasoning took the case for the statue out of the realm of history entirely. She would be not a representation, but a symbol.

Borough President Shulman had no choice but to withdraw public support. Inevitably, her decision drew criticism. Both the *New York Post* and the *Wall Street Journal* published editorials expressing dismay. The *Journal* wrote that the "handsome statue seems to be the latest casualty in the ever-accelerating campaign to delete most of European history as insufficiently caring of the future feelings of sensitive Black children in America." Apparently, "the flabbergasted president and the large Portuguese community, which raised the money, failed to investigate Queen Catherine's position on slavery in the 17th century. Even a proposed relocation to private land has not appeased the statue haters whose mantra is: 'Nowhere on this planet.'"[35]

The *Post* dismissed the reason for opposition as "an off the cuff statement by a local historian that Catherine's family had been involved in the slave trade. That was it." The slave trade, of course, was far from trivial. The point was not the cancellation of European culture but to consider what history should be enshrined. Further, opposition to a statue of Queen Catherine was entirely different from demanding the removal of historical monuments already in place, for that is nothing less than the erasure of the past and an assault on American memory and identity.

This episode revealed how historical issues could grab the public's imagination, but in an emotional rather than an intellectual fashion. The media eagerly grabbed onto a story they readily simplified and polarized. In the end, a debate over history was resolved in the political arena, where all nuance is lost.

Revolution and Retribution

The inhabitants of the Province of New York enjoyed the benefits of self-government and freedom of conscience, but that did not mean there was no cause for conflict. The Ministry Act of 1693 permitted towns to tax themselves to fund a minister, and in 1701 Jamaica elected to do so. The residents built a church and a house and invited a Presbyterian minister to preside. The newly installed governor, Edward Hyde, Viscount Cornbury, would have none of that, however, ordering the ejection of the Dissenter sect and the installation of an Anglican cleric, William Urquhart. His action was rather more self-interested than pious, however. Historian Carl Bridenbaugh wrote that "Cornbury pandered to the Church of England solely for his own private purposes and without regard for sectarian harmony in his government." From Boston, the influential Puritan clergyman Cotton Mather complained that a hundred families of "Christian knowledge and goodness" in Jamaica had supported a minister, but when ten families requested an Anglican minister, Lord Cornbury dispossessed the Presbyterians of the church, the parsonage, lands, and salary. Smoldering for decades, the Dissenters finally seized the property in 1727 for good. A Church of England appointee declared that the Presbyterians had taken possession "by their sly tricks and quirks of common Law." Liberty of conscience proved as important to Long Islanders as self-rule, and the identification of the established church with the provincial authorities contributed to the weakening of the loyalties of the Long Islanders and to the crown.[36]

In a letter to London in 1705, Cornbury frankly laid out the connection between freedom of conscience, self-government, and, more, self-determination in economic affairs. "In the country, and especially in Long Island," he wrote, "most of the English are dissenters, being for the most part people who have removed from New England and Connecticut, who are in no wise fond of monarchy, so that they naturally incline to encroach, as often as they can, upon the Prerogative, so it is no wonder if they are willing to extend the power of their assembly as far as they can." Rather than accept and work with that independent spirit, however, Cornbury concluded that they

> ought to be kept entirely dependent upon and subservient to England, and that can never be if they are suffered to in the notions they have, that, as they are Englishmen, so they may set up the same manufactures here as people do in England. I am well informed that upon Long Island and in Connecticut they are setting up a woolen manufacture; and I, myself, have seen serge made upon Long Island that any man may wear. The consequence, therefore, will be that if once they see they can clothe themselves, not only comfortably but handsomely, too, without the help of England, they, who are not very fond of submitting to Government, will soon think of putting into execution designs they have long harboured in their breasts. This will not seem strange when you consider what sort of people this country is inhabited by.[37]

Lord Cornbury's warning was certainly prophetic. In July 1775, Governor William Tryon took refuge on an English warship as New Yorkers supplanted English authority. He wrote to London that the situation was beyond repair. "Oceans of blood may be spilled, but America will never receive Parliamentary taxation," he stated.[38]

Self-government was embedded in the Long Island towns from the earliest settlements. A 1669 petition to Governor Nicolls's successor, Governor

Francis Lovelace, requested a voice in making the laws, "by such deputies as shall be yearly chosen by the freeholders of each town and parish." Throughout the years of English governance, the Long Islanders repeatedly asserted their right to tax themselves and to assent to all laws, all the while maintaining their loyalty to the Crown.[39] Such democratic sentiments did not translate into devotion to the cause of independence. While Suffolk County was solidly behind the Patriot cause, the mass of residents in Queens and Kings preferred to remain loyal, or rather to be left alone. Between loyalty to King George III and their insistence on the right of self-governance, however, there could be no compromise, and that fault line cut through Queens.

In September 1775, Patriots in the northern part of Hempstead, that is, above the terminal moraine, moved to separate from the Loyalist-dominated town. Referring to those Loyalists, they resolved "that during the present controversy, or so long as their general conduct is inimical to freedom, we be no longer considered as a part of the township of Hempstead than is consistent with peace, liberty and safety; therefore in all matters relative to the Congressional plan, we shall consider ourselves as an entire, separate and independent beat or district." The state legislature made that break official in 1784.[40]

After learning of the Boston Tea Party, Queens men met in a tavern in Brushville (Queens Village) east of Jamaica on December 7, 1774, and approved a series of resolutions declaring their allegiance to the Crown as loyal British subjects while approving "the measures of the late General Congress in Philadelphia" and declaring "that it is our right to be taxed only by our own consent, and that taxes imposed on us by Parliament are an infringement of our rights."[41] As the crisis deepened, it proved impossible to honor both truths at once.

When the Provincial Assembly met in the city in April 1775, Queens towns not only refused to send representatives, but forwarded statements opposing the intent and purposes of the delegates. In November, months after the Battle of Bunker Hill, Jamaica, by a vote of 221 in favor to 788 opposed, again refused to send a representative to the new Congress. Facing such pronounced opposition, the Provincial Assembly declared the counties of Kings and Queens to be in a state of insurrection against the Patriot cause, and the Committees of Safety intensified the harassment and arrest of Loyalists. The aggression with which they carried out their task further alienated the farmers and merchants of Queens.[42]

Twenty-six citizens of Queens were to be arrested, and the 788 who voted against sending representatives to the Provincial Congress were effectively banned, deprived of their rights and privileges, removed from the protection of the law, and forbidden to leave the county. In January 1776, soldiers under Colonel Nathaniel Heard and Major William De Hart marched from Hell Gate to Jamaica, robbing Loyalists and ransacking their homes. Though those arrested were soon released, the incident served to harden Tory opposition and Patriots' resolve. When General Charles Lee took charge of building the defensive lines in Brooklyn, he increased the pressure. In March 1776, he wrote, "I should be in the highest degree culpable, I should be responsible to God, and the Continental Congress of America, in suffering at so dangerous a crisis a knot of professed foes to American liberty to remain any longer within our own bosom, wither to turn openly against us in arms, in conjunction with the enemy, or covertly to furnish them with information, to carry on a correspondence to the ruin of their country."[43]

By his actions, Lee made it certain that those people would perform the very actions he feared, and when the British finally arrived that summer, they found many loyal residents willing to render them aid. Such was the situation in August when the British began landing troops at Gravesend. The Americans observed the landing, but there was little they could do. One officer later wrote, "As there are so many landing places and the people of the island generally so treacherous, we never expected to prevent the landing."[44]

On August 27, the British assaulted the main American line stretching from Gowanus to Fort Putnam (now Fort Greene). During the night, a force of ten thousand regulars marched east below the moraine to Jamaica, where they poured through the only unguarded pass. The Americans were caught from behind unawares, and they retreated as best they could. The battle was a disaster, with a thousand men killed or wounded and as many captured. Miraculously, General Washington evacuated his entire army to Manhattan during the night.

In Jamaica, General Nathaniel Woodhull, commander of the Suffolk militia, was charged with moving livestock and supplies out of the reach of the enemy. The great-grandson of Richard Woodhull, founder of the Town of Brookhaven, Nathaniel was born on Mastic Neck in 1722. He served with the rank of major in the French and Indian War, and in the 1770s he assumed leadership of the Patriot cause in Suffolk. He was elected president of the Provincial Congress in 1775, and was responsible for asserting rebel authority on Long Island.[45]

General Woodhull sent 1,400 head of cattle east, and remained at a tavern in Jamaica awaiting reinforcements. Unaware that he had been cut off from the main army by General Howe's flanking maneuver, he finally headed east after his men. He was quickly surrounded by British dragoons, slashed with a saber, and severely wounded by one of the horsemen, his arm nearly severed. How it happened is not entirely clear, and sources offer several versions, some more legend than fact. One account has a Tory dragoon claiming to have cut him down in the tavern's barn. A history from 1839 records that when Woodhull offered his sword in surrender, a dragoon "ordered him to say *God save the King*; the General replied, 'God save us all'; on which he most cowardly and cruelly assailed the defenseless General with his broad sword, and would have killed him upon the spot if he had not been prevented by the interference of an officer of more honor and humanity (said to by Major Delancy of the dragoons) who arrested his savage violence." That account was an embellishment of an 1826 history by Silas Wood, who records an officer who encountered Woodhull on a prison ship stating that he named Tory leader Oliver De Lancy as the slasher. James Fennimore Cooper, who married into the De Lancy family, claimed that Oliver always denied having done so.[46]

The wounded general was put aboard one of the hulks the British used to hold American prisoners, and his condition worsened under the foul and filthy conditions. Finally, in September he was transferred to a home in Brooklyn used as a hospital, where he died on September 20. Long Island's own martyr to the cause of independence has been all but forgotten. His noble cry, "God save us all," apocryphal though it is, might have joined the pantheon of other legends of the Revolution, such as Nathan Hale's "I regret I have but one life to give for my country," but it never did. Nathaniel Woodhull lacks even a modest memorial to remind the generations that followed of the sacrifice of the founding generation.

The long years of British occupation were hard for the people of Queens, however much the majority may have welcomed the return of English authority. Tory and Patriot alike suffered abuse and the loss of property. Thousands of soldiers were quartered in Newtown, with ten or twenty billeted in each farmhouse. Between the day in August 1776, when the American army abandoned Brooklyn, to the day when the last troops marched out of Jamaica in December 1783, Long Island was under military rule and military law, with no recourse to superior civil authorities. While some officers tightly controlled their men and fostered good relations with the locals, others permitted them to despoil and plunder at will. They took livestock, occupied the best rooms in their homes, and demanded blankets and food for soldiers and fodder for horses, often without compensation. Writing in the 1820s, Silas Wood commented that the administration of justice suspended, the army was a sanctuary for crime and robbery.... Those who remained at home were harassed and plundered of their property, and the inhabitants generally were subject to the orders, and their property to the disposal, of British officers. They compelled them to do all kinds of personal services, to work at their forts, to go with their teams in foraging parties and to transport their cannon, ammunition, provisions and baggage from place to place as they changed their quarters; and to go and come on the order of every petty officer who had the charge of the most trifling business.[47]

Even churches were appropriated for use as hospitals or stables, and the pews and furniture used as firewood. Wood wrote, "The British officers did many acts of barbarity for which there could be no apology. They made garrisons, storehouses or stables of places of public worship in several towns, and particularly of such as belonged to the Presbyterians." Anglican churches were used as storehouses or stables. In Flushing, the Quaker Meeting House became a prison and storehouse; St. George's in Hempstead became a military storehouse. Henry Onderdonk Jr. offered a more favorable picture of the soldiers, noting that the Hessians especially were more sociable, and that "as the soldiers received their pay in coin they were flush, and paid liberally for what they bought, such as vegetables, milk, or what they could not draw with their rations." Their presence on outlying farms also provided a safeguard against robbers and the occasional American whaleboat men.[48]

Table 1
Pre-1800 Survivors in Queens County

Year	Structure	Landmark designation
1661	Bowne House, Flushing	1966
1694–1719	Friends Meeting House, Flushing	1970
ca. 1709	Vander Ende-Onderdonk House, Ridgewood	1995
ca. 1729	Abraham Lent House, Steinway	1966
1733–1806	Rufus King Manor, Jamaica	1966; interior 1976
1735	Cornelius Van Wyck House, Douglas Manor	1966
1735, 1772	Old St. James Church, Newtown	2017
1772	Creedmoor (Cornell) Farmhouse, Bellerose	1976
1774	Kingsland Homestead, Flushing	1965

SOURCE: Jeffrey A. Kroessler and Nina S. Rappaport, *Historic Preservation in Queens*, Queensborough Preservation League, 1990 (designations prior to 1990).
For a complete list of Landmark properties and dates in Queens, see https://www.nyc.gov/site/lpc/designations/designation-reports.page and type in Queens under Borough.

That Kings and Queens had preferred to remain loyal to the Crown and rejected the rebels brought retribution when the British occupation finally ended. An act of the legislature in March 1783 excluded from actions for property damages incurred during the occupation those who had participated in the damage, even under military compulsion. A second act in May 1784 imposed a fine of 37,000 pounds on Long Island "as a compensation to the other parts of the State for not having been in condition to take an active part in the war against the enemy." Wood comments that both acts were "violations of public law, and the immutable principles of justice; were partial and oppressive in their operation, and fully proved that an abuse of power was not peculiar to the British parliament, but a common infirmity of human nature; and in conflicts of local interests, fomented by local jealousies, might sometimes occur under the freest forms of government."[49]

The wounds of the Revolution healed, though only after many Tories were obliged to yield their property and abandon Long Island. In the spring of 1790, President Washington toured Long Island, visiting towns and inns from Jamaica to Setauket. He found a country of great agricultural promise, though he did comment on the sandy quality of much of the soil. The final leg took him from Oyster Bay through Queens. He wrote, "From Flushing to Newtown, eight miles, and thence to Brooklyn, the road is very fine, and the country in a higher state of cultivation and vegetation, of grass and grain, than any place I had seen, occasioned in a great degree by the manure drawn from the City of New York."[50] The president thus recognized the true character of Queens—a prodigious agricultural community developing its potential to the fullest to supply the ever-growing needs of the City of New York.

2

The Rural Landscape

Canal Fever on Long Island

Until the middle of the nineteenth century, transportation links between Long Island and the metropolitan center were inadequate. Access to market was not as easy as it appeared on the map. Ironically, the completion of the Erie Canal in 1825 made new farms in Genesee and Cayuga Counties more profitable grain producers than the long-established farms of Kings, Queens, and Suffolk. Long Islanders bridled at the realization that their tax monies and bank deposits had helped finance the enterprise that now threatened their prosperity. The Erie Canal greatly extended New York City's economic reach, cementing the city's position atop the nation's hierarchy of cities, and it assumed that Long Island's resources and economic potential were rightfully its own. With all that, it is remarkable that Queens grew as slowly as it did in the 1800s, given the exponential rise of New York and Brooklyn.

From the earliest colonial settlements into the nineteenth century, the pattern of development always reflected the quality of transportation, and from the earliest Dutch and English settlements transport by water was the most efficient way to bring agricultural produce to urban markets. The earliest schemes for internal improvements on Long Island, therefore, centered on canals.

David H. Burr, *Map of the counties of New York, Queens, Kings, and Richmond* (New York: David H. Burr, 1829). (The New York Public Library Digital Collections. 1829–1839, Lionel Pincus and Princess Firyal Map Division.)

Farming practices in Queens changed as the cities grew, and internal improvements extended their economic sphere deeper into the hinterland. When the Erie Canal was proposed, Long Islanders were among the most vocal opponents. They feared that the canal would open new and more fertile lands to commercial agriculture and Long Island's farmers would lose long established markets, driving down the value of their land. Within a few years, the upstate region did indeed replace Long Island as the state's premier wheat region, and the young city of Rochester was soon known as the "flour city."[1]

In January 1825, farmers and merchants organized the Long-Island Canal Company and applied to the state legislature for a charter authorizing them to dig canals to connect the bays on the South Shore of the island and improve the "navigable communication" with the city. Not so incidentally, the charter also permitted the company to operate a bank. In this they followed the path blazed by Aaron Burr when he organized the Manhattan Company in 1799 with the announced intention of supplying fresh water to the city. But Burr and his colleagues were primarily interested in organizing a bank; the resulting company is a direct ancestor of J. P. Morgan Chase.[2] The canal company envisioned a waterway 110 miles in length along the

South Shore, with 100 miles already "formed by the hand of nature." It would require no locks as the entire route was at or very near sea level. The incorporators believed that their enterprise would connect Long Island more efficiently with the city and extend their reach to the Great Lakes and surrounding regions opened up by the Erie Canal.

The island's agricultural interests were keenly aware of the changes wrought by the Erie Canal. Their petition stated:

> Whilst other districts have not only experienced the benefits of artificial navigation, but the additional advantage of having several millions of dollars expended amongst them, the farmers of Long-Island have felt it as a weight upon them, in the depression of the value of their farms and produce. As faithful members of the body politic, they have contributed to the burthen of its construction.
>
> The wealth of an agricultural county, may be fairly measured by its surplus produce; but the value of that surplus depends upon the facility of its transportation to a market. The city of New-York is now almost as accessible to the farmers of Cayuga and Ontario [counties], as to those on the south shore of Long-Island. The necessary and the inevitable tendency of opening the market to such extensive regions, has been to depress the value of those districts whose wealth consisted in their access to the metropolis. Nor is this all; the immense quantities of produce which have been poured into New-York, from the west, and the north, have depreciated its value, as well as the value of the land on which it was raised.[3]

The original petition by Abraham G. Thompson and his associates was signed by 644 men, "chiefly farmers." Of that number, 225 were from Queens, while the others hailed from Suffolk. "Individuals of extensive wealth, immediately interested in the navigation of the bays, are comparatively few," they explained. Thus, "the persons most to be benefitted are the industrious farmers and other resident inhabitants." The legislature failed to act, however, and the company resubmitted their petition again in 1827. "Patient, unassuming and uncomplaining, they have yielded to the destiny which seems to be crowding them behind their sister counties," they wrote, "but when they discover an apparent disregard of their reasonable requests, it becomes them, in the bold and honest language of freemen, to urge and expostulate." Ideally, the petitioners suggested, "the work should be undertaken at the public expence, and that the public should have the benefit of it, either in the shape of a free passage through the canal, or by the payment of the tolls into the public treasury." At the same time, however, they recognized "that it might be regarded as a troublesome precedent," and thus suggested that the state "reimburse such a proportion of the expenditures, as that a probable receipt of tolls may be thought to equal an interest upon the reduced capital."[4]

The petitioners were "not a little unwilling to ask for a bank. They do not wish to be confounded with the speculators and stock jobbers of the day. A bank is with them a secondary object—the means, and not the end." They therefore based their request for a bank on the premise that "these canals would be of more benefit to the public, than profitable to the individuals who might make them, and that therefore it was not to be expected that private funds could be raised for their construction unless the legislature gave some encouragement, beyond a right to receive tolls." The Long-Island Canal Company listed the Bank of New-York and the Phenix Bank as willing to subscribe to portions of the stock and issue loans at 3 percent interest.[5]

Beyond the political and financial issue of the bank charter, the canals linking the Great South Bay and Jamaica Bay with New York Harbor would offer great economic benefits. "For want of convenient access to market," a committee of the state senate reported, "no inconsiderable part of the south side of Long-Island, remains uncultivated. Mastic, in the township of Brookhaven, is situated sixty miles from New-York, and transportation thither from that city costs more per ton, than it does 400 miles to Rochester: the wood also, on the south side of the island, bears only one half the price it does on the north, where it can be conveyed to New-York through the waters of the sound." The citizens of the island would prosper, of course, but the canals would also prove "an essential and lasting benefit conferred upon the city of New-York." Governor DeWitt Clinton concurred. In his annual message to the state legislature on January 6, 1826, he endorsed the proposal as "a measure vastly important to our population in that quarter, and to the city of New York."[6]

The South Shore canals were never dug, and another proposal in 1848 also came to naught. With the introduction of the railroad in America in the early 1830s, canal fever began to cool.[7] By the 1840s, the agricultural prospects of Queens had improved considerably, and the dire predictions voiced in the years immediately after the opening of the Erie Canal were never realized.

Commerce and Agriculture

From the eighteenth century into the twentieth, a defining industry in Queens was the nursery business, particularly in and around Flushing.

Horticulturalist William Prince founded the first, the Linnaean Botanic Garden, in 1732, and by 1767 he was offering for sale "a great variety of fruit trees, such as apple, plum, peach, nectarine, cherry, apricot and pear," noting that "they may be put up so as to be sent to Europe," as passage boats left for New York on Tuesdays and Fridays. A notice from 1774 offered many more varieties, including "one hundred and ten large carolina Magnolia flower trees, raised from the seed—The most beautiful trees that grow in America—4s. per tree, four feet high." He also sold almond, fig, mulberry, and filbert trees, as well as many varieties of strawberries, grapes, and currants. In October 1789, six months after his inauguration, President Washington journeyed to Flushing to examine the nurseries, but the entry in his diary shows that he was scarcely impressed: "I set off from New York, about nine o'clock, in my barge to visit Mr. Prince's gardens and shrubberies at Flushing. These gardens, except in the number of young trees, did not answer my expectations. The shrubs were trifling and the flowers not numerous. The inhabitants of the place showed us what respect they could, by making use of one cannon to salute."[8] The president may have been disappointed then, but in the following decades the nursery industry flourished in Queens and expanded to national prominence. An 1820 catalogue for the Linnaean Botanic Garden listed a dazzling selection of trees and plants, both fruit and ornamental, including 33 varieties of cherry trees, 59 peach, 12 nectarine, 12 apricot, 44 plum, 72 pear, and 44 varieties of apple, four of which were touted as best for cider, and two others that had distinctly local associations—the Flushing Spitzenburgh and the Newtown Spitzenburgh. The catalogue also described a great many ornamental trees and shrubs for planting around private homes or estates, including eighty-eight different varieties of roses. Not confined to New York, Prince boasted agents in every major city from Portland, Maine, to New Orleans, Louisiana.[9]

The 1850 census lists many gardeners, nurserymen, and laborers in Flushing, ranging from immigrants apparently trained in the British Isles to Robert E. Parsons, who listed his occupation as horticulturist. In 1847, nurseryman Samuel Bowne Parsons planted a weeping beech sapling he brought from Belgium, and it grew into a magnificent specimen that was the progenitor of all weeping beech trees for generations after. The tree survived until 1998 (in 1968, the 1785 Kingsland Homestead, now home of the Queens Historical Society, was moved to Weeping Beech Park). In 1887, Samuel Bowne Parsons Jr. became superintendent of parks for the City of New York. Working closely with Calvert Vaux, Parsons was responsible for much of the planting in Central Park at the turn of the century. The

Kissena Park Grove, Parsons Nursery, Flushing, 2024. (Laura Heim Architect.)

Greensward connection actually went back to the 1840s, when Frederick Law Olmsted, then a gentleman farmer on Staten Island, purchased fruit trees from the Parsons nursery. Olmsted later met Parsons in London, where the nurseryman was buying trees for Central Park. The Parsons and Sons Company nursery remained active until 1906. The next year the city acquired the property for Kissena Park, where exotic, hundred-year-old specimens still stand in stately rows.[10]

In an address before the Flushing Horticultural Society in 1844, William Prince said that it was time for the people of Queens to decide on the future of their lands, "these being no longer able to compete with the mighty prairies of the West in the production of wheat and other grains." He told the assembled members, "Happily our peculiar position gives to us a pre-emptive right to the production of all articles required by the adjacent cities of New-York and Brooklyn, whose bulk or perishable nature prevent their distant transportation. And henceforth we may look to our Fruit Orchards, our Vineyards, and our Vegetable Gardens to make up the deficiency in the amount which we formerly derived from other sources."[11] Prince did not mention that Queens had another asset that brought the metropolis within easy communication: the railroad. While it had initially bypassed Flushing, the residents of that town, as with other villages on the island, were not slow in recognizing its potential to bring greater prosperity.

John A. King of Jamaica, the son of the respected Federalist and former U.S. senator Rufus King, delivered the major address at the 1848 Queens County Agricultural Fair held at Jamaica, and discussed those same issues:

Before the Erie Canal was completed, wheat, and barley, and rye, were largely raised for sale, and the flourishing mills on the Island had as much business as they could attend to; the quality of the grain raised was excellent, and the reputation of the mills on the North shore was well established for the quality of their flour. The construction of that great work of internal improvement, very soon caused a radical change in the husbandry and crops of the County. We could no longer compete with the rich and virgin lands of the west, in the production of cereal grains; and it was at one moment feared that the value of our lands, and the prosperity of our farmers, would be seriously affected by the cheapness, fertility and great extent of the western lands. Such, however, was not the case.

King described the new and extremely profitable relationship between Queens County and the metropolis:

The result and effect of these new and varied elements of wealth poured into the city of New York, was immediately felt, in the extension of her commerce, the increase of her population, and in the enlargement and improvement of the city itself. This impulse, so powerfully felt by the city, was soon communicated to the surrounding country; and as the number and means of the citizens increased, the demand for those productions which the farmers in its neighborhood alone most easily and profitably supply, was soon greatly augmented. Hence, as the growth of New York, and subsequently Brooklyn, continued to increase, it followed that the lands in the immediate vicinity of these cities must advance in value—first for the erection of houses and buildings, and next for the cultivation and supply of those articles most needed from day to day for the consumption and support of two large cities.

He made special mention of peach trees, "whose fruit has been abundant, fair, and finding a ready market."[12] But he did not mention the railroad, which was odd as he was the founding president of the Brooklyn and Jamaica Railroad Company.

Speaking in Flushing at the eleventh annual exhibition of the Queens County Agricultural Society in 1852, Charles King, president of Columbia College, described the dramatic transformation of agriculture in Queens after the canal opened fertile lands in the west. Until then, Queens had been known for its excellent wheat and "the best flour then made in the state." He pointed out that

> now, instead of flour and wheat, Queens exports hay, and oats, and corn, and potatoes, abundant poultry, and more abundant garden stuffs. The canal, which was to ruin the county and depreciate its lands, has turned it into a garden, and added two or three times, and perhaps more, to the value of every tillable acre in it. Bathed by two sides, indented along either coast by deep bays, and intersected in its whole length by a railroad, which affords cheap and rapid conveyance to and from the great metropolis, Queens County cannot be interfered with in its prosperity, as long as there are in that great metropolis hundreds of thousands of mouths to be daily supplied, and hundreds of thousands of dollars to be expended for what may be called, perhaps, articles of luxury, early flowers, fruits, and vegetables, and flowers, fruits and vegetables raised out of season, and by artificial climates; and herein indeed is mainly to consist in the future the profitable employment of the soil and the industry of Queens County, or at any rate, of that large portion of it immediately contiguous to its railroads and bays.[13]

The situation was the same in Kings County. Writing in 1880, Gertrude Lefferts Vanderbilt described the transformation of farming in Flatbush since her youth. "Where formerly wheat, rye, buckwheat, oats, corn, flax and barley were the products of the farm, with only so much of cabbage, peas, potatoes, and turnips as were necessary for the family use," she noted, "all this is now reversed; only so much hay and grain as the farmer needs are raised, while he depends upon his market produce for remunerative sales."[14]

To take advantage of these promising new opportunities, Long Islanders needed improved transportation. While rutted farm roads were perhaps adequate for local business, the only direct route to Brooklyn was via one of the privately owned turnpikes or plank roads. Chartered by the state legislature, these corporations collected tolls and were responsible for maintaining the gravel, stone, or wood-plank road surface. For a farmer bringing a wagon of hay or fresh produce to the market in Wallabout Bay, the smooth surface of the plank road must have seemed infinitely superior, although perhaps not worth the cost of the toll. By one account, the opening of the road from the bridge over Flushing Creek to Newtown "was accomplished only after much opposition on the part of the farmers," but once the road was finished, a stage began running between Flushing and Brooklyn, by way of Newtown and Bedford.[15]

All chartered in the early decades of the nineteenth century, the turnpikes usually followed established, if ill-maintained routes. This early example of privatization relieved the county of responsibility for the condition of the roads, and, by midcentury, all of the major roads leading to Jamaica were privately owned, making it impossible to travel between the villages without paying a toll. Onerous as the 1807 New York State turnpike law may have been to farmers accustomed to free travel, the law did allow many exemptions: "No tolls might be collected from a person when going to or returning from public worship, a funeral, the grist mill with grain for family use, his usual blacksmith, when a person lived within one mile of the toll gate, when going to town to vote at a town meeting or election. No toll was to be paid by physicians, midwives, jurors, United States or State troops." An 1859 map identified the Flushing and Bayside Plank Road (Northern Boulevard), the Williamsburgh and Jamaica Turnpike (Metropolitan Avenue), the Jamaica Plank Road (Hillside Avenue west of 168th Street, Jericho Turnpike eastward from 212th Street), the Hempstead and Jamaica Plank Road (Jamaica Avenue to Hempstead Turnpike), and the Jamaica and Rockaway Plank Road (Rockaway Boulevard). Conceived as monopolies, the plank roads could not survive competition, and they fell into unprofitability and disrepair soon after the introduction of the steam railroad and streetcars.[16]

Queens at Midcentury

In 1850, New York City stood alone atop the nation's hierarchy of cities, having achieved pre-eminence in politics, finance, and culture, as well as population. Its population surpassed Philadelphia in the census of 1810, and twenty years later it outpaced Mexico City to become the largest metropolis in the Americas. At midcentury, Brooklyn, too, was a rapidly growing city. As late as 1800, Kings County held fewer than 5,800 inhabitants, a smaller population than Queens (defined as it has been since 1898). But Brooklyn expanded at an extraordinary rate following the introduction of steam-powered ferries to Manhattan in 1811. The Village of Brooklyn was incorporated in 1816, and it received its city charter in 1834. In the antebellum decades, Queens had no great or growing urban core, only small village centers and no suburban districts to speak of.[17]

The most obvious contrast between rural Queens and urbanizing Brooklyn was the latter's street grid. Mapped for four miles from the Fulton Ferry, the streets existed for the most part only on paper; maps of the period show natural features, farm lines, and country roads visible beneath the superimposed grid. But the topography in the City of Brooklyn was becoming less and less relevant, as the only important feature was the rationalization of property for sale as standard city lots. In truth, much of the area within the Brooklyn city limits would hardly differ in appearance from property just across the line in Kings County, though the streets closest to the waterfront and the ferries were densely built. Beyond the city line the historic towns of New Utrecht, Gravesend, Flatbush, Flatlands, New Lots, and Bushwick remained almost entirely agricultural until the last decade of the century. In his 1870 *History of Brooklyn*, Henry Stiles described Kings County as "one immense garden" serving the "vast and increasing demand of the city of New York for vegetables and fruits of a perishable nature." Once among the most productive agricultural landscapes in the nation, Brooklyn saw virtually all of it vanish between 1890 and 1910.[18]

Just north of Brooklyn was the City of Williamsburgh. This industrializing district, stretching along the waterfront from the Navy Yard to Newtown Creek, split away from the Town of Bushwick and incorporated as a city in 1852. City leaders clearly identified their fortunes more closely with the port of New York than with a rural backwater where many inhabitants still spoke Dutch. In 1855, Brooklyn annexed Williamsburgh, with its 50,000 inhabitants, dropping the "h" from its name, as well as Bushwick, which had about 7,000, bringing Brooklyn's total population to more than 202,000 and making it the third-largest city in the nation.

One reason for the annexation was to gain control over the water sources on Long Island. Incorporated in 1852, the Williamsburgh Water Company bought up sources of supply on the south side of the island, the very streams and ponds Brooklyn had sought to acquire. This would seriously impede

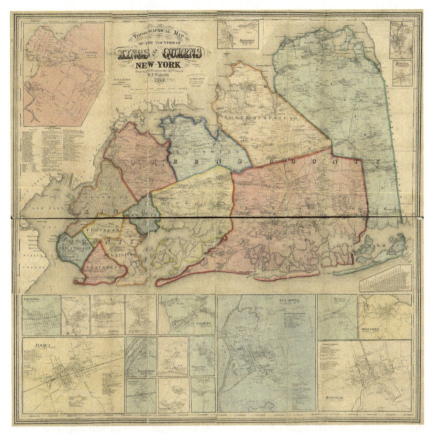

Henry Francis Walling, *Topographical map of the counties of Kings and Queens, New York* (New York: W. E. and A. A. Baker, 1859). (Library of Congress, Geography and Map Division.)

the economic prospects and future growth of Brooklyn. Annexation was the only solution. Brooklyn built its water system at once. An aqueduct conveyed the water from southern Queens to the base of the moraine, where a steam plant pumped the water up to the Ridgewood Reservoir, massive basins dug out atop the hills. From that height, gravity distributed the water through pipes under the streets to the residents. The water improved the lives of Brooklynites immeasurably, while also supplying industry.[19]

In striking contrast to the rapid growth of Brooklyn, the three western townships of Queens together had fewer than nineteen thousand inhabitants in 1850. Until about 1820, the populations of Kings County and the three western towns of Queens were about equal. Within a decade of the opening of the Erie Canal, however, the population of Kings was three times that of western Queens, and Brooklyn was emerging as an urban power in its own right, spinning a web of metropolitan expansion into the Long Island. Queens did grow nearly 350 percent between 1810 and 1860, but that amounted to just over twenty-six thousand people. Such a slow increase paled in comparison with Brooklyn's growth rate of over 3,200 percent.[20]

Long Island's roads funneled traffic to the East River ferries. In the 1850s, five ferries plied the waters between Brooklyn and New York, and four more ran from Williamsburgh. Only two ferries served Queens, however. One was the Calvary Cemetery route, bringing funeral parties and Sunday picnickers directly to the rural cemetery. The other crossed between the Village of Astoria (incorporated in 1839) and Yorkville, a sparsely populated but growing section of the city. Other boats made daily trips from communities along the North Shore. One steamer ran from Flushing to the Fulton Market Slip, with a stop at Hallett's Cove in Astoria, and another provided daily service between Manhasset and New York, with stops at Great Neck, Whitestone, and College Point.[21]

Who lived in Queens then? The 1850 federal census reveals an ethnic and class picture offering few surprises. Native-born Americans, a great number of New Yorkers among them, listed their occupations as gentleman, farmer, gentleman farmer, and none, as well as merchant, lawyer, miller, innkeeper, and such skilled crafts as blacksmith, carpenter, machinist, "segar maker," and carriage and wagon maker. Almost without exception, however, Black Americans were listed as laborers.

Slavery had been present in Queens almost from the beginning, though nothing like the plantation system of the South or the Caribbean took root. According to the 1790 census, 14 percent of the population were slaves; in Kings County, a third of the population were slaves. New York State enacted a law providing for the gradual elimination of slavery in 1799, freeing all children born to slave women after July 4, 1799, the males to be freed when they reached twenty-one, the females at twenty-five years of age. Still, slave labor was common on the county's farms. In 1817, the legislature decreed that "every slave born before July 4, 1799 was freed as of July 4, 1827." The last loopholes permitting visitors to bring their slaves into New York were closed in 1841, finally abolishing involuntary servitude entirely. Queens had a tradition of free Blacks from colonial times, and the position of that population among the propertyless laborers in the 1850s is for that reason all the more striking.[22]

With its Quaker heritage, Flushing had a strong tradition of abolition. In 1814, members of the Society of Friends and others founded the Flushing Female Association to provide free education to the children, both white and Black. Support for abolition, however, did not translate into an embrace of racial equality. In his *History of the Town of Flushing*, Henry Waller

Table 2
Population, 1800–1860

	1800	1810	1820	1830	1840	1850	1860
New York	60,515	96,373	123,706	202,859	312,710	515,547	813,669
Increase		35,858	27,333	79,153	109,851	202,837	298,122
Percentage increase		59%	28%	64%	54%	65%	58%
Kings	5,740	8,303	11,187	20,535	47,613	138,882	279,122
Increase		2,563	2,884	9,348	27,078	91,269	140,240
Percentage increase		45%	35%	84%	132%	192%	101%
Brooklyn	2,378	4,402	7,175	15,394	36,233	96,838	266,661*
Increase		2,024	2,773	8,219	20,839	60,605	169,823
Percentage increase		85%	63%	115%	135%	167%	175%
Percentage of Kings County	41%	77%	64%	75%	76%	70%	96%
Queens**	6,642	7,444	8,246	9,049	12,480	18,593	32,903
Increase		802	803	803	3,431	6,113	14,310
Percentage increase		12%	11%	10%	38%	49%	77%

SOURCE: *The Encyclopedia of New York City*, 170, 1019.
* Includes the City of Williamsburgh and the Town of Bushwick.
** Queens County defined as it has been since 1898.

describes an unpleasant incident from 1825, around the time when the last slaves in New York were emancipated:

> The slaves of Flushing had always, as a rule, been kindly treated. The Quakers had been working for nearly a hundred years for the abolition of slavery. Their sympathy for the slaves and their interest in the negroes' education and general well-being were widely known. Flushing became the rendezvous of freedmen, who hoped to secure the blessings of freedom without its responsibilities. A very undesirable element was thus added to the population of the village. These negroes became so numerous, so aggressive, so lawless, that the peace and quiet of the community were greatly disturbed. They filled the streets at night; they held out-of-door dances and barbeques, which generally degenerated into drunken brawls. Town ordinances and the mild influence of the Quakers were without avail. The apprentices and other young men of the village took matters into their own hands. They formed a sort of vigilance committee and attacked with volleys of rotten eggs, these noisy gatherings which made sleep impossible. A few attacks of this sort had the effect of breaking up the gatherings, or at least transferring the orgies from the public square to the shanties on Crow Hill and Liberty street.[23]

Unknown artist, *Landscape of Newtown, Long Island*, 1839 (today Elmhurst, Queens). (Preservation Long Island.)

Table 3
Population of New York, Kings, and Queens, 1790–1860

	1790	1800	1810	1820	1830	1840	1850	1860
New York	33,131	60,015	96,373	123,706	202,859	312,710	515,547	813,669
Percentage growth		81%	59%	28%	64%	54%	65%	58%
Kings	4,495	5,740	8,303	11,187	20,535	47,613	138,882	279,122
Percentage growth		28%	45%	35%	84%	132%	192%	101%
Queens	16,014	16,916	19,336	21,519	22,460	30,324	36,833	57,391
Percentage growth		5.5%	14%	11%	4.4%	35%	21.5%	56%

SOURCE: *Census Bulletin No. 38, Twelfth Census of the United States*, January 22, 1901.

The truth of this account is impossible to determine, not the least because the voices of the African Americans are silent. The episode does, however, reveal quite a bit about racial attitudes in the village. While Flushing certainly embraced abolition, racial equality was another matter.

Though there were many skilled craftsmen among the English, Scottish, and German immigrants in Newtown, Jamaica, and Flushing, few had

Table 4
Population of Queens County, 1790–1860

	1790	1800	1810	1820	1830	1840	1850	1860
Total	16,014	16,916	19,336	21,519	22,460	30,324	36,833	57,391
Newtown, Flushing, and Jamaica	6,159	6,642	7,444	8,246	9,049	14,480	18,593	32,903
Percentage growth		7.8%	12%	11%	10%	60%	28%	77%
Percentage of total	38.5%	39.3%	38.5%	38.3%	40.3%	48%	50.5%	57.3%
Hempstead, Oyster Bay, and North Hempstead	9,855	10,274	11,892	13,273	13,411	15,844	18,240	24,488
Percentage growth		4%	16%	11.6%	1%	18%	15%	34.3%
Percentage total	61.5%	60.7%	61.5%	61.7%	59.7%	52%	49.5%	42.7%

SOURCE: Demographics of Queens, https://en.wikipedia.org/wiki/Demographics_of_Queens.

Table 5
Population by Race, 1790–1860

	1790	1800	1810	1820	1830	1840	1850	1860
New York	**33,111**	**60,489**	**96,373**	**123,706**	**202,589**	**312,710**	**515,547**	**813,669**
White	29,619	54,122	86,550	112,820	183,136	296,352	501,732	801,088
Percentage	89.5%	89.5%	89.8%	91.2%	92.9%	94.8%	97.3%	98.5%
Nonwhite	3,462	6,367	9,823	10,886	13,976	16,358	13,815	12,574
Percentage	10.6%	10.5%	10.2%	8.8%	7.1%	5.2%	2.7%	1.6%
Free	30,738	57,621	96,687	123188				
Percentage	92.8%	95.3%	98.3%	99.6%				
White	29,619	54,122	86,550	112,820				
Nonwhite	1,119	3,499	8,137	10,386				
Slave	2,373	2,868	1,686	518				
Percentage	7.2%	4.7%	1.8%	0.4%				
Kings	**4,549**	**5,740**	**8,303**	**11,187**	**20,535**	**47,613**	**138,882**	**279,112**
White	3,021	3,929	6,450	9,426	18,589	44,767	134,817	274,123
Percentage	66.4%	68.5%	77.7%	84.3%	90.2%	94%	97.3%	98.2%
Nonwhite	1,528	1,811	1,853	1,761	2,007	1,846	4,065	4,999
Percentage	33.6%	31.6%	22.3%	15.7%	9.8%	6%	2.9%	1.8%
Free	3,067	4,261	7,185	10,308				
Percentage	67.4%	74.2%	86.5%	92.1%				
White	3,021	3,929	6,450	9,426				
Nonwhite	46	332	735	882				
Slave	1,482	1,479	1,118	879				
Percentage	32.6%	25.8%	13.5%	7.9%				
Queens	**16,013**	**16,891**	**19,336**	**21,519**	**22,460**	**30,324**	**36,833**	**57,391**
White	12,886	13,932	16,173	18,312	19,352	26,815	33,382	54,004
Percentage	80.5%	82.5%	83.6%	85.1%	86.2%	88.4%	90.6%	94.1%
Nonwhite	3,127	2,959	3,163	3,207	3,108	3,509	3,451	3,387
Percentage	19.5%	17.5%	16.4%	14.9%	13.8%	11.6%	9.4%	5.9%
Free	13,705	15,363	18,527	20,960				
Percentage	85.6%	91%	95.8%	97.4%				
White	12,886	13,932	16,173	18,312				
Nonwhite	819	1,431	2,354	2,648				
Slave	2,308	1,528	809	559				
Percentage	14.4%	9.1	4.2%	2.6%				

SOURCE: *1870 Census: Volume 1. The Statistics of the Population of the United States*, https://www2.census.gov/library/publications/decennial/1870/population/1870a-08.pdf.

reached the propertied class by 1850. The Irish, on the other hand, remained disproportionately represented among unskilled laborers, although every group had a significant number of laborers. Furthermore, the majority of the immigrants dwelled in the town centers, with only a minority living and working on farms, a residential pattern of class and ethnicity that held true across the county. There was no dense urban settlement in Queens, the three town centers possessing street plans notable for the absence of an urban grid and for the easy transition to the rural landscape. While Jamaica grew after the opening of the Long Island Railroad, Flushing's population remained stable at about two thousand from its incorporation as a village in 1837 into the early 1850s. Newtown achieved neither the size nor the prominence of the other two town centers. Even so, it had a number of resident craftsmen—English masons, a Scottish weaver, Irish shoemakers, German glazers and tailors—and native-born merchants and professionals. One of the more prominent residents of Newtown was Samuel Lord, cofounder of the Lord & Taylor department store.[24]

For two centuries, New York City had been a rather distant influence on Queens County, a market for agricultural produce and the source of manufactured and imported items but not generally a direct concern for Queens citizens. The coming of the railroad, however, pushed Queens into a period of suburban development and commercial growth, gradually but inevitably changing the rural landscape.

3

The Railroad and Long Island

A series of canals linking the bays along the South Shore of Long Island would certainly have proved a boon to farmers, but it would not have been in any sense transformational. Railroads promised to achieve just that by opening Long Island to new economic and residential opportunities. It was indeed ironic, however, that the first railroad on the island was intended not to serve the agricultural hinterland but urbanites traveling between New York and Boston.

The Long Island Railroad (LIRR) made its first run between Jamaica and Brooklyn in 1836. Jamaica prospered as the fulcrum of the line stretching from the Brooklyn waterfront to the North Fork of Long Island. Other parts of Queens, however, were not served by any rail lines until the Flushing Rail Road began running in 1854. An important function of the railroad in its earliest years was to carry agricultural produce from Long Island farms to the hungry cities of New York and Brooklyn, and manure for use as fertilizer in the opposite direction. The railroad stimulated economic growth, both by serving farmers and eventually stimulating the construction of new suburbs.

The Long Island Railroad

The Brooklyn and Jamaica Railroad Company was organized in 1832 to build a line between those two places, a distance of about ten miles. Capitalized at $300,000 with shares valued at $50, the company was authorized to lay a single or double track and to appropriate property required for the right of way if it could not otherwise be obtained, with damages to be assessed by an independent panel. The charter stipulated that the railroad could not use existing streets in the Village of Brooklyn, nor use steam power there without permission from the village.[1]

Two years later, the LIRR received a charter to construct a line westward from Greenport on the North Fork to a terminal on the East River, and to raise $1,500,000 through the sale of stock. The concept behind the enterprise was to speed travelers between New York and Boston, not to foster the economic vitality of Kings, Queens, and Suffolk. The right of way ran through the center of the island, distant from the farms and villages on either shore. From Jamaica, the line ran east across the unbroken Hempstead Plains to Hicksville (named for Valentine Hicks, one of the original directors of the company) and out to Greenport, where passengers boarded steamers to Connecticut. There they would meet the Norwich & Worcester Railroad to continue on to Boston. Before this route was completed, travel between New York and Boston took about seventeen hours, the first leg via Cornelius "The Commodore" Vanderbilt's steamers to Providence, then on the cars of the Boston & Providence Railroad (incorporated in 1835). The route through Long Island promised to cut travel time to ten hours.

The charter also permitted the LIRR to acquire the Brooklyn and Jamaica Railroad and utilize that company's tracks down Atlantic Avenue to the East River ferries. The LIRR agreed to pay $33,300 per annum for forty-five years, a sum representing "10 per cent. of the cost" of constructing the road.[2]

Brooklyn was one of the six original townships in Kings County. In 1816, the Village of Brooklyn was incorporated, encompassing the densely settled section near the ferry landing. With construction of the railroad imminent, Brooklyn received a city charter in April 1834, taking in all of the old town. The village had roughly doubled in population each decade since 1800 and counted about three-quarters of the population of Kings County. In 1830, there were 15,394 residents in Brooklyn; a decade later, after the railroad commenced operation, the population stood at 36,233, and it would stand just shy of 100,000 in 1850. During that same period, the population of Queens grew by the dozens. In 1800, the county counted 6,642, and forty years later it had not quite doubled to 12,480. Growth remained modest, reaching only 18,593 in 1850; rural Kings County beyond Brooklyn held more than double that number.

The *Ariel* made its initial run on April 18, 1836, covering the distance between Brooklyn and Jamaica in only twenty-three minutes. Alighting from the four open cars, two hundred invited guests attended a groundbreaking ceremony for the next section of the road, which would extend the tracks as far as Hicksville, and then retired to the new Rail Road Hotel for refreshments and speeches. John A. King "congratulated the Long-Island company on the spirit in which they had taken hold of this great work, and the auspicious prospect of its speedy accomplishment and complete success." He then congratulated his fellow citizens "on the new era which was opening not only to those in the immediate vicinity of this road, but to the Island, and to the state at large." As was customary, the speeches were accompanied by a series of toasts reflecting not only the pride in this undertaking, but also the vision, interests, and concerns of those in attendance. Beginning with a toast to "native enterprize," others followed, such as "Railroads: may they extend and bind together, beyond the possibility of separation, this whole Union"; and "The Brooklyn and Jamaica rail-road—the republican method of uniting Kings and Queens."[3]

The once sleepy village of Jamaica (incorporated in 1814) and the increasingly dynamic city of Brooklyn were indeed "bound together by bands of iron," as one toast put it. Over the next half century, the railroad expanded the length and breadth of Long Island, presenting entrepreneurs and investors new opportunities to develop the economic potential of Queens. The county's rich agricultural hinterland would emerge as a natural outlet for the rapidly growing urban populace in the decades to come. Jamaica prospered with the opening of the railroad, and residents expected greater prosperity ahead. Only four years after the coming of the railroad, an editorial in the *Long Island Democrat* boasted:

> If any old residents who departed from this village prior to the existence of our rail road, should now reappear among us; it might, in some parts of the village, be difficult for them to recognize the location where they had formerly lived. Within a few years some streets have been built up entirely new; and improvement is everywhere visible throughout our bounds. There are now eight Churches in this town. In the village, we number eight stores—two apothecaries shops, and others of various descriptions, two printing offices publishing weekly newspapers—three law offices; and what is better than this latter a very

great increase of artizans, mechanics and manufacturers of various kinds. For academies, Schools and Seminaries of learning; and good Inns; we are not behind any equal population elsewhere.[4]

After completion of the line between Brooklyn and Jamaica, workers began laying a single track to Greenport, eighty-five miles away. By March 1837, the fifteen-mile stretch to Hicksville was finished, but all work stopped abruptly on April 5. The Panic of 1837 made capital scarce. The directors were hard pressed to fulfill the terms of their lease of the Brooklyn and Jamaica road, let alone resume work. Staggered by the financial collapse, the LIRR directors sought to secure a loan from the state, and in 1840 they finally received loan guarantees worth $100,000. Only this assistance from the State of New York permitted the insufficiently capitalized road to resume construction. In its 1843 report to the stockholders, the board of directors boasted of the assistance from the government. "It is one of the great, as it was one of the earliest works patronised by the State," they explained, "to secure for this State and City the leading avenues to and from its commercial capital, and to be a connecting link, in the great chain of internal improvements." At this time also "new life and greater financial ability [was] infused into the direction of the road as new members appeared in the Board of Directors." One of them was Commodore Vanderbilt, who owned the steamboats the railroad depended upon to carry passengers across the Sound from Greenport. This, Vanderbilt's first venture into railroading, was a logical extension of his growing steamboat empire.[5]

Newspapers began trumpeting the newly accessible wonders of Long Island. The *Brooklyn Star* declared, "We are confident there are thousands of families, who are deterred by various causes from penetrating into the western wilderness, who would gladly locate themselves on Long Island, if they properly understood its real advantages." The paper reported that "there is now a rail road in operation, extending 50 miles into the centre of the island. There are more than fifty thousand acres of land adjourning this rail road in a state of nature—never having been subjected to cultivation. It is true, this is mostly light land, a thin soil, but the neighboring farms which have had industry and capital bestowed upon them, show of what the land is susceptible. But the advantages of location are an ample compensation for the poverty of soil." Among those advantages, the *Star* noted "fish in any quantity, and sea weed and creek mud for manuring, healthy throughout the whole distance, very few locations for disease [and] the best market for her productions." The editor added that many farmers "now avail themselves of the rail road," and expressed surprise "that our grounds and fisheries are not improved and cultivated by some of the thousands who are seeking a comfortable home."[6] An early bit of boosterism, this piece set the tone for subsequent publications championing the opportunities to be found on Long Island. As for the railroad, there were greater profits in transporting agricultural produce than in serving passengers from sparsely populated villages.

In 1844, the line was finally complete, stretching the length of the island from the East River to Greenport. On Saturday, July 27, a special train made the trip in just three and a half hours, a journey that had formerly taken three days. Upon arrival, George B. Fisk, president of the LIRR, entertained five hundred guests at dinner.[7]

It was not long before the railroad encountered problems from the residents of Suffolk, however, many of whom had been employed in the construction of the road. Sparks from the locomotives set fire to fields and woodlands, causing severe economic hardship. Writing a century later, David Robinson Georger, a publicity director for the LIRR, trivialized this problem by commenting that the farmers objected only because the noise frightened their livestock "and disturbed their rest, and the smoke sprinkled their wives' wash with cinders. Furthermore, the trains had the audacity to run on the Sabbath. It was too much." The reason for the angry reaction went far beyond petty personal concerns or a Luddite rejection of the machine in the garden. A contemporary observer described forest fires "eight or ten miles in length, and from two to four in breadth [devouring] every vestige of vegetation [and] thousands of cords of wood that has been cut and piled and hundreds of deer and rabbits, and other game." The Suffolk men reacted quickly and decisively: "With lightening retaliation the farmers banded into groups and tore up the tracks, burned stations and pulled spikes, wrecking whole trains. The law, enlisted by the railroad, was of no assistance against vigilantes who struck in the middle of the night."[8]

Suffolk resident Preston Raynor recalled that the fires also killed livestock. "My father had a number of sheep killed in this way," he said. "Local people became so enraged that they began tearing up sections of track, causing several accidents. The railroad kept watchmen on duty nightly between Yaphank and Riverhead. Although local men were recognized tearing up the tracks the watchmen did not report their friends." The railroad agreed to pay half the damages, and apparently "that settled the trouble." Vincent F. Seyfried, historian of the LIRR, could find no records of derailments or wrecks from the sabotage and doubted whether farmers and woodsmen did any significant damage. So common were these fires that it was newsworthy when the railroad was not the cause. The *Flushing Journal* in 1846 reported on a great fire in the forest of Long Island near Huntington, noting, "This fire having originated at a distance of more than a mile from the Railroad, and the trains not being run on Sunday, will probably exonerate the Railroad Company on this occasion."[9]

These were not exaggerated claims. A major source of income in Suffolk, particularly in the Town of Brookhaven, was lumbering and woodcutting. Before the coming of the railroad, a quarter of Long Island was forested, and as late as the Civil War Suffolk was listed as the foremost woodcutting county in the state, sending annually no fewer than a hundred thousand cords of wood to the city. The devastating fires that followed in the wake of the railroad destroyed much of the young timber that remained after cutting.[10]

For a very brief time, the LIRR was the principal passenger and mail route between New York and Boston. But competition was fierce. The steamboat lines slashed their rates, forcing the company to lower the fare from Brooklyn to Greenport from $2.25 to 50 cents. In truth, the route involved at least three breaks in travel and was so cumbersome as to render the saving in travel time negligible. Passengers from New York had to take a ferry to Brooklyn, then transfer for the train to Greenport, where they boarded steamers to Norwich, where they again boarded a train. By comparison, the steamboats left from Manhattan piers, and passengers spent the voyage in relative comfort. In 1847, Commodore Vanderbilt resigned from the board of the LIRR and sold his interest in the road. Completion through southern Connecticut in 1850 of a new railroad in which Vanderbilt had an interest rendered the route uncompetitive. After a decade of effort, an expenditure of nearly $2 million, and only six years of service, the LIRR suspended the Boston train. The company was forced into receivership on March 4, 1850.[11]

The Flushing Rail Road Company

As the LIRR had neither an interest nor the capital to construct a line to Flushing, residents of that village organized their own. The Flushing Rail Road Company received its charter from the legislature on March 2, 1852, and its brief corporate existence demonstrates the financial perils of building a railroad in the antebellum era. The company began laying tracks from Flushing to Hunters Point in 1853, and the road opened to the public on

June 24, 1854. Within three years, however, the Flushing Rail Road was in the hands of a receiver, its property sold at auction.[12]

The Village of Flushing was relatively wealthy, dominated by old Flushing families upholding traditional social values. Many substantial villas were situated on generous 50-by-200-foot lots. An 1841 map commissioned by the village featured illustrations of the Italianate homes of prominent citizens. One in particular was the estate of Gabriel Winter adjacent to the Linnaean Botanic Garden. However romantic the landscape, Flushingites understood that property was essentially wealth. After the coming of the railroad, Winter subdivided his nursery into building lots.[13]

These first families set the tone and controlled the civic culture. Nurseryman Samuel Bowne Parsons, who was introduced in chapter 2, , was active in the temperance movement and served on the local Board of Education. In the early 1850s, they resisted efforts by Father McMahon to have the King James Bible removed from the schools. Catholics protested that one teacher reportedly forced all children to recite a Methodist prayer, telling parents who objected "that their children must either quit the school or learn and recite these prayers." The *Flushing Journal* answered with an editorial expressing nativist sentiments: "Before your advent, Mr. McMahon, these people were at peace with their neighbors and were subject only to the moderate exactions of your predecessors. Now the case is entirely altered. You have thrust them into antagonism with a school, of which they were satisfied,—and have almost prevailed to provoke against them the ill will of a republican people between whom and them there existed the best understanding."[14] This issue festered, but in the end the Bible was removed from the schoolroom.

Before the coming of the railroad, Flushing depended on steamboats for direct communication with New York. Located on a sheltered bay, the village benefited from this water-borne communication as travel by land was so cumbersome. Part of a vibrant coastal communication network along the East River and Long Island Sound, boats from Flushing called at Whitestone, Great Neck, Manhasset, and Glen Cove; Northport, Stony Brook, and Port Jefferson in Suffolk County; New Rochelle in Westchester; and New Haven, Hartford, Norwalk, and Bridgeport, Connecticut.[15]

Other boats were designed for the market and freight business. Tredwell Sands advertised that his sloop *John L. Franklin* would leave Flushing every Monday, Wednesday, and Friday, and sail from New York the other days. The owner guaranteed that he would "superintend the Sale and delivery of every article entrusted to his care," adding that "those who have surplus Fruits,

Vegetables, etc., can put them in charge of the subscriber, who will sell them on the best terms, and charge only a small commission for his trouble."[16]

In the *Flushing Journal*, "A Friend of Improvement" noted that better service was essential if the village was to advance. He opined that "the beauty of its scenery, the advantage of being nearly surrounded by its Bay, the East River & Sound, its high order of Public and Private Schools, its many Nurseries and Flower Gardens, its romantic elevation, with its Chalybeate Springs, its fine roads and beautiful drives, renders Flushing one of the most beautiful towns in the vicinity of the metropolis, and to insure what it should be, we now want good, frequent and cheap communication to the City."[17]

By 1850, the possibility of a railroad from Flushing to Williamsburgh or Brooklyn was a "topic of animated conversation." The *Flushing Journal* was behind the idea, and a correspondent signing himself "Kings and Queens" urged "substantial citizens" to "consult the true interests of their property, and unite in some settled policy in regard to the promotion of our internal prosperity." The writer estimated a running time from Flushing to Williamsburgh of no more than fifteen minutes, with only a short ferry ride to Grand or Houston Streets or to Peck Slip. "Thus we are made more handy to the business and amusements of the city, than those who dwell above 20th street," he concluded, "especially if there be trains run from early morning until 10 ½ in the evening." The desired result would be "in a few years one continuous village along its whole line—a great increase in the villages of Newtown and Flushing, and of the whole country within say three miles. Can any man doubt that hundreds of merchants and others, would be seeking our lots and our acres, erecting cottages, becoming our citizens, immediately increasing our tax-paying numbers, and increasing nay doubling our passengers." To drive home his point, he compared Flushing with the region served by the recently completed Hudson and New Haven lines, with new villages "springing up where there were naught but forests and rock land which was not worth $50 now commands from $300 to $500 per acre. Let us try to turn a portion of this mighty torrent of migration from New York City, from the Hudson and New Haven, to our own beautiful region, a region replete with every beauty and convenience desired, except that conveyance which will bring us in quick and certain proximity with the city."[18] A railroad would generate demand where there was little and increase the value of land.

Meeting on April 11, 1850, public-spirited citizens resolved to acquire a right of way to Williamsburgh or Brooklyn and to apply to those cities for permission to lay tracks over the streets to the ferries. The men further resolved that no cars should run on the Sabbath. The issue of the Sabbath was especially acute in Flushing, long known as a conservative, religious community. This was quite in contrast with Jamaica, which seemed more commercially minded and less overtly concerned with religious matters. Flushing also leaned heavily toward temperance, and the license question often animated local politics.[19]

In the summer of 1851, the owners of the *Island City* proposed to run their boat on Sundays. The *Flushing Journal* responded with a firm editorial titled "Sabbath Money Making," warning against

> disastrous results to the property and morals of our residents. For years our village had not been profaned by such desecration as the landing here on Sundays of the pleasure-seekers of the City.—When such was the case, years ago, our streets were filled with spectacles of drunkenness, our orchards and gardens were ravished of their choicest treasures and that citizen liable to be beaten who dared vindicate his rights to his property. We are now threatened with a renewal of these scenes, doubly aggravated by the enhanced viciousness of the City Sabbath breaking population. We deprecate the attempt to prostrate our beautiful village to the desecration of the city vandals who will make up the freight of the Island City.[20]

A correspondent identifying himself as "Vlissingen" saw the connection between his pleasant village with the distant city in an entirely negative light, asking, "Why is Flushing to become as one of the suburbs of New York and our citizens to be annoyed by the lawless of a large city?" Another letter writer commented, "I do not know the arguments which the millionaires of the Island City put forward to justify their subjecting this community to the yoke of their money power." Despite editorial denunciations, however, the *Journal* accepted an advertisement for the new service: "Sunday Excursion to Flushing," 25 cents.[21]

Samuel Bowne Parsons stepped to the forefront of the opposition. "The running of the Island City upon the Sabbath," he wrote, "will be in direct violation of Divine and human law and of the clearly expressed wishes of this community." The boat's owners replied that they would run a "moral boat" and prohibit the sale of liquor, adding that the relatively steep fare would "effectually prevent the class of persons so much dreaded by Mr. Parsons."[22]

At least one voice supported the new service. "JDT" of Bayside wrote with sympathy of the plight of the urban workers who toiled six days a week:

There are in New York many thousands mechanics and laborers who are orderly citizens and do esteem it an inestimable privilege, to visit with their wives and children on the only day which they can call their own the country, to enjoy its pure air and invigorating scenery, and who considering how confined and unhealthy their habitations in the city are, religiously believe it a duty thus to avail themselves of that privilege. I think it would be worse than selfish to prevent them.

New-York is becoming every day more and more unhealthy from overcrowding, rendering this relaxation a question of vital importance to her citizens; and it seems evident to me that if we and others who live near them do not furnish them with the proper facilities for this purpose, it cannot be very long before they will take the matter in their own hands; how much better then is it for us to give it to them cheerfully and thus exercise a more restraining power over those who would take unlawful advantage thereof. It is evidently more dangerous to the morals of the community to shut up a class of evil-disposed persons in a city, where there are thousands of groggeries and other dens of iniquity open on that day, than to dispence them for miles around its suburbs.

The editor noted that the writer was a relative newcomer who lived far from the village.[23]

For further evidence of the evils a Sunday steamboat service would surely inflict on Flushing, the residents had only to point to the result when in 1848 the Catholic Church opened Calvary Cemetery along Newtown Creek near Blissville. Ferry boats departed every half hour from the city, bringing dozens of mourners and picnickers. "The people in the neighborhood of the Penny Bridge are worried to death by the scamps, rowdies and thieves which this ferry boat brings there on Sunday and other days. Gardens, orchards and even houses are pilfered by them. After funerals there are highway robberies, fights, in which at times there are hundreds of persons engaged, and which results in alarming and terrifying the neighborhood. A complaint against this ferry will be laid before the next Grand Jury in our County." The *Flushing Journal* called this situation "aggression upon our county by the authorities and people of New York," a characterization tinged, perhaps, with at least a hint of nativism and anti-Catholicism.[24]

In March 1852, the Flushing Rail Road received a charter "to construct, maintain and operate a Rail Road from the village of Flushing in the County of Queens, to some point on the East River, within Kings County, opposite the city of New York," a distance of about nine miles. The *Journal* commented that "the names at the head of the enterprise are in earnest that everything will be done that can be done by wealthy and energetic men to accomplish the great work in which they have enlisted."[25]

The Flushing Rail Road opened its books for stock subscriptions and took in $32,300 from ninety-six investors in Flushing, but they remained an entire day at Newtown without receiving a single subscription. The *Flushing Journal* was indignant:

> New-York is fast becoming the financial centre and commercial metropolis of the world, and is centralizing in it and around it a rich and industrious population, which is increasing in almost geometrical progression. Quickness of access is of immense importance to every locality who for purposes of thrift seek an increase of population from the great outflowings of the city. Give us then rail roads and plank roads and locomotives and omnibuses and steamboats, as essential elements to our immediate and future prosperity, and we shall within a year see the lands of Newtown and Flushing quadrupled in value, and in another ten years covered with a dense population.

Evidently, this was not the future the citizens of Newtown wanted for themselves. At an anti-railroad meeting held at Wheeler's Hotel, they objected that the railroad would "not materially" shorten travel time and would prove of little benefit to their market gardens; they also feared that the railroad crossings would endanger lives and contended that all thickly settled towns in the vicinity of railroads had been injured and not benefited by the steam trains. "We regret," they stated, "our neighbors of Flushing have not evinced a more friendly feeling by ascertaining our views on the subject, before embarking in the enterprise, and that we also regret, the interests of this Town renders it necessary that we shall strenuously oppose the construction of said Rail Road through this Town." If Newtown, through which the railroad would necessarily run, did not immediately embrace the idea, Flushing certainly did. Residents of that town subscribed at the rate of about $15,000 a week, although only 10 percent of that figure was actually paid into the company's coffers at the time.[26]

Construction began in the spring of 1853, even though the location of the western terminus had yet to be determined. The directors assumed that their line would meet the river in either Williamsburgh or Brooklyn. They did not even consider the possibility of siting their depot in Queens. The East River shoreline in Queens was almost entirely undeveloped, while the shoreline running south from Newtown Creek was alive with industry.

The possibility of the Flushing Rail Road terminating at Fulton Ferry was unlikely from the start, since the citizens of Brooklyn were increasingly vocal in their opposition to the LIRR running steam trains through their streets. In Williamsburgh, too, despite the advocacy of business interest, the citizens rebuffed the railroad. In support, the *Williamsburgh Times* argued that the railroad would reduce those places "to suburbs of our city, and thereby enlarging our local trade. The objection raised that railroads are injurious to property in their vicinity now longer holds good.... Old grannyism is opposed to railroads and all other improvements, but Young America leads on the spirit of progress and believes in locomotion after that fashion." The *Independent Press* opposed the road, however. "A Rail Road track tends greatly to destroy the usefulness of a street, particularly if it is a business one," they proclaimed. "The matter in our opinion should be decided by the property owners along the streets through which it proposes the track shall run."[27]

Both Brooklyn and Williamsburgh rebuffed the railroad. Only then did the directors consider Hunters Point. The place was not especially promising, despite the apparently ideal location just across the river from 34th Street, for the swampy ground presented an engineering problem. Further, there was no industry, and the area was sparsely inhabited.

Ultimately, the selection of Hunters Point made the most sense. First, the route was almost completely level, which meant the road would be much cheaper to build. Second, the company would be able to run over its own right of way the entire distance, avoiding the necessity of a franchise for laying tracks on city streets. Most importantly, this was the only route that brought the steam trains directly to the water; the routes through Greenpoint or Williamsburgh would have compelled passengers to disembark at the city limits and board horsecars for the connection with the ferries. The main problem with the selection was that much of the line along Newtown Creek was marshy, necessitating the use of pilings and the construction of several bridges.[28]

In September 1853, the board finally voted in favor of Hunters Point. It was "simply a question of time and money, the Hunters Point route being cheaper and fifteen minutes nearer Fulton market by ferry boat" than a route necessitating a transfer to horsecars at Bushwick. The president of the Flushing Rail Road, James Strong, announced to the board that Crane, Ely and Company of Hunters Point "would give us the right of way, grounds for depot &c, and would take $10,000 in our stock; also let us own the Astoria & Williamsburgh Turnpike Co., for which they would take the stock of this

Borden Avenue, Long Island City, as it Appeared in an Earlier Day, Looking from the Roof of the Long Island Railroad Station, n.d. (The LaGuardia and Wagner Archives, LaGuardia Community College/The City University of New York.)

Company at par." The Flushing men considered the turnpike company an asset because it owned the Manhattan Avenue Bridge over Newtown Creek, which offered connections to the horsecar lines to ferries in Greenpoint, Williamsburgh, and Brooklyn.[29]

Jonathan Crane and Charles Ely were involved in the development of Hunters Point in the early 1850s, buying farms, leveling hills, grading streets, and filling in the shoreline. The *Astoria Gazette* was prompted to report, "The large hills that have become so familiar to our travelling neighbors are rapidly disappearing and a second Greenpoint will soon take their place. Already several portions of this property have gone into private hands for ship-building and manufacturing purposes and a number of lots have been sold for the purpose of erecting dwelling houses thereon. Our Rip Van Winkle neighbor Astoria may awake some morning and behold a flourishing little village where now nothing is to be seen but a collection of barren sandhills." Though virtually unpopulated, Hunters Point was nonetheless the scene of considerable speculation.[30]

As for the eastern terminus, all agreed that it would be near the company's office on Main Street. But the public objected to trains crossing thickly populated streets. The *Flushing Journal* argued, "If Main street shall be traversed by locomotives, it will become a nuisance to the travelling public. The scream of the locomotives will cause it to be shunned by other vehicles." The board then resolved to fix the terminus at Parsons' Nursery. After years of controversy, the line was set. The tracks began at Main Street, crossed the creek and ran in a more or less straight line to Winfield, curving southwest to Newtown Creek. The company still had to secure the right of way through Newtown; it still had to secure passage of a bill in the legislature granting the right to bridge Dutch Kills Creek, which flowed into Newtown Creek; and it still had to purchase or lease steamboats to ferry passengers to New York. Above all, it had to acquire capital.

The company offered to pay $50 an acre for salt marsh, and between $300 and $600 an acre for other land. Property owners, however, had other figures in mind. In Newtown, Samuel Lord initially refused to negotiate, but he eventually agreed on $5,300, and was later approached to "convey or lease the land required" for a depot. Other property owners suggested they might settle for $1,000 an acre, and one asked $1,500 for his half acre. William Prince objected to the line running through his nursery, and the *Journal* referred to him as "the only obstacle in regard to the right of way." In response, Prince published an open letter addressed "To the Inhabitants of Flushing," explaining that he had suggested to the directors a route that would not have taken his property. "I had hoped," he wrote, "to improve that part of the town by regular streets running from Main street to the creek, but such streets will be of little value to build upon, if they are to be crossed every few minutes by locomotives, and my anticipations would thereby be blighted." He eventually settled the matter for $3,200, including $1,200 for his considerable stock of trees, which the railroad sold at a public auction. This marks an important moment in the history of Flushing. Portions of both the Parsons and Prince Nurseries were sacrificed for the railroad. Nurseries remained an important business in Flushing for decades after, but the town's future lay elsewhere. Nevertheless, the Flushing Rail Road latched onto that heritage and adopted a seal featuring a tree.[31]

In March 1854, the company acquired two steamboats, the *Enoch Dean* and the *Island City*, now partially owned by William Prince. This was as much to eliminate potential competition as to serve the public. On the recommendation of Gouverneur Morris Jr., secretary of the Harlem Rail Road, the company hired E. T. Dudley as superintendent of the line at a salary of $100 a month.[32]

Despite the positive developments, financing remained a constant challenge. Stock subscriptions never kept up with the pace of construction and land acquisition, and many subscribers were several installments behind in their payments. In September 1853, the company issued $165,000 in first mortgage bonds.[33] This bond issue was crucial because there was no cash on hand to pay the contractors or the owners of property along the right of way, but it was also the first installment of what became a crushing debt.

The contractors rushed to finish the road in time for the races scheduled for the last four days of June at the National Race Course in Corona. There is no record of any public ceremony celebrating the opening, but perhaps none was necessary. The company ran trains every thirty minutes from Hunters Point to the racecourse over the not quite completed line. Thousands of sportsmen paid the 25-cent fare, and this immediate success warmed the insides of the company's coffers far better than any toasts and speeches. In July, the contractor turned over the finished single-track road to the company, which initiated a regular schedule of three trains daily in each direction. In April, the directors had magnanimously voted free passage to themselves and the officers of the road, Joseph H. King, the captains and pilots of the company's steamboats, the editors of the *Flushing Journal* and the *Public Voice*, the widow of Captain Curtis Peck, the proprietors of the three principal hotels, the principals of the three boarding schools in the village, and the clergymen of Flushing.[34]

The trains stopped at the National Race Course (during the season); Newtown; Winfield; Penny Bridge, where passengers could transfer to horsecars for the Williamsburgh ferries; and Hunters Point, making the trip in about thirty-five minutes. A "speed run" covered the seven and a half miles in eleven minutes on one occasion. The ferry from Hunters Point reached Fulton Street in twelve minutes. The next year, the Flushing Rail Road added a stop at Maspeth, where speculators had been buying farms and subdividing them into building lots. Even before the company began laying the rails, farms in Newtown were being purchased at inflated prices. The *Journal* reasoned that "Newtown might as well be laid out into avenues and streets at once. It will be wanting for building purposes shortly. If avenues and streets are laid out now at right angles, it will save a world of trouble hereafter, while it will greatly facilitate the settlement of a large population."[35] The suggestion was beyond Newtown's ability to realize, and one need only examine the map of Queens today to see that the street grid was imposed by individual developers in different places at different times.

Other speculators laid out a new suburb along the line of the railroad, just across the meadows from Flushing. Visiting the spot in May 1853, the editor of the *Journal* reported that "a better site for a village cannot be selected," and praised especially the "small sylvan lake the borders of which are beautifully wooded" that was to be enclosed in a park of about four acres. In January 1854, the West Flushing Land Company approached the railroad's board with a proposition to subscribe to $5,000 worth of stock if the railroad would give them a depot near their property. They also offered to sell land for the right of way for $300 an acre (a bargain compared to the sums demanded by other landowners) and sell posts and rails for fencing at only seven cents each. Short of cash, the Flushing Rail Road accepted this offer on the condition that the depot be named "West Flushing" and that the trains would stop only upon a signal from the passengers. That place is now Corona.[36]

Against all odds, the Flushing Rail Road was a modest success. During the summer months the road carried as many as a thousand passengers a day. The number of commutation tickets was disappointing, however. While the income was adequate to operate and maintain the road, the interest on the company's debt grew faster than the operating revenues and in the end proved fatal.[37]

On September 1, 1856, the Flushing Rail Road defaulted on its first mortgage bonds. The finance committee reported that "there were no monies in their hands for the payment of the interest due this day on the first mortgage bonds and that said interest has therefore not been paid." By February 1857, the company had instituted "the strictest economy," moves that included the discharge of almost all of the hands on the *Island City* and many of the railroad workers. In March, the treasurer reported that "an execution had been served upon the Company by the sheriff, who had levied upon all the rolling stock and personal property of the road on behalf of the Delaware & Hudson Coal Company and others." To make matters worse, several of the directors, including the president, William Smart, sued to recover funds they had advanced to sustain the enterprise. In April 1857, the company went into receivership, and a year later a syndicate headed by Peter Cooper purchased the bankrupt railroad.[38]

The new owners reorganized the company in March 1859 as the New York & Flushing Railroad Company.[39] New Yorkers now dominated the board, as control of the road passed out of the hands of the Flushing men. Oliver Charlick, then the manager of the Eighth Avenue Rail Road Company in Manhattan, became president. Elizur Brace Hinsdale, longtime counsel to the LIRR, respected neither Charlick's business practices nor his character. In his history of the company he wrote, "The new corporation continued to operate this road about the same as the old one had done, but its management was about as bad as any management could be, and the

Table 6
Flushing Rail Road, Expenses and Revenue

Item	9/30/1854	9/30/1855	9/30/1856	Total
Railway revenue	8,591.38	39,432.88	40,072.52	88,096.78
Operating expenses	6,690.38	38,902.60	41,566.29	87,159.27
Net revenue	1,901.00	530.28	1,453.77	937.51
Interest on debt	2,000.00	16,589.80	12,706.44	31,296.24
Net income/debit	99.00	−16,059.52	−14,200.52	−30,358.73

SOURCE: H. C. Lewis, *Corporate and Financial History*, 53–56.

service was totally inadequate to the wants of so large a community as that residing at Flushing and in the adjacent country."[40]

Charlick improved the Hunters Point terminal, built a new seven-hundred-foot pier for the ferries, and initiated ferry service to 34th Street and to James Slip. But he soon alienated the traveling public, the editors of the local papers, the people of Flushing, and, finally, the stockholders. He changed the schedule to the convenience of no one, making it impossible for passengers on the stages from communities east of Flushing to make their connections. He shut out laborers from rush hour trains by limiting those with commutation tickets to specific trains, and raised fares into the bargain. And to the consternation of the people of Flushing, Charlick instituted Sunday service, fanning the fears of residents that hooligans from the city would arrive to disturb their heretofore quiet Sabbath. The Sunday trains proved unprofitable, however, because the village stationed deputies at the depot to discourage violations of the local liquor laws.[41]

Only three months into Charlick's belligerent management, Flushingites purchased a steamboat to compete with the now unsatisfactory railroad. The new company was entirely capitalized by June, with Conrad Poppenhusen of College Point subscribing to $20,000 of the $50,000 required. Poppenhusen was a German immigrant who had arrived from Hamburg in 1843. Starting out with no capital of his own, he became a partner in a company that worked whale bone into combs, corset stays, and other such accessories in a small factory in Williamsburgh. As the supply of whale bone dwindled, Poppenhusen joined with Charles Goodyear, inventor of vulcanization, a process that produced "hard rubber." He opened a large factory in College Point, then a small, quiet village of middle-class respectability, and became a benefactor of the place. He built brick row houses for his workers and their families, most of them German immigrants, and financed civic improvements. He donated to the community the impressive six-story, mansard-roofed Poppenhusen Institute and funded the cultural and educational activities there, including the nation's first kindergarten. Poppenhusen made his fortune in the 1850s, and, as he prospered, College Point grew. When the Civil War came he received government contracts to equip the Union Army. He encouraged his workers to volunteer and provided for their families in their absence.[42]

With ridership down, the result of poor service and competition from the steamboat, Charlick was forced out on February 7, 1860, replaced by Electus B. Litchfield. The Flushing line chugged along until corporate consolidation united all the railroads on Long Island.

Manure by Rail

A cornerstone of the LIRR's early business was carrying agricultural produce from Queens and Suffolk to urban markets. In the last half of the nineteenth century, local papers in Jamaica, Flushing, Hempstead, and Brooklyn contained more advertisements for agricultural products than for building lots. One touted the benefits of using generous applications of lime on heavily farmed land:

> Lime for Land. Of excellent quality constantly on hand, or supplied at short notice at the Lime Factory, near the South Ferry in Brooklyn. Farmers who have not tried Lime on their land for a manure, and who are in the habit of putting on from thirty to sixty loads of manure to the acre at an expense of as many dollars or more, will find it decidedly to their interest to try Lime—as 100 bushels, which costs but eight dollars delivered on board the Rail Road Cars has been found to produce as much as 40 or 50 loads of manure. The utility of it with other manure, in making a compost is known to every Farmer who has tried it.[43]

Addressing the Queens County Agricultural Society in 1848 on the occasion of their seventh annual exhibition, John A. King, president of the society, described the crucial role of manure:

> Long Island in all its length and breadth, particularly in its western counties, depends essentially upon a supply of the richest manures, from the cities and towns on the North and East Rivers—which is brought by water and railway to the nearest point where it is required; and the farmers of this county proceed

upon the principle that it is better and more profitable to sell the corn and the oats, the straw and the hay, for cash in the market, and with it, to purchase the manures required for the growth of their crops.

A typical farm in Queens needed approximately thirty to forty cart loads of manure and one hundred bushels of ashes per acre to keep the soil fertile from season to season. Henry Stiles, the nineteenth-century historian of Brooklyn, observed, "The farmer could afford to buy stable manure, street sweepings, lime and ashes from the city to apply to his land. Guano and artificial or manufactured fertilizers have been largely used with good results, but stable manure is the great staple manure for market gardeners, for they raise double crops each year, a draft no land can endure without constant manuring."[44] This symbiotic relationship between the city and its agricultural hinterland in Kings and Queens benefited both—the farms of Long Island would prosper and the populace of New York would enjoy fresh produce.

In 1880, there were more than 150,000 horses in Manhattan and Brooklyn, each producing fifteen to thirty pounds of manure daily. These waste products could easily be transported by railroad, but at the time of King's address there was only a single track running through the center of the island, with a branch from Mineola to Hempstead (served by a single passenger car pulled by horses), far from most fertile farms. Indeed, the landscape through which the road travelled—the Hempstead Plains and the Pine Barrens—was decidedly inhospitable to agriculture; neither had yet been successfully farmed.[45]

The manure and fertilizer business became an increasingly important part of the freight traffic during the 1850s, generating loud and persistent cries of opposition from the citizens of Brooklyn. Throughout the decade, they pushed for the removal of the railroad from Atlantic Avenue, unhappy with the noise, smoke, and danger, not to mention the odor of manure piles. The people of Flushing faced a similar problem, for sailing vessels brought street sweepings from New York and deposited great piles of the stuff near the town dock. According to the *Flushing Journal*, the composition of that matter had changed from the beneficial manure to a repulsive mixture of urban and industrial waste:

> The article of manure is now manufactured by having incorporated with it the blood and offal of slaughter houses and ingredients when in a state of fermentation by heat, absolutely pernicious to health, and diffusing a nauseous effluvia

Percy L. Sperr, *Queens: Little Neck Parkway—74th Avenue 1922–1927*, 1927. (The New York Public Library Digital Collections, Irma and Paul Milstein Division of United States History, Local History and Genealogy, Photographic Views of New York City, 1870's–1970's.)

over a large surface. Last week a whole neighborhood was sickened by the landing of a quantity of this manufactured manure when the thermometer was at 94 degrees. The article of manure is very different in its constituent parts from what it was twenty years ago, or until quite recently when it might be deposited with impunity any where, and without detriment to the public health.[46]

Thus manure profited the railroad and spurred economic growth, even as it discomforted residents. Jamaica grew as a regional hub, the fulcrum of the railroad's commuter lines and an increasingly important center of financial and commercial enterprises. It boasted the finest shopping street in the county and emerged as an entertainment center as well. Capitalizing on the advantages of their location, firms in Jamaica looked to dominate business on eastern Long Island. J. and T. Adikes, for example, dealt in all aspects of agricultural products—hay, tools, groceries, and seed, especially seed potatoes:

> A great specialty is made of the seed trade. The peculiarity of climate and soil on Long Island make it of great advantage to use new seed supplies every year, and this naturally constitutes an immense business. The superiority of this house lies in the great variety of its stock and the quickness of its deliveries. Seed potatoes are grown especially and shipped here by the house from the "newlands" of Maine, Minnesota and South Dakota, as well as those of Michigan, Vermont, Northern and Western New York. And can ship through all orders to any part of the island on the day of receipt of same. No other house, even the largest in New York and Brooklyn, can do this, as the transfers west of Jamaica make it impossible.

Railroads had created a national market resulting in the increasing specialization of farmland and changed the nature of farming. Long Island farmers grew potatoes for the urban markets but found it more profitable to buy seed potatoes from afar rather than reserving part of the crop for the next year's planting.[47]

The nuisance of manure only compounded the ire of Brooklynites. Originally, the tracks had been set down the center of Atlantic Avenue, and the iron rails broke carriage and wagon axles with distressing regularity. In 1855, the LIRR agreed to widen the street and reset the rails flush with the road surface. Two years later, the Brooklyn Common Council investigated the matter, in part because of accusations that the contract had been made under "circumstances of suspicion." The majority report summarized the arguments against the railroad's privilege of using Atlantic Avenue:

> The use of locomotives in public streets, especially of densely populated cities, is a nuisance, which ought not to be tolerated; and which neither the State Legislature nor the Common Council should have aided or connived at the introduction of. In no case should the use of steam be permitted in public streets, except under the most peculiar circumstances of urgent necessity, and then only when accompanied by the most stringent constraints. The principal article of freight conveyed by the Long Island Railroad being manure is necessarily offensive to the residents along the road, even apart from the danger arising from the use of steam itself.

H. R. Pierson's minority report contended that "fraud" invalidated the contract entirely.[48]

Despite accusations of fraud, and while admitting "that the petitioners are subjected to a very grievous nuisance," the Brooklyn Common Council's majority report concluded that they did not have the power to ban the locomotives, noting that the state legislature had given the City of Brooklyn authority to regulate only those railroads established since January 1, 1853. They concluded that the legislature had therefore intended to exempt the LIRR from Brooklyn's regulation and suggested the petitioners seek redress in the courts. Pierson ridiculed such reasoning on the grounds that "no ordinance or mere contract by the Common Council can permanently restrict their successors from exercising their usual legislative jurisdiction over the subject of regulating the streets of the city." As he argued, "The power of the city to abate nuisances is unequivocal and absolute. The power to prevent and remove obstructions and incumbrances in and upon all streets, wharves, public places &c., is equally definite and absolute."[49]

The citizens of Brooklyn took their grievance to court and obtained Grand Jury indictments "against both the Brooklyn & Jamaica and the Long Island Railroad, for maintaining a public nuisance, in running steam locomotives in said street [Atlantic Avenue], and also for maintaining the approaches to the Tunnel in said street." It was becoming increasingly difficult, and dangerous, to operate the trains on the crowded city streets, but that was only one aspect of the public's opposition. The citizens' report also mentioned the introduction of "omnibus cars" (a horse-drawn street railway) and the desire to remove the railroad "so as to allow the city cars to be put on." These "citizens along Atlantic street" proposed that the company relocate its terminus to Hunters Point. By purchasing the Flushing Rail Road and constructing a new track from the existing line of the LIRR to Winfield, the company would secure several advantages, not the least of which would be an end to the constant conflict with the people of Brooklyn: "Hunters Point is outside the city of Brooklyn, the approach to the River would be through the middle of the blocks, and not along the streets," the petitioners argued. "It is thought that no interference would ever occur here, to the business of the road or the use of locomotives." Besides the connection to docks along Newtown Creek, the company could actually improve service to its passengers, for although the ferry ride would be somewhat longer, the overall travel time would be shorter by forty minutes.[50]

On April 19, 1859, the state legislature rescinded the LIRR's franchise to operate steam trains within the city limits. For the next two years the locomotives had to stop at the city line in East New York, and passengers endured an inconvenient transfer to slow horsecars to the ferry. In 1861, the company finally bowed to the inevitable and relocated its terminal to Hunters Point. Three hotels at South Ferry closed their doors almost immediately, and Brooklyn merchants saw millions of dollars of Long Island business lost to firms in New York because their customers now rode to Hunters Point and took the ferries into Manhattan, bypassing Brooklyn's merchants. A thriving farmers' market at the corner of Atlantic Avenue and Columbia Street withered and soon disappeared. Brooklyn achieved its purpose, but within a few years regretted its action. Hunters Point grew rapidly as a transportation hub, and in 1870 became the heart of a new municipality, Long Island City. The LIRR secured permission to resume service into the City of Brooklyn by an act of the state legislature in 1876, but only to a terminal on Flatbush Avenue (where it remains).[51]

The South Side Railroad Company

Another problem soon faced the LIRR Company. While the south side of Long Island had many thriving villages and prosperous farms, the railroad had no plans to construct a new line to serve them. To fill this void, Charles Fox of Baldwin, Willett Charlick of Freeport (Oliver Charlick's brother), and other investors organized the South Side Railroad (SSRR) Company of Long Island in March 1860.[52]

By September, the new company had completed surveys for a twenty-seven-mile route from Jamaica to Babylon and had obtained sections of the right of way. The Civil War set back the enterprise, and in 1862 the directors notified the state that the company "not having expended ten per cent of the amount of its capital in the construction of its road within two years from the time of its filing its articles of association, its corporate existence and powers have ceased. The affairs of the company have been closed." The state legislature granted two-year extensions of the company's corporate charter in 1864 and 1866.

After the war the SSRR moved quickly. Iron rails, long scarce, were suddenly plentiful, and by early 1866 the company had acquired the entire right of way. Several owners donated their property in expectation of a rise in land values. Laborers began laying the single-track road in April 1866, and it was ready for business in October 1867.[53] The line from Jamaica to Babylon presented no difficulties, but the question of an outlet on the East River proved as vexing as it had for the Flushing Rail Road.

The directors hosted a formal opening on November 14, 1867. A special five-car train conveyed prominent citizens and public officials over the length of the road from Jamaica to Babylon. Among the guests were politicians from both Queens and Kings, including, significantly, the entire Common Council of the City of Brooklyn.[54]

Still, the South Side Railroad needed a terminal on the East River. Their first choice was Williamsburg, the industrial heart of Brooklyn. Hunters Point, now the terminus of both the LIRR and the New York & Flushing Railroad, was their second option. They opened negotiations with Brooklyn for a franchise to run their cars into that city, while simultaneously negotiating to lease the tracks of the old Flushing Rail Road along Newtown Creek. Whether the terminal was to be in Hunters Point or Williamsburgh, it was still necessary to build a line through what is today Richmond Hill, Glendale, and Ridgewood to the Brooklyn line.

Settling on a route was one thing; negotiating with Oliver Charlick was another matter, for he had gained control of the LIRR. Elizur Brace Hinsdale was present at the meeting. The directors of the SSRR desperately needed the deal, but it was impossible. "Every consideration was urged upon the Long Island Railroad Company to enter into such an arrangement," he wrote, "but Mr. Charlick was obdurate. His motive was not easy to define, except that it is highly probable he anticipated that at some future time this railroad would become more embarrassed and better terms could be made."[55]

Rebuffed, the SSRR abruptly abandoned the Hunters Point option in December and approached Brooklyn. The Common Council had previously rejected an application for a terminal in Williamsburg, reiterating the arguments that had driven steam trains from Atlantic Avenue, but also bowing to the interests of Peter Cooper, who owned a glue factory in the path of the route, and the Kalbfleisch family, who owned much of the adjacent property. The company gained permission to run their trains to Bushwick at the northeastern edge of the city and convey the cars to the Williamsburg waterfront "with Horse power only." This cumbersome route went into service on November 4, 1868, bringing the entire south side of Long Island into direct contact with Brooklyn, albeit in a clumsy fashion.

In March 1869, the railroad was indeed finished. Passengers could board the cars near the East River ferries in Williamsburg and travel out to Patchogue. Over the objections of some local residents, the SSRR gained permission to use "dummies," small steam engines with a low gear ratio that limited their speed to no more than eight miles an hour, through the city streets. The company was relieved of the necessity of conveying the cars to the ferry by teams of horses, but the dummies only heightened local opposition.[56]

Breaking up the trains at Bushwick was obviously inefficient, and it was scarcely possible to convey freight cars through crowded city streets, especially since the SSRR had only a single track. Local residents often placed obstructions on the tracks, angry that the rails damaged their carts and carriages. Furthermore, carrying manure, the most profitable freight business, was forbidden by law.[57]

The SSRR had long struggled under a mounting debt, and finally succumbed to the cutthroat competition, despite steadily growing ridership. In August 1872, President Fox announced to the directors that the road was $300,000 in debt. When a reorganization plan failed in 1873, the company went into receivership.[58]

Table 7
Traffic on the South Side Railroad, 1868–1873

Year	Passengers	Freight (in tons)
1868	No figure	None in operation
1869	246,660	51,645
1870	586,375	76,530
1871	611,782	67,077
1872	617,899	83,671
1873	679,055	65,663*

SOURCE: Seyfried, *The Long Island Rail Road: A Comprehensive History*, vol. 1.
* January–November.

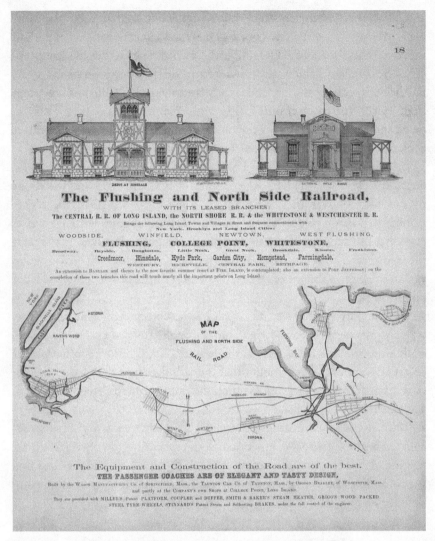

F. W. Beers, *The Flushing and North Side Railroad, with Its Leased Branches* (New York: Beers, Comstock and Cline, 1873). (The New York Public Library Digital Collections, Lionel Pincus and Princess Firyal Map Division.)

Destructive Competition

Looking back at the turn of the century, Elizur Brace Hinsdale wrote in his history of the company that Charlick's management "nearly ruined the Long Island Railroad Company. In a very short time there sprang up between the railroad corporation and the citizens' antagonistic feelings, which resulted in great changes in the railroad map of Long Island." A new group of capitalists from northern Queens, among them Conrad Poppenhusen of College Point and John Locke of Whitestone, owner of a tinware factory, mounted an aggressive challenge to Charlick's attempt to monopolize rail traffic. Their only object was to provide efficient railroad service to the north side, and they had the resources and connections to successfully challenge the LIRR.[59]

In 1868, the men incorporated the Flushing and North Side Railroad to build a new line from Hunters Point to Woodside, and from Flushing to Whitestone. In August, realizing he was beaten, Charlick sold the New York & Flushing Railroad for $500,000, but considering that he had bought the property for $300,000 only a year before, he did not fare badly in the exchange.[60]

Poppenhusen brought in several other investors from the rising and prosperous German American community. Hinsdale described him as "a gentleman of very large means, of the highest character and of a sanguine temperament. He had a very limited experience in railroad matters, and for a few years was a very important factor in the railroad affairs on Long Island until he came to financial grief." In October, the Flushing and North Side Railroad began running their trains between Hunters Point and Flushing.[61]

The SSRR now renewed its quest for a terminal on the East River. The Flushing people naturally had no objection to the SSRR entering Hunters Point. In fact, they welcomed the prospect, for it was an effective competitor of Charlick's road. In October 1869, the SSRR bought the old New York & Flushing Railroad's right of way along Newtown Creek and then built a connection to their tracks at Fresh Pond.[62]

The plan brought an immediate conflict with William E. Furman, former sheriff of Queens County and owner of Furman's Island at the head of Newtown Creek. The SSRR surveyed a line only five feet from his house, for which he claimed damages of $8,000 (he was eventually awarded $2,250). Of equal importance, Furman maintained a trout farm on his grounds; the "fresh water from springs passing west into Newtown Creek was diverted through a series of S-shaped sluices, bedded with gravel and sand for spawning." This proved only a minor obstacle, compared to what awaited the SSRR at Hunters Point. Oliver Charlick refused to grant the South Side permission to cross the tracks of his railroad. The company was able to build only a freight depot on Furman's Island, not the passenger terminal in Hunters Point they had anticipated. In 1873, the company finally voided the contract with the New York & Flushing Railroad on the grounds that they had been "unable to make use of said road as a passenger road and the annual rental agreed to be paid therefore is more than the use of said track by this company is worth."[63]

Writing decades after these events, Hinsdale marveled at the disastrous competition. "A person who will take a map of Long Island and look at the lines cannot fail to observe that the three systems of railroads cross and intersect each other at numerous points, and competed on the same ground for travel and business that one railroad could easily handle. The effect of this situation was to have the sharpest kind of competition to secure business, with the result that wherever competition could reach it was done at ruinous rates."[64]

This lesson was lost on the directors of the LIRR, for on March 8, 1872, they incorporated yet another road to compete for the Flushing business. "Immediately upon its opening," wrote Hinsdale, "the rates were reduced about one-half. It became a formidable rival to the North Side system at its most vital point, reducing the revenues of that road to a very material extent." The new "White Line" began running on November 11, 1873, and siphoned off about a thousand passengers a day from the Flushing and North Side Railroad. Both lines had initially charged a 25-cent fare, but within months this had fallen to 15 cents. Charlick's White Line also sold books of a hundred tickets for $8; these were often bought by merchants who then resold the tickets for 10 cents; he also dropped the ferry price for White Line riders to 4.5 cents. The public benefited greatly from this rate war, not only because the fares dropped, but also because the number of trains increased. Charlick ran fifteen a day and Poppenhusen nineteen.[65]

Another field of competition was the Rockaways. In 1868, the SSRR interests formed the Far Rockaway Branch Railroad Company to construct a feeder line from Far Rockaway to Valley Stream. The route opened on July 29, 1869, and by September the tracks had been extended to the railroad-owned South Side Pavilion, which offered a restaurant, picnic grounds, bath houses, and entertainment. The next year, eyeing the profitability of this seasonal traffic, the LIRR organized a rival, the New York and Rockaway Railroad to run from Jamaica to the beach. It met the line of the SSRR at Springfield, and the two tracks ran parallel to Far Rockaway. The LIRR received land for a depot from Benjamin A. Lockwood, owner of Lockwood's Grove. This competition prompted the SSRR interests to incorporate the Rockaway Railroad, a four-mile track running through the dunes to the Sea Side House. Denied direct access to the shoreline, Charlick's line terminated at Far Rockaway, inconveniencing the passengers but delighting local businessmen who opened saloons, restaurants, and hotels near the depot.⁶⁶ This contest for the summer traffic to Rockaway perfectly illustrates the redundant and mutually destructive railroad business on Long Island.

A third point of competition was Hempstead. For many years, the LIRR served that village via the branch from Mineola, but in 1869 the SSRR interests incorporated the Hempstead and Rockaway Railroad to run from Hempstead to the SSRR line at Valley Stream (today the West Hempstead branch).⁶⁷ In 1870, there were two competitors for the Hempstead traffic, and a third was about to enter the lists.

Alexander Turney Stewart and the Central Railroad

Alexander Turney Stewart was one of the most successful merchants in antebellum New York. Born of Protestant stock in the north of Ireland in 1803, Stewart came to America when he was sixteen. After investing most of his $5,000 inheritance in Irish lace, he opened his first shop on Broadway in 1823. Within ten years he was worth an estimated $1.5 million. In 1846, he opened a large, marble-faced store on the corner of Broadway and Chambers Street near City Hall (later the home of the *New York Sun*, the building still stands). At the start of the Civil War, Stewart's fortune was estimated at $20 million. In 1862, he opened a new emporium on Broadway and 10th Street. A six-story marvel with a cast-iron facade, it was the largest store in the world, with a workforce of two thousand and generating an estimated $33 million a year in retail sales. During the Civil War, he received profitable contracts from the government, but he also donated $100,000 to the Sanitary Commission, having announced he would match Cornelius Vanderbilt's contribution and goading the Commodore into ever greater generosity. After the war, Stewart built one of the largest and most opulent mansions in the city on the corner of Fifth Avenue and 34th Street.⁶⁸

In 1869, Stewart turned his eye on Long Island, where he intended to build his "Garden City," a new suburb for families of "refined and cultivated tastes." He offered $55 an acre for the Hempstead Plains, the unique prairie that since the seventeenth century had been held largely in common by the citizens of Hempstead. A town referendum approved the sale, and Stewart purchased 7,150 acres, and acquired an additional 1,500 acres from private individuals for a tract ten miles long and two miles wide. In 1869 and 1870, he awarded contracts to grade nearly 500 miles of road, to be lined with rows of maples and oaks. Key to the success of Garden City was the railroad. This was one of the first examples of a planned suburb in the United States, but unlike Llewelyn Park in New Jersey, Garden City was not immediately successful. Part of the problem was Stewart's insistence on maintaining total control over his village, to the extent that he refused to sell the houses and only rented to carefully scrutinized middle-class tenants. Garden City's prospects indeed improved once the homes were offered for sale, but the most dynamic period of its growth came after the railroad was electrified in the early twentieth century.[69]

Stewart met with Oliver Charlick to discuss a cooperative venture, but, not surprisingly, could not come to terms. In April 1870, he met with Poppenhusen and Hinsdale, who were at once more than willing to work with him. By the end of the year, they had agreed to organize the Central Railroad Company of Long Island, to be capitalized at $500,000 (5,000 shares of $100). Poppenhusen subscribed to the lion's share, 1,500 shares, with Stewart holding 250. Most of the twenty-six investors came from College Point and Flushing. Stockholders subscribed to only $298,000, however, and, as with all other lines on the island, construction had to be financed through the sale of bonds. The Central Railroad mortgaged its property and franchises to secure a $1 million bond issue, but it is doubtful that the entire issue was ever sold. The new railroad was to run the length of the Stewart property to Farmingdale, with a branch to Hempstead, and would link up with the Flushing and North Side Railroad in Flushing. The tracks ran through what is now Kissena Park, the Kissena Corridor, and Cunningham Park.

In 1872, Stewart fulfilled his contractual obligations to build "a first class single-track Railroad from the Western boundary of the main body of his Hempstead Plains purchase to a point in or near Farmingdale and a single track railroad from the above line to the Village of Hempstead." The Flushing and North Side then agreed to lease the Central and operate the new line together with its own "substantially as one railroad." It guaranteed to pay that road's financial obligations to Stewart and to run at least one freight train and two passenger trains daily to Garden City and Hempstead; one freight and one passenger train to Farmingdale; and one freight to Bethpage, site of Stewart's brickworks busily producing materials for the houses in Garden City. To encourage new residents, they further agreed to "issue to every newcomer who intended to make his home in Garden City or Hempstead a free ticket over the road for one year."[70]

Map Showing the Route & Connections of the Central Rail Road Extension Company of Long Island, New York, 1873. (Library of Congress, Geography and Map Division.)

As at Flushing, the introduction of a rival road in Hempstead brought a rate war. The Central offered thirty tickets for $10.50 and ran "mechanics trains" that honored tickets costing 20 cents; the SSRR sold books of fifty tickets for $15. Despite capturing much of the traffic at Hempstead and practically destroying the LIRR's business there, the Central proved entirely unprofitable.[71] It was simply not possible for three roads to remain in the field. Furthermore, Poppenhusen and his partners had leased the Central on unrealistic terms, a miscalculation that eventually caused the collapse of their railroad empire. After acquiring the Central Railroad, the Flushing and North Side Railroad, which had been a modest success, began to lose between $150,000 and $200,000 a year.

Bankruptcy and Consolidation

The railroads of Long Island proved an investor's nightmare. There was business enough for one to operate profitably, but by the 1870s three railroads were in direct competition. Nothing less than the agricultural present and the suburban future of Queens was at stake, but the three companies could not peacefully coexist, let alone agree to merge into one rational system.

Table 8
Finances of the Flushing, North Shore & Central Railroad

October 1, 1873, to May 3, 1876	
Income from railway operations	$957,401.11
Operating expenses	$910,053.91
Railway taxes	$34,691.90
Balance	$12,655.30
Mortgage payments and interest on bonds	$705,151.04
Loss	−$687,116.07

SOURCE: H. C. Lewis, *Corporate and Financial History*, 74–91.

In August 1874, Conrad Poppenhusen moved toward consolidating the competing lines. He and his associates formed the Flushing, North Shore & Central Railroad Company, combining the several roads already linked by operating agreements and interlocking directorates. While a sound undertaking in principle, the new company was awash in debt. They attempted to issue consolidated mortgage bonds to retire its funded debt but found no buyers. That was not surprising given the state of the market since the onset of the Panic of 1873. Jay Cook & Company had invested heavily in railroads, and the firm's collapse made investors wary of such offerings. The Poppenhusen interests took the entire $750,000 issue. The bonds were retired in 1877 by exchanging them for promissory notes payable to Conrad Poppenhusen. Consolidation did enhance operating efficiency, but the Flushing, North Shore & Central could never overcome its mounting debt.[72]

In September 1874, the SSRR was put up for sale at auction. Hinsdale, with Conrad Poppenhusen's sons Herman and Alfred, bought the company for only $200,000, but at the same time assumed its $2.5 million debt. They then conveyed the property to a new corporate entity, the Southern Railroad Company of Long Island. There were now only two competitors in the field. According to Hinsdale, "The railroad fight was now on against the Long Island Railroad by the combined roads on the north and south, although legally the two corporations were still distinct properties. A war of rates continued with unsatisfactory results to the railroads. In 1875 the earnings of the Long Island Railroad were only $798,000; the Flushing, North Shore & Central $429,691; and the Southern Road $340,000, making a total of $1,567,691." Oliver Charlick died in April 1875, and the following January the Poppenhusens purchased a majority of the LIRR's outstanding stock, 35,000 shares, from his successor, Henry Havemeyer. "Thus," wrote Hinsdale, "for the first time were all the railroad properties on Long Island brought under one harmonious control." In April 1876, Conrad Poppenhusen became president of the LIRR.[73]

While owned by the same individuals, the three corporations remained separate entities. In May 1876, the LIRR leased the Southern Railroad for ninety-nine years, for $173,250 for the first year, increasing to $233,450 for the sixth and each succeeding year. The Flushing, North Shore & Central leased its property to the LIRR on similar terms, with the rental increasing yearly from $229,250 to $351,050. The monies collected by the LIRR were to be applied first to operating expenses, second to the interest on the bonded indebtedness of the LIRR, third to the rental owed the leased roads, and lastly dividends on the stock of the respective roads. These rates were clearly excessive, and the revenue would never be sufficient to meet those obligations.[74]

Despite the shaky financial foundation, consolidation did greatly improve the operating efficiency. First, the terminals at Hunters Point were united. Then, redundant routes were eliminated and double-tracking went forward, a particularly crucial improvement because trains often had to wait on a siding to allow another heading in the opposite direction to pass (there had been several head-on collisions and many more near misses).

Other innovations included the introduction of newspaper trains by the Union News Service. A special train left Hunters Point on Sundays at 4:40 A.M. carrying a passenger car crowded with newsboys and a baggage car filled to the ceiling with New York papers. The boys were dropped off in twos and threes at several points from Mineola to the East End, where wagons carried them to the fashionable watering spots on Fire Island, the Hamptons, and Shelter Island. The return train left Greenport at 7 P.M. Rockaway excursion trains also proved popular with the riding public. During the 1877 season the railroad carried 200,000 day-trippers to the beach. Another innovation was the publication of the first promotional guidebook, *Long Island & Where to Go!!* The company distributed thousands of complimentary copies of this brochure, which described each suburban locale and resort served by the railroad.[75]

Although there were successes, the company's financial situation worsened, and Conrad Poppenhusen went bankrupt attempting to keep it afloat, a victim of his own unrealistic expectations no less than the generally depressed economic conditions.[76]

In October 1877, Colonel Thomas R. Sharp was named receiver at the insistence of Drexel, Morgan & Co., which held much of the debt. During the Civil War, Sharp served as the number-two railroad man in the

Confederacy, and after the war he became the Baltimore and Ohio Railroad's master of transportation, in which capacity he tried to protect the railroad's property during the destructive strikes in the summer of 1877. Perhaps Drexel, Morgan reasoned that any man who had contended with General Sherman in Georgia and faced the strikers in Baltimore was more than capable of running the LIRR.

Colonel Sharp proved an imaginative and capable helmsman. Under his three-year receivership, he not only made existing lines pay, but also introduced new services that expanded the ridership. From the start, of course, he had the advantage of a consolidated system unchallenged by competitors and liberated from unrealistic leasing agreements. Achieving that end had bankrupted Conrad Poppenhusen, but the system could now grow and prosper in a rational direction. Sharp eliminated redundant routes but added trains when justified by the demand. For example, he introduced Sunday excursion rates to the cemeteries. While the horsecar line charged a 7-cent fare from the ferry landing to Calvary Cemetery, the LIRR offered a round-trip excursion for 10 cents. The excursion fare to Fresh Pond, near Lutheran Cemetery, was 20 cents, and 30 cents to Cypress Hills Cemetery in Glendale.[77] This proved quite a lucrative business, as visitors from the city appreciated the rural, parklike qualities of the cemeteries.

Another shift was an active interest in the leisure business. Sharp instituted steamboat excursions from Hunters Point to Coney Island in 1879, charging 50 cents. The railroad also operated its own picnic ground on Atlantic Avenue in Woodhaven. On opening day, May 25, 1879, ten thousand visitors crowded Morris Grove, many of them taking advantage of the railroad's 25 cent excursion fare. Although Sharp abandoned the Central Railroad route from Flushing to Floral Park, the company continued to provide special trains to the shooting range at Creedmoor, excursions that were extremely popular with the German shooting clubs. The railroad also instituted "Rapid Transit" along Atlantic Avenue between Jamaica and Brooklyn; the nickel fare spurred ridership, especially among working men. One change that proved less popular with the public was an overdue fare increase. Poppenhusen had stubbornly kept fares at rate-war levels, believing that it was only competition that had rendered the lines unprofitable. In his second year as receiver, Sharp ordered an increase of 20 cents to 25 cents on all routes, with the exception of the rapid transit on Atlantic Avenue.[78]

The LIRR had finally become a profitable enterprise and an attractive property. In 1880, Austin Corbin purchased the 35,000 shares Drexel,

Table 9
Long Island Railroad Traffic, 1877–1883

Year	Passengers	Tons of freight
1877*	3,063,431	272,086
1878*	4,157,715	254,580
1879*	5,043,848	286,071
1880*	6,228,292	320,837
1881	6,512,270	339,252
1882	8,878,543	380,349
1883	9,024,370	416,153

SOURCE: [J. E. Ralph], *Long Island of To-Day* (New York: LIRR, 1884), 14.
*Years when the LIRR was in receivership.

Morgan had acquired from Poppenhusen (there were 65,212 outstanding shares at the time), and thus gained a controlling interest. Corbin had himself appointed receiver and ran the railroad in that capacity until October 1881, when the court ordered the property returned to the control of the board of directors. Corbin then became president.[79]

Austin Corbin was born in New Hampshire in 1827. After graduating from Harvard Law in 1849, he headed west and settled in Davenport, Iowa. He opened a bank that remained solvent during the Panic of 1857, one of the few such institutions in the west to survive. During the Civil War, he developed strong ties with New York banks, and in 1865 relocated Austin Corbin and Co., later the Corbin Banking Co., to Manhattan. His interest in railroading began in 1874 when he spent the summer at Coney Island. Convinced that this spot, so close to the steaming cities, was destined to become a great resort, Corbin formed a company to build a line from Prospect Park to Manhattan Beach, where he constructed a mammoth hotel. By the mid-1870s, as Poppenhusen was consolidating his railroad empire, Corbin was quietly expanding his holdings and gaining expertise in the complex affairs of local railways.[80]

Corbin's ultimate dream, which he outlined in an article in the *North American Review* in 1895, was to develop a deepwater port for transatlantic liners at Fort Pond Bay, six miles west of Montauk Point. The chief advantage was the saving in time; he estimated travel time of six days, six hours, and twelve minutes between Liverpool and New York, but claimed that by changing to the train at Montauk the trip could be shortened by as much as ten hours, and even longer if fog caused the ships to lie at anchor off Sandy Hook. Another argument in favor of this project was that "the risk from

William J. Rugen, *Old Jamaica LIRR Station*, circa. 1909. (Courtesy of the Queens Borough Public Library, Archives, William J. Rugen Collection.)

collision on the much frequented North River and New York Bay is escaped, and the long delay at Sandy Hook and the slow passage through the twenty-five miles of tortuous and crowded channels from Sandy Hook Lightship to the New York piers are done away with."[81]

The problems with such a development far outweighed the benefits, and Corbin neglected to suggest how the essential support services might be provided. As a 1923 report noted, each ship required about 5,000 gallons of fresh water; 120,000 pieces of laundry had to be serviced within 48 hours, a task that then employed 400 persons at a facility in Hoboken. Supplying foodstuffs would also put Montauk at a disadvantage. Then there was the matter of constructing facilities for emergency repairs. Finally, where would the hundreds of longshoremen, laborers, and other personnel live, not to mention the 193 customs inspectors, 62 examiners, and 16 guards needed to process each ship?[82] How would a new city rise out of the sand dunes?

In June 1896, Austin Corbin died in a carriage accident near his home in New Hampshire.[83] The Pennsylvania Railroad purchased a controlling interest in the LIRR in 1900 to realize its long-term objective of direct access into New York City. The company also inherited Corbin's scheme, and soon put an end to it. Alexander Cassatt, Pennsylvania's president, actually made a personal inspection of Fort Pond Bay. As he stared at the desolate vista and the sparsely inhabited fishing village, Cassatt surely must have questioned Corbin's sanity.

The Pennsylvania Railroad revitalized the aging system with an unprecedented infusion of capital, digging tunnels under the rivers; building Pennsylvania Station, the magnificent urban monument designed by McKim, Mead & White; and electrifying several lines. The railroad entered the twentieth century on the express track.

4
The Verdant Suburbs

Between the mature, agrarian environment of the early nineteenth century and the metropolitan landscape of the twentieth, new patterns of land use emerged in Queens. Some of the earliest examples of the classic railroad suburb arose there, and the availability of large tracts of open land encouraged manufacturers to relocate or open factories in western Queens, most intensively along Newtown Creek. With industry, of course, came the rise of the first working-class communities, usually built close to the factories. Both suburbanization and industrialization were made possible by more efficient forms of transportation.

At midcentury, agriculture dominated the Queens economy, and most landowners anticipated that the railroad would enhance the profitability of their farms. Indeed, for decades transporting agricultural produce from Long Island and delivering urban manure to the farms represented the bulk of the railroad's business. Others envisioned a different future for Queens. Speaking to the Queens County Agricultural Society in 1852, Charles King, president of Columbia College, commented that the same elements that benefited the county's farms—"the character of the soil, its general salubrity and its pure water, combined with its proximity to the great city"—also "invite to a residence here" for the citizen "who looks forward eventually to spend the serene evening of his days beneath his own vine and his own fig tree."[1] The appearance of a few country retreats for the urban gentry, men retiring to live the life of the "gentleman farmer" as several men identified themselves in the 1850 census, does not herald a new suburban age, but it does point to Long Island's future.

Along the East River

Brooklyn Heights is rightly considered the first true suburb of New York. Located directly across from the city's commercial core, the area developed quickly once steam ferries went into operation in 1814. While Brooklyn and Williamsburgh urbanized, however, the East River shoreline in Queens retained its rural character. As late as the 1830s, the only communication with Manhattan was via rowboat or sailboat ferry. In 1834 Stephen A. Halsey, a New York merchant living in Flushing, purchased land around Halletts Cove with the idea of founding a new village. The next year he replaced the sailboats with a horse ferry (four horses were tethered to a pole on deck and walked in a circle; the rotating pole turned a propeller). In 1840, Halsey launched a steam ferry, the first step toward suburban development.[2]

Under Halsey, Astoria became an incorporated village within the Town of Newtown in 1839. The name honored John Jacob Astor, the richest man in New York, in hopes that he would donate $2,000 to fund the female seminary Halsey planned. Astor sent only $500 and the school never opened, but the name stuck. Astoria grew slowly, as it was rather remote from the business section of Manhattan. Not until the 1840s was there even a good road between Astoria and Flushing. Progress was meager indeed.[3]

Unlike Brooklyn Heights, which prospered as the archetypal ferry suburb of the era, Astoria grew not as a bedroom community but as a distant retreat where members of Manhattan's merchant elite kept summer homes. Overlooking the East River, these stately residences insulated the families from the unhealthy conditions in town during the summer months. Among those who summered on this, Long Island's first "gold coast," was the family of Edith Wharton. Her great-grandfather, Ebenezer Stevens, was a successful New York merchant, and in her 1933 autobiography, *A Backward Glance*, Wharton describes her ancestor's home: "The Mount stood, as its name suggests, on a terraced height in what is now the dreary waste of Astoria." Her mother spent summers there as a girl and remembered "stately colonnaded orangery, and the big orange trees in tubs were set out every summer on the upper terrace."[4]

Ravenswood, the shoreline between Astoria and Hunters Point, was soon lined with mansions. The men of commerce who built homes along the East River included Samuel Gouverneur Ogden; Pliny Freeman, founder and first president of the New York Life Insurance Company; George W. Beebe, of the Wall Street banking firm of Parshall, Beebe and Company; Anthony W. Winans, founder of the 34th Street ferry; Charles Parshall, president of the Harlem Railroad Company; Francis Palmer, president of the Broadway Bank; J. Lee Smith, president of the St. Nicholas Bank; shipbuilder John Inglis; and the wholesale grocer John A. Bodine. The Bodine Castle, a crenellated wonder built in the fashion of an English manor house, dominated the shoreline until its hasty demolition to make way for a Con Edison training facility in 1966, just before the Landmarks Preservation Commission could designate it. Ravenswood was also the subject of a rare Currier & Ives print depicting the fanciful if unrealized vision of architect Alexander Jackson Davis.[5]

Lydia Maria Child, author of the popular domestic guide *The Frugal Housewife*, visited in October 1841, and was pleasantly surprised by the charms of the place. "Last week we went to Ravenswood, to visit Grant Thorburn's famous garden," she wrote. "We left the city by Hell-gate, a name not altogether inappropriate for an entrance to New-York. The garden at Ravenswood is well worth seeing. An admirable green-house, full of choice plants; extensive and varied walks, neatly kept; and nearly three thousand dahlias in full bloom—the choicest specimens, with every variety of shade and hue."[6]

Ravenswood's era of elegance lasted but a few decades. By the 1890s, almost all of the mansions had been either torn down or converted for industrial use. During the last quarter of the nineteenth century, the shoreline lost its bucolic charm and was transformed into a heavily industrialized and increasingly polluted environment. New York's gentry moved further east in search of more remote and exclusive watering spots. In 1895, the *New York World* reported that several of the mansions remained "in a fair state of preservation" but added that others were "occupied by manufacturies and other industries. The smoke of adjoining factories now assails the greater part of the old landmarks. In many cases the carved stone and iron fences have been demolished and the grounds laid waste." The industries included a chemical plant adjacent to the Bodine Castle, the New York Architectural Terra Cotta Works (the company's office survived and was designated a city landmark in 1982), the New York Sumac Extract Company, the East River Light Company, the Harris Zinc and Lead Company, and a cordage works.[7]

Nathaniel Currier (American, 1813–1888), *Ravenswood, Long Island, Near Hallet's Cove*, 1836, 19th century. Lithograph, hand colored, on wove paper, Image: 11 1/4 × 49 3/4 in. (28.6 × 126.4 cm). (Brooklyn Museum, Dick S. Ramsay Fund, 51.239.)

The advance of the city also promised to change the character of Shore Road, a scenic drive between Hunters Point and Astoria, though the realization of the change never resembled this optimistic vision:

> The true lover of nature will regret the disappearance of this pretty bit of road, or rather its transformation into a broad paved highway with artificially made flower beds, fountains and ornaments, and bordered by carefully trimmed trees. When all this has been introduced and the multitude crowds the new drive, the world will be richer by a beautiful piece of work, but a bit of nature, precious to many, will be lost. But we must not complain for it is unavoidable that the growth of cities does away with many things which we would like to retain, and which ought to be retained, but must make room for the inexorable demands of stern necessity.

By 1900, most of the mansions had been abandoned, reworked into rooming houses and industrial sites, or torn down, and the Astoria shoreline no longer attracted visitors by its natural charms. It is no wonder that Edith Wharton dismissed the place as a "dreary waste." Much of the traffic was of a commercial nature, "long lines of trucks and wagons which wend their way toward the ferry in the morning and return empty in the evening."[8]

Railroad Suburbs

Middle-class railroad suburbs sprouted across Queens after the Civil War, coinciding with the consolidation and expansion of the Long Island Railroad. A second wave of suburbanization, more extensive than the first, followed electrification in the early 1900s and the opening of the tunnels under the East River that eliminated the inconvenient break in transportation in Long Island City.

Bloodgood Haviland Cutter was a member of one of the oldest families in Flushing and a resident of Little Neck. Known as the "Long Island Farmer Poet," Cutter journeyed to the Holy Land in 1867 with a group that included Mark Twain. In *Innocents Abroad*, Twain dubbed Cutter the "Poet Lariat" for his habit of putting his every thought and impression into "barbarous rhyme." Cutter penned a bit of strained verse about the new North Side Railroad:

And then when all the track is laid,
We will be more than doubly paid.
Our land will then take such a rise,
'Twill us agreeably surprise.

In the end, thought the poet, both landowners and new residents will benefit:

Then citizens will out remove,
And then the North Side will improve;
How much better that will pay,
Than raising either corn or hay.

Cutter was not the only local versifier. In 1873 an anonymous realtor-poet praised the virtues of "Fair Bayside":

Then come out to Bayside, Long
Island's fair garden,
Come away from the turmoil of
business and strife,
Own your own happy home, 'tis
the glorious guerdon,
The only true rest, peace, and
comfort in life.[9]

In the absence of reliable transportation, communities blessed with the natural advantages that might entice new residents remained immune from urban pressures. Steamboats connected villages on Long Island's North Shore with the city, but those places were more in the nature of summer retreats than bedroom communities. A letter to the editor of the *New York Herald* reprinted in the *Long Island Democrat* described one such place. Dated Manhasset, July 31, 1839, the correspondent points out the pleasures of this charming but remote village in North Hempstead:

> I see frequent references in the papers to this, that and the other watering place, and charming retreat from the heat and bustle of the city—to Rockaway, Coney Island, New Brighton, New Rochelle, Glen Cove, Oyster Bay, and various other delectable spots, where visitors will have nothing to do but enjoy themselves in eating, drinking, sleeping, driving, sailing, sporting, dancing, etc.—but have not seen a single allusion to this pleasant region, where I have taken up my abode for the summer, and find it combining as many, and in some respects, greater advantages than anyplace I have heretofore visited in the vicinity of New York.
>
> The steamer Sun leaves here every morning at seven o'clock, and New York on her return at half past four in the afternoon, except on Tuesdays and Fridays, when the boat goes on pleasure excursions to the Sea Bass Banks, on which days she leaves here at five in the morning, and New York on her return at six P. M. This arrangement, you will perceive, gives those who have business or calls in the city, a good long day there, as the boat makes the passage generally in two hours and a half, including her stops at Great Neck, Throg's Point, White Stone, West Chester, and College Point.

One can only imagine the olfactory joys of traveling to and from New York on those days when the steamboat doubled as a fishing boat. The correspondent, after praising the "beautiful and varied scenery," adds that "unfortunately, there are but few places of accommodation here. The inhabitants generally being wealthy farmers, but few are disposed to give themselves any extra trouble in the way of boarders."[10] Despite this bit of boosterism, the suburbanization of Manhasset would not commence for several decades hence.

As described in chapter 3, in 1877 the Long Island Railroad published its first promotional booklet, *Long Island & Where to Go!!*, with descriptions of every community served by the railroad and advertisements for resorts and real estate. One advertisement offered five hundred "choice building lots" at Manhasset directly across from the depot, where "the ground is in condition for immediate improvement, being elevated and free from rock." The notice went on to describe the place in glowing terms for potential homeowners. "The society here consists of the best American elements, old families resident over 100 years, churches for all denominations," it boasted. "Here is the spot for the over-worked business man—clerks, book-keepers, and others, where pure air can be enjoyed, imparting the necessary rest and vigor to the overworked brain and muscle, on the shore of one of the loveliest and safest bays, with fish, oysters, and clams in abundance. The roads are perfect, drives in every direction." While the wilds of Manhasset had not yet been tamed by suburban development, there were many other locations in Queens County that did enable "the business man from the city to reach a quiet retreat in the country by a short and pleasant ride."[11] Still, many of the communities praised in *Long Island & Where to Go!!* were described as ideal for summer excursions rather than year-round residence.

The arrival of the railroad did stimulate growth across Queens. Jamaica and Flushing in particular attracted new residents, but the first real suburb, a community built expressly for commuters along the railroad, was Alexander Turney Stewart's Garden City, also mentioned in chapter 3. Homes went up on streets around the train station, and a grand hotel rose there in 1874, which was replaced by an even grander hotel designed by McKim, Mead & White. That structure burned, and a magnificent hotel designed by Stanford White rose in 1901, which endured until it was demolished in 1973. The Garden City Cathedral, the seat of the Episcopal bishop of Long Island, was dedicated in 1885, a gift from Stewart's widow, Cornelia. She also donated land and funds to build St. Paul's, a school for boys. Sadly, the Village of Garden City had been a rather poor steward of its heritage, and many historic buildings have been lost.[12]

Richmond Hill

It is in Richmond Hill that the railroad suburb found its earliest and most complete expression in Queens. Located at the convergence of the railroad lines from Brooklyn and Long Island City, the site combined convenience with beauty.

In 1869, Albon Platt Man, a New York attorney and onetime director of the New York & Flushing Railroad, purchased farmland just west of Jamaica. Together with landscape architect Edward Richmond and real estate developer Oliver Fowler, he set out to build a suburban community. Man had been much impressed by Stewart's plans for Garden City, but while Stewart had to build a spur to his new community on the Hempstead Plains, the railroad's main line ran through Man's property. Rejecting the name of a nearby station, Clarenceville, an earlier and until then unsuccessful subdivision, Man

Bird's Eye View of Richmond Hill Arcade #3 and Lott Manor, circa. 1910. (Courtesy of the Queens Borough Public Library, Archives, Maps Collection.)

named his suburb Richmond Hill, evoking an association with the stylish suburb near London, while also acknowledging Edward Richmond, who had recently died.[13]

Long Island & Where to Go!! offered an enticing description: "The eye takes in at once the beauties of that portion of the place lying nearest to the [rail]road. This includes a number of commodious dwellings and many neat cottages, with the handsome church, schoolhouse, and depot; but not half the beauty of the place can be seen without visiting the hills which overlook all that part of the island and the ocean itself." The site was ideal, hugging the wooded hillside of the terminal moraine and benefiting from the cool, healthful breezes rising off Jamaica Bay a few miles to the south. It was "far enough away from the city to escape its deleterious and confined features and at the same time near enough to reach all its interests, of business, instruction and amusement within a few minutes."[14]

The combination of exceptional natural features, convenient rail lines, and the fact that the entire tract was under the control of a single owner made the realization of the suburban ideal possible. The environment presented a contrast to Brooklyn's urban grid and suggested the parks of Olmsted and Vaux. A later promotional brochure described the verdant environs: "We enter upon rich, warm fields as soon as we are clear of Brooklyn, and directly we find ourselves among a congeries of new parks, pleasant places, very delightful to the man of moderate means, with perhaps a number of children who need the educational advantages of the town, but are the better for living in fresh air and having green things about them. These parks are restricted against nuisances of all kinds."[15]

The railroad station faced an open green in the village center, giving those arriving from the city an immediate sense of the verdant and uncrowded landscape. A small village of shops surrounded this core. Man donated large amounts for a school, a church (the Church of the Resurrection, 1874), and the village green. In 1905 a Carnegie library was built facing the green; it features Philip Evergood's 1938 Works Progress Administration (WPA) mural *The Story of Richmond Hill*. Fanning out from this commercial center were the residential streets leading to the village's own park on the slope of the picturesque, and more difficult to develop, moraine. The City of Brooklyn later transformed those acres into Brooklyn Forest Park (now Forest Park) and hired the Olmsted firm to produce the original design. Man's sons donated fourteen acres to that end, recognizing that "a nearby 'central park' could only increase the value of their remaining real estate holdings as well as serve as a greenbelt/buffer against the urban sprawl" of expanding Brooklyn.[16]

Man brought his vision to every street. Restrictive covenants written into the land titles mandated that houses be built well back from the street line and prohibited fences. Trees were planted along property lines, so each street presented the spaciousness and leafiness of a linear park. In the era before zoning regulations protected residential neighborhoods, covenants were adopted to define standards of construction, identify prohibited uses, and, in many cases, mandate the exclusion of racial and religious minorities. Man "understood that good planning makes for a good development, and that in turn attracts the 'right kind' of people."[17]

Long Island & Where to Go!! noted that as Richmond Hill was "intended specially for private residences, the whole place has been restricted against nuisances of every kind," including tenements, factories, and warehouses. An 1873 map displays the section adjacent to the park and just north of Richmond Hill with curvilinear roads, but this land was not yet subdivided. Man later built a golf course there for the residents, a beneficial use of otherwise idle land, but the course lasted only a few years. In the 1910s, the new main line of the Long Island Railroad cut through the Richmond Hill Country Club, and the site was developed as North Richmond Hill, soon renamed Kew Gardens.[18]

Designed in deliberate contrast to the row houses lining the grid-iron streets of Brooklyn and Manhattan, the large-frame houses, many built in the eclectic Queen Anne style in the 1880s and 1890s, often had a separate entrance for servants, further evidence of the economic standing of these suburbanites. As a later railroad booklet described them, the homes were "obviously the abodes of taste, if not wealth." The social characteristics of the residents also merited comment. A booster publication of 1894 described Richmond Hill as possessing "some of the most attractive characteristics of a suburban point":

> The refinement and long standing of its people afford a basis upon which has been built up a most delightful and valued social life. There are no extremely wealthy people in the village proper, which adds rather than distracts from the cordial and unrestrained relations between the residents who are all of our well to do and most progressive American stock. A visitor is impressed with the uniform comfort and even elegant taste displayed by its people both in the architecture of their homes and in all those little details which go so far to lend charm and variety to life. The streets are neatly kept, the lawns carefully trimmed, while flowers and shade trees abound in all parts of the village.

The description concludes by noting that "careful limitations and restrictions have been devised which afford a secure guarantee of the most select and refined associations. It is therefore an easily calculated problem to count upon the steady upward growth and rapid increase of the town in all those interests and features which constitute the best wealth of our American life." In the 1890s, most of the two-and-a-half-story wood-frame homes sat comfortably on 75-by-100-foot lots, and a few were even larger. At the turn of the century, a builder appealing to the less well-off offered new eight-room homes on 50-by-100-foot lots costing between $3,800 and $4,200, "according to finish."[19]

Jacob Riis was one of the early residents of Richmond Hill. In great demand as a lecturer, Riis brought his lantern slides and tales of life in the slums to middle-class audiences in Queens, accentuating the distance between the comfortable suburban qualities of Richmond Hill and the grim existence of the urban underclass. Riis built his reputation on his accounts of life in the immigrant neighborhoods, but his intimate knowledge of those conditions effectively alienated him from city life. While he was at war with the squalor of Mulberry Bend, using his photography to expose the slum's conditions, he settled his family in a rented home near Prospect Park. Each night he traveled "from the slum to my Brooklyn home or I do not think I could have stood it. I never lived in New York since I had a home, except for the briefest spell of a couple of months when my family were away, and that nearly stifled me. I have to be where there are trees and birds and green hills, and where the sky is blue above." Riis obviously equated a proper home with life beyond the urban grid. In his 1901 autobiography, *The Making of an American*, he described his move to Queens in glowing terms: "It was winter when all our children had the scarlet fever that one Sunday, when I was taking a long walk out on Long Island where I could do no one any harm, I came upon Richmond Hill, and thought it was the most beautiful spot I had ever seen. I went home and told my wife that I had found the place where we were going to live. The very next week I picked out the lots I wanted."[20]

Even this well-known journalist could not immediately afford to build his dream house. Only a timely commission of $200 to translate some insurance policies into Danish and generous loans from friends made his move possible. The Riis family was soon situated in their snug new house, "with a ridge of hills, the 'backbone of Long Island,' between New York and us. The very lights of the city were shut out. So was the slum, and I could sleep." There is no question but that Riis identified the ultimate victory over the

Jacob A. Riis, *Our House in Winter*, glass negative, between 1890 and 1914. (Library of Congress.)

slum with a suburban future. Each year he and his wife opened their home to children from the crowded tenement districts of the Lower East Side, certain that their deprived visitors could only benefit from a day in a wholesome suburban environment: "Even as I write the little ones from Cherry Street are playing under my trees. The time is at hand when we shall bring to them in their slum the things which we must now bring them to see, and then their slum will be no more." Clearly, for Riis there was an undeniable connection between life in the suburbs and the making of an American.[21]

The Expanding Suburban Landscape

After Conrad Poppenhusen consolidated the three competing railroads on Long Island in 1876 (see chapter 3), he negotiated to regain access to a terminal in downtown Brooklyn. His railroad now offered service from Jamaica and East New York "at a rate of fare identical with that now charged on the horse railroads" while cutting travel time substantially. To allay the fears of the local citizenry, the railroad fenced the tracks from the terminal to the city line. The company anticipated that the reintroduction of service into Brooklyn would benefit both that city and Long Island. "The metropolis of New York," the railroad's booklet stated, "connected by its railways with the neighboring localities, has by its extensive commerce, hitherto eclipsed Brooklyn; making the latter more noted for its beautiful residences than for its commercial enterprise." The new service on Atlantic Avenue, however, "will bring Brooklyn within easy reach of the people of Long Island, and make it for them the most convenient business center; while the residents of Brooklyn will find all parts of Long Island readily accessible both for residences and pleasure excursions. This new Railway interest, and that of the people within reach of it, are identical; the advantages arising from rapid transit are incalculable, and should be the means of developing constant traffic between Brooklyn, East New York, and Jamaica." Indeed, a string of suburban communities, "the outgrowth of Brooklyn, Williamsburgh, and East New York," did arise along this line.[22]

The railroad capitalized on the new suburban ridership by offering such new services as theater trains: "For the accommodation of persons desiring to visit theatres, friends, or attend lectures or concerts, several night trains are run, the last train leaving Long Island City at midnight. These trains run every night in the week, except Sundays, to Woodside, Winfield, Newtown, Corona, Flushing, College Point, and Whitestone; and every Saturday to

Glendale, Richmond Hill, Jamaica, Frankiston, Creedmoor, Hinsdale, Garden City, Hempstead, Broadway, Bayside, Little Neck, and Great Neck. These trains are very popular, and offer inducements to many to live in the country all year round."[23]

Until the opening of the East River tunnels, when a new line was built through the Sunnyside Yards and central Queens to Jamaica, the main line ran from Hunters Point along Newtown Creek, through Maspeth, Ridgewood, Glendale, and Richmond Hill. The railroad's 1877 promotional booklet noted that "among the surrounding hills" at Fresh Pond [Ridgewood], only four miles from Hunters Point, "may be found many desirable villa sites." This section did not grow into a middle-class preserve, but developed as a working-class streetcar suburb, an extension of Brooklyn's street grid. Glendale, two miles further along this line, offered "many attractions to mechanics and others whose business requires them to be in the City at an early hour. The location is healthy, and remarkable for its freedom from all malarial infections."[24] There, too, vigorous suburban development had to await the boom in the early 1900s.

So successful was Albon Platt Man with Richmond Hill that other developers purchased farms in the vicinity and even appropriated the name for their subdivisions: Richmond Hill Terrace, Richmond Hill South, and Richmond Hill Estates. Richmond Hill Park was sited nearer Jamaica Bay than the terminal moraine, and Richmond Hill Circle was so far toward the bay that it was in all likelihood wetland.[25]

William Ziegler developed Morris Park just south of Richmond Hill. An 1890 advertisement for the place boasted such amenities as stone sidewalks, water mains, shade trees—"real shade trees, none of your two-for-a-cent saplings that die as soon as planted"—and promised that "electric lights will soon be introduced." The notice also described the benefits of raising children in the new suburb, "where a puny boy or girl is as rare as a white crow." The "beautiful residences" sold for between $3,000 and $12,000, and unimproved lots were offered for $200. "If you are a man of moderate means," the advertisement concluded, "and yet desirous of living in a refined neighborhood, visit Morris Park." The agent was conveniently located across the street from the railroad station on Atlantic Avenue.[26]

In 1891, about forty wood-frame homes lined the streets of Morris Park. In 1894, a booster publication declared that "during the past three years several hundred houses have been erected, aggregating in the neighborhood of a million dollars of real property. The character of the people who have become interested and taken residence here fixes definitely the growth of

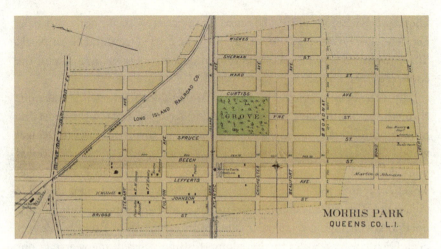

New Map of Kings and Queens Counties, New York: From Actual Surveys, detail (New York: J. B. Beers and Company, 1886). (The New York Public Library Digital Collections, Lionel Pincus and Princess Firyal Map Division.)

Morris Park as one of the most refined and advanced suburban towns of the metropolitan district." This author, while exaggerating the number of new homes, was certain that Queens was destined to become part of the proposed Greater New York and thus assured potential buyers that the elevated line from the Brooklyn Bridge would be extended. "The advance in value of real property here is as certain as the revolution of the seasons," continued the author, "and by 1900, what Henry George calls the unearned increment should amount to a very respectable sum. There may not be a palace or immense hotel erected, but what will be far better will be the large number of select and handsomely arranged American homes, one of which is the center of more real happiness than all the palaces in the world." By 1901, some blocks in Morris Park were completely built up with two- or two-and-a-half-story wood-frame houses, most of them on generous 40-by-100-foot lots; a few had street frontage of 50, 60, or even 100 feet. But there were also a number of smaller homes, sometimes attached, on 20-foot lots on the edges of the development.[27] In 1895, Morris Park and Clarenceville merged with Richmond Hill into one village, which lasted only two years before being swallowed up by Greater New York.

One line of suburbs stretched eastward from Long Island City along the north side. Patches of a rational street grid overlay the rural topography, but not according to any common plan. Developers apparently built their new suburbs without considering how their streets would intersect with others.

But the landscape was so open that it must have seemed that the intervening spaces would never be completely filled in. A similar pattern emerged on the south side along the railroad's main line from Richmond Hill through Jamaica and into the Town of Hempstead. In general, developments closer to the city attracted blue-collar homeowners, while commuting costs limited residence in more distant suburbs to professionals.

The topography east of Jamaica Village and south of the moraine was remarkably flat. In early maps it was sometimes marked as "Little Plains," to distinguish it from the vast Hempstead Plains to the east. At Hollis and Queens Village, the rural landscape yielded to suburbanization in the 1890s, but it was not a sudden transformation, and older economic activities persisted. A promotional booklet from 1895 pointed out that Hollis was "an attractive place, where the houses stand at independent angles to each other, the Queen Anne style of architecture, that was so persistent about ten years ago, is still popular; but its rigors have modified, and if a Hollis man has a fondness for some other style, say the colonial or even the plain modern American, the neighbors will not send out a vigilance committee." At Queens Village, the appearance of suburban subdivisions was not so advanced as to warrant comment on architectural styles, but even there "the local muscle of the place is concerned in the building of houses and the raising of fruits and vegetables for the towns and the satisfaction of the appetites of boarders in these precincts." The author makes clear, however, the difference between this spot and the city by commenting on the view from the moraine, "seen through the incessant vapor and smoke that drift from the chimneys of New York—the incense that is burned at the altar of commerce and industry."[28]

Because the land was so flat and lent itself so readily to subdivision, development costs were relatively low. The primary advantage of this landscape was that "whole districts may be laid out without the necessity of removing a single cubic yard of earth for grading the streets; it was only necessary to trace the streets and drive the surveyor's stakes into the ground." One writer praised the "pretty and substantial cottages" and added that the "custom of doing away with fences, now so prevalent, is here strictly adhered to. We do not see single houses with small gardens, separated from each other, but one continuous large garden with pretty houses between the trees and shrubs." He concluded that the entire section along the railroad line east of Jamaica offered "striking examples of what modern cottage colonies should be." Even so, in 1909 there were few dwellings in Queens Village, and none at all only a few blocks beyond the railroad. The most prominent resident was undoubtedly Tammany Hall boss "Big Tim" Sullivan, whose summer home was located on a spacious 130-by-330-foot lot not far from the Metropolitan Jockey Club's racetrack, in which he held an interest.[29]

The creation of Greater New York in 1898 spun the forces of urbanization into these suburban districts. The Williamsburg Bridge (1903) and Queensboro Bridge (1909) connected Manhattan's streetcar network with Brooklyn and Queens, places that until then had endured a cumbersome commute into the city. This fostered a land boom and the construction of semi-detached two-family homes and row houses instead of detached, single-family homes. The extension of the elevated lines in the 1910s yielded even more dramatic changes, including higher population densities and the construction of smaller suburban homes and apartments for working-class families. The tracts beyond the railroad retained their rural character well into the twentieth century, and parts of eastern Queens remained undeveloped until after World War II, when the automobile emerged as an affordable and distinctly American form of mass transit.

Lots offered at auction were of value only insofar as they were adjacent to efficient transportation links to the urban core. In 1903, an exuberant advertisement for Auburndale, a new development between Flushing and Bayside, boasted that the depot was located in the center of the tract: "No Walking!" It was, however, something of an exaggeration to claim that the site was "only 30 minutes from Herald Square." If a would-be suburbanite did purchase a lot, he would find the commute far more involved than the route today. It was indeed an advantage that the depot was an easy stroll from his new home, but to reach his destination in the city, a commuter first took the train to Hunters Point, where he transferred to the ferry across the East River. Now to reach Herald Square he could either board one of the crosstown trolleys or walk. Even under the best of circumstances, it was not possible to complete this journey in thirty minutes. Within a decade, however, our hero's life improved significantly. Completion of the Penn Tunnels in 1910 and the opening of that grand urban monument, Pennsylvania Station, indeed cut the commute to about a half hour. The advertisement merely anticipated the completion of the tunnels, already under construction. Auburndale was not immediately successful, however; in 1909, fewer than a dozen homes were scattered through the subdivision.[30]

Between 1918 and 1922, two hundred single-family houses went up at a development called Richmond Hill South, within walking distance of the railroad station but, more significantly, close to the new Fulton Street elevated line that opened in 1915. Richmond Hill South offered such expected amenities as sidewalks and curbs, streetlights, water mains and sewers, and Norway maples planted in front of each house. Set back twenty feet from the street to provide lawns, these "detached cottage type" dwellings were smaller than their Victorian predecessors, but even here the developer offered "many varying architectural designs, giving a pleasing individuality to every home."[31] These were clearly designed for families of modest means, however, and that points to the ultimate destiny of Queens. Development in the early decades of the twentieth century followed the mass transit lines, not the railroad stations. The homes were smaller, but homeownership remained fundamental to these new suburbanites. Those more prosperous families who in earlier generations might have moved to Richmond Hill or Flushing now bought homes further east in suburban Nassau County, Long Island, which over time had become separate from Queens, which will be discussed in chapter 7.

A substantial volume put out by the *Flushing Journal* in 1908 described the varied features of the Queens landscape and the borough's commercial life, praising especially the suburban qualities: "Here are, indeed, still found the charms of true rural life with all the advantages the near neighborhood of a big city can supply. We find meadows and fields, copses and stretches of woodland, brooks and ponds in abundance. The noise of the bustling city cannot be heard but an occasional shriek of the locomotive or the buzzing of the electric car as it dashes past reminds us that we are not in a distant solitude but only very little removed from the activities of modern life at its highest tension." The author added that "the expanse is so vast that another generation at least will pass before Queens had lost its principal charm, its truly rural aspect as far as a large part of its territory is concerned. And it will never lose this entirely, because its shore line is of such a nature that it lends itself freely to every attempt of beautifying the city." He greatly underestimated, of course, the intensity of the next wave of development, which would be far more urban than the bucolic suburbs of previous decades.

Older, established residents of Queens no doubt expected that their suburbs would remain "part and parcel of the city and as important as the other districts but just a trifle more charming, a little quieter and certainly more agreeable to everybody who does not set utility above everything else."[32] But the twentieth century brought unprecedented changes to Queens. After consolidation in 1898, the fantastic resources of Greater New York financed construction of an urban infrastructure that the old townships and villages could never have dreamed of, and the advancing metropolis inevitably eclipsed the suburban qualities of Queens.

5

The Noxious Industries

Beginning in the 1850s, as land became more expensive in Manhattan, manufacturers looked to Queens to expand their enterprises, especially if the factory emitted foul odors or other pollutants. They selected relatively isolated spots rather than long-established villages, expecting regulation to be lax. The three historic villages—Newtown, Flushing, and Jamaica—had only a few workshops and no factories of any size even into the 1890s. The local economy was based on wholesale and retail commerce, much of it tied to agriculture. Jamaica prospered as the major transfer point for the railroad, Flushing grew into a fine suburban retreat, while Newtown remained essentially a quiet country village of general stores and churches.

In the second half of the nineteenth century, industrialization came to dominate large sections of the county, and by the turn of the twentieth, Queens had emerged as one of the leading industrial centers in the country. The industrial landscape took various forms. In Astoria, College Point, and Woodhaven industrial villages grew around new factories. Conrad Poppenhusen established his hard rubber company in College Point and became the benefactor of the place. Henry Englehardt Steinway built a new factory complex at an isolated spot along the East River just beyond Astoria; the community that arose around the factory was immediately known as Steinway. In Woodhaven, located between Jamaica and East New York, Charles

Lalance and Florian Grosjean built a large facility to manufacture tinware.[1] In each case, the industrialists fostered the growth of communities around the factories, in some cases actually building homes for the workers and donating schools, libraries, and churches.

A second pattern flourished in Hunters Point along the East River and Newtown Creek, where oil refineries, distilleries, smelters, and other resource-processing facilities were established. Industry also emerged near the Brooklyn city line in Ridgewood, or, as it was originally known, East Williamsburgh, where breweries and street railways based in Brooklyn expanded their operations.

Industrial Villages

In 1854, Conrad Poppenhusen acquired the rights to use Charles Goodyear's vulcanization process to produce hard rubber. With options for expanding his operation in Williamsburgh limited, he built the Enterprise Hard Rubber Works in College Point, then a small, isolated community of only a few hundred inhabitants along the East River shoreline, separated from the Village of Flushing by wetlands. A German immigrant, Poppenhusen, quickly transformed the place into a thriving settlement, and his success prompted the establishment of breweries, silk mills, and other factories, as well as saloons and beer gardens patronized by the largely German workforce. By 1860 the population had grown to more than two thousand. Poppenhusen erected barracks and private houses for workers across the street from the factory. Originally the homes were available only for rent, but soon workers were given the chance to buy them. In general, the place enjoyed years of labor peace, in no small measure because Poppenhusen was the very model of the paternalistic industrialist. He provided for the families of workers who served in the Union Army in the Civil War, and in 1868 donated to the community a five-story mansard-roofed building for use as an educational institution.[2] The Poppenhusen Institute still serves the community and is a designated city landmark. College Point continued to thrive even after Poppenhusen's financial empire collapsed in 1877 (see chapter 4). The India Rubber Comb Company and the other factories provided employment into the late twentieth century, and for many years the owners of those enterprises continued to live within walking distance of their factories, just as the workers did.

Another successful transplant, and still the most well-known industry in Queens, was the Steinway & Sons Piano Company. In 1853, three years after

Village of College Point, 1876. (Courtesy of the Queens Borough Public Library, Archives, Borough President of Queens Photographs.)

arriving in New York from Germany, the Steinwegs founded their company under their anglicized name. Working out of a rented building on Varick Street, they sold eleven pianos that first year. In 1859, they exhibited in the Crystal Palace exhibition and won great acclaim (four pianos were lost when that structure burned). The company expanded, and in 1858 the Steinways purchased the entire block between Park and Lexington Avenues, 52nd to 53rd Streets, and erected a 175,000-square-foot factory at a cost of $150,000. The complex was turning out pianos within two years.[3]

Manhattan may have been where the company's business was, but the location had its own problems. In the first place, there was no room to expand within the confines of the dense street grid. The urban context created another problem for the manufacturer. "We sought a place outside the city to escape the machinations of the anarchists and socialists," wrote William Steinway, "continually breeding discontent among our workmen, and inciting them to strike." Lamenting the harmful effects life in the tenements imposed on his employees, he thought the only way to secure the future of his business was "to remove [his] very large factory requiring much room and many men from the City of New York to the suburbs."[4] The site had to be large enough and sufficiently remote to accommodate a foundry to produce

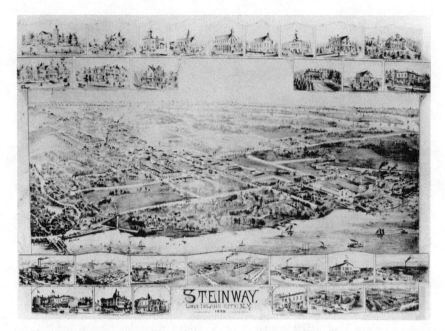

Lithograph print of Steinway Village, 1896. (The LaGuardia and Wagner Archives, LaGuardia Community College/The City University of New York.)

the iron frames for the pianos and space to store wood as it seasoned prior to being dried in kilns.

In 1870, William Steinway purchased a large nursery in Astoria and the adjoining estate of optician Benjamin Pike, whose 1856 mansion became the family's summer home (now a city landmark). The next year, he purchased additional acreage for a half mile of waterfront, ideal for delivery by barge of wood, sand, coal, and pig iron. During 1872 and 1873, the company erected an iron and brass foundry, a sawmill, boiler and engine houses, and the first factory building; other buildings were added in 1876 and 1879, as the company moved more of their operations from the city. Soon there were four hundred workers crafting pianos in Queens, in addition to the six hundred employed in Manhattan. Steinway installed a private telegraph line connecting the two sites.[5]

To encourage the workers to move to Queens, Steinway built blocks of two-story brick homes. This was a means to profit from the land he purchased, but it could also serve as a means of social control, using threats of foreclosure or eviction in times of labor unrest. In reality, however, few Steinway workers lived in the houses. New streets were opened and paved, and the main thoroughfare to the complex was renamed Steinway Avenue

Steinway and Sons Factory, 1895. Astoria, NY. (Courtesy of the Queens Borough Public Library, Archives, Illustrations Collection-Astoria.)

(now Steinway Street). Steinway also built a streetcar line to the Astoria ferry. By 1876, the burgeoning village had a school, provided by William Steinway, and in 1890 he funded construction of a Protestant church and a building to house a kindergarten and library, to which he donated the books. By the turn of the century, the community had grown to more than seven thousand inhabitants, the majority of them European immigrants connected to the piano company, and the post office had officially recognized the place as Steinway.[6]

Following the lead of the Steinways, the Sohmer Piano Company moved from 14th Street in Manhattan to a waterfront site in Astoria in 1886, purchasing part of the Stevens estate along the East River. The *Long Island City Star* predicted that there would "be an exodus of manufacturing firms and their works from New York to Long Island City. Here, particularly in the outskirts, there is room for the expansion, rents are lower, land cheaper." Obviously trying to allay fears of Astoria residents about the pending influx of immigrant workers, the paper added that Sohmer employed about three hundred men, "nearly every one of them is married and the father of a numerous family. They are good citizens, steady, honest and industrious and they would prove a valuable addition to any community." The paper soon reported that Sohmer employees, "over from New York, looking for houses,

The Piano Industry—The Factory of Sohmer & Co., at Astoria, Long Island, Opposite Ninety-Second Street, New York, ca.1890. (Jeffrey Kroessler Print Collection.)

express themselves as delighted with the idea of coming where they can afford fresh air." The workers were undoubtedly familiar with Astoria, as they probably ventured over for picnics, but there was no possibility of moving to Queens unless they had employment nearby as the cost of a daily commute by ferry and streetcar made the realization of such dreams prohibitive. Like Steinway and Poppenhusen, Sohmer & Company also built homes for their workers, and even erected the Sohmerville Hotel adjacent to the six-story brick factory.[7]

From Ravenswood to Newtown Creek

The new industries crowded out the estates that had dominated the shoreline since the 1840s. There was of course no zoning to protect the owners of those once magnificent residences from intrusion by the noisome factories. The 1873 Beers *Atlas of Long Island* shows only one industry in the Ravenswood vicinity, J. McAloney's carpet factory, which had been in operation since the 1850s. By the mid-1880s, however, industrial concerns, some of them moving into the former mansions, dominated the entire shore from Hunters Point to Astoria. In 1886, John Goode decided to remove his cordage works from Brooklyn and bought the Brooks mansion. The *Star* reported that fifty men have been "digging away the hill back of the old mansion—or where the old mansion stood—and leveling all the ground to five feet above high water. Early this week the masons began their work and soon another great manufacturing structure will rise above the trees and houses of Ravenswood." In early 1887, the New York Iron & Chemical Company purchased the Noble estate, and the Harris White Lead & Zinc Company bought the Beebe estate, joining the New York Architectural Terra Cotta Company, which began operations the year before.[8] Each of the new industries had access to the waterfront to receive raw materials, and, in the absence of any environmental controls, used the river to dispose of industrial waste.

The same process played out in Hunters Point and along Newtown Creek, as large-scale industries crowded out of Manhattan and Brooklyn or pushed out by growing complaints about their obnoxious pollutants sought new sites. Lumber and coal yards, lime works, oil refineries and storage tanks, distilleries, and bone boilers (the production of glue by boiling dead animals, a process resulting in especially obnoxious fumes) lined the shores of Newtown Creek. Forced out of Brooklyn by that city's Board of Health, some industries simply moved across the border into Queens, which had a weak governmental structure and ineffectual enforcement of what regulations there were. Hunters Point attracted varnish works, soap factories, ink manufacturers, a lard oil works, and other chemical plants. One chemical company built its works at the head of Dutch Kills Creek, which flowed into Newtown Creek, no doubt relying on the tide to remove by-products and pollutants. By 1873, the Standard Oil Company, which acquired Charles Pratt's holdings, was one of the largest concerns in Long Island City.[9]

The casual pollution of Newtown Creek "had the effect of spoiling the area of shore and East River, Hell Gate and beyond, which once produced large quantities of fish, oysters and clams." The *Newtown Register* noted that this was a growing problem in the region, and referenced the pollution of Newark Bay and its impact on the oystermen: "The fear is that the leakage from the pipes will injuriously affect, if not entirely destroy, this important industry. The fear is not without just foundation but the petroleum industry is of such overwhelming magnitude and importance and is operated by such heavy combinations of capital that it is doubtful whether even by an appeal to the State Legislature the New Jersey fishermen will be able to arrest the evil which threatens them."[10]

There was also a constant danger of fire. As early as 1863, an insurance survey of petroleum depots in New York harbor noted that "petroleum vapor has a powerful tendency to permeate every crevice and even the pores

Harway Dyewood and Exterior Manufacturing Company Factory, circa. 1898. (Courtesy of the Queens Borough Public Library, Archives, Jacob F. Wieners Jr. Photographs.)

of wood, [and] it will also accumulate in any confined space, and then, like gas, it acquires an explosive quality, if mixed with oxygen or air in certain proportions." The report also mentioned that "the leakage of Petroleum and its products from wooden barrels is worthy of notice," as was the hazard of empty barrels that had been saturated by the substance. There were, in fact, several large conflagrations in the refineries on both sides of Newtown Creek throughout the period.[11] The environmental problems still remain, the most intractable an immeasurable pool of petroleum floating beneath Greenpoint, the residue of a century of leaking tanks. In 2010, Newtown Creek was designated a Superfund Site, and in 2022 the underground petroleum and chemical plume was so designated.

By the 1880s, East Williamsburgh, or Ridgewood, attracted fireworks manufacturers, bone boilers, fertilizer plants, breweries, and the facilities of the street railways, including offices, depots, stables, and car barns. In 1873, there were only about three dozen homes in the area, but within ten years the opening of the breweries and the expansion of the streetcar companies gave employment to hundreds and fueled a rising demand for building lots. This also brought growing complaints about the noxious fumes some industries emitted. The *Register* reported, "Fat boilers, bone burners and dead animal dissectors, whose establishments have been driven out of Kings County as vile nuisances, have squatted in this Town and are permitted to pursue their health-destroying avocations without hindrance. The air of this Town, in many localities is polluted to an alarming extent by the nauseating stenches and disease-breeding effluvia, of which complaints are daily made to the Board of Health." In one instance, the State Board of Health certified that George W. Baker's fertilizer establishment was "clean and odorless," and used "no decayed animal matter." Long Island City also had to address the problem of the bone-boiling and fat-rendering establishments situated along Newtown Creek. According to historian Vincent Seyfried, "The odors that emanated from these plants were so fetid and stomach-turning that no one could live near them; when the wind was right, the odors wafted into the city and even travelers on the Long Island R. R. were taken sick from the fumes." One of the first acts by the Long Island City Board of Health was to ban these plants "from locating near routes of public travel."[12]

With Ridgewood becoming more populous, nuisance industries had to move again. In January 1893, the Good Citizenship League notified the Flushing town board that bone boilers, "driven out of the vicinity of Brooklyn," were looking to set up their operations nearby, and requested that the board "prevent the establishment of such nuisance within three miles of our village limits." The village trustees did not seem alarmed by the prospect, and one member suggested that the ladies "be thanked for their interest in the matter." Two months later, however, Newtown officers raided a bone-boiling factory "which had threatened the villages of Flushing and Corona with the worst of smells." In May, the *Flushing Journal* reported that wagon loads of dead horses were delivered every Sunday to bone boilers located near the Flushing-Jamaica line, adding that the animals were cut up for rendering and "much of the flesh that is not used is thrown in the woods to rot in the open air."[13]

Not all industries proved a burden on the local neighborhoods. Beginning in the 1890s, German immigrants opened knitting mills in Ridgewood, and by the 1950s approximately 25,000 workers were employed in more than 1,100 mills. In succeeding decades, as more production was moved overseas, the industry contracted; still, in 1990 the area had 400 mills employing 13,000. The German flavor may have faded with each generation, but the mills provided employment for succeeding waves of immigrants.[14]

Queens very rapidly emerged as one of the nation's most productive industrial centers, ranking fifteenth in the nation by the 1930s. According to the census of 1909, the growing borough already contained 771 factories employing 23,891 men and women.[15]

Garbage

For decades, noxious industries had relocated from crowded urban neighborhoods to Queens, and in the early twentieth century the city looked to its largest borough for a solution to its problem of waste disposal. There had long been a symbiotic relationship with regard to manure—the city generated tons of manure daily, which was transported to farms on Long Island to fertilize the market gardens that produced food for the cities. Prosperity and a rising consumer culture yielded more and more garbage, but finding sites to dispose of the tons of food waste, ashes—the residue from coal-burning stoves and boilers—and rubbish—paper, rags, wood, and metal—was more challenging, both in the composition of the waste stream and in disposal. The solution was not a form of ecological recycling, but a dump.

There was, of course, money in refuse. In 1859, private entities began using Barren Island, located on the western shore of Jamaica Bay in Kings County, to process waste, mainly animal carcasses, into fertilizer and oils. An inlet there was called Dead Horse Bay. The site was ideal, for it was beyond the control of municipal authority and in theory the tide would flush the residue out to sea. In reality, of course, much of the residue that flowed out with the tide flowed back into the bay, and the foul odors wafted inland and over the resorts at Coney Island and the Rockaways. Far from addressing such pollution, the city added to it. In 1896, a municipal processing facility was built, but it handled barely 10 percent of the daily total, about two thousand tons.[16] Profiting from waste was the dream, but the facilities could handle only a fraction of the daily tonnage, and the reality was that the problem of garbage disposal would only grow worse as the population grew.

Waste processing at Barren Island continued until 1933. By then, new uses were imagined for Jamaica Bay. In 1930, the city opened Floyd Bennett Field, its first municipal airport, and in 1934 Robert Moses created the Marine Park Authority, with himself as the only member, to create and provide access to new parks. The first piece of his vision was the Marine Parkway Bridge (now the Gil Hodges Bridge) connecting Brooklyn and the Rockaway Peninsula. Portions of every toll went toward the construction of Marine Park. The wasted landscape of Barren Island would become an urban oasis. Using the same funding stream, Moses then pushed through the Rockaway Improvement to remake the beachfront along the lines of Jones Beach.[17]

In 1884, the city acquired Rikers Island, intending to construct a new prison there. Before construction began, however, the island had to be enlarged, and in 1893 dumping commenced. A report of the Department of

Street Cleaning that year stated, "Final disposition of the city's refuse is the most difficult problem to be solved. No adequate provision for it has ever existed." At the start, much of the material consisted of street sweepings—still largely manure—and ashes, for the city burned approximately seven hundred thousand tons of coal annually; as much as 60 percent was sent to Rikers. Later, however, the composition of the material was less "clean."[18]

By the 1930s, Rikers was the primary site for municipal waste, with twelve dumps rising 40 to 120 feet high. A self-appointed good government group called the Committee of Twenty on Street and Outdoor Cleanliness tasked Dr. George A. Soper with investigating the issue. Summarizing his work in the *New York Times* in 1931, he called the place "perhaps the worst and most extensive nuisance of its kind anywhere to be found. It is a mountain of ill-smelling waste. Fire from spontaneous combustion has existed in this dump for years and cannot be quenched. The offensive odor from Rikers Island is sometimes noticeable for a distance of more than ten miles." Dumping at Rikers did not finally cease until 1943, and by then other sites had been opened.[19]

For decades, the city relied on ocean dumping as a solution to urban refuse. In the 1880s, the city began dumping in the upper bay, which of course polluted the harbor, and the debris impeded shipping. Later it was dumped further out to sea at a point approximately ten miles from Long Island and New Jersey. A quarter of all garbage collected, between 2,000 and 2,500 tons a day, was dumped from barges offshore. Not all sank immediately to the bottom, of course, and it was inevitable that some of this material would drift back to shore with the tides. An investigation by the Metropolitan Sewerage Commission in 1910 revealed that "refuse was washed upon the beaches in considerable quantities for fifty miles along the New York Shore and for seventy-five miles along the New Jersey shore." Dr. Soper recognized the greater implications of this failure. "Millions of persons seek these beaches in hot weather," he wrote, "only to find the sand and surf now strewn with garbage and rubbish."[20]

In May 1929, the State of New Jersey filed a federal complaint against New York's ocean dumping. The U.S. Supreme Court appointed Edward Campbell, a retired federal judge, special master. In December 1931, he ruled in favor of New Jersey and ordered that the city cease ocean dumping by July 1, 1934. Dr. Soper thought the decision "one of the most fortunate things that have ever been accomplished," for "it hastens New York's tackling of the whole problem of refuse disposal with a thoroughness hitherto lacking as because it seeks the preservation of the invaluable bathing and recreation resources which mean so much in the vicinity of the metropolis."

The solution was not immediate, however. Complying with the letter of the ruling, the city sent the last garbage scow to sea on June 28, 1934.[21]

Incineration appeared to be a promising solution. By 1930, there were nine incinerators operating in Queens, five in Brooklyn, three in Manhattan, and three on Staten Island, each handling between 60 and 500 tons daily. Only one was utilized to generate electricity, however; all the others were just intended to dispose of the waste. But burning garbage had its own problems. First, there was the city's short-sighted policy of granting only short-term contracts for waste removal, generally three to five years, a period far too brief to justify the investment of private capital. As ever, polluted air and unpleasant odors were a source of constant complaints. Further, there was the matter of transporting the garbage to the incinerators; there was no way to hide that. Finally, "they do not solve the whole problem of getting rid of the waste. The cinders, ashes and metals remain to be taken care of, and are disposed of by dumping, either at sea or on land."[22]

As early as 1913, as Rikers accepted most of the city's waste, a report from the Department of Docks and Ferries noted that "many thousands of acres of waste lands exist in all the Boroughs of Greater New York, as well as in the adjoining sections of New Jersey, which are susceptible of being filled in by the City waste, and are now being filled in as rapidly as the necessary arrangements can be made by the street cleaning bureaus of the different Boroughs, as practically none of it is going to sea." The report added that "the most extensive opportunities for riparian public reclamation are to be found in the marshes surrounding Jamaica Bay."[23]

By the 1930s, dumping in saltwater wetlands was presented not as merely expedient, but as a public benefit. The "low swampy areas within the City limits," particularly around Jamaica Bay, could be transformed into usable land. The Department of Sanitation's annual report of 1938 boasted that these "mosquito-breeding marsh lands at locations within economic hauling distance of the regular collection" actually create value, "and the disposal cost is only a fraction of what it is by other methods." From a public relations standpoint, the primary goal of these bayside landfills was not a cost-effective way to dump the garbage, but to create usable land for parks or development.[24]

Over the first three decades of the twentieth century, Flushing Meadow was turned into an enormous landfill. Unlike other landfills, however, this was not a municipal operation. Michael Degnon, who built bulkheads along Dutch Kills in Long Island City and erected factories and warehouses, envisioned Flushing Meadow as a grand industrial park, and for this he needed fill. He secured a contract to remove the street sweepings and ashes from

Brooklyn, and dumping began in 1910. Not long after residents of adjacent neighborhoods complained about the "nauseating stench of rotting garbage decomposing in the summer heat." The healthy wetland became the Corona Dumps.[25]

All told, over the first half century after the creation of Greater New York, Queens came to have the largest area given over to landfills and other waste processing in the five boroughs. Staten Islanders took the presence of the mammoth Fresh Kills landfill as a personal affront, evidence indeed that theirs was the forgotten borough. For decades prior to the opening of Fresh Kills in 1948, however, the wetlands and waters of Queens accepted most of the city's waste, even as the borough grew to a city of a million inhabitants.

The intrusion of nuisance industries threatened the rural landscape and suburban tranquility of Queens, but this was to be expected as New York and Brooklyn grew and Queens lacked an effective county government. After Queens became part of the greater city, its undeveloped, seemingly empty landscape promised an immediate solution for the waste of the city. Wetlands were deemed of no use unless they could be filled to create buildable land, and the city scarcely considered questions of pollution, water quality, or any other environmental issues. Residents of the borough had the burden of the ill effects of industry and waste disposal. However vocal they may have been, their concerns scarcely influenced the city's needs and plans.

6

The Leisure Landscape

Queens beckoned as a landscape for leisure activities even in the seventeenth century. The open land provided opportunities for activities that would have been impossible in the city, and distance only enhanced the experience for day visitors. Almost from first, those activities were commercialized. As a defining feature of Queens, the leisure business was a constant, even as the spaces, participants, and events evolved over time.

Horse Racing

The English seized New Netherland from the Dutch in 1664, and not a year later Governor Richard Nicolls established a racecourse on the Hempstead Plain, for the purpose, he explained, of "encouraging the bettering of the breed of horses, which, through great neglect, has been impaired." Impressed by the flat and open terrain, he called it Newmarket, after a racecourse in England. A few years later, his successor, Francis Lovelace, appointed "trials of speed" to be run in May, a "crown of silver, or the value thereof in good wheat" to be awarded to the winner.[1]

Other tracks opened in the eighteenth century, but it was in the early decades of the 1800s that the sport attracted great crowds. In 1821, the New

York Association for the Improvement of the Breed of Horses opened Union Course in Woodhaven, three miles west of Jamaica. In 1823, it was the scene of the first match race pitting champion horses of the north and the south, Eclipse from New York, and Sir Henry from Virginia. The event brought out over fifty thousand spectators, Andrew Jackson, Aaron Burr, and Vice President Daniel Tompkins among them, and as much as $200,000 was wagered on races. Sir Henry won the first heat, but Eclipse took the next two. In 1842, again at Union Course, running for a $20,000 purse, Fashion, champion horse of the North, bested the southern champion, Boston, in two four-mile heats, taking the first by a length in the record time of 7:32½, and the second by sixty yards. The crowd was estimated at between fifty and seventy thousand, and the railroad strained to carry the sporting crowd to the track.[2]

The most famous match race of the antebellum era was run at Union Course on May 13, 1845. A crowd estimated at more than seventy thousand witnessed Fashion run against Peytona, a challenger from the South. The underdog Peytona won both very close heats. A Currier and Ives print immortalized the event, with the Cypress Hills and the Long Island Railroad in the distance. The businessman and bibliophile Daniel M. Tredwell wrote that after the results were officially announced, "the railroad company exhausted its capacity and left thousands on the grounds to wait for a return train." Referring to this match race, Dr. Nathaniel S. Prime, in his 1845 *History of Long Island*, condemned the sinfulness of the spectacle:

> But the gambling, expense and loss of time attending these scenes of dissipation, form only a part of the evils with which they are connected. The drinking—the swearing—the licentiousness—the contentions, and other nameless crimes, which are here periodically committed, with the countenance of law, are enough to sicken the soul of every man that fears God, and is disposed to reverence. His commands; and must induce him to wish most devoutly for the time to come, and that speedily, when this crying abomination, with all its accompaniments, shall be banished from this once sacred soil of Puritans and Huguenots.[3]

Leaving aside the reference to Puritans and Huguenots, of whom there were very few in colonial Queens, Reverend Prime evidenced a cultural divide between the traditional values of those with deep roots on Long Island and the rising commercial culture of the nineteenth century. Still, the economic benefits of horse racing went far beyond the enthusiastic wagering on every race. Farmers and merchants benefited from the sale of food and beverages,

Peytona and Fashion: In their great match for $20,000. over the Union Course L.I. May 13th. 1845, won by Peytona, time 7:39 ¾ 7:45 ¼ (New York: N. Currier [between 1835 and 1856]). (Library of Congress.)

and the breeding of race horses was another generator of wealth. Coaches, railroads, and ferries enjoyed increased ridership on race days, when the Fulton Ferry took in as much as $1,000.

Fashion Race Course, later renamed National Race Course, opened in West Flushing, now Corona, in 1854. The Flushing Rail Road had been rushed to completion in time to deliver crowds to the races. Apparently, the farmer who sold the property tried to buy it back once he learned of the sinful purpose. The site accommodated other sports as well. In July 1858, all-star teams—"Picked Nines"—from Manhattan and Brooklyn met in a best-of-three series there. Thousands of fans paid admission—10 cents per person, 20 cents additional for a one-horse vehicle, 40 cents for a two-horse vehicle. This may have been the first time fans paid to see a baseball game, ostensibly to support the widows and orphans of firemen. New York won that first game 22–18, and the teams met again in August and September. The *New York Times* published an account of the game on page one, a first.[4] Oddly, almost always the most important baseball games in that era were played in Brooklyn.

Centreville opened near Union Course as a trotting track in 1825. In addition to the regular racing season, on at least one occasion it was the scene of remarkable animal cruelty. In 1847, Albany Girl was put up to run a hundred miles over ten straight hours. She was pushed until she broke down after 9.5 hours, having covered 97.5 miles. One can imagine the fevered betting involved in that spectacle. Cruelty was an inescapable feature of sports involving animals. In January 1866, a sizable crowd of "genuine sportsmen" attended a grand fox chase at Union Course. Six foxes were released in turn, each torn to pieces by a pack of hounds. A *Times* editorial exclaimed, "If that is deemed 'manly sport,' we must plead to a dullness of vision quite unable to see it."[5]

In the last quarter of the nineteenth century, the center of the racing industry shifted to south Brooklyn. The Coney Island Jockey Club, organized in 1879 by Leonard W. Jerome, with investments from such prominent figures as William K. Vanderbilt, opened a track in Sheepshead Bay the next year, and other tracks soon opened in the vicinity. Horse racing in Queens was by no means at an end, however. The Queens Jockey Club opened Aqueduct Racetrack in 1894 along the line of the historic aqueduct carrying water from Long Island to the Ridgewood Reservoir atop the terminal moraine. The Metropolitan Jockey Club, organized 1901, opened Jamaica Race Course near the Locust Manor station of the Long Island Railroad in April 1903, and in 1905, August Belmont and members of the New York Jockey Club opened Belmont Park, just over the line in Nassau County. Jamaica closed in 1959 and Rochdale Village, a high-rise cooperative-apartment complex rose on the site. Belmont Park, of course, continues to host the Belmont Stakes, the third leg of the Triple Crown.[6]

Resorts at Rockaway

While Rockaway had attracted visitors since the early 1800s, its reputation as a stylish resort began with the opening of the Marine Pavilion in 1834. Former New York mayor Philip Hone, the politician John A. King, and other investors formed the Rockaway Association and expended $43,000 on a large and well-appointed hotel built in the Greek revival style. A local historian writing in 1839 described the Marine Pavilion as

> a large and splendid edifice, standing upon the margin of the Atlantic, and kept in a style not excelled by any hotel in the Union. The main building is 230 feet front with wings, one of which is seventy-five and the other forty-five feet long. The peristyles are of the Doric order, the piazza being 235 feet in length by 20 in width. The sleeping apartments number 160. The dining-room is eighty feet long and the drawing-room fifty. The atmosphere here is fresh,

cool and delightful; invalids soon find themselves benefited, and all experience fresh inspiration and increased vigor by repeated plunges into the ocean.

Those who visited Marine Pavilion included Henry Wadsworth Longfellow, Washington Irving, and the painter John Trumbull. The hotel burned to the ground on June 25, 1864, but its success had already brought other investors to Rockaway.[7]

In the 1850s and 1860s, entrepreneurs built bigger and more elaborate resorts. James S. Remsen of Jamaica began buying sections along the beach in 1853, and in 1863 he opened Seaside Park. By the end of the decade Michael P. Holland and Louis Hammel were also planning parks. To reach this isolated resort, patrons traveled by train to East New York, where they transferred to another line that brought them to Canarsie; a steamboat ferried them across Jamaica Bay to the beach. Of course, the expense of such a journey limited patronage to the relatively well-off. By the time William Wainwright's Surf Pavilion opened in 1874, a string of villages and hotels catering to summer visitors dotted the entire strip of beach. By the 1880s, the Rockaway Line's *Grand Republic* and *General Slocum* offered regular service to Rockaway pier; in 1902, the round-trip fare was 50 cents, making an outing possible for working people.[8]

The largest and most ambitious undertaking was the Rockaway Beach Hotel, a 1,200-foot-long structure costing more than $1 million, a sum that included $90,000 for plumbing fixtures alone. The mammoth resort was modeled after Austin Corbin's successful Manhattan Beach Hotel (1877) and Oriental Hotel (1880) on the eastern end of Coney Island. Describing the season in August 1880, the *Newtown Register* reported:

> Far Rockaway cottages are all occupied and permanent guests crowd the hotels. At Rockaway Beach, the hotels are full and the number of transient visitors and guests is unprecedented. The big hotel was either started too late or not pushed with sufficient vigor and capital to be a success this year, yet it is one of the chief attractions of the beach and unfinished, draws multitudes weekly. The iron pier is completed and is the second great novelty of the beach. Steamers discharge and receive full complements of passengers daily and in the evenings its broad flooring furnishes a fine dancing platform for cotillion parties.[9]

The grand hotel was never finished. It opened briefly in August 1881, but that was all. It "proved to be a financial failure and the thousands of workmen who had received nothing but a lot of receiver's certificates in pay for

Bird's Eye View of Far Rockaway in 1900, in Bellot, *History of the Rockaways*, 97. (Cornell University Library.)

their labor, at one time threatened to burn it down. It was with the utmost difficulty they were satisfied. Drexel and J. Pierpont Morgan bought up a large number of the receiver's certificates and paid off the men." Apparently, it proved to be an unwise investment, however. After paying $175,000 for the hotel in 1883, Morgan had to dispose of it at auction in April 1889; it fetched less than $30,000. The building was torn down, the separate pieces sold to local builders who erected dozens of smaller hotels and houses with the estimated 1 million bricks and 6 million feet of lumber.[10]

Despite this spectacular failure, other hotels attracted a prosperous clientele. For a sense of how extravagant the ill-fated Rockaway Beach Hotel was, the Arverne Hotel, erected in 1888, cost only about $200,000, and it was sufficiently successful to attract New Yorkers who built spacious summer "cottages" nearby. Illustrations from the 1880s and 1890s depict well-dressed ladies with their parasols on the pier and the beach, and suited gentlemen on horseback, a pronounced contrast to the boisterous crowds attracted to Coney Island.[11]

Most of the Rockaways remained an upper- and middle-class preserve until the advent of mass transit, but the shoreline was so long that each section developed a distinctive character. Some welcomed working-class families out for a day at the beach, and others catered to millionaires "who in former years leased cottages for the summer season but who are now buying and building beautiful residences and living in the beautiful 'City-by-the-Sea' all year 'round." One of those who built a cottage in Rockaway was Otto Huber, owner of a successful brewery in Bushwick. Wealthier families

Arverne Hotel, Arverne, by the Sea, L. I. ca. 1915. (Jeffrey Kroessler Postcard Collection.)

congregated in Arverne, which had none of the saloons or picnic parks that attracted day visitors. Seaside offered row after row of small wooden bungalows rented by middle-class families, plus hotels and an iron pier extending into the ocean. The railroad, of course, brought thousands of visitors every Sunday, and this summer traffic actually accounted for a major portion of its annual ridership in the decades before it became a profitable commuter line. More than two dozen saloons and chowder houses sprouted in the vicinity of the Far Rockaway terminal, a neighborhood that also had a large Catholic church and orphanage. Board at the larger hotels ran about "$10 a week and upward, and in the boarding houses for even less," a sum that was certainly out of the range of most working people. Within walking distance from the depot were the exclusive suburban streets of Wave Crest, Ocean Crest, and Bayswater, where new cottages, "some of them being plain in appearance and designed more for comfort than show," cost from $4,000 to $40,000.[12] These substantial year-round cottages set Rockaway apart from Coney Island.

In the early 1900s, summer at the beach became manageable for families of modest means. Bungalow colonies arose, with row after row of small cottages. For those with more limited means, tents erected on wood platforms accommodated an entire family. Quite often, the mother and children would remain all summer, while the father commuted to the beach on

Bungalow Colony, Rockaway, 1910. (Library of Congress, Prints and Photographs Division, George Grantham Bain Collection.)

weekends. Sections developed into distinct ethnic enclaves—Jewish, Irish, Italian. At the far west end of the Rockaway Peninsula was a summer colony called Breezy Point. Originally, families rented tent sites for the season for about $20, and later many erected modest bungalows. For decades Breezy Point and its neighbors, Roxbury and Rockaway Point, remained almost exclusively Irish.[13]

In 1961, a developer purchased all the land west of Jacob Riis Park, intending to construct apartment towers. The residents of Breezy Point formed a cooperative to purchase their land, but the city intended to incorporate the entire western end of the peninsula into the Gateway National Recreation Area. A political compromise allowed the communities to remain, and only then did some convert their cottages into year-round homes. While a few bungalows remain scattered across the Rockaways, the largest concentration is along Beach 24th, 25th, and 26th Streets. Several have been made year-round, but their survival is by no means assured as development pressures, encouraged by the city, intensify.[14]

A final feature of recreation at Rockaway was the appearance of rides and attractions similar to Coney Island. The Rockaway Beach Amusement Park opened in 1901. Rockaways Playland finally closed in 1987.

Escape from the City

While bargain prices for land and the relative absence of government regulations brought manufacturers to Queens, the picturesque features of the rural landscape, together with lax enforcement of Sunday blue laws attracted thousands of working-class men and women who flocked to the cemeteries and picnic groves or spots along the shoreline. The influx of day-trippers certainly offered business opportunities for some, but it did not necessarily please local residents. In the summer of 1874, the *Flushing Journal* reported, "A lot of drunken rowdies from New York, calling themselves 'chowder' parties, go through the village every few days. For the most part these fellows come from the city to enjoy a good 'drunk' and escape arrest."[15] Although the very spirit of the Gay Nineties could be found in Queens, enforcement of the Sunday closing laws and the behavior of the city dwellers who swarmed into the county every weekend remained a contentious issue into the early twentieth century.

Many city dwellers were accustomed to taking occasional trips into the nearby countryside. The trip by ferry and streetcar could take as long as two hours, but that only heightened the experience, accentuating the differences between the home environment in the tenements and the rural recreational spots. A turn-of-the-century guidebook noted that the trolley itself could be a form of recreation:

> Trolleying has a thousand fascinations, and is the most inexpensive of sports. It can lead the explorer into a hundred and more pleasant places, and make him forget his cares. He has scenery, history, fresh air for his objects. By train but a fraction of this countryside is revealed. The bicycle laid it open to a few but by no means to all. To those who most needed these glimpses on the skirts of the city—the tired women, the mothers, the babies, the restless children, the men worn out by days of work—they might as well have been hundreds of leagues away.[16]

Visiting the rural cemeteries was among the more popular activities. The 1847 Rural Cemeteries Act banned new graveyards in Manhattan, leading to the establishment of large cemeteries in counties around the city. The act also permitted the creation of commercial cemeteries not associated with a particular church or denomination. The most beautiful, well-designed, and prestigious of all was Brooklyn's Green-Wood Cemetery, a nonsectarian city of the dead laid out in 1838. In Queens, the Catholic Church opened

Calvary Cemetery near Newtown Creek in 1848 (Governor Al Smith, Senator Robert F. Wagner, and Mayor Robert F. Wagner Jr.); the nonsectarian Cypress Hills Cemetery opened in 1848 (Elizabeth Jennings Graham, who integrated streetcars in New York, and Jackie Robinson are there); Lutheran Cemetery opened in Middle Village in 1852 (unidentified victims of the *General Slocum* disaster); Flushing Cemetery opened in 1853 (Louis Armstrong, Dizzie Gillespie, and Bernard Baruch); and Machpelah, a Jewish cemetery opened in 1855 (Harry Houdini). Many more opened in succeeding years.[17]

Paying respects to the departed was only one reason for the popularity of cemeteries in the nineteenth century. Visiting those places was a free activity, an all-important consideration for many families, and though owned by the churches or corporations, the cemeteries were in a general sense public spaces, wide-open and, in the early years at least, not overly cluttered by monuments. Above all, these outings offered a temporary escape from urban conditions. The Sunday traffic was so great that the enterprising owners of the streetcar lines raised fares to 10 cents, compared to 5 cents during rush hours. There was also a confluence of politics and business, for Long Island City mayor Patrick Jerome Gleason controlled the Calvary Cemetery line that ran along Newtown Creek from the ferries in Hunters Point.[18]

Families often brought picnic baskets from home but bought beer and ice cream from the many saloons and restaurants established at the end of the street railways. A hotel had opened across from Lutheran Cemetery in the 1850s, specifically to cater to the funeral trade. In 1888, Niederstein's restaurant opened on the site, tapping into the thirst of the German families who had just laid loved ones to rest. The last of the hotels and restaurants serving the cemetery trade, that venerable establishment remained until 2005, when the estate of the last owner closed the doors and sold the property.[19]

Another popular destination was the picnic park. Astute farmers fenced off part of their land and invited visitors to bring their baskets, the farmer providing the ice and beer. Soon more imaginative entrepreneurs built elaborate parks that offered music and dancing, vaudeville acts, athletic contests, bowling alleys, and an indoor hall. These parks still permitted patrons to bring their baskets, for that was the only way many families could afford such outings. While there was certainly some mixing at these places, each ethnic group generally patronized its own park. In Queens, the Germans had Schuetzen Park in Steinway, the Irish had Celtic Park in Woodside, and the Czechs their Bohemian Hall in Astoria (established in 1910 and the last

Niederstein's Restaurant and Hotel, Middle Village, Queens, 1922. (Courtesy of the Queens Brorough Public Library, Archives, Eugene L. Armbruster Photographs.)

authentic beer garden in the city), but the parks were often rented by members of other ethnic groups, and on at least one occasion Schuetzen Park hosted a picnic by a Black organization.

These places were especially popular with labor unions, ethnic clubs, and political associations. Tammany Hall sponsored annual picnics that attracted thousands. In July 1891, for example, the General Committee of the First Assembly District of the Tammany Association of New York, five hundred strong, journeyed to Whitestone; the annual Tammany-sponsored picnic for the voters took place the next month, a day when "the whole First district is depopulated." The *Flushing Journal* reported: "They left Rector street early in the day and arrived at Whitestone before noon. Corks flew and beer streamed in goblets to thirsty lips until the boat touched at Whitestone. Then there was a scramble for Stimmel's Hotel, for lunch was announced for half-past twelve." One man whose day did not start well was Tammany boss "Big Tim" Sullivan: "Before lunch was over Assemblyman 'Tim' Sullivan put in an appearance. He was wrathful, too. Not only did he miss the boat, but he was mulcted by the Long Island Railroad, a corporation which he has so often befriended in the Legislature. 'I paid seventy cents for an excursion ticket when the price is fifty-five,' said Sullivan, 'and I had to pay ten cents from Whitestone to Whitestone Landing when the fare is five. Just wait until I get to the Senate next year.'" Despite Big Tim's sweaty wrath, the picnic was a grand success, with athletic contests, dinner, a concert, and dancing with "a swarm of village maidens."[20]

Sabbath-Breaking and Alcohol

Although popular with working-class families and single men and women, the parks could cause problems for local residents. One stated in exasperation, "There is no protection for property and as the fruit season approaches, the inhabitants pray for rain on Sunday, as that seems to be the only thing that will allow them to enjoy a quiet day." This Woodside resident also accused the local constabulary of accepting bribes to permit the activities to continue. "One of the constables arrested a number of ball players who came from New York," he complained. "How these parties escaped without being before the magistrate is certainly puzzling. On Sunday last there was a crowd of young ball players from Winfield who filled the air with their shouts and profane language, but as there was probably no money in it, no officer appeared." A surprising element in this episode is the objection to baseball. The main reason, according to the locals, was that "the players appear careful to select a place for the game in the immediate vicinity of some dwelling or church where their noise will be most calculated to disturb the public peace and offend other citizens who desire to observe the day. This, together with past experiences, with drunken brawls so often accompanying the pastime, has determined our citizens to put a stop to the sport."[21] Others complained of the profanity and public drunkenness, the theft of fruit and vegetables, public urination, and casual damage to property.

One particular source of problems was William Monteverde's Grand Street Park in Maspeth, where as many as three thousand fans attended games on Sundays. In 1882, the *Register* described the crowds leaving Monteverde's after the games: "On Sunday afternoons and evenings it has been unsafe for a lady to ride from Maspeth to Williamsburgh in a Grand Street car. The rowdies crowd on top of the cars, putting their feet through the windows and defy the efforts of the conductors to collect the fares. The traffic is composed of crowds that any respectable lady will shun and render walking more preferable than riding."[22]

In 1886, in response to complaints by the neighbors, the authorities finally clamped down and arrested Monteverde for "keeping a nuisance at Grand Street." One witness testified that "during the games there had been loud shouting and obscene language used by the persons in the grounds," adding that the patrons annoyed him by "trespassing on his property, destroying articles owned by him, exposing their persons and when remonstrated with, replying 'Go to hell, you son of a bitch.'" Another stated that he had actually "paid 10 cents to go inside. Had seen intoxicating liquors sold in the park and drank them himself." Asked the nature of the profanity coming from the ball grounds, another witness replied, "Run, you son of a bitch." Despite testimony from other property owners in the vicinity of the park that they did not consider it a public nuisance, Monteverde was convicted and fined $250. Within a few weeks, however, citizens were again complaining of illegal baseball games at parks in Maspeth, including Monteverde's Park. The presence of the sheriff was enough to stop the games one week, but it was clearly impossible for him to be present at every park, every Sunday. Monteverde was arrested again the next year, as were the proprietors of other parks. But shutting the parks had economic consequences as significant as the perceived social ills of keeping them open. By one account, the streetcar lines running from Brooklyn lost $2,500 every Sunday the parks were shut down.[23]

Throughout the period, newspapers in Queens, and occasionally New York, commented on the rowdy and at times violent behavior of the visitors. An 1891 article in the *New York Times* entitled "Long Island's Curse—Lawless Visitors That the Authorities Cannot Catch" described numerous complaints about the influx of Sunday visitors, without providing either specific examples or the particular location of the problem. The *Times*, of course, was only just discovering what Queens had known for years:

> Thousands of people from New-York and Brooklyn swarm over Long Island on Sundays. Many seek legitimate pleasure and recreation, but many more seek beer. Many get intoxicated and boisterous Saloons, liquor stores, lager beer gardens, and parks are thicker in many parts of Long Island than farmhouses. Saloons and beer gardens occupy the corners of every crossroad; the village streets are lined with drinking places and even in the country lanes and bypaths through the woods beer signs meet the gaze. Sunday ball playing and "Wild West" shows are indulged in the rough-boarded inclosures called parks.

The small local constabulary in Long Island City and the towns of Newtown, Flushing, and Jamaica were hardly equipped to control the crowds, but there was also a question about their willingness to enforce the laws, not to mention suspicions regarding their honesty. The *Times* piece concluded by suggesting that "many officials are directly or indirectly interested and that large sums of money are contributed by the proprietors of the parks and disorderly houses to a fund used as 'hush money.'"[24]

Ballplayers had to resort to these measures because there were then no ball fields in public parks. In both Central Park and in Prospect Park ball playing was prohibited, as was the consumption of beer. The Central Park Board of Commissioners recognized the conflicting constituencies who would enjoy the park but showed little sympathy for those seeking fields for active recreation. They insisted that it would be impossible to accommodate those interests "and at the same time preserve in the grounds an appearance that would be satisfactory to the much more numerous class that frequent the park for the enjoyment of the refined and attractive features of its natural beauties." Ball playing was not permitted in Central Park until 1920, and not until 1922 was it legal to play baseball in the City of New York on Sundays.[25]

One politician repeatedly linked to corruption and violations of the blue laws was Patrick Jerome Gleason, the mayor of Long Island City. While Newtown tried repeatedly to shut down the parks, Gleason permitted such activities to flourish in Long Island City. The previous mayor, George Petry, had attempted to enforce the law and suppress ball playing, but early in his term Gleason announced that the games would go on. His police force did not interfere with cock fights, boxing matches, or gambling, either. While New York suffered under the "strict enforcement of the Excise law," the saloons in Long Island City did a thriving business. As the *Long Island City Star* reported, "Thirsty New Yorkers came over in droves and the consumption of beer was enormous. One well-known hotel keeper in Hunters Point sold 34 kegs during the day and a like increase in the local trade was observable in other sections. Men even came over from New York by the Astoria Ferry with large tin pails hidden in market baskets and after having the pails filled with beer returned to New York."[26]

On one occasion, Gleason personally visited his city's main park, the People's Recreation Grounds, and "after a pleasant chat with the manager drove away." As the only park guaranteed to be open on Sundays, the People's Recreation Grounds attracted, according to the *Star*, "the disorderly elements of New York City and the roughs of this city who delight in disorder and disturbance," and "when the police attempted to interfere with their right 'to do as they pleased,' they turned upon the officers and attacked them." Outside the grounds, wagons were stocked with "kegs of lager and an ample array of beer glasses and the owners combined the pleasures of baseball with the liquid refreshment furnished by the contents of these kegs." On one Sunday, spectators saw a game "between nine colored gentlemen, the Gorhams, and a team of white trash called the Senators. The Blacks were from Sullivan and Thompson Streets. The entire place was filled by a noisy yelling mob whose shouts and curses were heard a mile away but no effort was made by either the 'mounted cavalry' or the footmen of the police to put a stop to the disgraceful proceedings." Gleason owed his election as mayor to the votes of the working-class Irish in the city's First Ward, Hunters Point and Blissville, and not surprisingly he declined to interfere with the saloons and picnic parks patronized by his constituents.[27]

College Point was also a favorite summertime spot for the organized picnics of Sunday Schools, political clubs, and labor unions; as many as ten thousand a day crowded the ferries and trolleys to visit Witzel's Point View Island resort and Donnelly's Grove. Both resorts were popular among politicians, regardless of party; Republican "political boss" Thomas C. Platt and Democratic Tammany leader "Big Tim" Sullivan attended events there. Despite the business generated by these visitors, the village was far from comfortable with the noise and disorder they caused, but as the German population there grew, the question of Sunday closings became increasingly difficult. Except for College Point, the Town of Flushing was populated largely by old-stock American Protestants. In 1875, the town's excise commission consisted of Benjamin Cox of Whitestone and George L. Gillette of College Point, both members of the Flushing Law and Order Association, a temperance organization, and Henry Kraemer, "keeper of a lager beer saloon" in College Point. Cox and Gillette favored strict enforcement of the law mandating the closing of saloons on Sundays, while Kraemer pointed out that "it will be utterly impossible to enforce this provision in College Point." Even the Law and Order men admitted "that it seems a hardship to enjoin the German from quaffing his Fatherland beverage to his heart's content on the day of all the week to him. It may be argued that the lager beer saloon is not, as a rule, the cause of any great crime or wickedness and that the whisky shop is. There is a difference in favor of the beer saloon in this respect, but is it a distinction that the law can recognize?" In practice, the Flushing authorities left enforcement up to the citizens of College Point. In 1887, however, conditions deteriorated to such a degree that the alarmed village trustees took the drastic step of temporarily banning Sunday picnics, due to "the lawlessness of the men and women who attended these gatherings," this in spite of the considerable financial loss suffered by hotels and parks that employed many of the villagers.[28]

William Steinway was well aware of the conflicts over drinking and the Sunday activities of workers, not only because he had an interest in North Beach, a resort that depended on Sunday business, but also because he was himself a German American. In an interview in the *Times*, he recognized that "rigorous enforcement of the Puritanical blue laws [fell] with the greatest severity upon the working classes, who are compelled to live in small, ill-ventilated rooms in which cooking, washing, and ironing are done—generally with a numerous family." Workers generally had only Sundays off, so enforcing the blue laws restricted the scope of their leisure activities and challenged cultural habits and practices. "Accustomed to take a glass of light, cool beer with his wife and grown up members of his family," argued Steinway, "that comfort was taken from him, and warm Croton water was his only drink. Instead of being able to go to some garden, where he and his family could listen to good music and take a glass of light cool beer or light wine mixed with seltzer water, the family is compelled to remain in the dingy tenement house rooms in rainy weather or walk the street in good weather."

Tempering his remarks with references to "light" alcoholic beverages and emphasizing the proper role of beer and wine within the family, Steinway was refuting the contention of prohibitionists and other supporters of Sunday closings that alcohol destroyed family life. The piano manufacturer saw that there was little room for compromise over this issue, which was as much a conflict between native-born Americans and the German immigrant community as it was between "wets" and "drys." He recognized that it would be "an exceedingly difficult task to suggest a liberal Sunday clause in the excise law that will uphold the sanctity of the American Sabbath and yet permit the opening of saloons and gardens where good music and light beverages may be dispensed in an English-speaking country." He noted that "disorderly persons, inclined to violence and ruffianism, are more prevalent in English-speaking countries." Moreover, it was "not a drinking question with German Americans, it is entirely a question of personal liberty."[29]

While economically successful and having achieved a prominent position in New York society, Steinway could still empathize with his workers who endured life in tenements and faced cultural pressures as German Americans; his sympathy did not, however, extend to accepting the unions formed by the piano workers or ameliorating the conditions that caused them to strike from time to time. Furthermore, as one dependent on the Sunday business to keep his streetcar line and resort profitable, he was speaking as much as a paternalistic capitalist as an immigrant libertarian.

Citizens in Astoria, College Point, Woodside, and other communities formed Law and Order Societies to combat these violations, but they were never effective in closing the saloons and parks for any length of time. The leading citizens of College Point, including Adolph and Alfred Poppenhusen, Hugo and Herman Funke, and A. P. Schlesinger, were behind the movement, but even their considerable economic power and social influence could not permanently close the saloons on the Sabbath.[30] By the mid-1890s, after more than a decade of conflict over the question, the Queens County authorities learned to balance the demands of residents and the rights of the Sunday visitors, in part by tacitly admitting that they could not strictly enforce the Sunday laws:

> Clergymen and other orderly people complain that settlements are overrun by pleasure seekers. Ball playing, beer drinking and dancing in the picnic parks are among the excesses complained of. The Sabbatarians demand that ball players be arrested, that the licenses of offending saloon keepers be revoked, and that the picnic grounds be summarily closed. Objections to interference is made by thousands of anxious persons who like the sort of outing the nearby villages afford. The problem for officials to solve is delicate and difficult. Their best course, under the circumstances, is to take a reasonably liberal view of their responsibilities. They should be no more ready to countenance disorder or encourage evil than they should to enforce unnecessarily a puritanism at variance with comfort and healthful relaxation for the masses of the people. District Attorney Fleming is commendably disinclined to interfere with the innocent amusements of the public.[31]

Many eventually accepted that the "parks or places of resort for the overflowing population of New York and Brooklyn have become almost a necessity to save the overrunning of the entire country embraced within the suburbs of these cities."[32] The Sunday visitors would come to Queens in any event, and it was certainly better to have them inside the picnic groves and ball parks than to suffer their depredations across the entire countryside.

North Beach

In the late nineteenth and early twentieth centuries, amusement parks and resorts dotted the fringes of all major American cities. Often situated near water and accessible by streetcar and steamboat, these parks offered working people the chance to escape the urban environment for an afternoon or evening in an exotic atmosphere. By bringing so many urbanites together, the trolley park was also, of course, an extension of that same environment. Amusement parks could be found in the Rockaways, at Fort George in Upper Manhattan, Classon Point and Starlight Farms in the Bronx, Glen Island in Long Island Sound, South Beach on Staten Island, and, of course, Coney Island, the most famous playground in the world.[33]

While the Rockaways evolved over several decades and remained largely middle-class until the arrival of mass transit lines in the early twentieth century, North Beach was specifically created to attract working people. From its opening in June 1886 until its decline in the early 1920s under the pressure of Prohibition and water pollution, North Beach remained an immensely popular pleasure spot.

Bowery Bay was about a half mile from Steinway, close enough to be accessible but just far enough to discourage vigorous development. The location was ideal for the urban picnickers who flocked there on Sundays, the only day of rest for workers who endured a six-day work week. One of the earliest depictions of the area, an 1877 oil painting by William Miller at the New-York Historical Society, shows the Lent Homestead on Old Bowery Bay Road, and in the background one glimpses the blue water of the bay and the green shoreline where picnickers have spread their blanket.[34] Even before the opening of the picnic parks and hotels at Bowery Bay, the place was a popular spot, attracting visitors who took the 92nd Street ferry to Astoria, and then a horsecar to Steinway; they had to walk the remaining distance to the secluded shoreline.

While Bowery Bay had no commercial entertainments, there were no fees, regulations, or constraints on the visitors, either. Local newspapers regularly carried articles condemning the urban crowds flocking to the place. The main cause of complaint, beyond the trampled flower beds and gardens, was the "indecent way in which bathing is permitted," making it "impossible for ladies during the hot weather to pass along the road abutting the bay in the afternoons and evenings. Full grown men bathe there without the slightest regard to decency, wearing no bathing suits or drawers, and naked men and boys may be seen running about or drying themselves after their bath without any appearance of shame and utterly regardless of the fact that they are within sight of a public thoroughfare." One incident from the summer of 1885 highlighted the situation. The *Long Island City Star* reported that a doctor and his wife were "accosted by several half drunken nude men who had been bathing in the waters of the bay. They demanded enough money to buy beer and the Dr. complied."[35] Not all of the weekend visitors engaged in disreputable or criminal activity, of course, but the reporting of even one crime was sufficient to alarm respectable residents.

On another occasion the *Star* reported, "A visitor to the beach at Bowery Bay last Sunday afternoon would have imagined himself at Coney Island or Rockaway, minus, however, the costumes on the forms of the bathers required at those places. From midday until late in the afternoon wagon after wagon drove up to the beach containing parties of men, women, and half-grown boys and children from all over New York and Brooklyn." The reporter went on to link the innocent family outings with crime and immorality:

> Only a few days ago a gentleman was stopped and robbed by a crowd of roughs as he passed the spot, but although the police of this city [Long Island City] and Newtown have made every effort to arrest the offenders, they have been so far unsuccessful. The indecent manner in which bathing is conducted is however apparent every week and can and should be promptly suppressed. The indiscriminate mingling of the sexes, the brevity of the covering and, in some cases, the entire absence of any on the part of some of the men and women is indelicate in the extreme, and will be likely, unless repressive measures are at once instituted, to lead to disorders of the worst character.[36]

The behavior and character of the visitors, working-class urbanites who neither conformed to standards of Victorian morality nor respected the "No Trespassing" signs, elicited numerous negative comments in the local press. Reformers and residents may have called for an end to the supposedly immoral activities there, but investors recognized an opportunity. If people went to Bowery Bay without the benefit of direct streetcar service or the gratifying joys of saloons selling cold beer, there was surely money to be made by opening a few parks and hotels.

In early 1886, William Steinway, George Ehret, owner of the Hell Gate Brewery in Yorkville, one of the largest in the city, and other investors, formed the Bowery Bay Beach Improvement Company. With $20,000 in capital, they opened an office above the Steinway showroom on 14th Street.[37] Work progressed quickly throughout the spring, as carpenters constructed bath houses, transformed estate houses into hotels, landscaped the picnic grounds, and graded the road from the car barns on Steinway Avenue to Bowery Bay.

On opening day, Saturday, June 19, the crowds were disappointing, but on Sunday "the groves and beach were literally thronged. The pleasure seekers commenced to arrive early in the afternoon and by 2 the horsecars leading from 34th St. and 92nd St. [the ferry landings in Hunters Point and Astoria] were packed with excursionists on their way to the beach. At 4 P.M. there must have been fully six thousand people scattered over the grounds. It was a noticeable and pleasant feature that the large assemblage was the most orderly and most respectable character."[38]

The first season was an unqualified success. The Bowery Bay Beach Improvement Company ran the resort and all of the concessions directly, both to maximize profits and to maintain complete control. The next year, however, the company leased some facilities to private individuals, on the condition, of course, that they sold only Ehret's beer. Bowery Bay was very much a monopoly for the investors, for while Ehret controlled the beer concession, Steinway owned the horsecar line that delivered patrons from the Astoria ferry. The Steinway workers held their annual festival there each summer, an event that began with a parade through Steinway Village.[39]

With the privatization of the shoreline, access to the water became limited to those with the means to rent lockers or bathing suits; there would be no nude bathing at Bowery Bay Beach. A week before the grand opening, the *Star* reported that the company had built 130 bath houses, "fitted up with every modern convenience and divided into two sections, one being reserved for the ladies and the other for gentlemen. By this arrangement," the article concluded, "the disgraceful scenes enacted on the beach last summer cannot possibly occur." Nude bathing remained a concern, if not an actual problem. Within a few weeks of the opening, a police boat was in operation, "managed by two men empowered by the sheriff to arrest any and all persons bathing without dresses at any part of the beach."[40] In this way, the company could control the activities at Bowery Bay, enforce standards of behavior and dress, and keep out those who did not conform.

For the first few seasons, the emphasis was on the wholesome and friendly atmosphere at Bowery Bay. There were dining rooms in the hotels, open-air dancing pavilions, and picnic grounds. The Northern European character and design reflected the taste of both the investors and the patrons. There was even a quaint "peasant's cottage" to remind visitors of the old country they had been so eager to leave behind. The management encouraged "basket parties," outings that enabled families to take advantage of the facilities while keeping expenses down.[41] Of course, this did nothing to lessen the labor of the mother on her day off, for she still had to prepare the food, pack the basket, and look after the children.

So successful was Bowery Bay Beach that each season brought new attractions, transforming the picnic ground into an amusement park, a reflection of both its steady popularity and profitability and the changing composition of the crowd. Bowery Bay Beach was originally designed as a rustic retreat that would uplift the spirits of visitors relaxing in the natural setting, but the new attractions offered boisterous amusements, with the patrons now active participants in the fun. In short, the changes demonstrated the eclipse of a genteel, almost refined environment and the noisy ascension of an urban working-class culture at a park evolving to accommodate their preferences.[42]

In February 1891, the resort was renamed North Beach to avoid the unfortunate association with the notorious Bowery in New York or Coney Island's Bowery, a street lined with saloons, hotels, and carnival attractions. Ironically, after the place was renamed North Beach, it came to resemble less a rustic retreat and more the loud and garish Bowery. At the same time, new rides and attractions opened, including the carrousel, a scenic railway (roller coaster), a Ferris wheel, a circle swing, and, in 1897, the shoot-the-chutes. At North Beach, the company created an artificial lake for the chutes, and the landscaped grounds around it were renamed Gala Park.

As North Beach changed in appearance, so too did the character of the crowds. A report in the *Star* from the first season had only praise for the patrons: "Family parties are frequent. Of the lovers going there for sweet communion with nature the majority are thrifty looking and quiet, apparently in that stage of courtship where the man is thinking seriously about the cost of furnishing the house and the prospective bride gives him good advice about the management of his finances. The rollicking young man with his 'best girl' seeking frolic only does not seem to have discovered Bowery Bay yet."[43]

The newspapers not only described the wholesomeness of the spot but stressed the efficient authority of the police, who "keep a sharp lookout for any objectionable intruders on the grounds and if any such appear, they are quietly but decidedly told to 'quit.'" Apparently, these trolley parks had a rather wild reputation, for even the promotional literature put out by the management emphasized the safety and security of the visitors: "A sense of security is the first element of civilization. Families desire innocent enjoyment, without unseemly hindrance or interruption. They will go places which offer the maximum of pleasure with the minimum of annoyance, and in this respect there can be no doubt that Bowery Bay Beach is beyond

North Beach Amusement Park, 1892. The Future Site of LaGuardia Airport, Astoria. (The LaGuardia and Wagner Archives, LaGuardia Community College/The City University of New York.)

comparison."[44] Concerns about rowdy, undisciplined, and drunken behavior were not entirely unjustified, and the owners publicized their efficient private constabulary.

In the early years at least, conditions at Bowery Bay remained wholesome, perhaps because of the police presence. An example of the effectiveness of the local constabulary was reported in the *New York Times* in August 1887. William Powers, visiting the beach in the company of "two respectable ladies of Astoria," had been there only a short time when "Sergt. Eagan and Officer Kerr, of the Steinway police force, which is a private concern, without provocation assaulted him, and when he resisted made him a prisoner and unmercifully clubbed him about the head and body. He was afterward locked up on a charge of intoxication, and kept without water for 17 hours, although he pleaded for it." Regardless of whether Mr. Powers was intoxicated, he was certainly not "quietly but decidedly told to 'quit,'" and he sued the company for $10,000, charging false imprisonment.[45]

This incident illustrates how police sought to head off trouble before it spread; the intimidation of a few honest citizens in the process was unavoidable. As the *Times* reported in an 1896 feature article about North Beach and the nearby village of Steinway, "The appearance of men in uniform has a wholesome deterrent effect on those who might be boisterously inclined. Under these favorable circumstances women, accompanied by their children, can visit this resort without the slightest fear of trouble or molestation, for they are looked after and protected as though they were the special guests of the management." The same orderly state of affairs was also to be found on the steamboats running between North Beach and New York, for a policeman was stationed on board each boat.[46] The article did not explain why it was necessary to take such precautions, but the difference between this and other resorts must have been obvious to the public.

After the turn of the century, newspapers were once again describing the terrible goings-on along the shores of Bowery Bay. According to one observer,

> Every Sunday the place swarms with the lowest class of East Side toughs and girls young in years but old in vice. Nevertheless we see girls of respectable parents going there perhaps out of curiosity, and thereafter, caught by the excitement and crowds and music, each succeeding visit is but one step nearer moral ruin. The Metropolitan policemen who are detailed to North Beach are unanimous in saying that it is the worst place and the most toothsome crowd they ever encountered. The Bowery or Coney Island in their palmy days were not the equal of North Beach for the evil influence it exerts on growing boys and girls. Any boy or girl who frequents North Beach is lost so far as her influence for good in the world is concerned.

Continuing, the article points out that the apparently peaceful resort catering to Sunday School picnics by day was quite another place after dark: "To one walking along the main thoroughfare the real conditions in the dance halls and dives are not apparent and in fact the devil to pay does not get into full swing until after dark. From that time until midnight pandemonium reigns. No attempt whatever is made to observe the Sunday liquor laws and persons of all ages are served with the vilest of compounds." For this moralist, much of the blame rested with strong drink; indeed, this was when the temperance movement was picking up steam, culminating in wartime prohibition in 1917 and ratification of the Eighteenth Amendment in 1919. The article concludes with an indictment of one of the men behind the park: "Mr. George Ehret, the product of whose beer factory is sold at just about every place in town, is largely interested in the money end of the place, but I am sure he knows nothing of the conditions existing there other than how many kegs of beer are sold each week."[47] Another Queens paper condemned the place in the classic rhetoric of the temperance movement: "The saloons there are wide open every Sunday. Men and women drink and get drunk there. Occasionally an arrest is made and the poor devils of drunkards are locked up, but the lawbreakers who sell them rum until they become crazed are never arrested to the shame of the police and to the shame of Queens County."[48] Contrary to the frightening evocation of demon rum, the most popular beverage at North Beach was beer.

Despite, or perhaps because of, the judgmental pronouncements on the dangers and rampant immorality of North Beach, it remained a popular spot, especially among young men and women. As one working-class woman told a reformer investigating conditions there, "My mother doesn't know I go out here, but I want some fun, and it only costs ten cents." Although she paid her own fare on the trolley or ferry, she undoubtedly expected that the young men she met there would treat her to rides and refreshments.[49]

Most of the patrons saw North Beach as a family resort offering good, clean fun. An 1898 advertisement for George W. Kremer's Silver Spring Carrousel, for example, boasted "Special Rates to Sunday Schools and Trolley Parties" and "Special Attention to Children and Ladies." In this way the concessionaires made a pitch for the family trade, pointing out the safety and wholesome fun of his carrousel even for those innocents on Sunday School outings. A 1905 advertisement for Henry Daufkirch's New Bay View Hotel went even further, noting the "Grand Continuous Sacred Concert on Sundays," an obvious but nonetheless clever appeal to those concerned that their trip to the amusement park might conflict with or negate their churchgoing; it was also a way to circumvent the laws restricting Sunday entertainment.

The trolley parties mentioned in both notices made up much of the regular business at North Beach. Although crowded on weekends, the resort struggled to attract large numbers of customers during the week. The management and individual concessionaires therefore encouraged these group outings. The Knights of Labor and other unions, social clubs, fraternal organizations, political clubs, and other voluntary associations held annual outings there, selling tickets that typically included transportation, entertainment, and refreshments. The ticket price for a 1901 outing of the Benchmen's Association of Retail Butchers was only $1 for a member and his guest, considerably less than an evening at the amusement park would normally cost. Indeed, the low cost of each item—10 cents for the ferry, 10 cents for the trolley, 5 cents each of the rides, and a nickel for a beer—often added up, especially when a young man was out to impress his date, or when parents took their children. An outing at North Beach, Coney Island, or any of the other trolley parks was a major event for most families, and it is doubtful they could splurge more than a couple of times a season. A 1907 survey of working-class families in New York City found that of those with any leisure budget at all, the average annual expenditure was only $8.50.[50] Single men and women, on the other hand, crowded the resort in the evenings, often as members of trolley parties, which kept the costs low and also reinforced group loyalties.

Middle-class families, such as the Geipels of Astoria, could enjoy North Beach more frequently. August Geipel had been a brewmaster for Ehret and then owned a saloon serving Ehret's beer, and his wife Wilhelmina was a midwife who had been trained in Germany. In 1897, they bought a season pass to Frederick Deutschmann's Silver Spring Bathing Pavilion, which featured bath houses and a cobblestone-bottomed pool fed by the East River tides. The family's season ticket cost $4, a modest fee for this successful family but an impossible sum for unskilled factory workers. Furthermore, the pass was good only on weekdays, not Sundays or holidays, presumably the busiest days and the only time workers could use the facilities. The Geipels not only went to the park often enough to make the ticket a worthwhile investment, but they also had the means to reach North Beach, either traveling by streetcar or taking their own buggy. A final point was that it was usually possible for Mrs. Geipel to take the children there, for her duties as a midwife only occasionally interfered, and in any event the family had a maid.[51]

What then was the true picture of this amusement park on the East River shoreline? Was it the wholesome and healthful resort advertised by the owners, or the pest hole described by reformers and prohibitionists? Through a nostalgic veil, we see it as we hope it was—clean, safe, friendly, and entirely innocent. Based on the hand-colored postcard views, North Beach seems the very image of the Gay Nineties, reminiscent of the innocence portrayed in the 1941 Warner Bros. film *Strawberry Blonde*. It is tempting to romanticize the place by focusing on images of hard-working immigrant families sipping beer in the outdoor gardens; digging into their baskets for cold cuts, bread, and pickles; singing and dancing; marveling at the dazzling electric lights; and applauding the fireworks. It is tempting likewise to sneer at the out-of-date Victorian sensibilities that sharply condemned those activities.

But even *Strawberry Blonde* had its darker side. William Kells, a man whose family leased a saloon at North Beach around 1900, after having a similar concession at South Beach on Staten Island, adds less pleasant details to the story of the resort. After a few seasons, Kells recalled, his father began showing movies—one- and two-reelers—instead of running the saloon because he preferred the relative quiet of sarsaparilla and the flicks to the more profitable, but rowdy, saloon. On too many occasions he had to intervene as a "boxing referee," breaking up the fights that started each night among the young men who crowded his drinking establishment. By opening a movie theater, Kells was actually on the cutting edge of the leisure business, and he and his partner later opened a regular theater in Astoria. At the time, however, he was less interested in the future of the movies than in the security of his investment. Kells also adds a racial dimension to the story of North Beach. He remembers a Black man who operated the steam engine that powered the chutes. When the man entered the saloons, the bartenders ignored him as long as they could, and then only reluctantly served him when it was clear he would not leave. Even then, the bartender stood over him and as a final insult smashed the empty glass on the barroom floor.[52]

The rowdiness was certainly real and not just the exaggerated reporting of sensationalist journalists. One important reason for the changing character of North Beach was the opening of the Brooklyn Rapid Transit trolley line from Williamsburg in 1896, which carried the hard-drinking crowds to the parks and saloons. *Appleton's Dictionary of New York*, an 1898 guidebook, described North Beach as "quiet enough in the daytime for ladies and children, but rather noisy in the evening, and somewhat frequented by the gambling fraternity."[53] The previous summer, front-page articles in the *Times* reported open gambling under the very eyes of the police, who pleaded "lack of instructions" and defended their inaction by declaring that the games were on private property; besides, they said, they had been hired to protect the property of the North Beach Improvement Company, not enforce the gambling laws. The bunko games described by the *Times* were common to carnivals and amusement parks across the country, but there was one that was particularly offensive. At several places, "baseballs were thrown at the heads of negroes, and here the competition was so great that one sign conspicuously informed the passer-by that he would get $100 in gold if he hit 'the coon' three times in succession."[54] The illegal games were halted within a week, but not before the integrity of the police had been damaged and the reputation of the resort tarnished, although not enough to prevent families like the Geipels from attending during the daytime.

North Beach remained popular until the Great War, when national prohibition forced the breweries to walk away from their investments. The attraction of a dry amusement park was quite limited, and in August 1925 even the trolley stopped running there. In the late 1930s, Works Progress Administration laborers tore down the abandoned structures, filled in part of the bay, and built LaGuardia Airport. No tangible evidence of the once glittering and boisterous amusement park remains.[55]

By the end of the nineteenth century, the Queens landscape had undergone an extraordinary transformation from a rural, agricultural county populated by a few slowly growing suburban villages to one of the most rapidly industrializing sections of any city in the nation. Pressures from New York and Brooklyn caused these dramatic changes, as the overflowing populations sought employment, homes, and leisure in Queens. Enforcement of the gambling, drinking, and entertainment laws was uncertain prior to consolidation. It was always possible that the authorities could endeavor to enforce Sunday closings and uphold local standards of behavior, but it was equally true that they could turn a blind eye. It was impossible to enforce the laws with any consistency, and the sheer number of visitors compounded the difficulties facing the sheriffs, even if they honestly attempted to do so. Moreover, many in Queens profited from these illegal activities, and the leisure business attracted entrepreneurs large and small.

Decisions made in the cities, whether by corporate managers or working-class immigrants, determined the future of Queens, and ultimately the latter would triumph in the clash of values between urban and rural, immigrant and native-born.

Part 2

Urban Borough

7

The Politics of Consolidation

In 1874, New York City annexed the southern Westchester towns of Morrisania, West Farms, and Kingsbridge, the area lying west of the Bronx River. Until then, the city encompassed only Manhattan Island. The urban grid was almost immediately superimposed over what was called the Annexed District. Construction of tenements quickly followed the extension of elevated lines across the Harlem River in 1888. In 1895, the city annexed the area east of the Bronx River, taking in the Town of Westchester and portions of Pelham and Eastchester, and the Village of Wakefield.[1]

In one sense, this action but continued the city's northward pattern of growth, but it also heralded a greater purpose. Annexation was the only way for the city to provide for future growth, and if New York was to remain the nation's premier metropolis, it could not be hemmed in by competing municipalities or rural counties. Many citizens reasonably expected that New York would continue its march into Westchester to annex the City of Yonkers, but New York fixed its gaze on the harbor, not the Hudson River towns. Historian David C. Hammack argues that commercial interests were the primary agents behind consolidation and suggests that "many of the merchants and bankers believed that if a single municipal government could gain control over New York harbor and all the surrounding territory, it could promote the unified, comprehensive development of shipping, railroads, and related facilities in such a way as to aid both merchants and property owners."[2]

The area envisioned for a Greater New York encompassed southern Westchester (the Bronx did not become a separate county until 1914), Richmond, Brooklyn, and Kings County, and as much of Queens to ensure the city's possession of Jamaica Bay and Little Neck Bay. That was crucial if New York City was to maintain control over future as well as existing harbor development. Another factor driving the move toward consolidation was the necessity of acquiring land for the future industrial and residential growth. Population density in several immigrant wards was already the highest in the world—in 1890 Manhattan's Tenth Ward held 522 persons per acre—and such unhealthy conditions caused genuine concern among reformers on both sides of the East River. Edward A. Bradford of the Consolidation League of Brooklyn reminded his peers that no matter where they lived, they were hardly immune to the evils of Manhattan's slums: "Let none imagine himself so rich, careless, or secure that none of these things can touch him. He may withhold charity, but he cannot dodge taxes swelled by crime and pauperism. And though he may establish himself in the costliest residence in the city, the sewer beneath his cellar and the breeze above his attic are freighted with germs from the tenements threatening alike his parlor and his nursery. The labor maxim 'the injury of one is the concern of all' is a thousand-fold true of this blot upon New York City." [3] To bolster his argument, he provided statistics for New York, Chicago, Philadelphia, and London, and New York did not fare well in the comparison.

For Bradford, the answer to unhealthy urban congestion lay in annexation, because the "cost of obliterating the water obstacle is trivial compared with the magnitude of the issues involved." The population and area of Long Island, he argued, "are New York's in fact, and may be so in name, if the voters so decide. Across the East River lie idle acres lacking only men and houses

Table 10
Comparison of Urban Conditions, 1890

City	Population in 1890	Area in sq. miles	Population per sq. mile	Families per dwelling	Death rate per 1,000
New York City	1,515,301	40	37,675	3.82	28
Chicago	1,099,850	160	6,849	1.72	21
Phil.	1,046,964	129	8,091	1.10	23
Greater New York	2,532,644	388	6,527	—	—
Greater London	5,656,909	689	8,210	(7 persons)	17

SOURCE: Bradford, *"Great York."*

to create values and taxable resources now scarcely dreamed of. This is Long Island's dowry in the union which shall produce Great York. New York can only reject the proposal at the cost of sinking to a second rate city." The question of whether New York, for almost a century the country's largest metropolis, would maintain its position was not idle conjecture. Its growth rate was slowing while Chicago's was on the rise. Chicago had ample room to expand, while New York was seemingly confined by geography. In the decade between 1880 and 1890, New York grew at a rate of 25 percent, and Brooklyn 42 percent. Chicago's growth rate, however, was an explosive 118 percent, and the second city showed no signs of slowing down.

Brooklyn and Kings County

Completion of the Brooklyn Bridge in 1883 had joined the first and third cities of the nation, and political union seemed only a matter of time. In July 1886, the *Long Island City Star* reported on a proposal to unify "New York and its suburbs into one grand city under the name 'Manhattan'":

> The scheme embraces Brooklyn, Long Island City, East New York, Yonkers, etc. and would give a metropolis which for extent of territory, variety of advantage and population, would rival and soon outstrip any of the great cities of the world. Annexation would bring many great and lasting benefits to property and business interests and much and incalculable good could not but result from the strong and far-reaching governmental regulations that would be brought about. A great city like New York cannot afford to have a number of petty and corrupt municipal corporations in its immediate suburbs and which are constantly in conflict with its police and sanitary regulations. The first step was taken in the opening of the Brooklyn Bridge. The next which will lead on to the final one of unification will be the building of the bridge across the East River at Blackwell's Island.[4]

For Brooklyn, with a population of 806,343 in 1890, consolidation meant it could share in the massive tax base of Manhattan; one large office building in the city paid more in taxes than did five hundred homes in Brooklyn.[5] But loyal Brooklynites also faced the traumatic prospect of the end of independence. Manhattanites expressed little sympathy for Brooklyn's fate. The *New York Post* stated it plainly:

> New York must retain its supremacy as the leading city of the New World, and it can only do this by enlarging its limits. It has for years been building up

Brooklyn and other adjacent territory with the overflow of its population, and the time will come when it will claim all this for its own. A great and important part of it, that which has gone into New Jersey, it cannot reclaim; but Brooklyn and Long Island, Richmond and part of Westchester Counties are within its reach, and must sooner or later yield to the inevitable and come into its fold.

The editor went on to describe the impact of new transportation links between Manhattan and Long Island:

It will not be many years before not one but many bridges over and tunnels under the East River will make Brooklyn and New York practically one city, and make the whole of Long Island almost as much a suburb of New York as Brooklyn now is. Brooklyn may as well resign herself to the loss of her identity, for the fates are against her preserving it. Her citizens ought to console themselves with the reflection that whatever greatness she possesses to-day is due to the fact of her nearness to New York, and that, after all consolidation will not be without compensation, for when the two cities are one, Brooklyn can no longer be spoken of as merely the sleeping room for New York.[6]

The contest over consolidation focused on Kings County. Since becoming a city in 1834—over the objections of New York City—Brooklyn embodied the principle of urban imperialism, having annexed the adjacent city of Williamsburgh and the Town of Bushwick in 1854, reached into southern Queens for water, and purchased parkland just over the border in Jamaica along the terminal moraine for Brooklyn Forest Park. Brooklyn steadily extended its influence over the rural towns of Flatbush, Flatlands, Gravesend, New Utrecht, and New Lots, and in 1869 the legislature mandated that the towns "plan and lay out streets, roads, and avenues ... conforming to the avenues and streets and plan of Brooklyn, as now terminated at the city line."[7] While it seemed inevitable that the city would absorb all of Kings County, the move took decades to accomplish due to resistance from the owners of the many still productive and profitable farms.

In 1873, the state legislature created a commission to devise a plan to consolidate Brooklyn with the rural towns, with authority to set "the relative rate of taxation" for different sections. Farming interests outlined their reasons for opposition in the *Brooklyn Daily Eagle*, arguing that it would "unjustly" subject "an agricultural people to the heavy expenses of a city government necessary in a densely populated community, but unnecessary and burdensome in a rural district." Taxes would surely rise, they argued, "the effect of which ... will have a tendency to compel the farmers in our midst to dispose of their premises at such prices as they can obtain" due to taxes exceeding the rents or the value of the produce. (Increasingly, landowners rented their farms to immigrants rather than work the land themselves.) This will "compel many of the farmers in our midst to dispose of their premises at such prices as they can obtain, abandon the homes of their ancestors and emigrate to more favored localities out of the reach of city burdens and oppressions, leaving their farms in the hands of speculators and non-cultivators and thrown out as common waste land ... in place of the present smiling fields and highly cultivated farms and gardens yielding in abundance and ministering to the wants of the population of the city."[8]

The rural voices prevailed then, but the advance of the city deeper into the county could not be stayed. In 1886, Brooklyn annexed the Town of New Lots, with the proviso that real estate "shall be assessed at the value of the land for agricultural purposes, unless the same shall have been ... divided into building lots." Identical language was included when the city annexed Gravesend and Flatlands in 1894. By then, of course, farmland was rapidly disappearing and agricultural interests had far less influence. In 1879, Queens ranked first and Kings second in agricultural production among all counties in the nation. Queens retained that top spot till the end of the century, while Kings dropped to twenty-third in 1890, and fortieth in 1899.[9]

By 1896, Brooklyn had annexed all of the old towns to make the city coterminous with Kings County, with a population of more than nine hundred thousand. In truth, New York had always been the primary city, and Brooklyn never seriously threatened Manhattan's economic, political, or social power, for while Manhattan had the entire continent at its back, Brooklyn could legitimately claim only Long Island for its hinterland. The 1686 Dongan Charter assured New York's primacy by granting the city control over all ferries. Brooklyn was prohibited from taxing them, so while her citizens paid the great majority of the fares, not a penny went into Brooklyn's coffers.[10]

Creating Greater New York

In 1888, the Chamber of Commerce of the State of New York initiated an earnest campaign for consolidation with the implicit approval of Mayor Abram S. Hewitt, who, in his annual message of January 1888 spoke of his city's "imperial destiny." The next year, Andrew Haswell Green, long an advocate of consolidation as the solution to the city's crowded and confined condition, traveled to Albany to implore the legislature to create a commission to at least study the proposal. The *Long Island City Star* once again loudly supported the bill, recognizing that consolidation meant that Long Island City would reap the "blessings" of costly urban improvements. Like a child on Santa's knee, the paper cried, "Come, gentlemen, hurry forward the 'Greater New York.' Long Island City is anxious to be taken in. We want the Blackwell Island bridge, a tunnel, some broad and handsomely paved streets and above all, a doubling and trebling up of the values of our factory and business sites and our magnificently situated building lands. The 'greater city' will bring all these blessings and many more, and we are hankering after them. How soon? What's the prospect?"[11]

This initial effort failed, but, undeterred, Green succeeded two years later. Green suggested six men for the Greater New York Commission, and Governor David B. Hill appointed five of them, almost guaranteeing that the pro-consolidation coalition of business and political interests would not be disappointed by the findings.[12] Green argued that there was "in the world over no other area of an hundred and fifty square miles whose welfare could be better promoted by one general administration, and yet there is not in the world over another like area so disturbed by multiplicity of conflicting authorities."[13]

The *Flushing Journal* praised formation of Green's commission and generally supported annexation, if only because it seemed inevitable:

> If New York cannot conveniently extend towards and into Westchester county, her overflowing population must find an outlet somewhere, and with the advantages which Long Island is offering the expansion must necessarily be this way. Any scheme which benefits Long Island, or any territory adjacent to New York, must benefit that city, for the time is not distant, in our judgment, when all territory indicated will become part and parcel of the greater New York which the Legislative Commission appointed last week is to investigate and report upon. Well-located property near to New York must improve rapidly in value.

About the commission, the paper commented, "We wish them godspeed in their task. The scheme is a gigantic one, but it is one that should be carried out if possible. It certainly will be, sooner or later. It is one of those things that must come, and the sooner the better." The *Star* also noted with approval Governor Hill's action on the bill. "The formal inquiry will acquaint the public with the difficulties and embarrassments which the present division of authority occasions in the community gathered about the port of New York," wrote the editor. "It will broaden their view of the future of the great commercial capital and give them lessons in sound and effective municipal government."[14]

From the start, the *Long Island City Star* was solidly behind the plan, in large part because local politics and government in Long Island City were shamelessly corrupt. In December 1886, the editor wrote:

> We are rejoiced to see that the project to raise one grand city has again been revived by the New York Aldermen appointing a committee to confer with the officials of the other municipalities interested and report. We hope all the parties interested in this movement may be able to decide upon some basis whereby the project may assume a definite shape and hasten the day when [they] will be incorporated into one grand corporation known as "Manhatta" or "Manhattan." We are not sticklers for any particular title; even plain New York will be agreeable to us.[15]

When the commission presented its work a year later, the Flushing paper exclaimed, "The change so contemplated is so radical, so revolutionary that it almost takes one's breath away to think of it." One of the first voices quoted in favor of the idea was former governor Richard C. McCormick of Jamaica, even though he thought that "a great difficulty in the way lies in securing proper care and attention at the seat of government for the districts on the outskirts" (perhaps the first, but certainly not the last time an outer-borough politician would decry the inattention of a Manhattan-centered city government). In actuality, the towns had enough difficulty providing services for themselves; as late as 1892 the road between Flushing and Jamaica was still unpaved.[16]

Queens County had a comparatively small population of 128,059 according to the 1890 census, despite being more than twice the size of Kings. Almost two-thirds of the county's population lived in Long Island City and the three western towns. Accordingly, Queens played a much smaller role in the drama than did Kings. As Joseph Witzel, owner of one of the most popular hotels in College Point, put it, if New York and Brooklyn united and sought to annex Queens, the people of Queens "would have very little say for or against the matter."[17]

At first, the plan excited little interest among the citizens of Queens, even though the progress of Green's Commission was covered regularly in the local papers. In early 1892, the *Flushing Journal* solicited the opinions of prominent Flushing men, and most disapproved of consolidation. Foremost among their objections was their fear of Tammany. One man replied, "Comparing methods of government I think it would be better for New York City to be annexed to Flushing." The paper noted that "the remedy lies with the people of New York; Long Islanders are powerless to do anything."[18] While recognizing the evils of Tammany, the *Journal* also acknowledged Flushing's deep ties with the city.

Another issue was the question of taxation and improvements. Voices opposed to consolidation emphasized home rule and reasoned that "the affairs of a single portion of the county" could not "receive proper consideration at the hands of a large city." Still, most businessmen recognized that annexation would ultimately bring economic advantages. Henry Clement stated that Flushing "would then have all the advantages that a metropolis has, the principal one of which is lower taxes. All the hue and cry about Tammany is mere chimera. The fact is Tammany would lose the balance of power that she now wields since it would revert to Brooklyn and the villages." F. P. Morris said simply, "It would help business and probably decrease our taxes. All large cities that have taken in suburban towns have prospered." Jere Johnson, one of the most active real estate developers in Flushing, envisioned a city of more than 8 million by 1950, and a city encompassing all the nearby counties. His optimistic prophecy was uncannily prescient. The 1950 census recorded 7,891,957 New Yorkers:

> The vast area will be densely peopled. The facilities for going from one part of the city to another will be far beyond anything our minds can now grasp. Scores of bridges will span the North and East Rivers, while beneath the waters numerous tunnels will have been constructed. New York will be the financial center of the world, as well as the center of intellectual and social life. Its magnificent public buildings and parks, its museums and art galleries, its theatres and coliseums, will render it the Mecca of all travelers. Rich and poor alike will delight to live within its limits.[19]

Local opinions ultimately carried little weight, however, for all major decisions were being made within Green's Greater New York Commission. Despite the testimony and editorials against particular features of the plan, the commission's work went forward without hindrance and with only a few modifications. During the 1893 session, the Greater New York Bill wound its way through the legislature, but the body adjourned before taking any action. Reintroduced the next year, the bill passed both houses and

Governor Roswell P. Flower immediately signed it. The Queens County Board of Supervisors had considered a resolution "that the representatives [of] Queens County in the senate and the assembly are hereby most earnestly requested and urged to cast their votes against said bill," but the matter was merely laid over. The county was split on the issue, and it is not surprising that the supervisors could neither approve nor reject the resolution.

The act called for a referendum to be held in November 1894 to gauge the sentiment of voters in the cities, towns, and villages that would comprise the new metropolis. Before the election, the Commission of Municipal Consolidation issued a statement regarding the meaning of the vote: "Your vote is only a simple expression of opinion. Actual consolidation does not come until the Legislature acts. Electors will please observe that this vote amounts to nothing more than a simple expression of opinion on the general subject of consolidation. It is merely the gathering of sentiment of the electors of each municipality advisory as to the future proceedings. If every ballot in a city or town were cast in favor of consolidation there would be no finality about it; no consolidation would result until further action by the Legislature."[20]

In the months leading up to the November election, opponents of annexation stressed two main points: first, the cost of improvements and tax assessments; and second, the power and influence of Tammany Hall. The *Newtown Register* editorialized against consolidation, warning that the citizens of the town "should not be misled by statements that the rate of taxation would be less. While the rate of taxation in New York and Brooklyn is somewhat lower than Newtown, the rate of assessments is three or four times greater. At present we would rather take our chances with Newtown as it is." The paper quoted approvingly an editorial in the *Brooklyn Eagle* that stated that even "if the proposed annexation of Brooklyn would result in lower taxes, such reduction would be a dear price to pay for loss of liberty and the miserable system of government which would invariably result." The *Register* added: "Municipal government of excessive magnitude is not only wasteful and expensive but popular control over the administration is proportionately diminished. Genuine elections by a huge district, the inhabitants of which are strangers to each other, is a moral impossibility. The inevitable result is the Ward politician with his machinery for collecting votes." Furthering the anti-consolidation argument, the *Register* tied the cost of improvements with the role of Tammany:

> Much has been said, and generally conceded, in regard to the benefits to be received by the cities of Brooklyn, New York and Long Island City but how the

suburbs will or can be benefitted remains to be seen. To be sure, we will have improvements to our hearts' content (some of which we could have had long since at moderate cost), and we will have to pay from double to five times their cost due to their heavy burden of the assessments levied to pay for these improvements. By the time of their completion one may look in vain for the original owners as few, if any, will survive the heavy expenses. Large owners, as well as small, will be compelled to sacrifice their property. Tammany, or some similar organization, will still exist and contracts will be given to favorite leaders whether the people like it or not. The Tiger must be fed and he has a capacious maw. In our present position we can jump on our derelict officials but would we dare to jump on the Tiger. Annexation does not mean lower taxation—it means the same taxation as paid today with the spending of these taxes in New York by New York officials. Newtown now gets the benefit of all her taxes. Then she will get only a percentage of them. Tammany, as usual, will have to have its share.[21]

Despite these arguments, voters in the Town of Newtown voted in favor of consolidation by about 57 percent in the November election. Long Island City, Jamaica, and the small portion of Hempstead included in the referendum likewise voiced their approval; only in Flushing did consolidation fail

Thomas Nast, *Something That Did Blow Over—November 7, 1871*. (The New York Public Library Digital Collections, Miriam and Ira D. Wallach Division of Art, Prints and Photographs: Print Collection.)

to win a majority. In all, more than 60 percent of the electors in Queens voted yes, with the greatest number of votes coming from Long Island City. As expected, the vote in Kings County was extremely close, a difference of only 277 votes out of almost 130,000 cast. Voters within the city limits of Brooklyn rejected the plan, while voters in the rural towns supported it. Overall, better than 57 percent of the voters approved of consolidation, enough of a mandate for pro-annexation forces to press forward.

By February 1896, the Greater New York Bill, originally put forward in 1893 and delayed by the approved caveat of a referendum to be held in November 1894, was still wending its way through the state legislature. Attempts to omit Flushing, Jamaica, and Hempstead from its provisions were turned back, despite an intensive lobbying campaign. The Flushing Village Association sent a delegation to Albany to testify against the bill, and seven hundred citizens of Flushing and Jamaica signed a memorial sent to the governor and the legislature protesting annexation, but their efforts could not stop, or even modify, the legislation. After passing both houses, the bill was sent to the three mayors. Mayor William L. Strong of New York

Table 11
Results of Consolidation Vote, 1894

County	For	Against
New York	96,938 (62%)	59,959
Kings	64,744 (50.1%)	64,467
Queens	7,712 (65%)	4,741
Richmond	5,531 (79%)	1,505
Westchester*	1,255 (56%)	1,034
Total	176,180 (57.2%)	131,706

*Towns of Westchester, Eastchester, and Pelham

Queens	For	Against
Long Island City	3,529 (82%)	792
Newtown	1,267 (57%)	946
Flushing	1,144 (45%)	1,407
Jamaica	1,381 (52%)	1,263
Hempstead (part)	478 (54%)	412
Total	7,599 (61%)	4,820

SOURCES: *Brooklyn Daily Eagle Almanac*, 1899, 135; *Long Island Democrat*, November 13, 1894.
NOTE: The Queens figures differ because there were discrepancies in the election returns reported.

and Mayor Frederick W. Wurster of Brooklyn vetoed it, but Long Island City's Patrick J. Gleason sent it back with his wholehearted approval. The legislature again passed the bill over the vetoes, and Governor Levi P. Morton signed the measure on May 11, 1896.[22]

In the end, Tammany Hall came out against the bill, possibly because it was not at all clear that they would control the new metropolis. The Republicans saw in consolidation the possibility that they could wrest control of the city from the Democrats, and by the end of 1895 party boss Thomas C. Platt was solidly behind the measure. In 1894, the Republican ticket actually carried the area that would become Greater New York, and some members of the party "believed that consolidation would actually help rather than hurt the party that accomplished it." It was Platt's control of the Republican Party that finally pushed the Greater New York Bill through Albany.[23]

When the bill first passed in March, the *Flushing Journal* lamented: "Of course the name Flushing will have to be dropped. Shall we have to call it 'New York, E. D.' (eastern district) and will our post office be 'Station X' or some other lowdown letter of the alphabet? Then, too, what will become of the proud and cherished distinction of belonging to the First Families of Flushing when it shall be known a Flushing no more?" After urging residents vote no, the *Newtown Register* was now resigned to the inevitable: "We can only hope that in the framing of the charter for the new city, and in other preparatory measures and arrangements, wise and patriotic counsels will prevail. If they do not, Newtown at least will have nothing to boast of in losing its time-honored identity."[24]

The consolidation bill established a commission to draft a charter for the greater city. On September 21, the subcommittee charged with preparing the document completed their work and sent the draft charter to Albany. The measure passed both houses, and on May 2, 1897, Governor Frank S. Black signed Chapter 378 of the Laws of 1897: "An act to unite into one municipality under the corporate name of the City of New York, the various communities lying in and about New York Harbor, including the City and County of New York, the City of Brooklyn and the County of Kings, the County of Richmond, and part of the County of Queens and to provide for the government thereof."[25] The law took effect on January 1, 1898.

Nassau County

In the 1830s and 1840s, a group of Kings and Queens men, many of them prominent in the island's social and political life and members of the oldest

Map Showing the Limits of Greater New York, 1896. (Courtesy of the Queens Borough Public Library, Archives, Chamber of Commerce of the Borough of Queens Collection.)

families, held "statehood conventions" at taverns in Brooklyn, Jamaica, Hempstead, and Islip. According to Daniel M. Tredwell, one of the most informative diarists of nineteenth-century Long Island, the group, after many hours of discussions and the "immolation of hecatombs of squab did solemnly vote and declare Long Island to be a free and independent state, and in the same spirit" elected Alden Spooner "Governor." Spooner was a member of the Queens County Bar, publisher of the *Brooklyn Star*, and in 1863 a founding member of the Long Island Historical Society (the Brooklyn Historical Society since 1985). The high point of this light-hearted campaign for statehood came at the grand national dinner and jubilee honoring president-elect William Henry Harrison at Niblo's Garden in Manhattan in early 1841:

> On the day and hour Governor Spooner at the head of his delegation formed in line at the entrance to the Garden to demand admission. The Massachusetts

delegates headed by Governor Winthrop was just in advance and as they entered and were announced the throng inside burst into cheers. As they passed in Governor Spooner advanced with his delegation behind him. They gravely marched up to the usher, who by the way was a Louisiana man. Governor Spooner solemnly handed out the credentials and whispered, "Delegates from the State of Long Island." Forgetting all his history and geography amid the confusion inside in consequence of the entrance of the Massachusetts delegation, the usher roared out, "Delegates from the State of Long Island please enter." They did enter and took seats amid thunders of applause, which broke out again and again as the ludicrous facts dawned on the convention. Spooner had the honor of replying to the toast "The Brand New State of Long Island" which he did in a manner said to have been the most consummate and finished piece of oratory of his life.[26]

Behind the high-spirited fun and Spooner's "unprecedented nervy humor" lay the hard realization that Long Island would never receive its due from the great state of New York or escape Manhattan's lengthening shadow. Tredwell wrote that Spooner "was one of the many old-time Long Islanders who never became reconciled to the rude and uncourtly treatment of the proposition to enroll Long Island on the galaxy of Union Statehood." Generously fueled by tavern spirits, the conventions were a tacit recognition of the folly of their quest.

Although statehood remained an unrealistic proposition, the idea of dividing Queens periodically surfaced. According to Nassau County historian Edward Smits, one reason was the emerging Republican majority in the eastern towns. As in other parts of the North, the party was organized in Queens in opposition to the Kansas-Nebraska Act in 1854. The Republicans carried Hempstead and North Hempstead in 1860, although the county as a whole went Democratic, as did New York and Brooklyn.

Differences between the agricultural hinterland and the commercial cities had always been apparent. At midcentury, the three eastern towns had a greater population than the western towns, but after the railroad terminals opened in Hunters Point, western Queens grew at a much faster rate than the rural towns. Not surprisingly, the interests of the two halves of the county began to diverge. The 1860 census revealed that for the first time the population of the three western towns surpassed that of eastern Queens, a development that presaged a shift in the locus of political power, especially after the incorporation of Long Island City in 1870.[27]

Table 12
Population Growth in Queens, 1850–1892

Year	Newtown, Jamaica, Flushing, and Long Island City,	Hempstead, Oyster Bay, and North Hempstead
1850	16,831 (46%)	20,002
1855	18,296 (39%)	27,970
1860	30,429 (53%)	26,962
1865	31,481 (54%)	26,516
1875	48,531 (59%)	33,490
1880	52,927 (59%)	37,147
1890	85,467 (65%)	45,760
1892	95,014 (67%)	47,184

SOURCES: Benjamin Franklin Hough, *Census of the State of New York for 1865* (Albany, NY: C. Van Benthuysen and Sons, 1867); C. W. Seaton, *Census of the State of New York for 1875* (Albany, NY: Weed, Parsons, 1877); *Flushing Journal*, March 26, 1892.

The growing rivalry burst open over the question of building a new county courthouse to replace the inadequate eighteenth-century structure located in North Hempstead along Jericho Turnpike, roughly at the county's geographic center. On July 10, 1869, the six county supervisors met at John A. Searing's inn in Mineola, and Edward A. Lawrence of Flushing introduced a resolution that the county build a new courthouse and jail:

> The Court House of this County is wholly unfit, from its location and construction, for the transaction of the business of the Courts of the County—there being no accommodations for those who are compelled to be in attendance at such Courts as Judges, Jurors, Witnesses, Counsel or Officers. And the County Jail is unfit in every particular for the purposes for which it was designed; and especially so from the miserable and disgraceful cells assigned to those unfortunates who are committed to the Jail—the apartments being over-crowded, badly constructed, illy ventilated, and poorly heated—from the necessity of the case, whites being confined with blacks, and girls, young men and boys indiscriminately incarcerated with old criminals and hardened offenders. The fact that the cells are unfit for the safe detention of criminals has been demonstrated by the frequent escapes during the past few years.

The existing structure was certainly inadequate, but the six supervisors could not agree on a location for a new one. After the western towns succeeded in getting a bill passed in Albany authorizing a new courthouse, the eastern towns began to lobby for the division of the county. In February 1869, Queens assemblyman James B. Pearsall introduced legislation to form a new county out of the three eastern towns and the western towns of Suffolk—Huntington, Smithtown, and Islip—but this measure gained no traction in the legislature and soon died.[28] The triumph of the western towns came two years later when the county supervisors, all of them Democrats, voted to locate the new courthouse in Long Island City, which had received its charter the year before. The deciding argument was that the railroad terminus was nearby, making the site equally accessible from all parts of the county (by that reasoning Jamaica would have been a better choice). The new courthouse, a magnificent stone and brick edifice topped by a gleaming copper roof, was dedicated on March 28, 1877. It was a fitting monument to an emerging urban center, and quite a change from its cramped, colonial-era predecessor.[29]

In 1891, Bloodgood H. Cutter, the "Long Island Farmer Poet," bought the old courthouse and had one wing moved to his estate in Little Neck, where he made it his "Poet's Hall." Cutter wished to preserve the place where he had once heard famed abolitionist Wendell Phillips speak.[30]

In 1876, as the new Queens County Court House was under construction, Townsend D. Cock of Oyster Bay introduced a bill in the state assembly to erect a new county from the towns of Oyster Bay, Hempstead, North Hempstead, and the Suffolk towns of Huntington and Babylon, which was formed from part of Huntington in 1872. The new county was to be called "Ocean," but the bill was amended and the name changed to "Nassau." The hearing held in Albany before the Assembly Committee on Civil Divisions brought out voices on both sides of the question. As expected, the only support came from representatives of the towns that would form the new county; both Jamaica and eastern Suffolk expressed opposition. After its second reading in March 1876, the bill died. Assemblyman Elbert Floyd-Jones reintroduced the measure the following year, but this too failed in the assembly by a vote of 42–56.[31]

The idea had gained influential supporters, however. Writer and poet William Cullen Bryant, a resident of the North Hempstead village of Roslyn, wrote, "The people in Roslyn and its neighborhood are strongly in favor of the project. I, for my part, am one of the numerous class who are in favor of the new county." The *Flushing Journal*, on the other hand, opposed the proposal. In a tongue-in-cheek editorial titled "The Division of the County," the paper suggested that Hempstead would soon gobble up North Hempstead and Oyster Bay. "What of the remainder," the editor asked. Long Island

City might "walk over the bridge and become part of Brooklyn," and Jamaica would "speedily absorb innocent and defenseless Flushing, and then Jamaica would represent in reality what it has long represented figuratively—the whole of Queens County." The *Flushing Journal* concluded, "We cannot consent to let our wayward sisters go."[32] For the next two decades, as resentment of Long Island City and the western towns festered in the rural townships, the question of a new county garnered little public interest.

The fate of Queens County was one of the thornier issues still to be settled with the creation of Greater New York, for unlike Kings and Richmond, borough and county were not coterminous. The committee that drafted the city's charter decided that the county's Board of Supervisors would continue and "provided for the equitable apportionment of that part of the county debt to be assumed by The Greater New York, and have further provided for the levying and collection, by the city, of taxes in that part of Queens County included within the city, and for the division of school moneys." The birth of Greater New York left the towns of Hempstead, North Hempstead, and Oyster Bay in the peculiar position of being part of a county that was half in and half out of the new metropolis. Overwhelmingly rural, dotted with small suburban villages along railroad lines, the eastern townships had never been included in discussions about the greater city's boundaries. For more than fifty years, however, Long Islanders had considered the formation of a new county or even statehood. As the Greater New York Charter worked its way through the legislature, state senator Theodore Koehler of Long Island City introduced a measure to divide the county, with the annexed portion to be added to New York County, just as the Westchester towns of Pelham, Eastchester, and Westchester had been soon after the 1894 referendum. His bill went nowhere, however.[33]

In truth, Queens had never been much more than a geographic expression. The sparsely populated townships were joined in a loosely structured, and thoroughly ineffective, county government. The Board of Supervisors did not even have a permanent home, and met at taverns across the county. In contrast to Kings County, which fell under the domination of Brooklyn, there was no city in Queens. Each town had its own village center, but not one of them emerged as the dominant social, political, and economic heart of the county. Only in 1892, in fact, did Newtown take the initial steps toward incorporation as a village.[34] Jamaica, it is true, prospered as the railroad's main transfer station, but the village never captured the county courthouse, the symbol of political power. Hempstead was the most populous township, but, as it was almost entirely rural, it could not compete with the gravitational pull of the dynamic economies of New York and Brooklyn. With the creation of Long Island City out of the western part of Newtown in 1870, Queens finally had its city, but the eastern townships soon perceived that their suburban and agricultural interests were not in harmony with the industrial economy and rough-and-tumble politics of Long Island City.

As the population in each section grew at a different rate, so, too, was there a marked difference in the relative wealth of the eastern and western townships. Most of the wealth was concentrated in Long Island City and, to a lesser extent, the western towns. In 1897, the area that became Nassau County contained only about 20 percent of the assessed valuation of Queens County; by contrast, Long Island City, with its growing industrial base, had over 50 percent of the total. Newtown, Flushing, and Jamaica accounted for the remainder. In the year after consolidation, the valuations in the eastern towns actually decreased, no doubt cheering the inhabitants and bolstering their belief that taxes from the rural districts had been siphoned off to finance improvements in urban and suburban sections.

Just as the wealth was concentrated in the annexed section, so was the county's indebtedness. Out of a total indebtedness of more than $10 million, the eastern towns accounted for only $642,500, or about 6 percent of the total, excluding their share of the county bonds and school bonds. The grossly mismanaged and blatantly corrupt administration of Long Island City incurred the bulk of the debt, almost 35 percent of the total. Not all of that figure could be charged to corruption, however, for this was also the most rapidly urbanizing part of the county, and the city had to let contracts for water and sewer mains, schools, and street paving. The incorporated villages of Queens accounted for more than a quarter of the debt, and the reason was plain. Under the new charter, Greater New York would assume "the valid debts, obligations and liabilities of the municipal and public corporations including the counties, towns, incorporated villages and school districts." Secure in the knowledge that they would not be held accountable for repaying what they borrowed, the several municipalities, whether in good faith or not, borrowed funds for all manner of public improvements. By November 1897, the Queens County Board of Supervisors had issued $375,000 in 4 percent bonds for county roads. The residents of Rockaway Beach, a square-mile section between Arverne and Rockaway Park, incorporated as a village on July 1, 1897, even though the area would become part of Greater New York within a few months. Almost immediately the new municipality issued $57,000 in bonds (10 percent of the assessed valuation) "to secure all the improvements they can before the city government takes

Table 13
Bonded Indebtedness, Queens County Governments, 1897

County of Queens	$1,849,000
Long Island City	$3,654,000
Town of Newtown	$400,000
Town of Flushing	$157,000
Town of Jamaica	$496,000
Town of Hempstead	$485,000
Town of North Hempstead	$131,500
Town of Oyster Bay	$26,000
Village of Jamaica	$700,000
Village of Richmond Hill	$330,000
Village of Arverne-by-the-Sea	$121,000
Village of Flushing	$414,000
Village of College Point	$700,000
Village of Whitestone	$500,000
Village of Far Rockaway	$100,000
County School District Bonds	$500,000
Total	$10,563,500
County Debt Limit	$8,543,500

Distribution of County Debt, 1897

Municipality	% of County Total
Long Island City	34.59
Newtown, Jamaica, Flushing	9.97
Incorporated Villages	27.12
Hempstead, North Hemp., Oyster Bay	6.08

Public Debt, Queens County, 1898

Borough of Queens	$3,862,116.79
Nassau County	$975,694.17
Total	$4,837,810.96

SOURCES: *Long Island Democrat*, December 7, 1897; *Queens County Review*, September 23, 1898.

away the local power and authority."[35] The *Newtown Register* commented that the towns and villages were obviously profiting from consolidation:

> Jamaica surpasses all her neighbors in this respect and throughout the town wherever one goes are found gangs of men building macadam roads, laying sewers or making other improvements. Newtown and Flushing have also indulged in the same line of business and all seem determined to get as many

local improvements as possible before going into the Greater New York. Controller Fitch of New York City has been very observant of the actions of the citizens of Queens County who are soon to be his fellow citizens of New York. He remarked that he did not blame the Queens County people in the least; that they are only doing what he would urge them to do if he lived among them; that they would not be likely to secure these improvements for many years if they did not secure them now.[36]

This luxury, of course, was not available to the towns excluded from the greater city.

Issues of taxation, public works, local politics, and county government only promised to grow in complexity and confusion if Queens County continued in its divided state. Although the new charter provided for Greater New York to acquire "all of the public buildings, institutions, public parks, water-works and property of every character and description," the courthouse and other public buildings in Queens located within the new city limits were specifically exempted. In practice, this meant that the eastern residents would be financing local government without receiving improvements bestowed on the annexed districts. The citizens of the eastern towns also recognized a crucial difference between the brand of politics practiced in the cities and, from their perspective, the more virtuous politics of Long Island, a distinction based on more than party affiliation.

After the Tammany victory in 1895 returned the "old ring" to power, the *Queens County Review*, a weekly published in the South Shore village of Freeport, asked, "Is the sense of morality so dead in New York that its citizens prefer corruption to business principles?" The unwelcome prospect of the Tammany machine, combined with fears that the growing urban population would dominate county politics, prompted citizens of Hempstead, North Hempstead, and Oyster Bay to organize a drive for secession. As an editorial in the *Queens County Review* noted, "The people do not relish the idea of having to support two separate governments with all the confusion and clashing of authority that would thus arise. From past experience it certainly seems advisable to reduce, not enlarge the number of conflicting governments in Queens County."[37]

As soon as the smoke had cleared from the fireworks set off to celebrate Greater New York, the citizens of the three eastern towns renewed their campaign. On January 22, 1898, they held a public meeting at Allen's Hotel in Mineola "to consider the most expedient actions to take to escape the dangers by which that portion of Queens County outside of the Greater New York limits is threatened by the operation of the new charter." P. Halsted Scudder defined five options for the assembled citizens. The first, annexation to New York, was "not to be thought of or discussed for a moment," and the second, annexation to Suffolk, was "a method repugnant to our sense of individuality and to all traditions of our people." Scudder then rejected the annexation of Queens to Kings as impractical and presenting too many financial, statutory, and constitutional barriers. The fourth option, erection of a new county to embrace the eastern towns of Queens and the western towns of Suffolk, could be considered only if the population of Suffolk gave its unanimous consent. Finally, he presented the fifth and final possibility, which was, "to those who have most carefully studied the situation in all its phases, the best, the wisest and surest way out of our difficulties—The erection of a new county out of that portion of the County of Queens which lies without the Borough of Queens." The assembly resolved "that it is the sense of this meeting that the Towns of Hempstead, North Hempstead, and Oyster Bay withdraw from the County of Queens and that a new county to include said towns be formed." At this excited gathering, they also voted that each of the towns would contribute $250 toward the expenses of drafting and preparing the bills "necessary to carry into effect the desire of the people to have a county free from any entangling alliances with the Great City of New York."

The citizens selected a seven-member committee to draft the legislation and select a name for the new county: P. Halsted Scudder, at-large; Lott Van de Water and William G. Miller of Hempstead; Dr. James H. Bogart and William Lewis of North Hempstead; and from Oyster Bay, James H. Ludlam and General James B. Pearsall. Names put forward for the new county were "Matinecock," after Long Island's dominant Indian tribe; "Norfolk," a complimentary if geographically inaccurate nod to Suffolk; "Bryant," in honor of William Cullen Bryant; and "Nassau," an "appropriate choice as Long Island had been named Nassau Island by an act of the colonial Assembly on April 10, 1693." When the committee met at Pettit's Hotel in Jamaica on February 5, they adopted the name Nassau and presented a draft bill to Assemblyman George Wallace.[38]

The issue moved forward with remarkable speed. On February 17, Wallace introduced the Nassau bill, and on March 25 it passed that house with three votes to spare, despite vigorous opposition from Assemblyman Cyrus B. Gale of Jamaica; the bill received unanimous approval in the senate. Governor Black signed the measure on April 27, and on January 1, 1899, exactly a year after the formation of Greater New York split Queens County in two, Nassau County was born.[39]

The Water Question

Formation of the new county promised to resolve one of Long Island's most serious long-term issues: control over the island's water resources.[40] New York's annexation of Brooklyn meant the integration of the water systems of the two cities. Long Islanders welcomed this news, for Brooklyn had pumped the south side dry and had designs on the water resources of Suffolk County. Beginning in the 1850s, the City of Brooklyn embarked on an ambitious program to secure a plentiful water supply for its rapidly growing population. The city paid the Town of Hempstead $12,000 for Hempstead Lake, and in 1853 and 1858 purchased additional bodies of fresh water, including Valley Stream. The water flowed through an aqueduct to the Ridgewood Reservoir atop the terminal moraine in Queens, just across the Brooklyn line. The acquisition of water resources continued into the last decade of the century. After all the ponds and streams had been tapped, the city's water department bought land and sank 150-foot wells to tap the water found in the layer of gravel below the 50-foot layer of clay; one such well yielded more than 5 million gallons a day.[41]

As Brooklyn thus assured its inhabitants of pure water, the South Shore communities confronted less immediate but equally dramatic consequences. The *Queens County Review* cried, "Long Island is literally pumped dry." Indeed, in 1896 Brooklyn pumped 50 million gallons of water a day from the wells and ponds of Long Island. Farmers, baymen, and homeowners on the south side witnessed the ecological impact of Brooklyn's thirst on the island. At the very least, Long Islanders had to dig deeper wells to compensate for the lower water table, but that was only part of the problem:

> It will not be long before the authorities of the City of Brooklyn will have to look elsewhere than Long Island for the source of their water supply. At the present time their system is taxed to its utmost capacity to furnish a sufficient supply, and a number of costly makeshifts have been added to the already large amount of expenditure. The fault of the matter is that the supply is not equal to the ever increasing demand, and the stoppage of our streams, and the reduction of the level of the surface and sub-surface by continual pumping is not only a source of expense to the citizens of this county but an absolute menace. Among the chief sufferers are the oystermen. Formerly the streams of fresh water seemed to keep the creeks free from mud, but they are now filling up; as it used to be there was a sufficient depth of water at low tide to prevent their oysters from freezing, but now, especially in the case of Freeport creek,

there is not enough water to cover them without the building of expensive "drinking houses."

On other occasions, the paper reported that several stagnant ponds "teem with germs" and had been reduced to "muck filled with vegetable matter, which, when exposed to the sun and heat, sent forth germs of disease endangering the health of the people." The editor implored Brooklyn to "cease pumping at Wantagh station until the heavy rains come."[42]

Brooklyn needed no convincing that it would soon require additional supply. In January 1896, Commissioner of City Works Alfred T. White issued a report on the prospect of future water supply that identified three options: Ten Mile River, a branch of the Housatonic River in eastern Dutchess County; the Ramapo River in Orange County; and the aquifer beneath the pine barrens in central Suffolk County, an area stretching for forty-three miles east of Massapequa, then the eastern limit of Brooklyn's system. City engineers anticipated that tapping eleven streams in eastern Long Island could yield 80 million gallons a day. White's report noted: "While the cities across the river feel that Brooklyn should hold to Long Island as its source of supply, our neighbors on the Island take an opposite view. Brooklyn must protect itself, but should give a fair hearing to these conflicting interests and serve itself with the least harm to others." The department anticipated that to protect "the unexcelled quality of the water from the south side streams of Long Island" from pollution, "as well as to prevent the denudation of the wooded swamps, liberal purchase of land should be made. The evils of a narrow or short-sided policy in this respect are every day apparent in our original works."[43]

This report brought an immediate reaction in Suffolk, and just a month later a bill was introduced in Albany to protect their resource from Brooklyn's designs. Indeed, that city's water department had "begun to skirmish along the north shore for water and the people do not welcome the prospect of having their lakes and streams interfered with." In June, the governor signed the law, preventing Brooklyn from drawing off Suffolk's water without the approval of a majority of the county supervisors. From this perspective, consolidation actually ensured Brooklyn's continued growth, for the city had been shut out of its most promising option and it was reaching the limit of its existing water sources. In 1896, Brooklyn's water system had a maximum capacity of 94 million gallons a day, but by 1899 daily use had reached 92 million gallons. With its rapidly growing population, Brooklyn would have faced a severe crisis. The *Brooklyn Times* suggested shortly before the governor signed the Suffolk water bill that "if there is a danger that the sources cannot be much further extended without impairing the rights of the residents, we cannot too soon make up our minds where we had best go."[44] Despite the looming crisis of supply, the water question scarcely entered into the debate over consolidation, dominated as it was by issues of taxation, home rule, party politics, and corruption.

While the City of Brooklyn developed its extensive water system, the towns and villages of Queens County still relied on local wells, and as the population in those places continued to grow, questions about the water quality and supply became more frequent. Long Island City relied on wells in Newtown owned by the Woodside Water Company, a firm controlled by the municipality's corrupt mayor, Patrick Jerome Gleason. The 1900 report on the city's water supply stated: "The Borough of Queens is in urgent need of additional supply. The quality of the present sources, which are driven wells near to the territory already occupied by dwellings and factories and which will each year become more thickly populated, must become continually less desirable."[45] With consolidation, Brooklyn was soon supplied by New York's system. After 1917, Queens, too, began receiving its water from the ample supply from the Croton system, and the baymen and farmers of Long Island were delivered from Brooklyn's unquenchable thirst. Still, wells on Long Island continued to supply Brooklyn and Queens for more than fifty years. The Ridgewood Reservoir was in use until 1959, and it was not formally decommissioned until 1989.

As many predicted, consolidation indeed lowered the tax rate in Queens and brought forward an unprecedented stream of urban improvements. In 1899, the rate per $100 of assessed valuation was $3.27 in Queens; by 1905 the rate had fallen by more than half to $1.55. At the same time, the borough received more than its share of city revenues. A pamphlet published to boost Borough President Joseph Cassidy noted that the tax rate in the borough had fallen, even as the assessed valuations and expenditures for improvements had gone up: "While the general city tax is $1,199,791.99, the borough will receive out of the general city tax fund about $3,500,000. This tax is levied on all boroughs according to their assessed values, and the Boroughs of Manhattan and Brooklyn, with their enormous assessed values, really donate these millions to Queens Borough. This explains why about $4,000,000 are expended annually in the borough for general improvements without taxing borough property to raise the money." His campaign brochure went on to claim: "This speaks volumes for the administration of Borough President Cassidy. It proves conclusively that the present chief executive of the borough has conducted the affairs of his office with careful consideration for the best interests of the property owners and the people generally. More improvements have been perfected and are now in progress under [his] administration than was ever recorded in the history of Queens Borough."[46] Cassidy later went to prison for attempting to sell a judgeship.

In truth, these improvements would have been undertaken regardless of who held the office of borough president. But the fact remains that consolidation quickened the pace of investment and construction in the boroughs, and with completion of the long-planned Blackwell's Island Bridge and extension of the city's rapid transit lines, the Borough of Queens urbanized at a faster rate than any other city in the nation. Consolidation set the stage for the passage from a rural county to an urban borough.

8

The Queensboro Bridge

The Queensboro Bridge fulfilled the promise of consolidation. Greater New York's first decade saw an unprecedented surge in municipal spending, with three East River bridges under construction simultaneously at one point: the Williamsburg, the Queensboro, and the Manhattan. Even as the spans rose over the river, a new subway tunnel connecting Manhattan and Brooklyn neared completion. In that same decade, the city also graded and paved miles and miles of streets, installed sewer and water lines, and created the world's largest school system. To build the twentieth-century metropolis, the city appealed to neither Washington nor Albany, and that is surely one measure of the city's greatness at the turn of the century.

Completed in 1909, the Queensboro Bridge had a dramatic impact on the Queens landscape and the borough's development. When it opened it was the fourth-longest bridge in the world, after the two earlier East River spans, the Brooklyn (1883) and Williamsburg (1903), and the Firth of Forth railroad bridge in Scotland (1890). The new bridge dominated the landscape, rising dramatically from Queens and silhouetted before Manhattan. Yet its impact on the transformation of the borough was even greater than its engineering grandeur. In 1900, the population of Queens barely exceeded 150,000; by 1930 it had topped a million. As an independent city, it would

The Great Forth Bridge, Scotland, C. H. Graves, publisher, 1900. (Library of Congress, Prints and Photographs Division.)

have ranked behind only Chicago, Philadelphia, and Los Angeles, which was larger by only about 100,000.[1]

The Blackwell's Island Bridge

The possibility of a Blackwell's Island bridge had been a topic of conjecture since at least 1836, when the *Long Island Democrat*, a Jamaica weekly, reported that "a project has been lately started, to build a suspension bridge over L.I. Sound near Hallets Cove or Ravenswood." The story pointed out that the suspension spans above the channels on either side of Blackwell's Island would not impede ship traffic, noting that the distance would not exceed the span of the 1826 Menai Strait Bridge in Wales, a 579-foot suspension bridge supported by sixteen chains of iron bars. Rejecting the possibility of a bridge "across the Stream from Brooklyn to New York" on the grounds that the "great distance will forever be an insuperable bar to its accomplishment," the paper reasoned that "a bridge at the proposed point would be a very great thoroughfare, and probably, would soon make Hallets Cove rival Brooklyn in population." The author estimated the cost at between $300,000 and $500,000.[2]

The next year, the *Democrat* reprinted an article from *Family Magazine* touting such a crossing. Roswell Graves, "while engaged in surveying the vicinity of Blackwell's Island, conceived the plan of a bridge to the city," commencing at a point between 65th and 75th Streets. His scheme called for three suspension spans of 700 feet, each rising 120 feet above the water. The accompanying illustration depicted an "iron hanging-bridge" resembling the Menai Strait Bridge. The proposed structure was to be only 45-feet wide, with a footpath between two carriage roads. The most persuasive argument in its favor concerned the poor communication between Long Island and New York:

> One of the greatest obstacles to the rapid and permanent growth of the city of New York [is] the fact that there is at present no certain and rapid mode of communication with the adjoining country. To be sure, the different ferries by which the inhabitants of this splendid city are able in the spring and summer months to enjoy the society of their neighbours, might, at first view, seem to render that objection futile; but when we consider the great expense of ferriage, and the uncertainty of the length of passage in the winter time, when the rivers are full of ice, it will be apparent to every one that if bridges could be thrown over the North and East Rivers, they would certainly be a public benefit, and contribute very much to the prosperity and comfort of the people.

The author estimated the cost at between $500,000 and $800,000, and confidently stated that the bridge could support a load of "upward of twelve hundred tons, a weight that beyond probability would never be upon the bridge at one point of time."[3] The author exuded the confidence of America's early industrial age but generated no action.

The idea was raised again in the mid-1850s, when Henry Kneeland, Archibald H. Lowery, and other New York businessmen approached John A. Roebling to request he submit preliminary designs for a bridge across the East River at Blackwell's Island. Based on his work in Pittsburgh and especially his Niagara railroad bridge completed in March 1855, Roebling was recognized as the pre-eminent bridge designer in the United States.[4] In June 1856, Lowery suggested a few guidelines. First, "the channel on both sides of Blackwell's Island are used. The very deepest water is on the N. Y. side of the channel but sufficient throughout all parts for large vessels." Obviously, the question of unimpeded navigation was paramount. Lowery added that he had discussed the question with Hell Gate pilots, and "an elevation of 150 feet above water would not be objectionable, not one vessel in fifty of the class that usually go that way would require a greater elevation." Finally, after questioning the wisdom of "starting at or near the Hill on the 3rd Avenue in order to approach the Bridge at an easy grade," he concluded, "The Bridge if built must be for use not ornament. Therefore if it cannot be gotten onto and off it will be of no use."

Within a week, Roebling sent off preliminary plans, complete with cost estimates and an enthusiastic conviction that "no other part of the East River offers a locality so favorable to bridging." He set the Manhattan end between 65th and 70th Streets, and Second and Third Avenues, "not quite opposite center of Island," and proposed a pair of 800-foot suspension spans, with a 500-foot island span between. His bridge would have an extremely narrow 22-foot roadway, and 6-foot sidewalks suspended outside the cables. The cost for this structure, including land for both approaches, he estimated at $1,216,740.[5] After this quick exchange of letters, however, the plan apparently dissolved, and when Roebling did finally build his East River bridge, it was not, of course, at Blackwell's Island.

A serious effort began after the Civil War. Thirty-five businessmen from New York and Queens organized the New York and Long Island Bridge Company and obtained a charter from the state legislature. The incorporators included Oliver Charlick, president of the Long Island Railroad (LIRR); Anthony W. Winans, owner of several ferry lines; and such prominent Queens landowners as B. S. Halsey, Archibald Bliss, and James Barclay. The company obtained a charter on April 16, 1867, the same day the New York Bridge Company acquired theirs to build the Brooklyn Bridge, but technically preceding the latter. The charters of the two companies were almost identical, excepting the particulars of location.[6]

The charter granted the company the right to borrow money and "to purchase, acquire and hold as much real estate as may be necessary for the site of said bridge, and of all abutments, approaches, walls, toll-houses, and other structures proper to said bridge." It fixed the rates of toll so that "the net profits shall not exceed the sum of fifteen per cent. per annum, after deducting the expenses of repairs and improvements and all just and proper damages." The bridge was to "commence between the Third avenue and East River, between Fiftieth and Ninety-second streets and shall be so constructed as to cross the river as near opposite as practicable to Long Island to such a point as will afford and give reasonable grade and facilities for approaches." The legislature thus left it to the corporation to fix the exact location for the structure.[7]

Neither the City of New York nor the rural county of Queens was in a position to finance such a bridge, nor was it deemed an appropriate government activity. Just as cities refrained from building and operating rapid transit lines, railroads, and turnpikes, municipal governments left the construction of bridges to private capital. However, the charter did contain a clause permitting New York and Queens, or either of them, to "take the said bridge and appurtenances, and acquire all property therein, by a payment to the said corporation of the cost thereof, together with thirty-three and one-third per cent. in addition thereto," with the provision that no tolls be charged either vehicles or passengers.[8]

The New York and Long Island Bridge Company amended its charter to extend the date for the start of construction to 1873 and the expected completion date to June 1879. This was to be the first in a series of applications to the legislature to extend the time frame of their charter, the last of which came in 1892, extending the date of completion to 1900.[9] In 1872, the company filed a survey of its proposed line with the Queens County Clerk. The Manhattan approach would begin at Third Avenue between 76th and 77th Streets; on the Queens side the approach began at 1st Avenue in Long Island City. For a time, that was all the company accomplished.

In June 1872, the legislature unexpectedly chartered a competing venture, the New York and Queens County Bridge Company. This charter was identical in all respects to the earlier corporation, with the exception that its field of operation was widened to include any point between 40th and 92nd Streets. The boards of directors shared only one name in common: Oliver Charlick. One of Charlick's favorite ploys during Long Island's railroad wars was to form a rival company to challenge an established franchise in the hopes of forcing them to either sell out to him or buy him out. Corporate records survive from neither company, but it is likely that Charlick engaged in a similar scheme with his bridge company. His New York and Queens County Bridge Company accomplished nothing, although it remained in existence into the 1880s.[10]

Many New York, Long Island City, and College Point businessmen and landowners became involved in this endeavor, among them John T. Conover, Herman C. Poppenhusen, Archibald M. Bliss, Pliny Freeman, Oswald Ottendorfer, Abram D. Ditmars, Charles A. Trowbridge, Herman Funke, and William Steinway, who became head of the board of directors.[11] The inclusion of prominent German American investors points to their economic influence and involvement in civic affairs.

The New York and Long Island Bridge Company took a major step forward in late 1875 when the directors appointed General J. G. Barnard, General Quincy A. Gilmore—both of the Army Corps of Engineers—and Oliver Chanute of the Erie Railroad as a Board of Consulting Engineers responsible for "recommending a design." On May 1, 1876, they announced a design competition, offering premiums of $1,000, $500, and $250 for the best submissions. Design specifications called for a single-track railway with the capacity for double tracking "without materially changing the general arrangement of parts or the loads imposed upon them, or interfering with the current use of the bridge." The bridge was to include two roadways for carriages, each ten-feet wide, from Third Avenue in Manhattan to Long Island City, two five-foot wide sidewalks, "either alongside or overhead of the main carriageways or the railway," and two steam-powered double elevators for foot passengers at Avenue A in Manhattan and Vernon Avenue in Queens. The specifications also stipulated that the Manhattan approach would include a 1,000-foot tunnel connecting with the tracks of the Harlem Railroad on 4th Avenue near 73rd Street. In all, the Manhattan approach was estimated at 4,580 feet, the single span over the west channel at 734 feet, the island span at about 700 feet, the eastern channel span at 618 feet, and the Queens approach at 3,900 feet, for a total of about 10,532 (the Roebling span would have been approximately 8,000 feet, and the 1830s proposal only 2,180 feet). The bridge floor would rise 150 feet above the high-water mark. By mid-December, the panel had received nine sets of plans. With the Brooklyn Bridge under construction, Washington Roebling, the son of John A. Roebling, did not submit a design; by late 1876, his crews had completed both towers and were preparing to spin the cables.[12]

The submissions included all manner of nineteenth-century bridge designs, but surprisingly, there were only two designs for a suspension bridge, and those would have utilized steel towers, rather than stone. The consulting engineers met in February 1877 and gave votes to four designs:

Delaware Bridge Company, New York	Cantilever
Henry Flad and Company, St. Louis	Derrick
Clarke, Reeves and Company, Philadelphia	Hinged arch
E. W. Serrell and Son, New York	Suspension

They rejected Serrell and Son's plan for a suspension bridge of wrought-iron link cables on the grounds that the design, though practical for a carriage road, would not be sufficiently flexible for "the heavy, concentrated loads of railway engines and trains at high speed." The plan for a double-track derrick bridge submitted by Henry Flad and Company received praise for ingenuity, but with an estimated cost of $2,610,785 it was not the most economical solution, especially as it involved untested technology. Clarke, Reeves and Company's Phoenixville Bridge Works submitted a design for a "hinged arch invented and patented by Capt. James B. Eads, distinguished engineer of the St. Louis Bridge." In this distinctive form, "the arch proper consists of two Lenticular struts or girders resting against each other in the centre, where they are hinged, and also hinged at the top of the piers. To sustain these hinge points, struts, made like girders, continue the arch form to abutments on the rock formation below." While admiring the design and praising the work of James Eads, the consulting engineers questioned whether the form, successfully utilized for the 515-foot spans across the Mississippi, was practical for the 749-foot distance across the East River.

The clear favorite was the Delaware Bridge Company's "novel modification of the Cantilever type of bridges." In their appraisal, the engineers explained the general principle behind this design: "In a Cantilever bridge, the two Cantilevers, balanced over each pier, form brackets, the shore ends of which are anchored down, and their outer ends sustain a central span, merely resting upon them, and free to expand and contract with changes of temperature. These brackets, therefore, perform a double function. They sustain their own weight and their proper rolling load to the extremity of their arms, and they also sustain the weight of the central span and its proper rolling load, extending between the ends of the brackets." This plan featured a twenty-foot-wide carriageway between the two railroad tracks, each built through an independent truss, and a walkway above. The consulting engineers concluded: "Not only is the structure rigid, economical and capable of erection with great ease and without danger of disaster or interference with the navigation, but it seems to us capable of still further improvement by revising the general proportions, the most economical arrangement of which, it may well be, the designer has not attained in so novel a plan." The estimate for double tracking throughout was $2,479,458.[13]

The board took no further action, however. In 1877, William Steinway stepped aside, and Dr. Thomas Rainey became head of the board of directors. Appointed to the board in 1876, Rainey immediately tried to interest Cornelius Vanderbilt; Drexel, Morgan and Company; and the Manhattan Elevated Railway Company in the Ravenswood Bridge but found no takers. On March 25, 1881, the New York and Long Island Bridge Company entered into a contract with Clarke, Reeves and Company for a "first-class double track railway, carriage and walkway iron bridge." Investors pledged about $1.6 million in stock toward an estimated total cost of $6 million; the company anticipated tolls of $2,000 a day. The exact cost could not be determined because it had not been decided whether to employ iron or steel in the structure. A "person connected with the enterprise" stated that "we shall use whichever is found to be the most economical," and estimated that the cost could be $5,000,000, "perhaps, however, half that amount will cover it."[14] Such comments suggest that from a managerial viewpoint, bridge building was far from an exact science. Despite such optimistic projections, the company never had the capital to carry out its plans.

Even though the Brooklyn Bridge was nearing completion, it was clear to Long Islanders that the beautiful suspension span would do little to solve the transportation problems that retarded the growth of Queens. Roebling's bridge linked the first and third cities in the nation and was a triumph of engineering and design without rival, but it "could never, by reason of its location, be made a part of any system of through transportation between Long Island and other parts of the nation." On the other hand, a bridge across Blackwell's Island promised to bring the LIRR into Manhattan.[15]

While the great East River Bridge forged the two cities into a single metropolis, it was not part of a regional transportation network. From the start, the interests behind the Blackwell's Island Bridge assumed that it would include tracks, even though the LIRR had no direct involvement. As one company spokesman, in all likelihood Dr. Rainey, stated in 1881, just as work began, "The rapid transit lines in New York and the LIRR will probably be only too glad to take advantage of our bridge and transport passengers and even freight across it without any additional charge upon either, making, of course, some satisfactory arrangement with us." He imagined transporting passengers directly from Westchester to Coney Island, and also anticipated a spur running down the shoreline to the Brooklyn Navy Yard, speeding communication between the industries in Williamsburg and Manhattan markets. Finally, Rainey expected that his railroad bridge would bring benefits to the home-seeking working class. "It is only when the narrow East River is crossed and free, open, high, healthy Long Island is reached," he claimed, "that the poor man's land is found, a place of refuge from tenement house life, quickly, easily, cheaply accessible—time, by the new bridge, ten minutes; fare, ten cents. Give these cheap home seekers a chance, and they will gravitate to it as by a natural law." Construction soon ground to a halt after the sinking of a cofferdam on the Ravenswood shore. Still, the company gained an extension of its charter and added an amendment permitting linkage with the tracks feeding into Grand Central Station.[16]

To the frustration of many citizens in New York and Queens, Thomas Rainey held tight to the franchise and cultivated the political connections necessary to maintain his control. In 1886, as Rainey left for England to raise capital for his bridge, the German American Citizens Association met in Astoria's Schuetzen Park and passed a resolution wishing him luck in his efforts, but in the same breath they pointed out that the recent charter extension mandated that the company spend a minimum of $100,000 in 1888, $200,000 in 1889, and $300,000 in 1890. The association had originally opposed the most recent charter extension and took credit for the insertion of the spending guidelines. The Germans in Astoria and Steinway were quite anxious for the bridge to become a reality. One man present at the meeting stated:

> Many people now living in the Fourth Ward bought property here and removed here under the supposition that the bridge was soon to be built. Look at this splendid tract of land, regular farming land, comparatively speaking, and almost within a stone's throw of New York. They are crowded over there and with the exercise of a little tact and the outlay of some money, we can catch the overflow and a great city will spring up here like magic. It has got to come some time and why cannot we see it in our day?

Another suggested that "men worth millions are ready to invest in this bridge if Dr. Rainey does not come on time."[17] The Steinways had relocated to Queens fifteen years before, beginning a movement of German immigrants to Long Island City and Newtown (see chapter 5). In Manhattan, Germans were filling the tenements in Yorkville on the Upper East Side. Thus, it was not surprising that representatives from both sides of the river should join to push forward the Blackwell's Island Bridge. It is quite possible that there was sufficient capital among the Germans in New York, no doubt taking advantage of connections to investors in Hamburg and Berlin, but they apparently did not trust Rainey enough to invest in his corporation.

The *Long Island City Star* also expressed impatience with Dr. Rainey. In an editorial published in December 1886, the paper criticized his unsuccessful attempts to obtain financial backing in London:

> For an undertaking which is manifestly of the greatest importance to New York and Long Island there should not be, and we do not believe there would be, the slightest trouble in getting all the money requisite for the work right here on Long Island if Dr. Rainey would take hold of the scheme in a business fashion. It is apparent, that, unable to start the bridge himself, he is unwilling to let others do so. If his plan is to trade on the franchise obtained from the Legislature, no progress can be looked for in some years and it looks very much as if that were his purpose.

The editor then added, "Long Island cannot afford to be retarded in its growth to suit the purposes of scheming speculators."[18]

Rainey, meanwhile, had turned his attention to Washington, and succeeded in having Congress pass a bill authorizing construction of a bridge across Blackwell's Island. Legally, this was hardly necessary since the span would be entirely within one state, but, as the *New York Tribune* reported, "the English capitalists who are to furnish the money to build the bridge insisted that the consent of the Federal Government should be obtained." The bill stipulated that work must be completed within ten years. Even this was not enough to spur construction.[19]

Austin Corbin had gained control of the LIRR in 1880, and soon turned his attention to the problem of bringing his trains directly into Manhattan. Despite its repeated failures, the franchise of the New York and Long Island Bridge Company was still an attractive prize. At the time Corbin acquired the railroad, the lucrative summer traffic was responsible for most of its ridership and income. The suburbs of Long Island, while growing, did not yet have sufficient population to support the line throughout the year. The inconvenient commute certainly retarded suburban development, involving as it did a cumbersome break in transportation at Hunters Point, where passengers transferred between train and ferry. In winter, when ice floes frequently clogged the river, ferry service could be interrupted for hours or even days, as happened during the Great Blizzard of 1888. The obvious solution was to bring the railroad directly into Manhattan, but this demanded capital beyond the means of the marginally profitable railroad. Another problem was that it was not feasible for steam trains to enter the city through a tunnel; smoke from the coal-fired locomotives would nearly suffocate the passengers, and it was clearly impossible to construct a terminal beneath the city streets until the transition to electrification. The railroad could cross the river only over a bridge. Accordingly, Corbin fixed on Rainey's New York and Long Island Bridge Company. Unfortunately, he linked construction of a railroad bridge with a grandiose, unworkable, and foolish proposal to develop a deepwater port for ocean liners at Montauk Point.[20] It is surprising that such a clear thinking, practical capitalist such as Corbin would fix on a fantasy.

One reason why Corbin became involved in the bridge was the incorporation of a new rival: the New York and Long Island Railroad Company. Organized in 1887, this enterprise proposed to build a system of tunnels beneath both the Hudson and East Rivers to connect with a "Central Union Station" to rise at Broadway and 42nd Street. The double-track railroad would link the Pennsylvania and other railroads then terminating at the Hudson River shore in New Jersey with the LIRR. Until now, the

Hudson and East Rivers proved a bar to efficient rail traffic between New York and the rest of the country. The New York and Long Island Railroad would more than pay for itself by eliminating the costly, time-consuming, and often unreliable ferries and barges and "permit the roads converging from all directions to enter the city. It will form a complete union and connecting line over which the traffic of all these roads can be exchanged in unbroken trains."[21]

The Boards of Aldermen in both New York and Long Island City approved the plans, and the directors of the company immediately went to London to raise the necessary capital. In 1891, the Steinways bought forty thousand shares of stock, and William Steinway was named to the board of directors. By any measure, Austin Corbin should have been interested in this project, but the two efforts went forward independently. Writing to William Steinway in 1896, Malcolm W. Niven, one of the directors of the bridge company seeking investment capital in London, explained that they had changed the name of the company to the Greater New York Union Terminal Railroad "to accustom our friends here to the scope of the enterprise, and get away from the idea that we are part and parcel of Corbin's road." In the end, this company abandoned the grandiose scheme to build a trunk railroad terminal and concentrated on a single tunnel under the East River (this eventually was utilized by the Interborough Rapid Transit (IRT) Company's Flushing Line).[22]

Challenged by this rival on the one hand, and apparently unable to reach an understanding with Rainey on the other, Corbin floated a bridge scheme of his own. In 1892, Elizur Brace Hinsdale, longtime counsel of the LIRR, testified before the state legislature on the company's application for a franchise to build a railroad bridge between Long Island City and New York ending at a depot at a point between 34th and 42nd Streets on Park Avenue, in the vicinity of Grand Central Terminal. It was to be "so constructed that the trains run into the second story; thence running by a viaduct or elevated road to the river front, spanning the river, with two piers in the middle [at Man-of-War Rock below Blackwell's Island], and thence on a viaduct or elevated road to Laurel Hill, Long Island."

In his testimony, Hinsdale emphasized that the company was not asking for "any concession by way of exemption from taxation to promote the enterprise. All the property that will be acquired and all the structures built will remain subject to taxation precisely the same as other like property is taxed within the state. The only favor asked is that capital be permitted to build the structure, and that it not be hampered or embarrassed so as to prevent its being constructed, and that it may have the same chance that other enterprises have that are for the benefit of the public and the benefit of the investors." One advantage of this bridge, he suggested, was that it would "enable all citizens of New York to proceed with the greatest rapidity to the most magnificent stretch of beach and healthy land that lies approximate to any city in the world," referencing the primary business of the railroad.

Hinsdale also noted the impact of the project on Brooklyn: "As a consequence of building the bridge," he suggested, "Brooklyn will be put in immediate and close connection by rail with the great lines that run east, north, and west from the Grand Central depot. Whether Brooklyn shall ultimately become a part of the Greater New York of the future, the material advantages will accrue just the same to that locality if it shall continue a separate municipality instead of forming part of New York." Hinsdale made clear that this was no mere speculative venture, nor was it intended to compete with any other bridge. The LIRR, he stated somewhat disingenuously, "does not propose to carry foot passengers or teams, but leaves that field to any capitalist who may seek to build a bridge for that character of service. In the near future, there will be a large city in the territory between the East River and Flushing Bay that will require a bridge for the local business, and the granting of the franchise for such a bridge would not in the slightest degree interfere with this enterprise, nor would it meet with any opposition from the promoters of this bridge."[23]

Was Hinsdale, an astute corporate lawyer well acquainted with the transportation situation and personalities on Long Island, being purposefully naive? He surely knew of the Rainey bridge, yet his testimony implied that the existence of another franchise would be news to him. The answer lay in Corbin's efforts to gain control of the New York and Long Island Bridge Company. If this was a ploy to compel Rainey to sell out to him, it was apparently successful, for by 1894 Corbin published plans for a bridge bringing his railroad into Manhattan at 64th Street and Second Avenue.[24] When Corbin died in 1896, his dream died with him.

The Queensboro Bridge

With the creation of Greater New York, the citizens of the new Borough of Queens began at once to agitate for their bridge. The city had assumed construction of the Williamsburg Bridge, and it seemed only right for New York to do the same with the Blackwell's Island span. Rainey began one final campaign to have the city buy his franchise, but once the city had obtained the enabling legislation to build the bridge itself, there was no need for such an expenditure, especially as it would have rewarded Rainey for a quarter century of inaction.

The citizens of Queens approached City Hall with demands for schools, sewers, water mains, police and fire stations, and street lighting. Using the wealth generated by Manhattan and Brooklyn, the city financed projects that Queens County could not have afforded on its own. Paramount among their requests was always the Blackwell's Island Bridge. Only Greater New York could carry that project forward by issuing bonds for its construction.

On February 14, 1898, influential Queens men met at Strack's Casino in Astoria and formed a Committee of Thirty to coordinate the effort, soon expanded into the Committee of Forty. All through the winter and spring of 1898, these dynamic citizens convened well-attended public meetings in Astoria, Winfield, and Hunters Point and lobbied elected officials whenever they could.

In October, a delegation met with Mayor Robert Van Wyck, who "expressed himself warmly in favor of more bridges over the East River and especially of this one." The *Newtown Register* complained in an editorial that the delegation went too far when, "in reply to the mayor's statement that no appropriation could be included in next year's tax budget they argued that the building of new school houses in the borough for which the issuing of bonds for $12,000,000 would have to be issued, should be deferred in order that the bridge project might at one be proceeded with." The editor stressed the absurdity of that argument, declaring, "We can wait a little longer for the Ravenswood Bridge but school accommodation for the rising generation is something that must be at once provided." When he met with Borough President Frederick Bowley a week later, Mayor Van Wyck mentioned that the Committee of Forty should follow the appropriate procedure, and first put the matter before the Board of Public Improvements, then the municipal assembly, from there the sinking fund commission and finally to the Board of Estimate. This the Committee of Forty ultimately did, while maintaining a high public profile. At one public meeting, the assembled voters resolved that "the citizens of Woodside in mass meeting assembled respectfully request that the present administration of the City of New York forward the work on the proposed Blackwell's Island Bridge; also that a further appropriation for rapid continuance of the work be made."[25]

The lobbying bore fruit, for in November Van Wyck informed the Board of Public Improvements that he favored immediate steps toward the construction of the bridge, followed by a recommendation that the board approve a second span between New York and Brooklyn, the Manhattan Bridge. In the background was Dr. Rainey, still holding his now worthless charter, claiming that he had an exclusive franchise for the work. The *Newtown Register* praised Mayor Van Wyck's stand that "the bridge ought to be built irrespective of the Charter which Dr. Rainey owns [which] should have been revoked years ago. Go ahead, Mr. Mayor, we want the bridge and as soon as possible. Let Dr. Rainey build his bridge if he can. It will do no harm to have two, but let us have one as soon as possible."[26]

Rainey's only hope was that the city would buy his franchise. Commissioner of Bridges John L. Shea stood in opposition, however, and after rumors surfaced that the city planned to "buy certain franchises at high cost," Shea stated publicly that the lines chosen by the city for the bridge "conflicted in no way with those fixed for the Rainey Bridge," and hence there could be no claim against the city, nor any reason to buy him out. The rumors were based in fact, for Rainey had convinced political leaders to endorse his charter. In Washington, Senator Thomas Platt introduced a bill to extend Rainey's charter, and the measure passed both houses. The Committee of Forty had written to both Senator Platt and Senator Chauncey M. Depew, to no avail. In Albany, Assemblyman Brennan introduced a measure designed to put the question of the Blackwell's Island Bridge under the control of a state commission, bypassing the city's Department of Bridges. The Committee of Forty successfully lobbied to defeat this bill. Meanwhile, state senator George Washington Plunkitt put forward a bill to authorize the commissioners of the sinking fund "to purchase from any corporation possessing it, a valid charter with authority to construct a bridge over the East River at Blackwell's Island connecting Manhattan and Queens. In case the Commissioners cannot agree with the owners upon the price, they are authorized to acquire it by condemnation. Upon the purchase of such charter all the rights of the corporation shall be vested in the city." This last-ditch effort was only a year before the expiration of the franchise, and the *Register* asked why it was at all necessary to pay Rainey the $1 million he claimed as the value of his charter. The legislature passed Plunkitt's bill, but in April 1900 Mayor Van Wyck vetoed the city's purchase of the "notorious Rainey franchise," an action praised not only "for his appreciation of the right," but, given the legislative pressure from Albany and Washington, "courage of the positive sort."[27]

At the end, the last gasp exuded the stale odor of political corruption, an aroma all the more offensive for coming just after the birth of Greater New York. The intervention of machine politicians, both Republican and

Democrat, only confirmed the fears that many Queens citizens had about the corrupt politics of the city. Defeating those forces in the matter of the Rainey franchise was an important victory for the Committee of Forty, to say nothing of the general principle of good government. All legal and political obstacles overcome, the city could now build the bridge.

Almost immediately after the mayor's veto, the Board of Aldermen passed the enabling resolution introduced by Queens alderman (and later borough president) Joseph Cassidy to provide the means to construct the bridge. But events did not move forward quickly enough for the Committee of Forty. In August, they sent a delegation to visit the two most important political figures in New York, Republican Thomas Platt and Democrat Richard Croker, to "acquaint them with the great irritation existing in Queens County because nothing was being done to advance the construction of the bridge." In November, the Board of Aldermen voted a $1 million appropriation for the Blackwell's Island Bridge; Alderman Cassidy, blamed by many boosters for causing delays for "political reasons," was "conspicuous for his absence."[28]

In January 1899, even before the political wrangling over the city's right to build its bridge had been settled, $100,000 was appropriated for soundings, test borings, and surveys for the Blackwell's Island and Manhattan Bridges. The engineers settled on a new line that began between 59th and 60th Streets on Second Avenue. The idea of linking up the LIRR with the Harlem Railroad tracks on Park Avenue was discarded in favor of a connection with the Second Avenue Elevated.

When famed engineer Gustav Lindenthal became commissioner of bridges, he brought in Henry Hornbostel as consulting architect. Their design was a unique hybrid. Like the Firth of Forth railroad bridge in Scotland, it would be a continuous, or independent truss, but the arms of the cantilever would be joined directly, without a suspended span between. The result was a cantilever bridge with a profile resembling a suspension bridge, complementing the other three East River spans. *Engineering Record,* which chronicled the story of the bridge down to the number and shape of the rivets, declared: "The Blackwell's Island cantilever may reasonably be expected to make it clear whether or not suspension bridges must hereafter be built for Greater New York on esthetic grounds. While even that bridge may not fully possess the same gracefulness or other esthetic qualities of a well-proportioned suspension bridge, it is believed that the advantages of this class disclosed by the final plans now being executed will be sufficient to indicate its adaptability to long spans in locations where esthetic requirements are most exacting."

The editors clearly endorsed its aesthetic qualities, praising the close integration of form and function. "The outlines of the entire structure are highly pleasing," stated the editor, "with rational accentuations in the design showing the changes from the parts of the structure of one kind to those of another, thus giving direct expression to structural truth."[29]

Engineering Record cited several unique features in the bridge, foremost among them the overall dimensions, which made it the longest "independent truss span so far completed on this continent"; the "omission of the center connecting spans usually suspended from the ends of the cantilever arms"; and the "peculiar design of the vertical posts," not to mention the extraordinary proportions of the nickel-steel eye-bars. The uniqueness of course created construction problems:

> No previous work furnished a precedent for the methods of construction necessary to adapt for the Blackwell's Island Bridge. Some of its members weigh over 120 tons each and are 50 ft. to 100 ft. long; some of them have to be assembled at a height of more than 300 ft. above the water, and a large proportion of the structure must be erected high over 1,000-ft. channels with deep water, swift current, constant navigation by steamers, barges, ferries and sailing vessels where it is impossible to sustain the superstructure of the longest spans on falsework, and the operations must be carried on continuously during the severe winter weather and high winds to which the site is exposed.[30]

The advantage of the connecting suspension span in a cantilever lay in the distribution of stresses. Its omission proved to be a serious design flaw, for "a load at any point on the bridge sets up stresses throughout the whole length, making it difficult if not impossible to determine the strains under various conditions of loading."[31] This critical miscalculation was only revealed as the work neared completion.

By the spring of 1901, the War Department had approved the plans, and the Board of Aldermen authorized condemnation proceedings to begin. On June 27, the firm of Ryan and Parker received a contract worth $745,547 to construct the six masonry piers; work began within the month. The stone piers on which the steel superstructure would rise were finished in June 1904, less than three years later, at a final cost of $858,565.01.

A unique engineering feature was that "the permanent structure [was] designed with special reference to the erection requirements." Before the superstructure could rise, it was necessary to erect an elaborate falsework on Blackwell's Island, the first section to be built "on account of the great

Queensboro Bridge during construction, July 12, 1906. (Courtesy of the Queens Borough Public Library, Archives, Chamber of Commerce of the Borough of Queens Collection.)

weight of the spans, and the enormous concentrated loads of the travelers in service." Workers began erecting the falsework in September 1904, and a year later all preparations for constructing the superstructure were complete. One crucial aspect of the falsework was that it was assembled with bolts instead of rivets, which facilitated its removal once the island span was complete and its reassembly on either shore for the anchor arm spans.[32]

On December 4, 1906, the last pin was driven home, and the 630-foot island span was complete. As a precaution, the engineers had ordered a specially constructed hydro-pneumatic ram to force into position the "unprecedentedly long and heavy pins, some of which weigh over three tons each," but because of the "nature of the design and the accuracy of the shop work" it was not necessary to use it; the pins were "driven in the ordinary manner."[33]

For the next six months, the public was treated to the spectacle of two travelers steadily advancing above the river. Each was a massive Z-shaped, 200-ton apparatus housing a 45-ton derrick to hoist the beams into position over the river. The beauty of the cantilever lay in its capacity to support itself,

Queensboro Bridge during construction, February 24, 1908. (Courtesy of the Queens Borough Public Library, Archives, Chamber of Commerce of the Borough of Queens Collection.)

and soon the crews had reached the middle of the channels, a web of steel suspended in midstream.[34]

By May 11, 1907, the west half of the 984-foot span above the east channel and fifteen of the twenty panels of the east half of the 1,182-foot span above the west channel had been assembled by a workforce of about 500 men. One gang of 20 men was "constantly employed in applying the first coat of red lead paint with flat brushes. This is often put on before the members are hoisted from the ground and care is taken to go over the work and touch up all rivet heads driven after painting." There were 22 four-man riveting gangs, each preceded by a four-man fitting-up gang making sure that each hole matched perfectly; by May 1907, they had driven about 151,500 field rivets.[35]

The Collapse of the Quebec Bridge

With the Blackwell's Island Bridge rising triumphantly above the East River, another cantilever was under construction hundreds of miles to the north. Spanning the St. Lawrence River, the Quebec Bridge would be even longer, 2,800 feet between each anchorage and a suspended center span connecting the cantilever arms. With the Quebec, Blackwell's Island, and Manhattan Bridges rising simultaneously, engineers had reason to cheer. The editors of *Engineering Record* proclaimed that the structures "constitute practically an epitome of the most advanced features of long-span design, construction and erection. All branches of the work are in the hands of highly trained specialists who have so far shown marked improvements in almost every successive span of great magnitude." The Canadian endeavor merited special praise:

> The excellence of field work in modern bridge erection has been reached by a kind of mutual interaction of the increasing demands of transportation and a concurrent development of capacity of the shop to produce greater and better bridge members. These statements are probably as fully justified by the field work in the erection of the cantilever structure being built across the St. Lawrence near Quebec, as by any iron or steel bridge construction yet completed. However carefully the members of a structure may be put in place in the field the erection of the structure would be impracticable if not impossible unless the design were carefully considered and the shop work accurately executed. Especially is this true of a great structure like the Quebec cantilever.[36]

The consulting engineer for the Quebec Bridge was Theodore Cooper, one of the foremost bridge builders in the world. As a young man, Cooper received his training under James Eads during construction of the St. Louis Bridge, and in 1907 Cooper was at the height of his fame. On this commission, however, he had been compelled to accept a reduction in the quantity of steel he had recommended.[37]

On August 27, 1907, engineers saw that one of the lower chords of the anchor arm was buckling, and immediately informed the Phoenix Bridge Company of Phoenixville, Pennsylvania. Officials there expressed surprise at this, not only because the members in question had been in place for over a year, but also, as chief engineer John Stirling Deans later testified, because the structure "was carrying only three-quarters of the working load for which it was designed and approved. The compression chords were failing under less than half the load for which they were designed and approved and were considered capable of sustaining without failure."[38]

Informed two days later, Cooper immediately cabled the engineers on site to stop all work and remove everyone from the bridge. The order arrived too late. At 5:30 P.M. on August 29, the entire superstructure of the Quebec

Bridge collapsed, carrying seventy-five men to their deaths. Some of the eleven survivors were "rumored to have said that rivet heads flew off before the disaster." It was all over in less than forty seconds.[39]

The Royal Commission of Inquiry found blame enough to go around. The Government of Quebec had issued the contract without complete specifications and had "intimated unofficially to the Phoenix Bridge Co. its desire that the bridge should be ready for the Quebec Tercentenary." The engineers had designed supporting members without an accurate understanding of the live and dead loads the structure would carry, but when the specifications were changed, they failed to alter the plans. The chords failed "due to their defective design." According to *Engineering Record*, "The real lack of knowledge is in connection with the design of latticing." It was later found that only two rivets had been used where as many as eight were called for. Finally, the report determined that Cooper "examined and officially approved" all designs, and in effect, "instructions given by Mr. Theodore Cooper from time to time were the specifications recognized as official and were so used." The report concluded, "The failure cannot be attributed directly to any cause other than errors in judgment on the part of these two engineers.... These errors of judgment cannot be attributed either to lack of common professional knowledge, to neglect of duty or to a desire to economize. The ability of the two engineers was tried in one of the most difficult professional problems of the day and proved to be insufficient for the task."

The commissioners concluded that the design itself was fundamentally flawed, and that nothing could have been done between August 27 and 29 to prevent the collapse. "A grave error was made in assuming the dead load for the calculations at too low a value and not afterward revising this assumption," the report stated. "The error was of sufficient magnitude to have required the condemnation of the bridge even if the details of the lower chords had been of sufficient strength because, if the bridge had been completed as designed, the actual stresses would have been considerably greater than those permitted by the specifications." As a young German-educated engineer, Othmar H. Ammann was part of the team investigating the disaster. Recalling the experience late in life, he concluded it was "a lack of knowledge on the part of the engineers of that day of the proper proportioning of compression members." Ammann later worked with Gustav Lindenthal on the Hell Gate Bridge and went on to design the Bayonne Arch and the George Washington Bridge.[40]

The tragedy reverberated in New York. The physical resemblance of the Quebec bridge and the Queens bridge was apparent to all—politicians, press, and public—and quite naturally questions arose about the safety of the Blackwell's Island Bridge, even as construction continued. In March 1908, the Board of Estimate appointed two teams of engineers to examine the plans and the condition of the cantilever, one headed by Professor William H. Burr of Columbia University and the other under the respected engineers Alfred Boller and Henry W. Hodge. Five months later, they submitted their findings to Commissioner of Bridges James W. Stevenson.

Engineering Record, having expressed unwavering confidence in the work of the professional engineers responsible for the two cantilevers under construction, had readily admitted in its columns the flaws in the Quebec Bridge and the failure of its architect, but expressed misgivings about the public debate over the safety of the Blackwell's Island Bridge. An editorial titled "The Public as an Engineering Critic" summarized the attitude of professionals faced with questions from "reporter-critics":

> There certainly can be no objection to the fullest information being given to the public in regard to any great public work, but at the same time it is only fair and right both to designers and constructors as well as to the public itself that that information should come through such channels as will guarantee of its accuracy and its proper proportions. This is especially true in the comparison of two different structures, some of whose main features may apparently be similar and yet in fact fundamentally different. Nothing is more common in such cases than the publication of the most confident statements that corresponding parts of two different bridges being in general outline quite similar they must of necessity have practically the same carrying power irrespective of the facts that the kinds of steel in the two members may be quite different and that their details of construction may be entirely dissimilar.[41]

In November, the investigating engineers published their reports and concluded that the Blackwell's Island Bridge was indeed safe. Furthermore, the quality of the nickel and carbon steel, the process of erection, and the mill and shop inspections all merited praise as "first class." However, both teams discovered "that the main truss members will not carry all the specified live loads for which this structure was designed." In other words, the current configuration of the span made it unsuited for the load it would carry.

Originally, the specifications called for four trolley tracks on the lower level, two within the superstructure and two on the outer roadways, and two elevated tracks and pedestrian promenades on the upper level. In September 1904, however, the design was modified to accommodate four elevated tracks, with the two 11-foot sidewalks to be cantilevered outside the main truss. The bridge had been erected according to the original specifications, without any modifications to accommodate the two additional tracks. Burr concluded that the computations for all main truss members showed stresses for a congested live load, combined with the dead load, "higher than prescribed as permissible in the specifications and higher than prudent to permit." Boller and Hodge stated that "the main truss members will not carry all the specified live loads for which this structure was designed."[42] In any event, it would be years before the city planned to extend the elevated lines over the bridge, and there was no reason to delay the opening.

There were two ways of interpreting these conclusions, and the *Long Island City Star* printed a version of each on its front page on successive days. First, the paper reprinted an editorial from *Engineering News* that claimed that the reports showed without question that the bridge was designed to carry specified loads and on completion was found "absolutely unsafe" for that load. The next day, the paper reprinted the conclusions of *Engineering Record*, which, "in direct contrast to the pessimistic tone of the editorial from the *Engineering News*," preferred to find satisfaction in the conclusion that the bridge could be opened as scheduled without any major reconstruction. "On the whole, notwithstanding some disappointment in that the structure is not fully up to its specified capacity," concluded the editor, "the public of the city of New York may be congratulated upon the outcome of this investigation." All agreed that had it not been for the tragedy in Quebec these flaws might have gone undiscovered. The cloud that had hung over the bridge since the previous August was lifted. As Commissioner of Bridges Stevenson wrote to William H. Williams of the celebration committee, "the bridge is safe," and the recommended changes "will cause no material delay in the opening."[43]

From the original idea for the bridge in the 1830s to the joining of the channel arms in 1908, the span had been known as the Blackwell's Island Bridge, or occasionally the Ravenswood Bridge. The day the east channel span was completed and inspected, the *Star* suggested that the official name be changed to the Queensboro Bridge. Realtor Edward Archibald MacDougall, a member of the celebration committee and "one of the bridge hustlers," successfully lobbied the Board of Aldermen to vote for this change. After all, Blackwell's Island was a penal colony, home to the city's dying and indigent, and a structure destined to transform the largest undeveloped expanse in Greater New York from, in the words of Borough President Lawrence Gresser, "a borough of villages" to "one great solid city, with a corresponding increase in the value of land," merited a more noble name. On September 29, 1908, the Board of Aldermen voted the Queensboro Bridge into being.[44]

The Grand Opening

In the autumn of 1908, the Committee of Forty formed a Queensboro Bridge Celebration Committee to plan for the grand opening and to raise the necessary funds, an estimated $25,000. This was not to be a parochial Queens affair, however. The committee met in the offices of the Long Island Real Estate Exchange, conveniently located at the corner of Fifth Avenue and 34th Street in Manhattan. Hearn's dry goods establishment on 14th Street and Bloomingdale's department store on East 59th Street and Third Avenue contributed to the planning; Samuel J. Bloomingdale was a member of the committee. The advantage for the Bloomingdale store, according to one of its own publications, was "too obvious for explanation."[45]

On October 15, 1908, several thousand attended the Celebration Committee's public convention at Astoria's Schuetzen Park, including, for the first time at such a gathering, women delegates. The *Long Island City Star* cheered this advance, adding that the women were as generous with their applause as the men. Before the fireworks display, which attracted thousands more onlookers, the delegates heard speeches by William H. Williams, chairman of the Celebration Committee; Patrick F. McGowan, president of the Board of Aldermen; Lawrence Gresser, Queens borough president; and August Belmont, president of the Interborough Rapid Transit Company. All praised the new bridge and the committee that promised a celebration "that will jar all of Long Island and melt the icicles off every roof between North Beach and Coney Island." Williams remarked on the unifying feature of the bridge. "There is now," he said, "civically speaking, no Flushing or Jamaica or Corona or Long Island City. All sections have been welded into one harmonious whole, one great, wide spreading city of opportunity, the Borough of Queens."

McGowan stated that "Queens has too long been held back, but with a continuation of such civic co-operation as this you will surely get all that is coming to you. It rests upon you people here to give Queens its rightful place in the sisterhood of boroughs. It requires push and co-operation, and that means progress." Former Brooklyn borough president Martin W. Littleton warned the assembly not to repeat in Queens the mistake made when the Brooklyn Bridge opened—that is, not providing adequate approaches:

Queensboro Bridge during construction, December 1, 1908. (Courtesy of the Queens Borough Public Library, Archives, Chamber of Commerce of the Borough of Queens Collection.)

"Don't repeat the awful fate of the Brooklyn Bridge, which is like a diamond ring on a dirty finger," he said. "It doesn't fit." The situation in Long Island City would be even worse, he added, for the Queensboro "connects Queens and Long Island with the rest of the world."

The highlight of the affair was the arrival of August Belmont, "head of the corporation that controls trolley service in Queens." He arrived "rather late in a huge automobile, and his appearance immaculately attired in evening dress." Belmont addressed the question of rapid transit service over the bridge, reminding the audience that "thus far there has been no definite provision made." He quickly added, however, "As a representative of the New York & Queens County Railway, I can promise you that the company stands ready and willing to run its cars across the bridge at the earliest opportunity, but when we recall the delays that ensued when the Williamsburg Bridge was opened, we may expect many months to pass before trolley cars begin to run over this new bridge."[46] Events proved him right, of course.

Littleton's comments also proved prophetic. While there was no need for concern about the plaza on the Queens side, many complained of the "extreme shortsightedness" in the treatment of the Manhattan approach. Failure to provide a plaza and permitting the approach to meet the sidewalk on Second Avenue would result in "disgraceful congestion." Although generous in its praise of the span, the 1909 *Bloomingdale's Diary*, published as a souvenir of the bridge celebration, claimed: "The consensus of opinion appears to be strongly in favor of a plaza in the block bounded by Second and Third avenues, Fifty-ninth and Sixtieth streets, with additional width in Second avenue, to be obtained by removing all the buildings in its westerly side to a depth of from 65 to 100 feet, comprising all the properties between the northwest corner of Second avenue and Fifty-seventh street to the southwest corner of Sixty-first street, inclusive."[47] No such plaza was created, of course, and the bridge roadways merge immediately with the city streets, resulting in endemic congestion.

At 2:30 P.M. on Tuesday, March 30, 1909, Mayor George McClellan opened the Queensboro Bridge with a modest, informal ceremony. According to one newspaper, "The mayor in an automobile followed by a procession of other cars and vehicles merely crossed the structure and declared it opened." The final cost was $20 million and fifty lives.[48] The moment came after eight long years of construction, forty-two years after the legislature chartered the New York and Long Island Bridge Company to build a Blackwell's Island bridge, and more than seventy years after the idea had been first suggested.

The Celebration Committee had rejected holding the official ceremonies at that time, preferring to wait until warmer weather in late spring. They scheduled the grand opening for the week of June 12, beginning with a colorful parade and culminating in a spectacular fireworks display. Some suggestions for the week-long celebration were fanciful, such as the idea to float enormous 100-foot paper figures above the center span representing the marriage of Father Knickerbocker and Miss Queens.[49]

Another feature considered and finally rejected was a leap by a daredevil from the roadway into the river. By February, almost 300 individuals had applied to the committee for the honor of being the official leaper at the ceremonies. The *New York Times* reported that of these applicants, 168 could be classified as professionals willing to jump "for a consideration"; 84 as "freaks" hoping to try a variety of flying machines, 9 as would-be suicides, women disappointed in love or trapped in unhappy marriages; and 24 as "unemployed" and hoping that the fame of their deed would lead to job offers. As June approached, Chief Inspector Max Schmittberger of the New York City Police Department put a damper on the idea when he notified the Celebration Committee that "Kearny Speedy, the bridge jumper, would not be permitted to make high dives from the centre of the structure as a daily feature of the bridge celebration." Leaping from bridges was against the law, and Schmittberger vowed to stop any attempts.⁵⁰

The highlight of the celebration was the parade on June 12, but many came to enjoy the carnival set up in Bridge Plaza. The *New York Times* reported that by June 11 the Queens side was alive with "frankfurter men flanked by the pie and milk men, the cane and knife ringers, and all those who cater to the fun-loving throng. The animal show barkers were in evidence, the merry-go-rounds were in action," and there was even a Ferris wheel powered by two sweating men. The carnival also included a variety of ethnic attractions, including the Old Plantation, the Hindoo Theatre, the Romany Camp, and the German Village, featuring a restaurant that could accommodate five thousand guests at a time. Though bridge jumping was banned, "Harry Six, Champion High Diver of the World," gave daily exhibitions of his prowess, plunging from a 130-foot tower into a makeshift pool only 36 inches deep.⁵¹

On the appointed day, the Queens side was packed hours before the parade came into view. With barely concealed condescension, the *Times* reporter commented that it was "Queens Borough's own day, and all Queens was there in best bib and tucker. Manhattan took it calmly, for all the bridges are Manhattan's and its citizens are used to them." Shortly after noon, 1,500 schoolchildren from Queens began the program in Bridge Plaza with a rendition of "The Star Spangled Banner." There followed several short speeches by John D. Crimmins, representing the Committee of Forty, Secretary of War Jacob M. Dickinson, and Governor Charles Evans Hughes. The governor said that Queens was the brightest of all the five boroughs because "so much of Queens lies in the future," adding that in his opinion here would be solved the problems of "municipal living." Unfortunately, almost none of the spectators heard any of these remarks for the police had earlier cleared the area directly in front of the reviewing stand. After the speeches, the eighty-five-year-old Dr. Rainey was introduced, few in the crowd having any notion of the frail gentleman's identity. By then, the parade had completed its crossing and was just entering the plaza.⁵²

The procession left Fifth Avenue and 34th Street at 12:30 P.M. behind Grand Marshal Major General Charles Roe and his staff, including one Cornelius Vanderbilt; immediately after came the Committee of Forty in ten carriages. There followed detachments of the Marines, the New York National Guard, the Navy Militia, public school children and floats, civic societies, mounted cowboys, fire companies, Irish Volunteers and the St. Patrick's Society, the "prosperity floats" of various manufacturers, Bohemian singing societies and bands, and, bringing up the rear, the political clubs.

Queensboro Bridge over Blackwell's Island, East River, New York. (Jeffrey Kroessler Postcard Collection.)

Queensbridge Houses under Construction in the Foreground, Next to the 59th Street Bridge, Aerial View Looking Due West, circa July 1939. (The LaGuardia and Wagner Archives, LaGuardia Community College/City University of New York, The New York City Housing Authority Collection.)

That night the public witnessed a spectacular fireworks display. The finale alone used two tons of gunpowder. The entire bridge was outlined in the flames of hundreds of torches set among the girders, and a rainbow of light cascaded over the side, an effect known as Niagara Falls. On the last day of the carnival, a crowd of about fifty thousand witnessed the crowning of Elizabeth Augenti, a nineteen-year-old Long Island City girl, as "Queen of the Queensboro Bridge." It was fitting that her prize was two building lots near Kissena Park in Flushing worth $1,500.[53]

The new Queensboro Bridge was indeed impressive. Never would it rival the Brooklyn Bridge for the affections of New Yorkers, but neither would it be an anticlimax like the Manhattan Bridge, which opened to little fanfare on the last day of 1909. Without a doubt, the Queensboro's beauty remains in the eye of the beholder. Gustav Lindenthal, for one, had no doubts about its aesthetic features. Speaking to the Municipal Art Society, he remarked, "In a bridge it is not possible to separate the architectural from the engineering features." Consulting architect Henry Hornbostel was less certain. On seeing the completed span, he exclaimed, "My God—It's a blacksmith's shop."[54]

The bridge has had its admirers, of course, among them Edward Hopper, who painted the subject from two perspectives, and Woody Allen, who featured it in a particularly romantic moment in *Manhattan*. F. Scott Fitzgerald offered perhaps the most evocative description in *The Great Gatsby*: "Over the great bridge, with the sunlight through the girders making a constant flicker upon the moving cars, with the city rising up across the river in white heaps and sugar lumps all built with a wish out of non-olfactory money. The city seen from the Queensboro Bridge is always the city seen for the first time, in its first wild promise of all the mystery and beauty in the world."[55]

Fitzgerald's Jazz Age image materialized in the two decades after the opening of the Queensboro Bridge. The city came to Queens.

9
The Booming Borough

The decade after the opening of the Queensboro Bridge was a time of phenomenal growth and change for the Borough of Queens. Private developers constructed thousands of one- and two-family homes, model tenements, and apartment buildings. Dozens of manufacturing concerns built new factories in Long Island City, which emerged as one of the leading industrial centers in the nation. The first three decades of the twentieth century saw extraordinary growth outside of Manhattan in every direction, and the development of Queens was part of that metropolitan surge. In 1900, the Bronx and Queens together represented little more than 10 percent of the city's population, but by 1930 those boroughs accounted for a third. During the 1920s, New York City accounted for a fifth of all residential construction in the nation. At the same time, Manhattan actually lost population. At the turn of the century Manhattan housed more than half of the city's residents; in 1930 it held just over a quarter. Even as it lost population, however, Manhattan extended its economic power and acquired its distinctive skyline.[1]

In spirit, purpose, and impact, the Queensboro and the Williamsburg Bridges had much in common, beyond the fact that they are often regarded as ugly ducklings next to the inspired Brooklyn Bridge. Both were designed to carry elevated lines, trolleys, and horse-drawn vehicles, and each span featured pedestrian promenades. Built to plans accommodating

Table 14
Population Change in New York City, 1890–1930

	Population in the Five Boroughs, 1890–1930 (in thousands)					
Date	Manhattan	Brooklyn	Bronx	Queens	Staten Island	Total NYC
1890*	1,441,839	89	87	52	2,507	
1900	1,850	1,167	201	153	67	3,347
1910	2,332	1,634	431	284	86	4,767
1920	2,284	2,018	732	469	117	5,620
1930	1,867	2,560	1,265	1,079	158	6,930

* for the area that became Greater New York in 1898.

	Decennial change, number (in thousands) and percentage					
Date	Manhattan	Brooklyn	Bronx	Queens	Staten Island	Total NYC
1890–	409	328	116	66	15	930
1900	28.4%	39.1%	125.6%	75.8%	29.7%	37.1%
1900–	481	468	230	131	19	1,330
1910	26.0%	40.1%	114.9%	85.6%	28.3%	38.7%
1910–	−47	384	301	185	31	853
1920	−0.02%	23.5%	69.8%	65.1%	35.6%	17.9%
1920–	−417	542	533	610	42	1,310
1930	−18.2%	26.9%	72.8%	130.1%	35.1%	23.2%

	Percentage of New York City's population in each borough				
Date	Manhattan	Brooklyn	Bronx	Queens	Staten Island
1900	53.83	33.94	5.83	4.45	1.95
1910	48.91	34.29	9.04	5.96	1.80
1920	40.64	35.91	13.03	8.35	2.07
1930	26.94	36.94	18.26	15.57	2.28

SOURCE: Rosenwaike, *Population History of New York City*, pp. 58, 133.

nineteenth-century needs, neither span was specifically designed for the automobile age.[2] The Williamsburg Bridge linked two highly developed and densely populated sections of Greater New York while simultaneously fostering urbanization beyond the urban core. The Queensboro rose from the crowded streets of Manhattan but set down on a relatively empty landscape on the Queens side.

Ridgewood, known at the time as East Williamsburgh, underwent a remarkable transformation in only five years as the rural and suburban landscape took on urban forms, especially adjacent to the trolley lines and in the vicinity of the new elevated running along Myrtle Avenue. A 1903 real estate

Semi-Detached Two-Family Houses—Casino Place, 2 Blocks from Astoria Park, Astoria.
(Jeffrey Kroessler Postcard Collection.)

atlas reveals a neighborhood of mostly wood-frame houses, picnic parks, dance halls, and baseball fields, as well as a half dozen breweries, including the Diogenes Brewing Company and the J. Geo. Grauer Brewery, which had its own picnic park, the Ridgewood Grove. The Brooklyn Rapid Transit (BRT) Company, with its large car barns, provided local employment. A few relatively large properties of between five and twenty acres were still given over to agricultural uses, but by 1910 those large plots had been subdivided and the street grid imposed. Blocks of two- and three-story row houses, a few in wood but all of the larger ones in brick, lined the new streets.

The G. X. Mathews Company was founded by German immigrant Gustave Xavier Mathews and two of his brothers in Ridgewood in 1904. They became the most active builders in Queens and erected hundreds of three-story yellow-and-orange-brick railroad flats. While undoubtedly attractive and certainly an improvement over housing available in the older working-class districts of New York and Brooklyn, the "Mathews Model Flats" nonetheless resembled urban tenements more than suburban homes. During these years, Ridgewood was one of the fastest-growing sections in the city, and by 1929 it had been completely developed, a clear illustration of the impact of the Williamsburg Bridge and the new mass transit lines.[3]

Railway Modernization

The Queensboro Bridge shifted traffic and business away from Hunters Point, the terminus of the Long Island Railroad (LIRR), to Bridge Plaza, particularly after trolleys began running over the bridge in September 1909. Compared with the longer, more cumbersome transfer to the ferry, and the expense of paying a triple fare, passengers logically preferred a convenient trolley ride that took them directly from their homes, over the bridge, and into Manhattan for a single fare. The *Newtown Register* reported in early 1910 that receipts in the stores near the ferry in downtown Long Island City had declined by half. "One of the loneliest places in the borough today are the famous hotels in that section," it reported. "Every old resident of the county remembers when, if it was desired to see any person in the public eye in the county, they could be found at Tony Miller's. But those days have gone and apparently forever." By the end of the year, the New York and Queens County Railway Company had abandoned through trolley service to the ferry and substituted a shuttle from Bridge Plaza. The *Register* compared the fate of Hunters Point with that of downtown Williamsburgh after streetcars began running over that bridge, noting, "There seems to be no immediate future in store for this section but that similar to the dead end of Brooklyn in the vicinity of the Broadway ferries."[4]

The opening of Pennsylvania Station in 1910 sealed the fate of Hunters Point. The Pennsylvania Railroad had acquired the LIRR in 1900 and invested millions to modernize the railroad. Several branches were electrified, the power supplied by a massive coal-fired plant in Hunters Point. A new station was built in Jamaica, the line's main transfer point. And finally, Pennsylvania Station, McKim, Mead & White's grand urban monument, rose at 33rd Street and Seventh Avenue. *Engineering Record* praised the work of this great architectural firm and outlined the two ideas that determined the design: "To express, in so far as was practicable, with the unusual condition of tracks far below the street surface and in spite of the absence of the conventional train shed, the exterior design of a great railway station in a generally accepted form; and also give to the building the character of a monumental gateway and entrance to a great metropolis. Apart from these two ideas, the plan of the station was designed to give the greatest number of lines circulation." The description concluded as only an engineering journal could, reducing one of the most magnificent edifices ever raised in New York to its functional essence: "The structure is really a monumental bridge over the tracks."[5]

Astoria Pool with Hell Gate Bridge in Background, New York: Wurts Brothers, ca. 1936–1950. (Museum of the City of New York.)

The Pennsylvania Railroad anticipated that the new station would serve a maximum of 144 trains an hour, or about 1,000 a day, the LIRR accounting for 600 of them. Modernization yielded enormous advantages for commuters, the most important being the saving in time over the transfer to the ferry and vastly improved comfort. The increase in ridership was phenomenal; between 1915 and 1928 the number of passengers rose from 43 million to 113 million, a figure that represented more than 14 percent of the total number of railroad passengers in the entire country.[6]

The final piece in the railroad system was the New York Connecting Railroad, a joint venture of the New York Central and Pennsylvania Railroads. Together, the longtime rivals funded construction of the Hell Gate Bridge, a massive steel arch designed by Gustav Lindenthal. Construction of the bridge was as impressive as the design. When the two arms of the arch met high above Hell Gate, they were only 5/16 of an inch apart. When opened on March 9, 1917, it was the largest such span in the world, built with 80,000 tons of steel. It was strong enough to carry on each of its four tracks a load equivalent to two 190-ton locomotives, each "followed by a train load of 5,000 pounds to the lineal foot and so stiff is the arch that under this load, the deflection at the center would be only three inches." Lindenthal believed this railroad bridge to be his finest creation.[7]

The Hell Gate Bridge provided the first direct connection through New York between New England and the south or west. Previously, freight cars had to be loaded onto lighters and ferried across the harbor from New Jersey to the Bronx, adding many hours and increased costs. Passengers, too, had endured an inconvenient break in their journey.[8]

Missing from this grand scheme was direct freight service between Long Island and New Jersey. A new spur from the Sunnyside Yards to Bay Ridge shortened the trip, but freight still had to be ferried on barges across the harbor to and from New Jersey. Business interests in Queens and Brooklyn had long proposed a Narrows Tunnel for railroad traffic as crucial "to prevent the City's isolation from the rest of the Nation, and maintain its commercial supremacy." For some local boosters, this was another aspect of a vision that saw Queens becoming the industrial and commercial center of the metropolitan region. The cross-harbor freight tunnel was never built, of course, though in the 1990s Congressman Jerrold Nadler of Manhattan reintroduced the idea, backed by the Regional Plan Association and various environmental groups. In 2022, he convinced Governor Kathy Hochul, but with the decline of industry on Long Island, it is unlikely that the tunnel will ever be built.[9]

Key to this vision of economic dominance was the transformation of Jamaica Bay as a deepwater port larger than the ports of Liverpool, Hamburg, and Rotterdam combined. Canals would cut across the borough from Flushing Bay and Newtown Creek to Jamaica Bay for a new terminus of the State Barge Canal. A Narrows Tunnel would link up with the New York Connecting Railroad to create a circumferential railroad system connecting Long Island to the mainland.[10] These grand proposals belong to an era of supreme confidence in the capacities of American engineers and when the environmental impact of such schemes was scarcely considered. Gustav Lindenthal boasted that he could build a bridge across the Atlantic. While the plans to develop Jamaica Bay were technically feasible, the result would have been an ecological disaster, and the cross-Queens canals would have surely filled with garbage, sewage, and other pollutants.

The Jamaica Bay Development, complete with new channels, islands, and pier lines, actually became part of the official map of Queens. Real estate speculators even used proximity to the bay as one of their selling points in advertisements, emphasizing the proposed harbor in contrast to the recreational potential and healthy breezes of the bay. A notice from 1914 described the property of the Jamaica South Realty Corporation as adjacent to "what the 'New York World' aptly calls 'America's New Front Door.'" In grandiose fashion, the company linked all the new transportation improvements with the prospects of this particular subdivision: "Every dollar in the Pennsylvania Tunnels and Terminals, in the city's Dual Subway System, in Jamaica Bay's great harbor, in the new Erie Barge Canal, in Hell Gate Bridge. Every dollar in each and all of these projects is a lever raising Jamaica Park South realty values to a higher level." Boosters of the harbor plan kept the proposal alive through the 1920s, and the Queens Chamber of Commerce persisted in advocating for it into the 1930s, long after it was economically feasible or politically possible. The decision by the Port Authority of New York and New Jersey to put its resources in the rebuilding and expansion facilities in Newark Bay finally ended all realistic hopes for a deepwater port in Jamaica Bay. In the early 1930s, the regional plan suggested that the area might be better suited for much needed recreational sites, adding that the government could better allocate its resources by addressing the problem of the 125 million gallons of raw sewage pumped into the bay each day.[11] The fantastic promise of a new city rising on the shores of Jamaica Bay was never more than a booster's mirage.

From Farms to Homes

Once the LIRR began running into Pennsylvania Station, Queens experienced a second and more intense wave of suburbanization. In contrast to the upper-middle-class railroad suburbs of the late nineteenth century, however, these subdivisions attracted less affluent, though still solidly middle-class families, as a promotional brochure for a development called Little Neck Hills made clear.[12] A 1907 LIRR publication, *The Home Builder on Long Island*, explained that "the development of the west end of the island as a section for suburban residence has extended eastward through Nassau and into Suffolk Counties." Nor was this growth the same as what had come before. Long Island, with "its fine estates and country clubs," had been known as "a rich man's play-ground," but in 1905 and 1906 the "healthy building growth consisted principally of homes built by wage-earners." The booklet also listed the number of new homes erected in the vicinity of each station, based on anecdotal evidence supplied by the station masters. Communities in eastern Queens and Nassau showed much more activity than neighborhoods closer to Manhattan. This, of course, reflects the economic realities of suburbanization. No matter how convenient the commute, estimated at only thirty minutes from Queens once Pennsylvania Station opened, working-class families were hard pressed to purchase new homes, and a commutation ticket on the railroad cost significantly more than the nickel fare on the trolleys and elevateds.

The promise of direct rail service into Manhattan spurred the division of farms and large estates into building lots. William Proctor Douglas had one such estate in the northeast corner of Queens facing Little Neck Bay. His father had purchased the property in 1835 and made his home in the substantial Greek revival mansion built by Wyant Van Zandt in 1819 (now the Douglaston Club). The son was a sportsman of renown, a polo player, and owner of the America's Cup yacht *Sappho*. In 1904, he sold the property for $500,000 to the Rickert-Finley Realty Company, the largest real estate concern in Queens, having purchased over a thousand acres in Astoria, Flushing, Bayside, and Little Neck, as well as Douglas Manor. The Douglas estate was divided into fifty-seven blocks with 2,473 lots, and sales began in 1906.[13]

Douglas Manor grew steadily and was almost completely built-out by the late 1920s. Individuals purchased lots and contracted to build homes, and the houses went up in every architectural style popular in the early twentieth century, including colonial revival, Tudor, Mediterranean, and Arts & Crafts. The place attracted families of means, but the deeds held no clauses excluding certain classes of people. Rickert-Finley made the unusual decision to hold the shoreline in common for all residents rather than sell lots that extended all the way to the water, and to maintain the old Douglas dock and boathouse for the residents. To emphasize the rustic charm of the grounds, fences were prohibited. These decisions made the Manor even more desirable. Soon after lots went on sale, the company organized the Douglas Manor Association to initiate projects for beautification, maintenance, and improvement, and "to maintain a clubhouse for the benefit and enjoyment of the members of the association, and for the promotion of social intercourse among them . . . and to preserve, maintain and improve the natural beauty and advantages thereof."[14] The new community cultivated a common design aesthetic and developed a lifestyle where leisure was integral.

Much of the new borough remained under cultivation. A 1901 U.S. Department of Agriculture report described the market gardens in Queens as a landscape "so thickly occupied by this industry that it virtually presents to the eye the appearance of one great truck farm; and the vast output of this section is almost entirely consumed by the millions of people located within a few short miles of the base of supply." Many farmers had acres under glass so as to deliver fresh produce all year round, competing with producers in the South. From 1850 to 1900, Queens ranked first or second among all counties in the nation in total agricultural and market garden production.[15] But as the city expanded, land values rose and farming all but vanished by the middle of the twentieth century, repeating the pattern of change in Kings County over the last quarter of the nineteenth century. This second wave of suburbanization brought an increase in land values, and this pushed agriculture further east on Long Island: "Good farm lands abound throughout the Island. The western section has for years produced all kinds of garden necessities and delicacies for the City market. The spread of suburban homes, however, is fast taking away this character, and the market gardens are being located farther east. The great crops of vegetables raised in the middle and eastern sections, some of which are moved in train loads during the season, distinguish Long Island as possessing some of the most productive farm lands in the Eastern States."[16] It was not entirely by choice that farmers in western Queens subdivided their land. As land values rose to $3,000 an acre, so did taxes, and it soon became economically impossible to continue raising crops. In an article headlined "High Taxes Squeezing Farmers," the *Newtown Register* reported that in the first year after consolidation assessors had advanced the tax rate on farmland to $1,200 an acre, up from the pre-consolidation rate of $200 in Newtown and $800 in Jamaica and Flushing. The local assessor, Richard Homeyer, stated, "I am determined to appraise all the property in my district at its full market value. I can do nothing else. I base my figures at what the farmers have been getting for their land where they have sold it." The only way farmers could continue working their land was to sell sections for building lots, with 25-by-100-foot lots priced between $100 and $250, but they could still earn enough from their farm to pay the taxes on the remaining land. When the entire farm was taxed at the higher rate, however, the farmers were forced to sell, flooding the market with cheap building lots.[17] While it was true that the development of Queens was financed in large part by taxes collected in Manhattan and Brooklyn, the increased tax rate on farmland certainly accelerated the pace of land sales.

One reason for the phenomenal rise in land values was the expansion of trolley service throughout the borough. Between 1910 and 1915, the population of the borough rose by over 160,000 to 394,351, an increase of more than 40 percent, and traffic on the streetcars reflected this extraordinary growth. Between 1913 and 1915 the number of passengers riding the cars of the Manhattan and Queens Traction Company, running from the Manhattan end of the Queensboro Bridge to Jamaica, increased from 2,753,000 to 6,855,000, a rise of almost 250 percent. According to *Queensborough*, the monthly magazine of the Chamber of Commerce, "Modern side-door passenger cars which make this trip in about 45 minutes have made accessible for greater home

Table 15
Streetcar Passengers in Queens, 1900–1913

Year	Number	Increase/decrease	Commuters
1900	12,837,649	610,444	—
1901	14,520,318	2,132,569	—
1902	16,611,102	2,080,884	—
1903	17,552,060	940,958	—
1904	18,815,977	1,263,917	—
1905	18,199,162	−616,815	76,644
1906	21,626,390	3,427,228	88,794
1907	23,950,574	2,324,157	106,208
1908	23,242,838	−707,709	108,429
1909	27,466,761	4,223,923	125,873
1910	30,978,615	3,511,854	142,427
1911	33,867,228	2,888,613	162,318
1912	37,319,812	3,452,585	182,046
1913	40,606,183	3,286,317	203,886

SOURCE: *Queensborough*, March 1914.

Table 16
Population Growth, 1910–1915

Borough	1910	1915	Increase	% Increase
Manhattan	2,331,041	2,351,757	20,215	0.86
Brooklyn	1,634,351	1,808,191	173,840	10.64
Bronx	430,880	590,955	160,175	37.17
Queens	234,041	394,351	160,310	68.49
Staten Island	85,969	100,058	14,089	16.39
Total	4,766,883	5,245,812	478,929	10.05

SOURCE: *Queensborough*, August 1915.

development thousands of acres of land through the center of the Borough, which formerly had no transit except one or two stations on the Long Island Railroad."[18]

Bridge Plaza was soon home to banks providing capital for the land rush. The Long Island City Savings Bank, the First Mortgage Guarantee Company, and the Corn Exchange Bank opened offices there, and in 1927 the Bank of Manhattan erected the borough's first skyscraper at the intersection of Bridge Plaza and Northern Boulevard. The bankers' optimism in the future of the city's largest borough was measured in the number of loans and mortgages issued. Once the country recovered from the brief recession after the end of the Great War, real estate investment in Queens jumped from less than $35 million in 1920 to almost $157 million in 1924, a rise of nearly 450 percent.[19]

The availability of large tracts of undeveloped and relatively inexpensive land encouraged construction on a grand scale, but it was only after the new elevated lines were complete that hitherto distant sections could be profitably developed. Richmond Hill, Elmhurst, and parts of Jamaica and Flushing grew as exclusive suburban enclaves in the late nineteenth century, but now those places sprouted two- and three-family row houses and apartment buildings for working-class families, as well as more modest single-family homes on smaller lots. The new mass transit lines opened in stages over the first decades of the twentieth century. Elevated lines in Queens (the subway only came when the Independent Line (IND) was built in the 1930s) converged at three points—downtown Brooklyn, the Williamsburg Bridge, and Queens Plaza.

Trains began running over the Williamsburg Bridge in 1908, and, in 1918, the Brooklyn Manhattan Transit (BMT) completed the line from the bridge through East New York to 168th Street in Jamaica; a connection from Myrtle Avenue to Lutheran Cemetery in Middle Village opened in 1915, and that same year the Liberty Avenue Line was extended from the Brooklyn line to Lefferts Boulevard in Richmond Hill. Also in 1915, service on the Queensborough Line began through the Belmont Tunnel (formerly the Steinway Tunnel) between 42nd Street and Third Avenue in Manhattan to Hunters Point; this was extended to Queensboro Plaza in 1916, and the next year to 104th Street in Corona. The line reached Flushing in 1928. The Second Avenue Elevated was extended over the Queensboro Bridge in 1917, and the tunnel bringing the BRT Broadway line into Queens was completed in 1920. The convergence of those three lines made Queensboro Plaza the most complex elevated station in the world. Queensboro Plaza was also the first Dual Subway System station in the city, served by both the Interborough Rapid Transit (IRT) and the BRT (the BRT became the BMT in 1923). Both companies sent trains from Bridge Plaza to Astoria and Flushing. The nickel fare connected Queens with the entire metropolis, and for the first time commuting to the city from Queens was fast, efficient, and affordable. Property values in the vicinity of these new mass transit lines soared.

Model Tenements and Garden Cities

As if the impetus of new rapid transit lines was not enough to spur real estate developers, in 1922 the legislature passed two measures to ease the city's endemic housing shortage. The first was a ten-year tax exemption for new homes and apartments begun before 1923. Ironically, the tax exemption would expire in 1932, the worst year of the Great Depression, and thousands of homeowners, already hard-pressed to keep up their mortgage payments, faced new tax burdens. A second act permitted insurance companies to invest up to 10 percent of their assets in new housing.[20] This legislative action quickly attracted an infusion of new capital, as corporations took advantage of the investment opportunity.

While much of the new housing consisted of conventional one- and two-family homes and apartment buildings, Queens was also the site of several famed housing experiments, ranging from model tenements to garden cities. These included Forest Hills Gardens (1912), arguably the finest expression of the suburban ideal; Jackson Heights (1909–1920s); the Metropolitan Life Houses (1922); and Sunnyside Gardens (1924–1928).[21] Forest Hills Gardens was conceived as a railroad suburb, while Jackson Heights and Sunnyside Gardens were built along the new subway lines, a difference reflected in the overall design and density of each community.

For Forest Hills Gardens, the Russell Sage Foundation utilized the talents of architect Grosvenor Atterbury and the Olmsted Brothers landscaping firm, as Frederick Law Olmsted's firm was known after his death. In the Foundation's earliest promotional pamphlet, Robert W. DeForest, president of the Sage Foundation Homes Company, explained its social, economic, educational, and aesthetic qualities:

> Mrs. Russell Sage, and those whom she has associated with her in the Foundation, have been profoundly impressed with the need of better and more attractive housing facilities in the suburbs for persons of modest means who could pay from twenty-five dollars a month upward in the purchase of a home. They have thought that homes could be supplied like those in the garden cities of England, with some greenery and flowers around them, with accessible playgrounds and recreation facilities, and at no appreciably greater cost than is now paid for the same roof room in bare streets. They have abhorred the constant repetition of the rectangular block in suburban localities where land contours invite other street lines. They have thought, too, that buildings of tasteful design, constructed of brick, cement or other permanent material, even though of somewhat greater initial cost, were really more economical in their durability and lesser repair bills than the repulsive, cheaply built structures which are too often the type of New York's outlying districts. They have hoped that people of moderate income and good taste, who appreciate sympathetic surroundings, but are tied close to the city by the nature of their occupation, might find some country air and country life within striking distance of the active centers of New York.[22]

Macklewood Road, Forest Hills Gardens, circa. 1915. (Courtesy of the Queens Borough Public Library, Archives, Illustrations Collection- Forest Hills.)

The Sage Foundation sought to erect a living example of an ideal suburb, but central as this educational aspect was to the plan, the company remained "a business investment conducted on strictly business principles for a fair profit." This reformist enterprise was hardly a philanthropic one. The profits would be limited to 5 percent, "far less," according to a contemporary real estate journal, "than that aimed at by the average tract or subdivision developer." This difference represented what the foundation was "willing to expend out of its own pocket in giving the home owner surroundings and advantages which cannot be obtained where the developer takes the higher profit." Still, John M. Glenn, general director, explained that the Foundation required "that its capital be kept undiminished, and that this scheme, like all other investments, must yield a good business profit. Any other basis of action would mean merely to give charitable aid to the individuals who might occupy the property," and that "would be demoralizing and contrary to the fundamental principles of the Foundation."[23] Regardless, the Sage Foundation never recouped what it invested in building Forest Hills Gardens.

Because the Sage Foundation expressed such lofty ideals, it has been assumed that the original intention was to build affordable, high-quality housing for working-class families. From the very start of construction, however, it was clear that the homes would be priced far above that income level. As General Director Glenn explained, the suburb would not be "for laboring people with small wages." Rather, the Foundation would "test, and if possible prove, the feasibility of creating and marketing a suburb combining aesthetic charm, economy of arrangement and commercial marketability."[24]

Proximity to the city pushed land values so high as to render single-family detached homes on generous lots affordable only to upper-middle-class families. The mandated open space and the quality of construction also dictated the final cost. In the "Declaration of Restrictions" published in 1913, the company stipulated that "no dwelling houses shall be erected or maintained which shall cost less than the amounts to be specified by the Homes Company in the several deeds." The same restrictions also barred buildings or rows longer than 250 feet, a restriction aimed at eliminating deadening blocks of tenements and row houses. As De Forest explained, "The Sage Foundation has not forgotten the laboring man. It may be ready to announce something for his benefit later on, but the cost of the land at Forest Hills Gardens, and the character of its surroundings, preclude provision there for the day laborer." All plans and designs pointed to the exclusive nature of this suburb, which was never intended to be a model for multiclass communities. In contrast with other suburban experiments, the Sage Foundation retained possession of the streets, public spaces, and lighting, and assessed maintenance charges on all property owners. To achieve its end, the company established a completely private enclave that endures to the present.[25]

Ten acres at the western edge of the community became the new home of the West Side Tennis Club. Founded in Manhattan in 1892, the club purchased the property in Forest Hills in 1912. Three years later, the club hosted the men's national championship, the forerunner of the U.S. Open. In 1923, a steel and concrete stadium with a capacity of thirty thousand opened, and this was the site of the Open until 1977, when the tournament moved to Flushing Meadows-Corona Park.[26] For decades, the private—and restricted—club remained an exclusive preserve within a borough fast filling with homes for lower-middle-class families. And it remained closed to Jews and Blacks in the 1950s, even as Althea Gibson won the women's singles title there. In 1959, the club refused a junior membership to the son of Ralph Bunche, the winner of the Nobel Peace Prize in 1950 and a resident of Kew Gardens, an incident that made national headlines.[27]

The reform impulse behind Forest Hills was thus limited to the design; the company did not aspire to social engineering. The subsequent construction of thousands of working-class homes and apartments in Queens

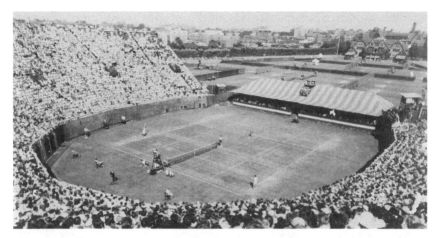

The West Side Tennis Club Stadium, Forest Hills, Long Island, N. Y., ca. 1958. (Courtesy of Michael Perlman, Rego-Forest Preservation Council.)

shows that the Sage Foundation could have attempted such a housing experiment, but the result would not have been the ideal realized in Forest Hills Gardens.

Architect Robert A. M. Stern has called Forest Hills Gardens, with its "unique combination of city planning and architecture," the "most complex and finely articulated" expression of the railroad suburb, "both a pinnacle and an end." Urban planner Alex Garvin noted that Olmsted "believed that successful communities depended on good roads and walks, 'pleasant to the eye within themselves and having intervals of pleasant openings and outlooks, with suggestions of refined domestic life.'" The result is a multidimensional delight. "One wanders his curving roads, never sure where they will end, constantly surprised and entertained by some aspect of his design," expounded Garvin. Susan Klaus, author of a book about the creation of Forest Hills, states its key attributes were "the caliber of its creators, the thoroughness of its planning and the quality of its architectural design, materials, and workmanship." Together these yielded an "extremely rare example of a suburb that's as intact now as when it was built."[28] Another factor, of course would be the restrictive covenants in place from the start governing all new construction and alterations to existing homes.

Immediately to the east of Forest Hills arose another suburb in the Anglo-American tradition. The Man family, who had built Richmond Hill in the last quarter of the nineteenth century (see chapter 4), developed land that had been their short-lived country club into Kew Gardens. The idea behind this walkable suburban community was much the same as the impetus behind Forest Hills. According to historian Barry Lewis, it would appeal to "a generation that had seen the city and felt it did not entirely work." This "cosmopolitan generation ... wanted the culture and opportunities a city offered but didn't know why they had to put up with the nerve-wracking assault on the senses and the demeaning lack of personal space." In that, Kew Gardens was akin to Riverdale, Prospect Park South, and, in Queens, Douglas Manor.[29] Unlike Forest Hills Gardens, which has been governed by strict design standards for the start, the integrity of Kew Gardens depended on the taste of individual homeowners, with the result that some historic homes have been demolished and replaced with new construction.

While Forest Hills Gardens represented the highest expression of the railroad suburb, Jackson Heights set the standard for urban housing along new rapid transit lines. The Queensboro Corporation was founded in August 1909, with William F. Wyckoff, descendant of one of Brooklyn's oldest families and president of the Homestead Bank and the Woodhaven Bank, as its president. The driving force behind the corporation, however, was the thirty-five-year-old general manager, Edward Archibald MacDougall, an experienced real estate man who had already been involved in Kissena Park North and South, Terminal Heights in Woodside, and Elmhurst Square. Activities of the Queensboro Corporation dwarfed those earlier ventures, both in scale and execution. In 1914, the Queensboro Corporation began constructing blocks of elegant apartment buildings for middle-class families. The first went up near Northern Boulevard, close to the trolley lines running to the bridge. Plans for the new Dual Subway System were well advanced, and for two full years before service began the corporation touted the subway as a prime attraction. Until then, the Queensboro Corporation arranged for the Fifth Avenue Bus Company to schedule service from Jackson Heights into Manhattan.[30]

The architects of Forest Hills Gardens planned their suburb to be set apart from the city and consciously rejected all urban forms. The curving streets, the spacious lawns, the emphasis on privacy, and the restrictive covenants combined to reinforce the distinctiveness of the place. Jackson Heights, on the other hand, fit into the urban grid and that influenced the architecture. Although the Queensboro Corporation would eventually erect some single-family homes, the predominant form was the apartment building. Unlike Manhattan, where the buildings went up without any consistent design, covered as much as 80 percent of the lot, and crowded together to utilize every inch of streetfront, the apartment buildings in Jackson Heights adapted the most innovative features of the English "garden cities" and pioneered the concept of the "garden apartment" in the United States. The buildings were set back from the street, creating small lawns in front, and the rear yards were treated as landscaped parks for residents. This arrangement guaranteed ample light and air, far more, in fact, than was mandated by the city's tenement laws.

The Queensboro Corporation erected few buildings before the war, but by 1919 construction was well underway again. Jackson Heights was soon recognized as offering the most innovative apartments in the city, with extraordinarily high standards of design and materials. Nothing articulated the distinction between Jackson Heights and Manhattan more than the introduction of free-standing apartment buildings and the generously landscaped inner courtyards that extended the length of the block. Even the most expensive new buildings along Fifth Avenue or Park Avenue lacked such features. To further enhance the appeal of Jackson Heights for the urban middle class, the corporation built tennis courts and set aside eight square blocks for a golf course. Residents could even putter in their own garden plots. Integral to the success of Jackson Heights was the introduction of a cooperative ownership plan, presenting families with the opportunity to own rather than rent, and thus combining a fundamental suburban trait with urban amenities.[31] Jackson Heights, like Forest Hills Gardens, offered nothing to the wage earner of moderate means. That segment of the housing market was left to builders like the Mathews brothers who, as noted above, constructed block after block of railroad flats across Queens.

In 1922, the Metropolitan Life Insurance Company launched an effort to build model tenements for working-class families. The company had lobbied in Albany for passage of the tax-exemption bill that permitted insurance companies to invest up to 10 percent of their assets in real estate, while limiting rents in the new housing to $9 a room. In 1922, Met Life approved loans of $2,750,000 to build 68 six-family buildings, 48 two-family homes, and 250 single-family houses in Long Island City, new housing for 800 families.[32]

By 1924, only two years after Governor Al Smith signed the law, Met Life had built apartments for 2,125 working-class families in Sunnyside, Woodside, and Astoria. For their architect, the company tapped Andrew J. Thomas, who had designed several of the buildings in Jackson Heights. Thomas presented a plan almost identical in outline to Linden Court, built in 1919.[33] The fifty-four identical U-shaped buildings featured modern kitchens, central heating, hot and cold running water, and excellent ventilation, with windows in every room facing either the street or the landscaped inner courtyard. Repeating the same design kept the costs low, and Met Life could thereby make the model tenements profitable.

The hopeful spirit of this enterprise was perhaps expressed best by seven-year-old Alberta Glenn, daughter of the project's construction foreman. At the ground-breaking ceremony in July 1922, the little girl stepped from the flag-draped bucket of a steam shovel and, presenting a shovel to Haley Fiske, president of the Metropolitan Life Insurance Company, said: "We the children of New York want to thank you ever so much for these beautiful homes. Now we needn't be shut up in the dark old tenements where we haven't any place to play; but we will come here to live in sunshine and see the wonderful garden and flowers all day. We hope that every little child in New York may have as fine a home as these."[34]

During this period of economic growth, a group of reform-minded citizens headed by Alexander M. Bing, a wealthy Manhattan realtor, formed the City Housing Corporation (CHC) for the purpose of building a model community, combining as far as possible the concerns of American housing reformers with the ideas of the garden cities movement in England. The idea for the CHC came from the individuals who founded the Regional Planning Association of America in 1923, among them architect Frederick L. Ackerman, Robert D. Kohn (later head of the Public Works Administration during the New Deal), Benton MacKaye (advocate for the Appalachian Trail), urban critic Lewis Mumford, and architects Henry Wright and Clarence Stein, who was chairman of New York State's Commission for Housing and the energy behind the group.[35] They met at least twice a week to talk about issues of housing reform and urban planning. Out of those stimulating and wide-ranging discussions came plans for Sunnyside Gardens.

Clarence Stein visited England after the war and returned a disciple of Ebenezer Howard and Sir Raymond Unwin, the leading figures of the garden cities movement there. In their design for Sunnyside Gardens, Stein and Wright applied Unwin's dictum: "Nothing gained by overcrowding." In community development, they believed, it was not the initial costs but the final costs that mattered.[36] The two architects attended to all aspects of the design, from the arrangement of the buildings to the layout of each unit; Marjorie Sewell Cautley was brought in as the landscape architect. Mumford lived in Sunnyside from 1924 to 1936 and described his experience in *Green Memories*, a poignant chronicle of his son Geddes, who was killed in combat in 1944. In design, appearance, and organization, Sunnyside Gardens was intended to provide an alternative to contemporary urban life, a conscious rejection of the values, disorder, and confusion of the city in favor of the healthy environment of small-town America. "None of us pretended that Sunnyside wholly fulfilled our dreams, but the main outlines of the community were right," Mumford wrote. "If we had to settle anywhere within a big city at the time Geddes was small, we are not sorry, at least on human terms, that we chose Sunnyside. It had been framed to the human scale. A little boy could take it all in."[37]

While the founders of the CHC were not primarily motivated by profits, neither could they ignore the example of Metropolitan Life, which received rentals in excess of $1 million a year, an 8 percent return on their investment in affordable housing. According to its promotional brochure, the CHC was animated by a sense of civic responsibility and recognition of the need for a "scientific attack on the problem of providing better homes for families of moderate income." Seeking to offer quality housing for wage earners as close to cost as possible, the CHC also embraced middle-class suburban values. Behind Sunnyside Gardens was the assumption that a community of homeowners was fundamentally more stable than a neighborhood where the majority of the residents rented apartments. Described by its incorporators as a "socialized business," the CHC was in fact a limited dividend company that would "operate without profit—that is to say, its dividends will be limited to six percent." The CHC counted Eleanor Roosevelt among their directors.[38]

The group moved quickly. In February 1924, they purchased seventy-seven acres from the Pennsylvania Railroad Company. The ground-breaking ceremony was on April 1, and the first units were ready for occupation in September. The entire development was finished within five years. Stein and Wright hoped to demonstrate the superiority of their innovative plans, but, given the booming housing market and the willingness of banks to provide mortgage money, it is likely that any homes built in that location would have found buyers.[39]

When completed in 1928, Sunnyside Gardens provided homes for 1,200 families. A 1926 survey determined that half of the new residents had left tenements on the East Side of Manhattan. Two years later, a survey of 504 residents, almost half of the community, found "184 blue collar workers, including 116 mechanics, 50 chauffeurs, and 18 restaurant workers; there were also 355 white collar workers, including 99 professionals (teachers, social workers, lawyers, and doctors), 79 office workers, 55 small tradesmen, 49 salesmen, and 35 government employees." Most of them were of German, Irish, or Jewish extraction, "with native Americans predominating." They chose the Gardens because of the facilities provided for the children, the quiet suburban atmosphere, the design and quality of the homes, and the community spirit, but for many the primary consideration was the convenient location.[40]

Sunnyside: A Step toward Better Housing, CHC brochure, 1927. (Cornell University Library, Division of Rare and Manuscript Collections, Clarence S. Stein Papers, No. 3600.)

The Gardens had rental apartments as well as one-family homes, anticipating that the suburban appeal cut across class lines. Capitalizing on this appeal, their promotional brochure proclaimed, "For most of us the ideal home of good taste and design, sound construction and with sunlight, air, a garden outlook and lawns for the children to play in safety is associated with the outlying suburbs and prices the average family cannot afford. Within a 20 minute subway ride of Times Square [are] attractive, substantial brick homes with acres of gardens and park at prices no higher than the rents they had been paying for ordinary city flats." This furthered the social ideals of the planners. Lewis Mumford thought that interacting "with a wide range of income groups . . . living side by side, has led me to believe that this is the best kind of community. In terms of education of the young and of making the institutions of democracy work, the arguments are entirely in favor of a mixed community."[41]

This pace was by no means extraordinary for Queens during the decade. In 1924 alone, developers submitted plans for 24,610 new buildings, and nearly 85,000 new homes went up between 1924 and 1928, three-fourths of them single-family or two-family houses. In eastern Queens, near the LIRR's Hollis station, the firm of Gross and Lemmerman purchased 700 lots, land that had been under tillage in 1923, and by early 1925 had erected 374 houses, with another 142 under construction. As at Sunnyside, the developers also installed the sidewalks, streets, curbs, and water mains. Queens developed a pronounced suburban character, more so than Brooklyn or the Bronx, which also grew exponentially during the Roaring Twenties. The borough averaged only 1.7 families per dwelling unit, compared to the citywide average of 3.5 families per unit. Commenting on this situation, Frank Mann, commissioner of the city's Tenement House Department, stated that one- and two-family homes were "oversupplied" in Queens and offered no advantage to the average wage earner. He added that the tax exemption had induced the construction of few homes at a low or moderate rental, defined as $8 to $15 a room; the building boom met the pressures of supply and demand only for those with more substantial incomes. In Mann's estimation, "The supply of low or moderate rental apartments has not yet been met." In fact, the vacancy rate for apartments in the borough was only 1.35 percent in 1925 (in 1923 the rate had been 0.04 percent, and in 1921 a scant 0.01 percent, representing a total of only two vacant apartments).[42] This meant, of course, that families were moving into the new homes as soon as the paint was dry.

While the CHC was building its progressive garden suburb, the aforementioned G. X. Mathews Company erected blocks of six-unit, three-story row houses nearby. Before the war the company had concentrated its efforts in Ridgewood, but after 1918 the Mathews brothers shifted their operations to Long Island City, building rows of tenements in Astoria, Woodside, and Sunnyside. The Mathews Model Flats were attractive, but differed little in design from other urban tenements, and lacked landscaping entirely. They boasted steam heat and hot water, electric lights (and in the earlier models, gas fixtures as well), modern kitchens, and tiled baths—in short, "all modern comforts"—but the primary attraction was the low price for buyers and the affordable rents for tenants. In its literature, the company explicitly compared its homes with the model development in Sunnyside, especially regarding the respective costs per room.

In actuality, the CHC and the G. X. Mathews Company aimed their homes at different sectors of the housing market. The CHC had no interest in low-rental apartments for owner-occupied investment, and the Mathews brothers did not build one-, two-, or three-family homes for the middle class. The Mathews brothers recognized their niche and excelled at filling it, as one of their brochures explained: "The safest of all real estate is that which caters to the masses—at lowest rents. This is the secret of the success of Mathews Model Flats. They supply an absolute necessity of life—shelter. Luxury buildings are a speculation—necessities are sure income producers."[43]

The collection of model tenements and planned communities in Queens generated significant interest from architects and planners beyond the five boroughs. In 1925, the city hosted the International Town, City and Regional Planning Conference, a weeklong gathering held at the Hotel Pennsylvania. A highlight of the event was a daylong tour of new housing in Queens, with stops at Sunnyside Gardens, Forest Hills Gardens, Kew Gardens, and Jackson Heights. Raymond Unwin, architect for Hampstead Garden Suburb in England, and head of the war housing program there during the Great War, was the featured speaker at the luncheon held at the Jackson Heights Country Club.[44] The meeting of the town planners brought even greater international recognition to the collection of model housing concentrated in Queens.

In terms of sheer numbers, the amount of housing built during the Roaring Twenties was unprecedented. Furthermore, the quality of the new homes intended for families of modest means was far superior to what had been available to them before. At the same time, it must be noted that all of this housing, as well the new transportation lines, was the product of the private sector. Even the young Queens Borough Public Library, rapidly expanding its services to the new neighborhoods through deposit collections and rented storefronts, was a private entity (as it remains, though today largely dependent on public funding).[45] Beyond the Queensboro Bridge, the primary work of the city was the building of schools to keep pace with the influx of new residents.

The Never-Ending Boom

The economic boom of the 1920s was nowhere more evident than in Queens, and much of the real estate explosion was built on credit. The result was an extraordinary period of residential construction. In the five years between 1924 and 1929, the city issued 73,656 permits for one- and two-family homes in Queens, providing housing for 93,000 families, or an estimated 400,000 persons. The erection of 4,400 apartment buildings provided homes for another 53,464 families, or an estimated 213,000 persons. This total of more than 600,000 newcomers was exceeded by the population of only eight cities in the country: Chicago, Philadelphia, Detroit, Cleveland, St. Louis, Boston, Baltimore, and Pittsburgh. The assessed valuation in the borough had also skyrocketed in the 1920s.[46] The city's economic vitality during the decade is seen in the enormous rise in values in Manhattan, the urban core,

Table 17
Assessed Valuation in the Five Boroughs, 1918–1928

Borough	1918	1928	Increase
Manhattan	5,094,601,238	8,141,520,095	3,046,918,857 (60%)
Brooklyn	1,826,813,885	3,780,468,290	1,953,654,405 (107%)
Bronx	726,129,198	1,614,294,910	888,183,127 (122%)
Queens	591,599,075	1,661,294,910	1,069,695,835 (181%)
Staten Island	100,459,455	268,588,055	168,092,600 (167%)
Total	8,339,638,851	15,466,183,675	7,126,544,824 (85%)
		% of NYC total increase	% of Growth outside Manhattan
Manhattan		42.75	—
Brooklyn		27.41	17.89
Bronx		12.46	21.77
Queens		15.01	26.22
Staten Island		0.02	0.04

SOURCE: Department of Finance, New York (N.Y.)

representing almost half of the total growth. Queens accounted for only about 15 percent of the increase in assessed valuation, but more than a quarter of the growth outside of Manhattan.

Experienced developers saw no reason to doubt the continuation of this boom. Interviewed in late 1926, A. F. Mathews, treasurer of the G. X. Mathews Company, did point to one unbalanced aspect of the housing market in the city:

> The problem for 1927 seems to me the adjusting of rentals of the many large projects in which big sums have been sunk. What is needed are low-rent houses and there is good reason to believe that the rental demands in the high-class buildings are greater in amount than the community can pay. We know that despite the amount of building during the past seven years, and tax exemption, although the production was of tremendous volume, it entirely failed to take care of the needs of the workers and the minimum priced rent payer. The reason was a simple one: there was more profit in high-rent types of buildings and this attracted most of the available capital and labor.

Beyond this structural readjustment, Mathews concluded that "no slump in real estate generally, however, seems possible."[47] The strategy of the Mathews brothers to concentrate on mass-market housing was certainly successful, for they prospered even after the market for luxury rentals had contracted.

But at the time of these comments, however, the downturn in Queens real estate had already begun. The high point in the value of building permits came in 1925, and by 1928 it had slumped from almost $200 million to less than $150 million. After racing upward in the early 1920s, mortgage investment, too, leveled off after 1926. Even the solid market of the Mathews brothers showed signs of a slump. A report of the State Board of Housing found that three-quarters of the city's 102,158 vacant apartments rented for less than $15 per room, though in Queens the increase in empty apartments "took place in the class above $13 a room and more particularly above $20."[48] The expansion of affordable housing in Queens, Brooklyn, and the Bronx meant that those who had a choice rejected "old law" tenements, and rents actually fell in that class of buildings. Builders like the Mathews brothers had been so successful that they had saturated the market even for low-rent apartments.[49]

But epic events sometimes come announced. The weather prediction printed in the newspaper for March 12, 1888, read "Generally fair and cloudy." What happened, of course, was the Great Blizzard of 1888. In the autumn of 1929, there were abundant expressions of business confidence. President Herbert Hoover assured the country that the business of the nation, "the production and distribution of goods and services, is on a sound and prosperous basis." In September of that year, V. H. Vreeland, the president of the Long Island Real Estate Board, stated proudly, "Yes, the future is bright."[50]

10

The Crisis of the Great Depression

For America's cities, the Great Depression brought an unprecedented level of unemployment and the nearly total collapse of one of the cornerstones of urban prosperity, the real estate market. While not exclusively an urban problem, unemployment was certainly more visible in the cities, and by their numbers and the nature of their needs the jobless soon overwhelmed all sources of private charity. Families had to make bitter choices between food, shelter, and other necessities, and with so many out of work, unable to pay their rent or keep up with mortgage payments, evictions and foreclosures, often enforced by city marshals, became tragically common. In 1932 alone, financial institutions across the nation foreclosed on a quarter of a million properties; by the time Franklin Delano Roosevelt took office in March 1933, the foreclosure rate was up to a thousand a day.[1]

For the real estate sector, the sight of a family forced out on the street, surrounded by their possessions, multiplied thousands of times, translated into that most unusual of urban problems, a housing surplus. The construction of new housing virtually ceased, leading to a crisis in the building trades and deepening the cycle of stagnation and unemployment. Existing apartments remained vacant as would-be tenants, if they were fortunate, doubled up with friends or relatives in already crowded homes, or lived in "Hoovervilles."[2]

Table 18
Permits for New Housing in Queens, 1921–1935

Year	Permits	Estimated $ in millions
1921	6,851	39.1
1922	21,321	133.1
1923	25,021	157.8
1924	24,610	160.3
1925	31,527	172.9
1926	24,151	186.6
1927	22,641	179.6
1928	18,710	146.5
1929	11,843	87.5
1930	11,213	70.0
1931	12,554	68.5
1932	4,015	12.8
1933	2,142	11.7
1934	3,314	10.1
1935	6,126	24.1

SOURCE: *Queensborough*, May 1936.

Unable to afford a place of their own, young couples moved in with parents or put off marriage altogether.

As the nation's greatest metropolis, New York City was perhaps unique in both the magnitude of its problems and in the scope of its solutions. Queens prospered mightily during the boom years of the 1920s, with new rapid transit lines carrying residents between jobs in Manhattan offices or Long Island City factories and new homes rising on land that only a few years before had been truck farms. After the stock market crash, however, the already slowing rate of real estate investment plunged dramatically. Banks that had eagerly granted thousands of mortgages during the twenties foreclosed on those same properties in the early thirties, and as a result they had little capital to invest in new housing, even if there had been a demand. Almost overnight, the mood of optimistic boosterism yielded to cries for government action to ease the crisis.

The impact of the Depression was felt almost immediately. Employment in Queens dropped by 20 percent in the first year after the crash and continued to fall in the years that followed. The business community in Queens embraced President Hoover's "Share the Work" movement, an attempt to deal with unemployment by encouraging businesses to each hire just a few more workers, maintain current wage levels, and cut back hours. "If every industry went on the thirty hour week," suggested Israel Silberman of the

Queens Share the Work Committee, "depression would walk out the back door." In March 1933, the month when Franklin Delano Roosevelt was inaugurated, the Queens Chamber of Commerce noted with pride that the borough's 227 industries employed 30,745 workers, 5,711 (18.6 percent) of whom were hired through Share the Work.[3] Such local efforts, however much they may have cushioned the full effect of the economic collapse, proved inadequate in the face of enormous structural failings manifest nationwide.

For Steinway & Sons, the crisis was especially acute. Obviously, pianos were a luxury item compared to rent and food, and sales fell swiftly and dramatically. In 1929, the firm employed two thousand workers. When the Depression hit, the paternalistic company had to lay off workers for the first time in its history. One worker saw earnings fall from $2,424 in 1929 to $670 in 1931. Steinway closed the factory completely between 1931 and 1933, and then reopened with only a skeleton crew of six hundred part-time workers kept busy repairing pianos. No new instruments were manufactured at all for years.[4]

The diary of one Queens man speaks with poignant eloquence of his own plight in September 1933. "We are flat cold stony broke and no place in the world to get any money," he wrote. "Have been living mainly on boxes of food from the Red Cross and received the last one yesterday as they have stopped giving them out. We owe 6 months rent. Resources all drained. I wonder what will happen now? God help us." What happened is explained in an entry from December 1935: "Two years on the WPA job. Grateful for it but hope to get on my own soon." What happened to him was the New Deal.[5]

The most pressing problem facing the city as the Depression worsened was, of course, relief. The Family Welfare Society of Queens, founded in 1923, was ill-prepared to cope with the crisis. In the whole last year of prosperity, the Society assisted only 1,912 families, but each month during the Depression winter of 1931–1932 they had on their books an average of over 6,000 families, representing about 30,000 individuals. The staff grew to 72, each handling as many as 200 cases, as compared to the normal caseload of 50.[6]

Active as they were, there was no way private charities could address the needs of the unemployed and their families. Within a very short time, the Welfare Society was reduced to offering only emergency aid to the very neediest cases. Across the city, one in four families was receiving some sort of assistance; in Queens, 36,000 families were on relief at the end of 1934, and a hundred a day submitted new applications for aid. The Queens Chamber of Commerce appealed to businesses and individuals to contribute an additional $300,000 to local charities, explaining that "the maintenance of these people in institutions operated at public expense will be far more on your tax bill than the cost of helping them now."[7]

The Business Community

As with the shortcomings of private charity, reliance on the private sector to provide jobs for the unemployed also fell far short of the need. While many businessmen reluctantly recognized that the economic crisis of the 1930s was profoundly different from the temporary downturns experienced before, others never did accept the idea that business alone could not pull the economy together again. They continued to blame the government, especially local government, for the collapse, and resisted New Deal programs as alien to the American spirit and a threat to the American system.

Nothing demonstrates the enormous difference between the stagnation of the private sector and the dynamism of the New Deal than the fact that by the end of 1933 public works programs in Queens had pumped $13 million into the local economy and put eighteen thousand men and women to work, more than three times the number employed through the private sector alone. The public works employees widened or repaved existing roads and built new ones, projects even the chamber of commerce admitted would not have been possible under the traditional method of assessment-based taxes. *Queensborough* reported that to confront the difficult conditions of the Depression, the federal government would "advance the payrolls, the city to make good the cost of materials and equipment either in whole or in part." The situation created a dilemma for the business community, for while they decried governmental intervention in economic affairs, they had to admit that the very actions they warned against also brought substantial benefits to the county and to themselves. It was indeed difficult to espouse the boosterism of the prosperous Coolidge years while requesting additional federal dollars for local public works. Still, this dilemma did not prevent the chamber of commerce from presenting Republican borough president George U. Harvey with a shopping list that included a Queens-Midtown Tunnel (a project the chamber had originally opposed on the basis of questionable funding when it had been approved by the Board of Estimate), a Bronx-Whitestone Bridge, the Queens Boulevard subway line, and parks, parkways, road improvements, schools, and hospitals. Reviewing the borough's needs in broad terms, chamber president Frank Ray Howe identified transportation and strike prevention as top priorities, not new housing.[8]

At their annual dinner at the Commodore Hotel in January 1933, President Howe stated flatly that the principal cause of the current economic distress was the unbalanced budget and the unacceptable level of government spending, adding on a homey note that government had to "cut back when hard times hit, just as individuals must." He prescribed the "elimination of all extravagance and waste, and doing away with all useless positions." He added that there would be no improvement "until real estate recovers from the depths of despair to which it has sunk." Congressman Joseph B. Shannon of Missouri, chairman of a House committee investigating government competition with private enterprise, was a special guest at the dinner and warned against the dangers of the state "departing from its high principles and promising to hamper and distress business men by setting up rival businesses conducted often by unfair and even secret methods." While the New Deal later embraced deficit spending, FDR presented himself as a budget balancer in the 1932 campaign, the candidate of fiscal responsibility as opposed to Hoover who had allowed the federal deficit to swell.[9] Even before Roosevelt had signed a single piece of New Deal legislation, however, conservative voices questioned his commitment to free market capitalism.

Borough President Harvey had greater cause for optimism at the start of 1934 than did the business community. In his annual message of December 1933, Harvey pointed out that "the depression, peculiarly enough, will result in more bridge and highway construction than took place in more prosperous years," as well as the erection of numerous public buildings, such as the new courthouse in the Rockaways. He specifically mentioned that work would resume on the Triborough Bridge; ground-breaking had taken place in October 1929, but within months all work ceased. These improvements, said Harvey, would be completed without placing additional burdens on the taxpayers of Queens, who were unable to meet higher assessments in current circumstances in any event. At the same time, he pointed out that none of these projects would be possible without federal dollars. "Our borough appropriations are so reduced," the borough president explained, "that it would not be possible to maintain roads and highways in anything like satisfactory repair were they not augmented by funds set aside by the City to provide materials and equipment with which emergency labor can be kept employed."[10]

Speaking at the installation of George W. Cassidy as new chamber of commerce president in April 1934, the borough president gave a sharp answer to those urging him to cut spending. "If I do any more economizing," he stated, "you won't have any more government. While I've been cutting my budget from $13,000,000 to $4,000,000 during the past four years, the population of the borough has increased 300,000." He reminded his audience "to thank the Federal and State governments for much of what we have been able to accomplish, particularly in the way of highway improvements." But the chamber was unconvinced. Both outgoing president Howe and his successor, Cassidy, voiced skepticism about the New Deal's activist government. By emphasizing spending cuts and the need for a balanced budget, business leaders ignored the fact that the city's budget crisis was due not to "extravagance and waste" but to declining tax revenues, a direct result of the collapse of the private sector. Cassidy went so far as to suggest that the New Deal was un-American. "The people of this country are confronted with a sociological change of the first magnitude," he asserted. "This change can be interpreted through some twenty-eight alphabetically symbolized laws and set-ups. Without going into the merits and demerits of these laws, such as the A.A.A., the P.W.A., and N.R.A., I would like to emphasize emphatically three letters which do not appear on the list and those three letters are U.S.A. Let us not forget them and what they mean to us." In his view, the proper role for the chamber of commerce in the current crisis was to work for "a better understanding and cooperation between individualism, business, industry and government."[11]

The chamber's position—warning against an un-American and anti-individualistic New Deal on the one hand while demanding construction projects for their own borough on the other—was obviously at its core contradictory. Cassidy admitted that "New York State, possibly because of its size and wealth [was] the very fountainhead of social reforms," but warned that if put into effect, many of those reforms "would operate to the disadvantage of the state and its business." Under his leadership, the chamber tried to limit the full implementation of the National Recovery Administration (NRA), giving assistance to businesses "in the preparation and interpretation of code agreements and to opposing rulings and regulations which [they] considered unjust."[12] Nevertheless, the September 1933 issue of *Queensborough* featured the NRA's Blue Eagle on its cover, complete with the "We Do Our Part" slogan. That symbol graced the masthead of the publication every month until the Supreme Court declared the act unconstitutional. The offending eagle unceremoniously vanished in July 1935.

Despite evidence of extreme cutbacks in city spending, Cassidy repeatedly called for a balanced budget and the elimination of "waste" and "useless jobs" before any tax increase could be considered, going so far as to call for a tax reduction. At the same time, he had only words of praise for construction of the Queens Boulevard subway line and the Triborough Bridge, projects moving forward through the "grant of federal funds" and bonds issued by the Triborough Bridge Authority. He listed other public works projects needed by the borough, including the Queens-Midtown Tunnel, the Bronx-Whitestone Bridge, road repairs, and new schools, all items, he claimed, "for which the Chamber is working."[13]

The New Deal and the Housing Crisis

Of course, it was not possible for private initiative to embark on construction projects on the scale of the Triborough Bridge. In the field of housing and real estate, however, the private sector strenuously objected to any governmental interference in what they saw as the cornerstone of the American way of life: the right of individuals to own and control their property. More than any other New Deal program, the idea of public housing—developments designed, built, and managed by the government—flew in the face of the American ideology of free enterprise and private property. The Queens Chamber of Commerce, the National Association of Real Estate Boards, the National Association of Retail Lumber Dealers, and the U.S. Savings and Loan League all opposed public housing, fearing that once in the real estate business, the state would become a direct and permanent competitor of the private sector.

Still, the unpleasant truth was that housing starts, a leading indicator of economic health, continued to fall nationwide from 134,000 in 1932 to 93,000 in 1933, with no end to the collapse in sight. In Queens, the number of plans submitted for new buildings fell from 3,898 in 1932 to 2,992 a year later, and the estimated value of those plans dropped nearly 45 percent ($12.2 million to $6.8 million).[14] Despite ideological uncertainties, it must have been obvious to all that emergency measures were necessary, the only question being the form those measures would take.

President Roosevelt's executive order of June 16, 1933, established the Public Works Emergency Housing Corporation, a new division of the Public Works Administration (PWA) authorized "to construct, finance, or aid in the construction of any public-works project," and to purchase or acquire through eminent domain any property needed for such construction. Within a fortnight, Congress had passed the National Housing Act (NHA), creating the Federal Housing Administration (FHA) to stimulate recovery by insuring mortgages. At this point, the New Dealers had no intention of competing with the private sector, their goal being first and foremost relief and recovery. The original purpose of the proposals for public housing, as with other public works projects, was to create jobs and consume materials. Providing new homes for the working poor was almost a by-product of the program, not an end in itself. Indeed, that is how Mayor-Elect Fiorello LaGuardia described his plans to the Queens Chamber of Commerce in late 1933. He promised "to launch a gigantic slum clearance program with Federal funds that would put thousands of unemployed building trades workers to work."[15]

The idea of using architecture and planning to effect fundamental changes in the social and economic fabric of urban life seemed inappropriate to conditions in Queens, which was then, and remains today, a borough of homes built and financed by the private sector. In 1930, about 45 percent of the nearly three hundred thousand families in the borough owned their homes, 40 percent of which were worth over $10,000. Nor were urban slums to be found in Queens, as three-fourths of the multifamily dwellings had been built since 1902. The problem facing Queens was neither a housing shortage nor the dilapidated condition of existing structures; it was the dreaded prospect of foreclosure. This was, in truth, a national problem, as the average homeowner by 1933 was two years behind in mortgage payments and local taxes.[16]

The problems in Queens were as severe as any urban section in the country. Since most of the housing had been built during the 1920s, families were strapped with inelastic mortgages. In Sunnyside Gardens, over half of the residents lost their homes to foreclosures and forcible evictions, events that made headlines and were captured by the newsreels. By 1933, nearly 40 percent of the residents there were unemployed, representing an estimated 50 percent loss of income and a 75 percent decline in net worth. In Sunnyside, however, the residents resisted the foreclosures and evictions as a united neighborhood instead of isolated homeowners. Ironically, the City Housing Corporation (CHC)'s effort to build a community instead of just houses was proven successful during the Depression, as residents organized and turned against the company, pressing for mortgage relief. But the CHC itself was in trouble and was headed into bankruptcy. It had originally obtained financing for buyers through third parties, including the Equitable Life Assurance Company and the Russell Sage Foundation, and those institutions held fast to the original terms of the contracts. In other neighborhoods, each homeowner arranged his own mortgage. This meant that several banks were involved and that the foreclosures would not hit everyone at once. In Sunnyside, however, one institution held all the mortgages, a situation that resulted in many homeowners facing foreclosure at the same time. In response, Sunnysiders initiated a mortgage strike. When the marshals

Sunnyside Gardens Eviction, 1936. (Queens Historical Society.)

arrived to dispossess the family, residents resisted. One woman who lived through those events recalled that "whenever the marshals would carry the furniture out the front door, we'd carry it around to the back door and put it back in the house." But even united neighbors could not stop the foreclosures. Finally, Mayor LaGuardia intervened and a compromise was reached, resulting in the mortgage terms being reset.[17]

Against this background, borough leaders identified as the path to recovery first mortgage relief and second new construction. When they considered federal intervention in real estate or housing, they envisioned loan guarantees or investment in limited dividend corporations. Large-scale public housing was not what they had expected, and the chamber of commerce opposed such projects every step of the way. On the other hand, they endorsed the goals of the Home Owners' Loan Corporation (HOLC), the New Deal agency created to purchase mortgages in default and offer delinquent homeowners refinancing or loans for deferred repairs or back taxes. The HOLC was financed through the sale of bonds, a device the private sector could support since it did not involve a direct outlay of federal funds and so kept spending under control, as well as holding out the prospect of a guaranteed return.

In June 1934, the Queens Chamber of Commerce wrote to FDR supporting legislation that would increase the capitalization of the HOLC by an additional $2 billion. They submitted this urgent request "because even now many are still unemployed, new groups of owners are defaulting constantly, having used up all of their savings from every source. Private mortgage money is not yet available to assist those homeowners. The United States Government, having undertaken to provide relief, cannot stop with the job half done—they must see it through." By September, over 75 percent of the applications of Queens homeowners had been approved, most for between $3,000 and $5,000. The chamber encouraged these short-term loans, and local banks offered full cooperation because they were a means to utilize idle capital and put unemployed tradesmen to work, thus stimulating the local economy while maintaining the existing pattern of private ownership in the borough.[18] Ironically, none of the homeowners in Sunnyside Gardens qualified for federal assistance. It is likely that the community was redlined because it was adjacent to industries and the railroad yard.

A. E. Horn, chairman of the chamber's Housing Committee, believed that the NHA was "designed as a bulwark against the continued outpouring of public monies for relief," adding that "it behooves all who are taxable to support every measure that will bring to a successful result the spirit of the Housing Act." If properly implemented, he suggested, the agency would not only stimulate recovery but also result in profits, a welcome marriage of "selfish interests" and "public spirited" actions. The chamber saw a threefold purpose in the NHA, in order of importance: "Renovisation [sic] and modernization of real property; Construction of homes to be occupied by the owners; Construction of residential buildings to be rented to people of low incomes."[19] The Queens Chamber of Commerce gave its qualified support to the NHA not because there was a pressing need for new homes in the borough but because of the benefits to property owners and the anticipated stimulus to the economy.

One of the tragic aspects of the Depression was the mismatch of housing demand and the available supply. In the late 1920s, the vacancy rate in Queens was less than 2 per cent; the fact that so many apartments remained empty in the 1930s was not evidence of a housing glut but the circumstance that thousands of New Yorkers could not afford to pay their rent. Unable to fill existing apartment buildings, owners feared that any new housing, especially state-sponsored projects, would only worsen their unprofitable predicament. Edward A. Richards, president of the Forest Hills-Kew Gardens Apartment Owners Association, declared, "There is no difficulty in any tenant finding fair quarters either in an apartment house or a one or two family house at a rental that will pay the operation expenses, taxes and interest on the mortgage and leave a few cents over to the owner of the equity. Under such circumstances I see no great inducement to build apartment houses in Queens." He stated emphatically that "no new buildings should be contemplated until an adjustment is made in rental income to a point where a fair return is insured. That point will be reached only when there are few vacancies in either apartments or small houses."[20]

In large measure, the housing problems facing Queens reflected the nature of the building boom of the 1920s. Nationwide, an estimated three-fourths of the new housing was intended for the top third of the population in household income, with almost no new construction for the bottom third. In 1929, only 38.8 percent of all Americans earned above $1,500; 42.3 percent earned below $1,000 a year. Given these basic facts, Secretary of the Interior Harold L. Ickes could claim that "by confining the work of the Emergency Housing Corporation . . . to the clearance of slums and the production of a like number of low cost units, limited as to rentals and restricted as to occupancy to the low income groups, the Administration can stimulate one of the basic industries without encroaching upon its field of future opportunity." When the anticipated recovery finally arrived, Ickes noted, the existing vacancies would quickly disappear and there would be a renewed demand for homes in both urban and suburban markets. Until such time, and in cases where local agencies were unable or unwilling to act, the PWA would take the initiative "in the interest of unemployment relief and recovery." Robert D. Kohn, director of the Housing Division of the PWA, stated that although the division was an emergency organization, there was nothing temporary about its program. Its aim was not just recovery but the "prevention of such conditions in the future." The PWA, according to Kohn, was not in competition with the private sector because, in the first place, they worked with local contractors, suppliers, and architects, and, in the second place, because "nobody is doing the job of providing adequate housing at rents the majority of the population can pay."[21]

The Housing Division offered up to 85 percent of the necessary funds to either limited-dividend corporations, such as the company that built Sunnyside Gardens, or municipal housing authorities. Cities and states were unable to form housing authorities immediately, however, and many of the proposals by limited-dividend corporations were impractical in that the projected rents were too high or else lacked provisions for substantial slum clearance. Like other states, New York lacked the legal apparatus to accept funds for public construction of low-income housing. Consequently, the first proposals came from limited-dividend corporations.

Several applications were in the works when Governor Herbert H. Lehman proposed legislation to create the New York City Housing Authority (NYCHA), legislation that passed during the 1934 session. Not surprisingly, the Queens Chamber of Commerce opposed this measure, as they opposed the local, state, or national governments "going into the housing business at all." Objections to Lehman's action focused on the prospect of New York City being put "perpetually in the housing business," as there was no provision for the liquidation of NYCHA "after the alleged emergency." The only exception they would admit was for an actual slum clearance program, "the replacement of dilapidated dwellings with up-to-date structures with limited rents" in the "exact areas" for low-income tenants.[22] In other words, the chamber would only support a program that did not compete with private developers and that kept slumdwellers in their existing neighborhoods and did not spread blight to other parts of the city, particularly Queens.

By the same token, the chamber found proposals to aid private real estate interests to be ideologically, politically, and economically acceptable, and companies in Queens aggressively applied for federal funds under those conditions. Within six months of FDR's inauguration, prominent architects and realtors formed limited-dividend corporations and applied for nearly $10 million in federally guaranteed loans for local projects. Of the hundreds of such applications submitted to the Housing Division, Harold Ickes approved only seven, committing about $11 million for the construction of 3,065 units. Convinced that the only solution to the crisis was for the federal government to build housing directly, Ickes hoped to outwit greedy land speculators and corporate investors, and thereby prevent, or at least minimize, the siphoning off of federal dollars into private pockets.[23]

One of the seven applications accepted was Boulevard Gardens in Woodside. The Housing Division signed a $3.21 million loan agreement with the Dick-Meyer Corporation on November 11, 1933, and work was completed within two years. Designed by architect Theodore H. Engelhardt and landscape architect Charles N. Lowrie, the 11-acre complex featured 10 six-story elevator buildings, a total of 968 apartments, covering less than a quarter of the site. Engelhardt based his plans on buildings he had earlier designed for Dick-Meyer in Forest Hills. In 1936, the chamber of commerce honored Boulevard Gardens in their annual Better Building Competition.[24]

The proposal of another Queens-based limited dividend corporation, Hallett's Cove Gardens, did not gain approval, however. The PWA had already funded one such project in Queens, and in any event Ickes was not inclined to fund other limited-dividend proposals. He favored direct governmental involvement in construction rather than working through the private sector. The problem, of course, was that at the start of the New Deal, there were no such authorities in existence, and most states were slow

Aerial View of Boulevard Gardens, Woodside, Queens, circa. 1930s. (Courtesy of the Queens Borough Public Library, Archives, Chamber of Commerce of the Borough of Queens Collection.)

to pass the necessary legislation. By 1936, the PWA had built or begun only forty-nine projects containing fewer than 25,000 residential units. This was hardly an admirable record in the face of the national emergency, but legal and political constraints obviously prohibited more rapid and far-reaching actions. Only with the passage of the Wagner-Steagall Housing Act in August 1937, part of the Second New Deal, did the federal government establish an agency to facilitate slum clearance programs and the construction of low-income housing.[25]

The Queensbridge Houses

In July 1936, NYCHA submitted plans to the Housing Division of the PWA for the Queensbridge Houses, the Red Hook Houses, and the Harlem River Houses. Mayor LaGuardia wrote to Ickes that he was "keenly interested" in furthering the three projects and hoped to hear from him favorably and to meet him again "when we put the old steam shovel to digging."[26]

Queensbridge Houses rose on 48.37 largely vacant acres along the East River just north of the Queensboro Bridge. In terms of construction costs, access to public transportation, and the present use of the land, the site offered clear advantages. However advantageous from NYCHA's perspective, the selection of the Queensbridge site was popular with neither the chamber of commerce nor the borough's political leaders. Borough President Harvey feared that the project would cause industries to flee to New Jersey, although he did not explain why they should fear the presence of such an available workforce near at hand. In fact, it was the location of the site near the factory district of Long Island City that NYCHA planners saw as one of its most desirable features. Another problem was that while the mostly vacant site in the shadow of the Queensboro Bridge offered the possibility of rapid construction, its selection contradicted one of the stated goals of the program: slum clearance. Responding to a telegram sent by the editors of the *Long Island Press*, FHA administrator for New York Nathan Straus placed responsibility for the selection of the Queensbridge site on the shoulders of NYCHA chairman Alfred Rheinstein. Straus explained that the site would be "materially less expensive to acquire than any built-up slum site," and that, in any event, "slum dwellings are being demolished elsewhere in the city equal to the number of new units to be constructed at Queensbridge." He did not mention where those slum dwellings were located, nor what would become of the newly cleared properties. It was clear that federal restraints on the cost of land to be acquired for public housing meant that it had to be constructed in the outer boroughs rather than Manhattan, where the need was greatest and where dilapidated tenements were concentrated.[27]

The Board of Estimate approved the Queensbridge Housing Project on April 22, 1938. In June, the sixty-five families living in scattered dwellings on the site were served with eviction notices to clear the way for the demolition of the half dozen four-story tenements and the few small factories and garages. The experts were wrong on one count. The cost of acquisition was actually higher than the cost of the Red Hook site, a tract that was approximately the same size and actually had slum buildings on it. Red Hook cost $1.48 million, compared with $1.95 million for Queensbridge, with $1.17 million of that going into the pockets of one man, Stuart Hirschman. Hirschman owed nearly a half million dollars in back taxes, leaving him a profit of nearly $700,000. Parks Commissioner Robert Moses commented sharply, "The city goes through the extraordinary farce of condemning property for public use which is wholly, or largely, eaten up by taxes."[28] Moses saw no reason why a man should reap windfall profits for failing to pay his taxes.

Vernon Boulevard. Queensbridge Housing Project # N.Y. 5-2, exterior of first unit finished, proof size, children on swing, October 23, 1939. (X2010.7.1.16661, Museum of the City of New York.)

Ground-breaking came on September 6, 1938, two years after the application had been submitted to Washington and three years after NYCHA had selected the site. But there the delays ended. The final cost for the twenty-six Y-shaped buildings was $14 million, $2 million less than the original $16 million estimate, and with that they were able to build 600 additional units, for a total of 3,149. NYCHA received 1,200 applications a week for apartments in the Red Hook and Queensbridge Houses, and by the end of 1939 they had received 104,000 requests. The first families moved in on October 16, 1939, just thirteen months after the ground-breaking.[29] Most of the new residents came from tenements in Manhattan and Brooklyn, which led to charges that Queens was being shortchanged. That Queensbridge benefited the city as a whole was to local critics less important than its impact on Long Island City and whether Queens residents and businesses benefited.

Even after construction was underway, however, criticism of the project persisted. Defending Queensbridge before the Queens Council of Social Welfare at the chamber of commerce, Chairman Rheinstein reiterated that public housing was not in competition with the private sector, which simply could not produce housing for low-income families. He explained that the apartments would rent for $5 a room and have "more cross ventilation than the finest residences in the city," adding that if they have gone too far in that regard it was "at the insistence of Washington." Catherine Bauer, long an advocate of municipal housing along the lines of Queensbridge, was in 1938 special assistant to Nathan Straus, and no doubt pushed for high standards. In 1934 she had written, "If you start with sun and air and biological requirements, you cannot say that because this family has only half the income of that family, they should only have half as good an outlook or half as big a playground or half as much water or half a toilet." Acceptance of "minimum standards," she explained, "precludes the possibility of modifying them in deference to class or income distinctions." After Rheinstein departed, city councilman Hugh Quinn attacked the project on by then familiar grounds—the alleged threat to industry, the absence of nearby schools, inadequate transit—and suggested that "some of the funds for this and similar projects could better serve housing problems if they were diverted into other channels, such as offering relief for present home owners and the owners of small tenements who wish to renovate their properties."[30] As far as Queens was concerned, he felt the needs of the borough could best be served by concentrating efforts for relief and recovery on private homeowners and the construction of single-family homes.

Borough President Harvey opposed not only Queensbridge, but the very idea of large-scale public housing. One reason was that between the cost of the land and the inclusion of such mandated features as elevators, the city would never get a return on its investment, a statement that evidenced his inability to comprehend the purpose of public housing. Harvey instead advocated government-sponsored construction of private houses to be purchased with a small down payment by wage earners, with city workers living in substandard housing getting the first selection. "You can buy good homes in Queens for $5,000," he said, and the government should help people buy them. Another advantage was that "it would not be necessary to make them tax exempt and otherwise subsidize the project," thus giving the state a chance to get a return on its investment. On an ideological level, the borough president believed that "any subsidizing of public housing will be following the same system and the same idea they have in Russia of one class supporting another."[31] This most damning indictment of public housing addressed the un-American principle of subsidizing those unable, and by implication, unwilling to support themselves. A vocal supporter of the Triborough Bridge and other public works, Harvey thought it was inappropriate for government to subsidize individuals at the bottom of the social ladder, although helping business recover was certainly in his eyes an admirable goal.

The bottom line, of course, is what the new projects meant to the residents—WPA workers, cooks and waiters, college graduates, and families on relief. First selected among the thousands who applied to live in Queensbridge were the Umlies, a family of three living in a three-story walk-up, a railroad flat on 26th Street and Second Avenue in Manhattan. Their rent was $20 a month. At Queensbridge, they would pay $21.65 a month for four and a half rooms, gas and electricity included. An upholsterer, Mr. Umlie earned $23 a week, two dollars less than the maximum allowable income. Another newcomer, a twenty-six-year-old mother of four who had been married for ten years, said:

> Why, it's been a godsend to us! Where we lived before we had to share the bathroom with another family on the same floor. I had to bathe the children in a tub in the kitchen—in front of the stove so they could keep warm. The rooms were dark and dreary and we paid $24 a month for them. At Queensbridge we have 5 and a half rooms, all of them bright and sunny—and a bathroom all to ourselves. We pay $5.70 a week for them—and that includes gas and electricity, too. The kids sleep better and seem healthier. I don't know what it is. It must be the air, or something.[32]

Queensbridge was undeniably a success. NYCHA could also take credit for the project, for it demonstrated the viability of large-scale developments designed to house the working poor, and the practicability of the ideas of Mary Kingsbury Simkhovitch, Nathan Straus, Catherine Bauer, Frederick Ackerman, and other reformers. Mayor LaGuardia could point to Queensbridge as evidence of the effectiveness of his administration, and even the New Dealers received a measure of political satisfaction; in the 1940 election, 77 percent of the vote at Queensbridge went to FDR.[33]

The city built a second public housing project in Queens in South Jamaica specifically for Black residents, because it was a Black neighborhood. There, NYCHA actually demolished blocks of run-down homes on the site and made clear that the blocks were blighted:

> The site selected had the worst conditions in a predominantly negro district where dwellings were badly overcrowded. There was a high venereal disease rate in the area as well as a high rate of tuberculosis, infant mortality and juvenile delinquency. Some of the buildings on the site had been closed by the Board of

South Jamaica Houses, 107 Avenue and 150th Street, Looking North. August 15, 1940. (Copyright New York City Housing Authority, the LaGuardia and Wagner Archives, LaGuardia Community College/City University of New York, The New York City Housing Authority Collection.)

Health. Other dwellings were so overcrowded that the rate of deterioration had become unusually rapid. The new development, consisting of modern buildings, attractively landscaped playgrounds, day nurseries, etc., should halt the spread of blight which had set in, and turn the tendency of the neighborhood from deterioration into improvement. There were about 100 families living on the site. The new project will take care of about 456, a gain of 356 families in a section where it is most difficult for negroes to find adequate low-rent dwellings.

Work began in the late summer of 1939, and the first families moved in the following August. There had been more than five thousand applications for the apartments, but precedence went to "families with low incomes living in sub-standard buildings at the time of application." What makes the South Jamaica Houses especially significant was that it was integrated, with 312 Black families and 136 white families; NYCHA photographs show Black and white children sharing the playground. By 1943, however, the manager stated that it was impossible "to keep racial distribution of families at the percentage current."[34]

The wrangling over public housing demonstrates the difficulties New Deal programs faced on the local level. Politicians had to consider their constituents, while businessmen expressed concerns over the perceived threat to the American way of life. Ultimately, NYCHA built Queensbridge over all local objections. In a sense, it was a victory of the city over one borough. It was also a victory for those planners who favored housing on a grand scale, animated by a commitment to social engineering, over development by the private sector.

Housing was only one aspect of the public debate over the implementation of New Deal programs, particularly with regard to the relationship between the government and the private sector, and how local concerns and political pressures entered into the final decisions. Many in the Queens business community never did accept the rationale behind the New Deal, even though government contracts kept many of them in business, kept many thousands of workers on the job, and meant that money would be circulating through neighborhood shops.

11

Building the World of Tomorrow

Robert Moses and the
New Deal Landscape

Public works transformed the Queens landscape from one end to the other during the New Deal, and from the Triborough Bridge to the Rockaway Improvement, Parks Commissioner Robert Moses played a central role. His considerable achievements depended on cooperation between several governmental agencies and, above all, the political will to commit the necessary resources toward their realization. The city was fortunate to have an energetic mayor in Fiorello H. LaGuardia and a friend in the White House in FDR.

LaGuardia understood better than anyone what the New Deal meant for cities. The era of the self-sufficient, revenue-generating city was over. From the 1930s onward, America's cities would be dependent on federal funds not only for new construction projects, but increasingly for operating expenses. Even before his inauguration, LaGuardia had approved contracts to employ workers through the new Civil Works Administration. Together, the mayor and his parks commissioner were adept at using the innovative programs of the

New Deal to the city's advantage. Under their creative leadership the city received millions of dollars in aid for dozens of construction projects, large and small. At the ground-breaking ceremony for the Queens-Midtown Tunnel during a campaign swing through the city on October 2, 1936, President Roosevelt remarked, "Every now and then I would hear that your Mayor has slipped off to Washington, and each time I say to myself, 'There goes another $5,000,000 or $10,000,000.' But I was glad to help, because everything that was initiated was a useful project."[1]

In Queens alone between 1933 and 1940, federal dollars built the Triborough and Bronx-Whitestone Bridges, the Queens-Midtown Tunnel, the Belt Parkway, a new Queens Borough Hall and Court House, Boulevard Gardens and the Queensbridge and South Jamaica housing projects, schools and post offices, sewage treatment plants, LaGuardia Airport, Astoria Park and Pool, Juniper Valley Park, the Rockaway Beach Improvement, Riis Park and the Marine Parkway Bridge, and, finally, the 1939 World's Fair, "Building the World of Tomorrow." These construction projects transformed the Queens landscape, but at the same time prepared Long Island for the automobile-based suburbanization of the postwar decades.

The key to the remarkable transformation of Queens during the 1930s is how Moses linked these various projects. That he was simultaneously chairman of the Long Island State Parks Commission, New York City Parks Commissioner, chairman of the Triborough Bridge Authority (TBA), and head of New York State's Emergency Public Works Commission made such linkage not only possible, but essential. As construction of the Triborough advanced, Moses appropriated a significant part of the "Corona Dumps" not only for the parkway leading to the bridge but also for new parks and playgrounds. Astoria Pool was built in the shadow of the new span, and on Randalls Island there rose a new municipal stadium. On the Bronx side, the approaches linked up with the Westchester parkways, and an additional highway signified by a dotted line on Moses's map closely follows the route of what became the Major Deegan Expressway, which was built after the war.[2]

It is paramount to remember that Moses's achievements came in the context of the New Deal. True, he did leave his mark on Long Island during the 1920s, as the parks and parkways in Nassau and Suffolk testify, but power, the kind of arrogant power that Robert Caro describes and that distinguishes his Moses the Dreamer from Moses the Power Broker, came during the 1930s, when the federal government made an unprecedented commitment to public works in response to massive unemployment.

The Triborough Bridge

The New Deal made possible projects like the Triborough Bridge and the Queens-Midtown Tunnel (one of the few public works projects in the city with which Moses was not associated), but the ideas did not originate with him. A 38th Street Tunnel had been proposed as early as 1921, when traffic on the Queensboro Bridge was already intolerable. Plans for the Triborough Bridge were drawn up in 1927; funding was approved by the Board of Estimate in 1929, and later that year Mayor James J. Walker presided at the groundbreaking. Unable to continue financing the bridge in the face of the demands of its citizens for relief and the collapse of the bond market during the early years of the Depression, the city abandoned the project. Only the massive infusion of $44 million in federal grants and loans in September 1933, and the reorganization of the TBA in 1934 with Robert Moses as one of the new members, allowed construction to resume. Of the $44 million, only $9 million came as an outright grant from the Public Works Administration (PWA), the remaining $35 million coming in the form of loans to the TBA.[3]

It is a testament to the dire economic circumstances of the city in 1933 that the federal government itself was compelled to purchase the TBA's first bond issue, since private investors either lacked capital to invest or confidence in the venture. But once the bridge was open, the TBA would prove an attractive investment. In July 1937, the PWA sold its TBA bonds, realizing a tidy profit of $1,365,000, and when the authority issued bonds for the Bronx-Whitestone Bridge that year, private investors quickly purchased the lot.[4]

One dimension of the story of the Triborough Bridge highlighted by Robert Caro in *The Power Broker* is the question of why the Manhattan terminus of the span was set at 125th Street. Caro contends that it was the pressure from Hearst interests that dictated the location of the entrance in Harlem, and suggests that Moses, while professing to battle private interests, actually capitulated to those interests. In fact, the terminus had been set in Harlem in the earliest plans for the bridge, long before Moses joined the TBA.[5] In the brochure published for the dedication of the bridge, Moses acknowledged this problem. "Since a good deal of the early pressure came from Harlem, that is, from the neighborhood around 125th Street," he wrote, "the Manhattan arm of the original plans was always located on this street, although it is obvious that it should not have been there. It should logically have been located on Wards Island as far downtown as possible, that is, in the neighborhood of 100th Street, and the junction should have been on Wards and not on Randalls Island."[6]

The Triborough Bridge and the Hell Gate Bridge, 1937. (Courtesy of the Queens Borough Public Library, Archives, Post Card Collection.)

While it was impossible for Moses to change the plans, he did make the most of the route by including fourteen miles of approach roads in the three boroughs, thereby transforming what might have been an essentially local project into a "modern metropolitan traffic artery" designed to knit the region together. The East River Drive brought traffic uptown from the heart of Manhattan, the Grand Central Parkway extension linked the bridge with the new North Beach Airport and the Long Island Parkway System, and in the Bronx provision was made for a connection with the Westchester parkways. The Triborough Bridge not only joined Manhattan, the Bronx, and Queens, but the network of approach roads stretched from the East River Drive to the Kew Gardens Interchange, where the Interboro Parkway, Grand Central Parkway, Queens Boulevard, and Union Turnpike meet in a complex interchange dubbed the Pretzel. Moses lured the distinguished engineer O. H. Ammann from the Port of New York Authority, and Ammann redesigned the bridge, rejecting existing plans for a two-level span with sixteen narrow lanes in favor of a single deck with eight wide lanes. In the process, the costly granite intended to cover the towers was eliminated, thus saving millions of dollars and enhancing the functional beauty of the steel span.[7]

True, Moses's part in the closing of the 92nd St.-Astoria ferry and the removal of "old hospitals for the feeble-minded" from Randalls Island exemplifies his penchant for disregarding legal, bureaucratic, or ethical hurdles in his drive to get things done, and in that sense Caro's criticism of Moses is justified. Even so, the resulting project was extraordinary.[8] The bridge opened in July 1936, as did the Astoria pool, just in time to host the Olympic swimming and diving trials. (Moses insisted that the venue again host the Olympic trials in 1964 in conjunction with the second World's Fair, of which he was chairman.) The Triborough Bridge was the first great public works project completed under the New Deal, and the first of Moses's transportation projects in the city. His insistence that landscaping, parks and playgrounds, and public access be essential components here set the pattern for his later projects across the city.

Moses actually increased his power during the New Deal despite President Roosevelt's personal animosity toward him. In 1934, FDR, acting through Secretary of the Interior Harold Ickes, threatened to hold up funds for the Triborough Bridge unless LaGuardia removed Moses from the TBA. When the story became public through a well-timed Moses leak, sympathy shifted to his side. In January 1935, the Queens Chamber of Commerce sent a letter to Ickes demanding that Moses remain on the TBA and that he keep his position as parks commissioner as well. After expending considerable political capital, the White House backed down, and Moses retained his power. The affair did not end there, however. Moses omitted the interior secretary from the list of honored guests and speakers at the opening ceremonies of the Triborough Bridge.[9]

The Rockaway Improvement

Jones Beach was probably the most successful and widely admired Moses project, and the expansion of public works during the New Deal gave him an opportunity to repeat that success at Coney Island, Orchard Beach in the Bronx, Staten Island's South Beach, and on the Rockaway Peninsula. At Rockaway, his goal was to eliminate the private interests that had crowded the beach with concession stands, hotels, and bungalows and return to the public a clean and uncluttered beach. According to Moses, "The Rockaway Improvement may not be a model to be followed in the development of unspoiled beaches. I believe, however, that it will be a guide to those who seek to reclaim beaches which man has spoiled, and to restore them at least measurably for the purposes to which they were intended by nature."[10]

The Rockaway Improvement featured a rebuilt boardwalk and new recreational spaces, all following the model of Jones Beach. Financing was linked to reconstruction of the Cross Bay Boulevard and construction of the new Marine Parkway Bridge (now the Gil Hodges Bridge) to Riis Park. The new Marine Parkway Authority, organized and controlled by its only member, Robert Moses, issued bonds to finance the projects. The master plan called for connecting Rockaway with the Belt Parkway, then under construction, and the future use of Jamaica Bay for recreational pursuits. At a time when plans for a deepwater port in Jamaica Bay were still seriously proposed in some circles, and when the proposed port had not yet been eliminated from the official city maps, Robert Moses envisioned a Jamaica Bay preserved "in its natural state for recreational and residential purposes."[11]

In 1938, the sanitation commissioner floated a plan to establish an ash dump and massive incinerator in the middle of Jamaica Bay. The refuse and material dredged from the bottom to create the channels would provide fill for two great islands in the center of the bay. With the closing of the Corona Dumps and the redevelopment of Flushing Meadows for the World's Fair, the city did in truth need a new site for its garbage, but Moses was vehemently opposed to spoiling the bay. In July, his Department of Parks issued *The Future of Jamaica Bay*, a booklet that laid out his civic values—public access to recreational facilities built to the highest standard, a clean environment, and removal of private interests. This was a vision of what the metropolis could, and in his eyes, should do.[12]

Moses called on the city to finally decide between the two seemingly irreconcilable visions of the bay. The choice was an industrial port (an idea that in fact had been dead since the mid-1920s when the Port Authority decided to concentrate shipping facilities in Newark Bay) or, in Moses's words, "a place within the limits of the city where the strain of our city life can be relieved, where the nerves of tired workers may be soothed, where the old may rest and the young can play." This was classic Moses rhetoric, espousing his own version of civic virtue. His reasoned—"What we need in this context is a little common sense"—and emotional appeal concluded, "Jamaica Bay faces today the blight of bad planning, polluted water, and garbage dumping. Are we to have here another waterfront slum, depriving millions of future inhabitants of Brooklyn and Queens of the advantages of boating, fishing, and swimming in safe inland waters? Must we continue the construction of expensive, artificial swimming pools in this region, where the waters of Jamaica Bay, protected from pollution, can meet the problem as nature intended it to be met?"[13] Moses was a master at setting up a straw man—"blight of bad

Jacob Riis Park. 1937. (Image Source Attributed to NYC Parks' Archived Collection. Neither the City of New York nor NYC Parks has endorsed, sponsored or are in any manner connected with Licensee's Published Materials.)

Jacob Riis Park. 1937. (Image Source Attributed to NYC Parks' Archived Collection. Neither the City of New York nor NYC Parks has endorsed, sponsored or are in any manner connected with Licensee's Published Materials.)

planning," "expensive, artificial"—to advance his own proposals, and of course, he was responsible for building those "artificial swimming pools."

Neither the Rockaway Improvement nor *The Future of Jamaica Bay* was an independent undertaking. Redevelopment of Riis Park, the new Marine Parkway Bridge, the widening of Cross Bay Boulevard, the Belt Parkway, and Canarsie Beach Park were initiated simultaneously and intended to fit together within a transformed leisure landscape, bridges and highways feeding into new recreational facilities. In retrospect, Moses deserves credit for saving Jamaica Bay from the blight of garbage dumps and industrial development, and today it is part of the Gateway National Park and a thriving wildlife refuge. With construction of new sewage treatment plants, the water is not nearly as polluted as it was in the 1930s. Portions of his vision have been realized, and the bay has been reserved for recreational uses. Nonetheless, from the 1940s into the 1960s a large garbage dump was active along the shore of Jamaica Bay near the Brooklyn-Queens border. Moses may have successfully opposed the construction of an immense ash dump and incinerator in the heart of the bay, but he did not, or could not, prevent the garbage piles adjacent to the parkway from compromising his vision.[14]

Flushing Meadows and the World of Tomorrow

Another set of projects focused on the World's Fair. As far as Moses was concerned, the primary virtue of the "World of Tomorrow" was the reclamation of the dumps and their transformation after the Fair into a great park. The Fair would also justify the construction of new roadways. How else would people get to the Fair?

A key piece of his plan was the Bronx-Whitestone Bridge. The span required only twenty-three months between ground-breaking and opening, just in time to speed visitors to the Fair. It was acknowledged as the most graceful suspension bridge ever built, at least until design flaws later forced the installation of steel stabilizers that eliminated the pedestrian walkways. The Cross Island Parkway, part of the Circumferential Parkway, connected the bridge to Northern State and Southern State Parkways. Since the Cross Island was for passenger cars only, Francis Lewis Boulevard, a new mixed-use artery, was built from the Whitestone Bridge through Cunningham Park, which was also slated for improvement.[15] The new municipal airport at North Beach, renamed LaGuardia Airport, also opened in 1939.

While these large public projects served to create jobs for many unemployed, they also significantly thrust Queens into the automobile age. Highways and bridges were planned as vital links in a modern, metropolitan system, rather than essentially local efforts addressing local traffic problems. The Regional Plan Association may have envisioned such arterials in the 1920s, but only the energy, commitment, and political will of Robert Moses, supported by generous federal funding, made their realization possible.

The New Deal construction projects marked the culmination of a historical process that transformed Queens from the rural landscape of the nineteenth century into a twentieth-century cityscape. From decades of prosperity as an agricultural hinterland, through the suburban passage forged by railroad lines, the development of Queens reached a momentary pause at the end of the Great Depression. The 1939 World's Fair celebrated the triumphs of the modern metropolis, but the most popular exhibits at the World of Tomorrow pointed toward the suburban future that would be realized in the postwar decades.

The 1939 New York World's Fair, "Building the World of Tomorrow," was a fitting climax to a decade that began with the American economy in collapse, the political system severely challenged by anti-democratic and authoritarian voices, and the citizenry expressing profound doubts and fears regarding the nation's future. The New Deal put many thousands of men and women back to work and restored faith in the republic's ability to endure and prosper. To be sure, the Public Works Administration (PWA), Works Progress Administration (WPA), Civilian Conservation Corps (CCC), Agricultural Adjustment Administration (AAA), and other alphabet agencies could not induce a return to prosperity, but they did stabilize the economy and instill a measure of confidence. Nothing demonstrated the achievements of the federal government and the capacities of the corporate sector better than the optimistic vision of the World's Fair.

In 1900, Flushing Meadows appeared much as it had two hundred years before—an expansive tidal marsh of salt hay, home to waterfowl, fish, shellfish, and fox, muskrats, and other wildlife. To the city, however, such wetlands were primarily useful as sites for dumping garbage. With the Rikers Island landfill approaching capacity (the island more than doubled in size), the city looked to Flushing Meadows.

In the first decade of the twentieth century, Michael Degnon conceived of dredging Flushing Bay to create a deepwater port and transforming Flushing Meadows into an industrial park. He already had impressive engineering credentials, having been the contractor for the Williamsburg Bridge and the Cape Cod Canal. He completed the Steinway Tunnel under the East River and used the rubble to fill in the marshes around Dutch Kills, creating Degnon Terminal, an industrial park with facilities for barges and railroad sidings. Turning toward Flushing Meadows, he set up the Borough Development Company and the Flushing Bay Improvement Company as subsidiaries of his Degnon Realty and Terminal Improvement Company. The Borough Development Company won a five-year contract with the city for the removal of ashes and street sweepings (manure) from Brooklyn, intending to use the refuse as fill to build up the meadows for his industrial park. The city not only received payment but was spared the expense of disposal. The Brooklyn Rapid Transit Company inserted itself into the deal, setting up its own subsidiary, the Brooklyn Ash Removal Company, to funnel refuse along their trolley lines overnight, and devising special trolley dump cars for the job. In 1910, John A. "Fishhooks" McCarthy, a well-connected Tammany man, obtained a franchise from the Board of Aldermen, the infamous "Forty Thieves," for the Brooklyn Ash Removal Company to fill the wetlands with urban refuse. According to Grover Whalen, president of the World's Fair Corporation, McCarthy's colorful "sobriquet came from his well-known inability to get his hands out of his pockets when the time came to pick up a tab." Dumping began in the winter of 1910, with as many as five garbage scows a day depositing their noxious cargo. It did not take long for neighbors to complain about the "nauseating stench of rotting garbage decomposing in the summer heat," for all matter of refuse was dumped with the clean ashes and manure, and to complain of rats "big enough to wear saddles." Over the next quarter century, McCarthy's company dumped 50 million cubic yards of garbage, as more than a hundred railroad cars a day unloaded ashes and rubbish. One pile rose over a hundred feet and became known as Mount Corona.[16]

Degnon's plans received a boost in 1913 when Governor William Sulzer signed a bill sponsored by Assemblyman Alfred J. Kennedy of Flushing "granting certain lands under the waters of Flushing Bay and Flushing Creek and vicinity, to the end that the city may cooperate with the Federal Government in straightening Flushing Creek for the advancement of commercial interests." The legislature then voted to fund an engineering survey for canals that would cut through the borough, linking Newtown Creek and Flushing Creek with Jamaica Bay, and further appropriated an additional $259,000 for the dredging of Flushing Creek.[17] Such massive transformation of the landscape to facilitate commercial interests, even to the extent of cutting canals clear across the island, was far from extraordinary. With the Panama Canal nearing completion, it seemed that any engineering feat that could be imagined could be realized. As Degnon maneuvered to create a port in Flushing Bay, other interests advanced proposals to develop the deepwater port in Jamaica Bay.[18]

The dredging pumped silt and mud from the bay bottom directly onto Degnon's property, and within a year the surface rose as high as fourteen feet above the original wetlands. By 1917, as much as 10 million cubic yards of fill had been deposited on the site, and nearly two miles of new bulkheads were under construction. The port and barge terminal, if not the canals, seemed well on the way to realization when World War I brought activity to a halt. Degnon ultimately defaulted on his obligations, and the property was sold at auction in October 1924; he died within months.[19]

In *The Great Gatsby*, F. Scott Fitzgerald described the Corona Dumps in such an evocative way that the place became an iconic American landscape:

> This is a valley of ashes, a fantastic farm where ashes grow like wheat into ridges and hills and grotesque gardens; where ashes take the forms of houses and chimneys and rising smoke and, finally, with a transcendent effort, of men who move dimly and already crumbling through the powdery air. Occasionally a line of gray cars crawls along an invisible track, gives out a ghastly creak, and comes to rest, and immediately the ash-gray men swarm up with leaden spades and stir up an impenetrable cloud, which screens their obscure operations from your sight.[20]

Pristine Flushing Creek had deteriorated into a "small foul river." In his autobiography, Grover Whalen described the site as "half tidal silt and half refuse, crisscrossed by streams of ooze. Nothing grew there. Beyond and above all the smell, which was evil enough, there were mosquitoes of a size you couldn't believe existed. Slime lay heavy on Flushing Bay. Swamps bordered the parkway (where LaGuardia Airport is now), and parts of the parkway itself were sometimes under water." Even so, wildlife persisted in what was left of the wetlands; as late as 1937, locals trapped foxes, but when construction of the Fair began, "rat refugees" invaded the neighborhoods around the dumps.[21]

But the Corona Dumps was more than a literary symbol. The filling operations were a genuine impediment to the growth of Queens during the interwar years as property values lagged in adjacent neighborhoods. In 1929, the Board of Estimate approved a 325-acre Flushing River Park, which would include a golf course, tennis courts, ball fields, and other facilities, acquiring the site from the Brooklyn Ash Removal Company by condemnation.[22] This was precisely the kind of small, and by implication corrupt, thinking that Robert Moses abhorred. He was even then completing the Grand Central Parkway, which cut through the dump, and envisioned in that valley of ashes a great public park, built on a scale to rival Central Park. At first, however, he could find no way to fund his vision. The answer, of course, was the World's Fair.

Selection of Flushing Meadows as the site for the Fair promised another great public works project for Queens. While the World's Fair Corporation was a private entity financed through the sale of bonds to be redeemed with receipts from the Fair, the roads, bridges, sewers, water mains, and other improvements were paid for by federal dollars and would remain long after the Fair closed. By condemning the dump, the city obtained a site for a new park, and for Parks Commissioner Robert Moses that possibility was the primary reason for the exposition.

Assessing recreational facilities in the 1920s, the Regional Plan Association noted, "The greatest lost opportunity in the city was the failure to provide Queens with a central park, corresponding to Central and Prospect Parks, before the building of the Queensboro Bridge." There had in fact been such a proposal in 1899 when the Topographical Bureau prepared the borough's street map; it called for a number of Olmstedian parks connected by tree-lined parkways. Such features were unfortunately omitted from the final approved map. When George McAneny, president of the Regional Plan Association and former Manhattan borough president, suggested a fair for Flushing Meadows, Moses "thumped the desk, and said, 'By God, that is a great idea!'" The parks commissioner had long had his eye on the site, and eagerly embraced plans for the Fair: "The Flushing meadow was almost the exact geographical and population center of the city. The opportunity to restore 1200 acres of land and an immense bay in the very heart of the metropolis was something to strike the imagination." He in fact hoped to create a string of parks eastward to the Nassau line, a vision more or less realized in the 1950s.[23]

The Suburban Future

The World of Tomorrow pointed the way toward postwar development patterns, but many of the themes and exhibits presented a profoundly anti-urban message and trumpeted a suburban future. "Democracity," the signature exhibit in the Trylon and Perisphere, which Moses called "two enormous gadgets"; Ford's "Road of Tomorrow"; General Motors's "Futurama"; and the "Town of Tomorrow," a cul-de-sac lined with single-family suburban houses featuring the latest furnishings and appliances each embodied the assumption that future of the American dream lay beyond the decaying cities of the present.

Grover Whalen was rather proud of the description of the Fair's statement of purpose included in the brochure distributed to visitors—"and not just because I wrote it myself." The Fair displayed the triumphs of the past beside hopeful visions of the future:

> By showing how the present has evolved out of the past—by giving a clear and orderly interpretation of our own age, the Fair will project the average man into the World of Tomorrow. By setting forth what has been beside what is, the Fair of 1939 will predict, may even dictate, the shape of things to come. For it will exhibit the most promising developments of ideas, products, services and social factors of the present day in such a fashion that the visitor may, in the midst of a rich and colorful festival, gain a vision of what he might attain for his community by intelligent, cooperative planning toward the better life of the future; and it will emphasize the vital interdependence of communities, peoples and nations.

The guidebook repeated Whalen's theme and boasted that this would be "everyman's fair," showing to "the plain American citizen" a vision of the possible. The message was clear: "Here are the materials, ideas, and forces at work in our world. Here are the best tools that are available to you; they are the tools with which you and your fellow men can build the World of Tomorrow. You are the builders; we have done our best to persuade you that these tools will result in a better World of Tomorrow; yours is the choice."[24] It was as if the country was awakening from a bad dream, and at "The Dawn of a New Day" (the title of the Fair's official song), citizens could finally get to work and start rebuilding along rational and humanistic lines.

The Trylon and Perisphere was certainly an inspiring symbol, but the exhibit within had an extraordinarily noble and preachy tone. Filling a space twice as large as Radio City Music Hall, Democracity was an enormous diorama presenting "a world fit for freemen to enjoy. Thirty or forty miles from where you are living today—about half an hour by the new safe-speed boulevard—lies the City of Tomorrow." Designer Henry Dreyfuss described his creation as "a center built in greenery, with a perfect traffic system—and surrounding it, separated by a green belt, are industrial and residential towns—and all these towns, with the business and social section at the center, together constitute Democracity." With an area of eleven thousand square miles and a million and a half people, Democracity combined the qualities of a Greek polis with an English garden city. Equally important, however, is what Democracity was not. It was not a reconstruction of an existing city, and in fact turned its back on contemporary problems by embracing a new urban frontier. This was not a vision of urban renewal, but an ideal that ignored history. Coming out of the Depression decade, many of those who paid their 25 cents admission undoubtedly found such a utopian vision appealing.

Instead of being concentrated in the congested urban core, citizens of Democracity lived in "Millvilles," industrial towns with a population of about 25,000 each, or the dozens of suburban villages of about 10,000 people. The narration intoned, "You live in a house of your own, in a town nearby, a town so agreeable that you call it Pleasantville. You'll wake in a cheerful room, on a garden in utter quiet and the air you breathe will be clean air. After breakfast you'll walk over to the school with the children. Not to protect them from accidents. They can't get run over. There isn't a single street they cross on which any motor traffic rides." This vision was a direct descendant of the English garden cities movement of the turn of the century. The City Housing Corporation, the limited-dividend company that built Sunnyside Gardens, actually constructed such a place in the late 1920s in northern New Jersey, a planned suburb they called Radburn.[25]

At the core of this "City of Tomorrow" was "Centerton," the commercial, social, cultural, and educational heart of Democracity. Here one found the university, the large department stores, and corporate headquarters. Connected to the Pleasantvilles, Millvilles, and farms by "safe-speed boulevards," Centerton was described as "a useful place," although "few live here." The one skyscraper, "a full twenty stories high," held government offices; the rest of Centerton consisted of office blocks, each one "on a park and on a parking lot as well." They lined both sides of the expressways, a model landscape for an automotive future. The Van Wyck Expressway, a Robert Moses highway built in the late 1940s, and Chicago's Dan Ryan Expressway, are nightmarish realizations of Democracity's "safe-speed boulevards."[26] The rise of sterile office parks and corporate headquarters in the suburbs seems to affirm this prediction.

Grover Whalen was thrilled with the inspiring display. In his 1955 autobiography, modestly titled *Mr. New York*, he wrote that it "foretold the decentralization taking place today. Nobody lived in the city proper but people were housed in an outer rim of garden suburbs, served by shopping centers; factories were in satellite towns or in the country. Belts of green encircled towns and city." But the stuffy tone of Democracity brought out an irreverent response in at least one man. Whalen related an incident on the closing night of the Fair's first season:

> After a nostalgic tour of the grounds, some of my staff and I hurried for one last visit to the Theme Center. Ahead of me, on the moving staircase, was a man whose spirits were high, or should I say strong? We emerged upon the balcony just as the lights came up brightly at the conclusion of a show. This gentleman pulled a bottle from his pocket, leaned across the railing, and prepared to hurl it into the center of Democracity. There was no time to remonstrate. I put my arms around him and held him in a firm embrace. "Good old Grover," he mumbled, returning my embrace, and very quietly and sentimentally, we departed.[27]

In the Education and Science pavilion, another of the fair's focal buildings, visitors could take in *The City*, a film produced by Clarence Stein and the American Institute of Planners. With text by Lewis Mumford and music by Aaron Copland, the forty-four-minute documentary began with contrived images of an idyllic, rural past. It moved on to the dangerous, dirty, overcrowded, and alienating cities of the present. Like the narration for Democracity, Mumford's text asked whether the city of the present was the best we could do. Moving on to images of Radburn, Chatham Village in Pittsburgh, and Greenbelt, Maryland, *The City* showed that Pleasantville was already here and was not merely a utopian fantasy. This film, too, turned away from the troubled city toward new towns, ending with, "Both are real; both are possible. The choice is ours."[28]

By far the most popular exhibit was General Motors's Futurama, designed by Norman Bel Geddes. A paean to America's automotive destiny, it projected "a basic theme of highway progress and possible trends in motor transportation facilities of the future." It showed the public that "by multiplying the usefulness of the motor car, the industry's contributions toward prosperity and a better standard of living for all are tremendously enhanced." Futurama offered a landscape rationally arranged around superhighways. "See how beautiful landscaping and architectural features conform to the modern engineering of the highways," intoned the narrator. Cities, too, were replanned "around a highly developed modern traffic system; the rights of way of these express city thoroughfares have been rerouted as to displace outmoded

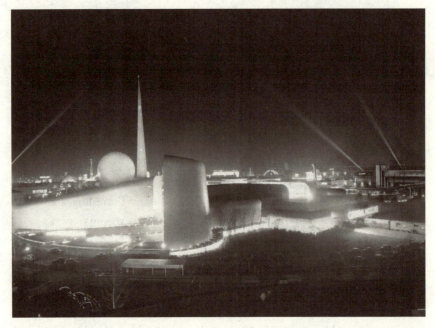

General Motors—Building—Aerial View at Night with Trylon and Perisphere in Background, 1935–1945. (The New York Public Library Digital Collections, Manuscripts and Archives Division, New York World's Fair 1939–1940 Records.)

business sections and undesirable slum areas." Like Futurama, Ford's Road of Tomorrow applied planning principles well known to highway engineers. The exhibit also highlighted "Village Industries" that resembled the "small Ford plants within fifty miles of the great Rouge plant at Dearborn [the] result of Henry Ford's desire to decentralize industry wherever possible, and bring about a closer union between farm and factory." These village industries were nothing less than Democracity's Millvilles, located far from the city's corrupting influences and its sometimes militant laboring classes.[29]

From this perspective, the city was obsolete, an obstacle to a more desirable, and, in the view of these visionaries, realizable, human environment. To realize this vision, people may have to be moved, their homes and neighborhoods bulldozed to clear the way, and their urban culture discarded. Indeed, this was the mandate of the postwar urban renewal programs. The city's lifeblood, mass transit, was also consigned to the junkheap, a relic of a discredited era. Futurama did have a provision for express buses to bring the residents of Pleasantville to work in Centerton, but in the city itself, no mass transit was visible. The private automobile was supreme.

Ford—Building—Aerial View, 1935–1945. (The New York Public Library Digital Collections, Manuscripts and Archives Division, New York World's Fair 1939–1940 Records.)

The Town of Tomorrow also glorified a suburban future. Unlike the utopian dioramas, however, this five-acre site featured new single-family homes. When Grover Whalen announced plans for the exhibit in 1938, the *New York Times* reported, "The homes will picture how modern materials and modern architecture can combine to create a dwelling of the greatest beauty and utility," with demonstration homes priced for different classes. The interiors were decorated with contemporary furnishings provided by major manufacturers, among them the American Gas Association, General Electric, and Johns-Manville, which installed a home featuring asbestos insulation, shingles, floors, roofing, siding, walls, ceiling tiles, and bathroom tiles. According to Whalen, the Town of Tomorrow was intended to be "the most extensive and practical home show ever developed [and] serve as a model for a far-reaching community for many years to come." *New York Panorama*, the work of the Federal Writers' Project, noted that the Town of Tomorrow would "show the average man how he may live under 'the nearly perfect flowing of Democracy' in the American small town of the future."

Town of Tomorrow—View of Three Houses, 1935–1945. (The New York Public Library Digital Collections, Manuscripts and Archives Division, New York World's Fair 1939–1940 Records.)

The twenty-one homes ranged in price from $3,500 to $35,000. As desirable as a suburban home might be, almost three-fourths of American families would still find it priced beyond their reach, despite the exhibitors' goal of showing a practical solution to the problem of how the average family "of moderate income can secure more house for its money right now." One critic called the Town of Tomorrow a "breach of faith," considering that the homes were far beyond what most Americans could afford, despite inclusion of "the small home of wood," a model touted as a "Dollar-a-day Home."[30]

When the Fair closed after its second unprofitable season on October 27, 1940, Queens did indeed receive its park, but the nation's entry into the war delayed construction for almost a decade. Moses had hoped that revenues from the Fair would pay for his park, but attendance had never approached the level that would have ensured a profit. Thus, there were no funds available for constructing the park, or even, it turned out, to remove the rubble after the buildings were demolished.[31]

The New Deal landscape found its most complete expression in the Borough of Queens, from neighborhood health care facilities to new parks and playgrounds, from insuring mortgages to public housing built on schedule and under budget. The new housing was first of all intended to put the building trades back to work, but also brought fundamental reforms aimed at eliminating the slums and improving the lives of their unfortunate inhabitants.

The World's Fair marked the culmination of decades of transformation, but it was also the end of a half century of change. The urban infrastructure was in place when prosperity returned after the war. Patterns of growth after 1945 would be markedly different from the built environment of the first half of the century, however. Democracity, Futurama, the Town of Tomorrow, and *The City* presented idyllic visions of the country's sprawling suburban future. They all suggested that urbanization, one of the strongest and most pervasive forces in American history, could be turned aside. The goal was the recreation of a democratic society of small towns and general prosperity distant from and transcending the corrupting influence of the older cities. The question of how the nation would pay for the superhighways, greenbelt suburbs, and new cities was never discussed, but that they were desirable was not questioned.

12

Prosperity and Stability in Postwar Queens

Domestic construction resumed with enthusiasm after World War II, and the vision presented at the World's Fair was precisely the fate awaiting America's older cities—urban renewal, expressways, suburban sprawl, and disinvestment. Robert Moses resumed his transformation of Queens, overseeing construction of the Long Island, Van Wyck, Whitestone, and Clearview Expressways. Built to ease congestion on the often-jammed Whitestone Bridge, the Throgs Neck Bridge opened in 1961. His proposed Sound crossing was never built, however. The Rye-Oyster Bay Bridge would have completed the Moses version of Futurama, but opposition by affluent residents of suburban communities in Westchester and on the island's north shore, a barrage of critical editorials, and the well-timed intervention of Governor Nelson Rockefeller ended such plans.[1]

After the war, millions of Americans moved to the suburbs. Many financed their new homes through the G.I. Bill and drove out there on new highways built with federal dollars. On Long Island, these new suburbanites arrived on the parkways built decades earlier by Moses. Intended then to speed city dwellers to clean, well-appointed recreational grounds like Jones Beach, the parkways now carried them to new single-family homes in the burgeoning suburbs. Just as Queens had been the fastest-growing county in the 1920s,

Table 19
Population of Queens and Nassau Counties, 1910–2020

Date	Queens	Nassau
1910	284,041	83,930
1920	469,042	126,120
Change	185,001	42,190
% change	65.1	50.3
1930	1,079,129	303,053
Change	610,087	176,933
% change	130.1	140.3
1940	1,297,734	406,748
Change	218,605	103,695
% change	20.3	34.2
1950	1,550,849	672,765
Change	253,115	266,017
% change	19.5	65.4
1960	1,809,578	1,300,171
Change	258,729	627,406
% change	16.7	93.3
1970	1,986,473	1,428,080
Change	176,895	127,909
% change	9.8	9.8
1980	1,891,325	1,321,582
Change	−95,148	−106,498
% change	−4.8	−7.5
1990	1,951,598	1,287,348
Change	60,273	−34,234
% change	3.2	−2.6
2000	2,229,379	1,334,544
Change	277,781	47,196
% change	14.2	3.7
2020	2,405,464	1,395,774
Change	175,100	65,420
% change	7.9	4.2

SOURCE: U.S. Census Bureau, *Census of Population*, 1910-2020, https://www.census.gov/programs-surveys/decennial-census/decade.html, Vol. 1.

Nassau emerged as one of the most rapidly developing in the nation during the 1950s and 1960s, growing more in absolute numbers than did Queens in the twenties.

While the suburban explosion in Nassau garnered the attention, development inside the city limits was not finished. Between 1940 and 1960, the population of Queens grew by more than half a million, and during the 1960s the borough grew by another 178,000. Vast stretches of eastern Queens, located far from mass transit lines, had resisted subdivision until the 1940s. When new communities did grow, they were overwhelmingly characterized by single-family detached houses; row houses, many of them with a driveway; or garden apartment complexes. At the same time, the pace of construction could barely keep up with demand. Homes could not be built fast enough for returning veterans and their growing families.

A 1948 article in the *World-Telegram* titled "Queens Has a Street Named Utopia" described the attraction of the borough's new neighborhoods, located geographically and stylistically between the "hard city streets" and "far distant suburban retreats." These outlying sections were "neither urban nor rural," but "a new kind of suburb in the city." The article concluded that "its one-family houses reflect idyllic living." It was the dream promised at the World's Fair, "a street of pretty, one-family houses, of backyard tomato patches and front yard flower gardens, of television sets in the living room and automobiles in the garages." An article from 1963 repeated this theme: "The big lure of Queens traditionally has been the suburban quality of the borough.... It's a place where parents could buy a backyard for the kids ... a place far removed from the teeming sections of the city they were glad to leave behind."[2]

But if this was "Futurama-come-to-life," as a *New York Times* story from 1955 put it, it was far from perfectly realized, for while there were no traffic jams on the Road of Tomorrow, in Queens "cars still pile up on the graceful network of smooth highways. Desolate, undeveloped patches and even marshlands prompt skeptical second looks at a map to be sure that the metropolis is still there. But the pattern of utilitarian communities abutting on an efficient crisscross of highways is discernable in central Queens perhaps more easily than in any other section of the city." Here, too, "émigrés from Manhattan, Brooklyn and the Bronx" moved "by droves into paint-wet developments." But their dreams of a suburban idyll were compromised, for "much of the shade of the North Shore-Central section disappeared with the uprooted trees." Although the population of this section had doubled between 1930 and 1955, a growth rate of less than 15 percent was forecast for the coming decades, for little unbuilt acreage remained. In a remarkably short time, the empty topography had been almost completely transformed, in much the same way the farms of western and central Queens vanished between 1900 and 1930. In the mid-1950s, it was already evident that "much of the traffic into Queens is not so much for Queens as by way of Queens, as motorists seek swifter access to Long Island or other areas."[3]

Regardless of the suburban character, the new residents were still dependent upon the city to provide basic services. How could the city possibly build schools as fast as the new housing went up? The answer is that it could not. Between 1946 and 1949, education accounted for 24 percent of the city budget, the largest single item. Of the $120 million allocated for school construction and modernization, a third was apportioned to Queens for construction of nineteen new schools and the modernization of several others. It barely kept pace with neighborhood growth. Built for 800 pupils, P.S. 46 in Bayside enrolled 1,600 when it opened in 1951. A few years later parents from Queens packed a hearing at the Board of Education to demand new schools. A school near the new developments of Electchester and Pomonok had 745 seats for 1,100 pupils. They demanded funding for a new junior high school be included in the budget, but even then it would "merely provide full-time attendance for children who have been nine years without a full day at school or a full curriculum. It would do nothing to meet the rapidly increasing enrollments."[4]

The new citizens of Queens were often frustrated, and feelings that City Hall would never prioritize their needs festered. Even something as seemingly simple as petitioning for a stop sign or traffic light became a long, involved process. Rather than accept that the residents were making a reasonable request based on their day-to-day experience, the traffic department would send out their own engineers to evaluate the situation, with the attendant delays and red tape.[5]

By the mid-1950s, the patterns of growth and change in Queens were unmistakable. In 1955, the *New York Times* published a series of articles titled "Our Changing City" in an effort to make sense of it. The article on the First Ward, old Long Island City, noted that "changes in the last generation have been of degree rather than kind. Long Island City remains an ugly, noisy, grimy heap of small factories." There were actually hundreds more factories than there had been in 1930, and this section contained 65 percent of the borough's industry. What the *Times* dismissed as "an ugly, noisy, grimy heap" actually employed tens of thousands, and the business community saw not blight, but prosperity.[6]

Garden Apartments

During the building boom of the early decades of the century, Queens became known for innovative and influential housing. Forest Hills Gardens, Jackson

Aerial View of Glen Oaks Village Complex, April 20, 1954. (Courtesy of the Queens Borough Public Library, Archives, Long Island Daily Press Photograph Morgue Collection.)

Heights, and Sunnyside Gardens were the most noteworthy (see chapter 9). Postwar Queens also sprouted planned communities of note—Fresh Meadows, Parkway Village, Glen Oaks Village, and, later, Rochdale Village, though that development was known more for the social values it represented than its architecture. In contrast to the housing of the 1910s and 1920s, which embraced historic styles, the postwar housing might be described as stripped-down modernism. Generally austere and devoid of ornament, these new communities nonetheless possessed a style of their own, combining efficient design with solid construction.[7]

Situated between Grand Central Parkway and Union Turnpike near the interchange known as the Pretzel, Parkway Village opened in 1949 for employees of the United Nations (UN). Robert Moses was instrumental in making the forty-acre site available. He had been lobbying to have Flushing Meadows Park become the permanent home of the UN—the General Assembly had been meeting in the former New York City Building on the former fairgrounds—and offered the promise of housing as an additional enticement. But John D. Rockefeller donated a seventeen-acre site along the East River in Manhattan and the question was settled. Still, plans for Parkway Village advanced, and when completed there were 110 two- and three-story buildings

Parkway Village, Kew Gardens Hills, 2024. (Laura Heim Architect.)

that covered no more than 20 percent of the site. Betty Friedan, later the author of *The Feminine Mystique*, lived there with her husband from 1950 to 1956. "It was almost like having our own home," she recalled. "The apartments had French doors opening on to a common lawn where the children could go out and play by themselves instead of having to be taken to the park."[8]

As the employees of the UN came from all parts of the world and were all different races, this enclave apart was essential. Embarrassingly, even the representatives of foreign governments faced racial barriers to securing housing in many neighborhoods. Still, the residents built a community and gained experience in the American way of self-government. The chairman of the Parkway Village Community Association was Dr. Djakal Abdoh, the representative from Iran. He found the place inspiring. "Because we have been able to live together—citizens of at least fifty countries, all races, religions, beliefs—in a friendly atmosphere, our children are growing up with no prejudice at all," he said. "It is proof that a future can be built on the basis of equality, understanding and cooperation of all people, and it is worth fighting to keep it that way." He made those remarks during a rent protest by residents in 1952. Both diplomat Ralph Bunche, winner of the 1950 Nobel Peace Prize, and Roy Wilkins, head of the National Association for the Advancement of Colored People (NAACP), lived in Parkway Village for a time.[9]

Glen Oaks Village was another notable garden apartment complex. The 175-acre site abutted the Nassau County line and was across from one of the last working farms in the borough. The land had been farmed since 1697, and in 1975 it became the Queens County Farm Museum. Built for veterans in 1947 by the Gross-Morton Company, Glen Oaks consisted of 2,904 units in 134 two-story buildings. The complex featured groups of garages behind the homes, but the front doors opened onto generous shared green space.[10]

The challenge in new neighborhoods like Glen Oaks was a lack of municipal services. Rarely, if ever, did the city proactively build the physical and social infrastructure required by the new residents. Always the city waited until the needs became clear, and even then responded in piecemeal fashion. When she lived in Parkway Village, Betty Friedan worked as a freelance writer. In a draft of an article later published in *Parents Magazine* in 1957, she wrote that those moving into Bell Park Manor and Bell Park Terrace in eastern Queens, new developments built south of the Grand Central Parkway, "paid $1,200 down to move out here, 20 minutes beyond the end of the subway line, so their kids could play in fresh air and sunshine and green grass." What they found, however, was that there was no "Y or a library or a candy store out here at the end of Queens—just miles and miles of new little houses and raw developments as crowded with kids as theirs."[11]

It took years before public libraries were built in this part of the borough. The Queens Borough Public Library did its best to serve the public, however, repeating what it had done during the building boom of the 1920s (see chapter 9). As soon as the first residents moved into Glen Oaks, the bookmobile began making regularly scheduled stops there, and a few years later a branch opened in a rented storefront. At Fresh Meadows, a new branch library opened in rented quarters in November 1949, only a few months after the first residents moved in, and a modern library building opened in 1958. At Bellerose, however, neighbors waited decades for a full-service branch. The building was completed in 1977, but its opening was delayed nearly a year as a result of the fiscal crisis.[12]

Among these new garden apartment communities, Fresh Meadows stood out. In 1946, the New York Life Insurance Company purchased the Fresh Meadows Country Club. A. W. Tillinghast designed the acclaimed course, which hosted the U.S. Open in 1925 and 1932, and the Professional Golfers Association Championship in 1931 (the club purchased a new site in Lake Success, a few miles east in Nassau County). The architectural firm of Voorhees, Walker, Foley and Smith designed a mix of two-story row house and three-story apartment buildings in a crisp modern style, together with a pair of

Fresh Meadows, 2020. (Jeffrey Kroessler.)

thirteen-story apartment houses; in 1962, a twenty-story apartment tower was added. When completed, Fresh Meadows was home to 11,000 residents, many of them veterans. It housed only seventeen families per acre, and Lewis Mumford noted with relief that had it been built with the density of recently completed Stuyvesant Town in Manhattan, it would have had 75,000 residents. As it was, "it sets a basic pattern for the ideal reconstruction of the outer metropolitan area: a vision of harmony, order, and joy."[13]

Mumford was effusive in his praise. In a pair of Sky Line columns in the *New Yorker* in 1949, he wrote, "Fresh Meadows is not just more housing; it is a slice of the City of Tomorrow." This new community was "what the residential neighborhoods of our cities would be like if they were planned not merely with a view to creating a safe, long-term investment but also to promote the comfort, the joy, and the equability of their inhabitants." New York Life gave the "architects a chance to show how humane and attractive a modern community can be if the designer's imagination can be applied not to isolated buildings but to the interrelationship of people, trees, greens, parks, streets, and buildings, so that they become an organic unity." In sum, Fresh Meadows was "not just 'housing' but a beautiful community—complex and many-sided and serene. This is the important difference between Fresh Meadows and all ordinary housing projects."[14]

Residents clearly appreciated the place. One man thought it "the best project in Queens," with "every facility for your daily wants and still you are not in a crowded city." A housewife described it as "an ideal place to live and a perfect location for people raising families."[15]

At the time it opened, neither Mumford nor any other commentators mentioned that New York Life restricted residency to whites. Perhaps they thought it unnecessary to do so. At the time, the borough was more than 96 percent white and only 3 percent Black; citywide the Black population was about 9 percent. Even so, the company believed that a policy of racial exclusion was essential for success. In 1983, after many instances of African American applicants being turned away, the NAACP filed suit in federal court. Helmsley-Spear agreed to a consent order to offer all vacancies to "qualified Black applicants whose applications are still on file."[16]

Exclusionary racial practices were hardly limited to Fresh Meadows. In 1982, the Open Housing Center of New York filed suits in federal court in Brooklyn against three real estate brokers and nine landlords, accusing them of discriminating against Blacks seeking apartments in twenty buildings in Forest Hills, Rego Park, and Kew Gardens, predominantly Jewish neighborhoods. Admitting no guilt, the defendants agreed to offer one out of every four vacant units to Black applicants and to pay the plaintiffs $40,000, to be given to Blacks seeking homes in those neighborhoods.[17]

The 1964 World's Fair

When the World's Fair closed in 1940, Robert Moses was ready to create his great park in Queens. All of the plans for the Fair had been approved with the successor park in mind. In "From Dump to Glory," an article written for the *Saturday Evening Post*, Moses declared that the park would be "more romantic and interesting than anything of a temporary nature... For like the mirage in the desert, the Fair will be gone in 1940, and at that time Flushing Meadow park will come into its own."[18] Francis Cormier and Gilmore D. Clarke, with consulting architect Aymar Embury II, designed the new 1,260-acre Flushing Meadows Park, incorporating "informal landscaped areas, formal gardens evocative of those of Versailles, a Japanese garden, a bird sanctuary, lakes, and a wide range of facilities for public events and active recreation, including a pitch-and-put golf course, a boat basin fronting Flushing Bay, bridle paths, bicycle paths." An ice- and roller-skating rink opened in the Embury-designed New York City

Building, which had been intended to remain as a permanent structure in the park. Money for the park was to have come from the profits generated by the Fair, but, for all its glory, the Fair repaid investors only 33 cents on the dollar. The federal government, the funding stream Moses had tapped so successfully in the past, was gearing up for the war. For years to come, there would be no funds for municipal parks.[19]

In 1946, the park might have been permanently derailed. The UN had selected New York for its permanent headquarters and was seeking a suitable site for its home. The UN leased space in Lake Success and held committee meetings at the Hunter College campus in the Bronx. As noted above, the General Assembly convened in the New York City Building in Flushing Meadows, where the body ratified the International Declaration of Human Rights and approved the creation of Israel. At the ceremony marking the transfer of the New York City Building to the UN, Mayor William O'Dwyer announced that the city was offering a 350-acre section of the former fairgrounds for construction of a world capital. The site had many advantages. It possessed the necessary infrastructure like water mains and sewers; there was ready access to the Long Island Railroad and the subway; it was already cleared—no businesses or tenants would be dispossessed; and because it was already city-owned there would be no issue with removing property from the tax rolls. As an additional inducement, the city volunteered to rezone adjacent neighborhoods to maintain a low-rise, low-density context.

Of course, Robert Moses was chairman of the committee charged with locating the UN's permanent home; committee members included Nelson Rockefeller, Thomas J. Watson of IBM, Democratic Party insider James A. Farley, Grover Whalen, Winthrop W. Aldrich, another member of the Rockefeller clan, and Arthur H. Sulzberger of the *New York Times*, together with Queens Borough President James A. Burke and Bronx Borough President James Lyons. In his remarks, Burke said that accepting the world capital would be

> an honor of which the people of Queens are fully conscious . . . for which I am sure they are willing to make sacrifices. . . . In presenting you with this home at Flushing Meadows we are not simply turning over to you so many barren acres. We are giving to you the best portion of a park which was becoming of more and more value in use to our people. We are willing to deprive ourselves of the use and enjoyment of this beautiful park with its many improvements so that you may have a proper and fitting setting for the capital of the United Nations and a beautiful place in which to carry out your all important work.[20]

Moses made his case for a world capital in Flushing Meadows in the *New York Times Magazine*. That site, he declared, was preferable to either Manhattan or Westchester because it "is central, but not crowded, equally accessible to city and suburbs, protected by parks, parkways, bay and lakes and other buffers and barriers and by zoning against future undesirable developments; because it is already furnished with most of the basic utilities and because it involves no disturbances of homes or business, no condemnation, no local tax problems and no unhappy suburban controversies."[21] To bolster the case, Moses commissioned renowned architectural illustrator Hugh Ferriss to create evocative charcoal renderings of the possible world capital. The UN, however, preferred a site in Manhattan, and, again as noted above, it was ultimately the wealth of the Rockefellers that secured the organization its home, purchasing property along the East River at the eleventh hour from William Zeckendorf.[22] Moses may not have had the chance to build the world capital, but at least he could complete his park, though on a much reduced scale.

Flushing Meadows Park scarcely had time to mature when ground was broken for the second World's Fair. As with the 1939 Fair, Moses saw an opportunity to further long-planned road projects by tying them to the Fair. The Van Wyck Expressway, running from the Pretzel in Kew Gardens to the Belt Parkway, was completed in 1952; in conjunction with the Fair, Moses planned to extend it north to the Whitestone Parkway, which would become an expressway to accept commercial traffic from the Van Wyck. At the same time, the Grand Central Parkway would be widened and improved.[23]

Even more than the 1939 Fair, the 1964 Fair was intended to leave monuments behind. The site plan, essentially unchanged since 1939, would remain, as would the fountains and sculptures. Where the first Fair's symbol, the Trylon and Perisphere, was demolished; the Unisphere would remain, and over time it emerged as an apt symbol for the increasingly diverse borough. Joining the two veterans of the 1939 Fair, the New York City Building, now with the popular panorama, a scale model of the five boroughs, and the Aquacade, which became a public pool, were the Federal Building, designed by Charles Luckman, the New York State Pavilion (the "Tent of Tomorrow") by Philip Johnson and Lev Zetlin, the Singer Bowl, the Port Authority Building with its rooftop heliport, and the Hall of Science, by Harrison and Abramovitz, intended as the home of the recently chartered Museum of Science and Technology.[24]

Shea Stadium was the final piece of this landscape, and the story of how it came to be was tied to the fate of the Brooklyn Dodgers. In the mid-1950s,

Dodgers owner Walter O'Malley demanded that the city condemn a site in downtown Brooklyn for a new stadium. Moses countered with an alternative. He bragged in *Sports Illustrated* that his "Park Department can build a first-class, all-purpose sports center at Flushing Meadow in jig time if we are given a green light." He claimed that he had wanted to build such an "all-purpose municipal stadium and sports center" in conjunction with the first World's Fair, but there was no funding for such a grand project. Moses pushed hard for his multiuse stadium, touting its many advantages over the Atlantic Yards site the Dodgers owner coveted. "It is large enough," he wrote. "It can provide all required parking on the surface without garages. It is accessible by way of major arteries, some of which are about to be substantially widened and improved as part of a federal-state-city arterial program.... The temporary Long Island Railroad World's Fair station can be easily restored. No money is required for land." He claimed the stadium would cost $8 million without a roof and $10 million with (he did not favor a roof) and could be ready for opening day in 1959.[25]

A further advantage was that the site was at the geographical and population center of the city, but Moses realized that the Queens location was "a fatal defect from the point of view of some Brooklyn fanatics." Still, the major point of contention was that O'Malley, in Moses's words, "from the beginning had been rooting for a strictly Dodger stadium custom-made to his own measurements and specifications, and with little or no regard for broader recreational use.... The notion of an all-purpose municipal sports center, with baseball as an incident, if the most important incident, has never penetrated his consciousness." If public land and public funds were to be dedicated to this purpose, he contended, then it must be designed to accommodate more than a single professional baseball franchise. Moses could not resist a dig at the Dodgers owner: "From the point of view of constitutionality, Walter honestly believes that he in himself constitutes a public purpose." He labeled O'Malley's suggestion that he use public monies to condemn private land for his stadium "a scandalous procedure."[26] With no commitment for a domed stadium in downtown Brooklyn forthcoming, O'Malley made good on his threat and moved his team to Los Angeles after the 1957 season.

William Shea, an influential and politically connected attorney, then launched plans for a new Continental League to challenge Major League Baseball. In truth, this was but a lever to obtain a new National League franchise for the city, which of course is what transpired. There was never any question that the new franchise, or the team from the phantom Continental League, would play in Flushing Meadows. Moses and his Parks Department had done significant spade work for a possible home for the Dodgers, and Mayor Robert Wagner could thus assure the National League that the city would build a new municipal stadium should New York be awarded a franchise. Indeed, that guarantee was key in negotiations for an expansion team, and considerable muscle was expended to secure the necessary approval from state legislature "to build on park land, lease the structure, and issue the bonds." With power brokers behind the legislation, opposition was doomed.[27] Moses was ready with his plans for a stadium in Flushing Meadows.

The Mets took the field in 1962 and played their first two seasons in the Polo Grounds, the ballpark abandoned by the Giants when they decamped for San Francisco. Shea Stadium was completed in time for the 1964 season, coinciding with the opening of the World's Fair. As finally built, Shea was the first of the new generation of ballparks: dual-use arenas surrounded by a sea of parking rather than squeezed into the urban grid. What also was new, however, was that it marked the first time New York City provided public land for a professional sports franchise, notwithstanding the fact that the Mets paid rent to the city. Moses got his stadium, and New York got the Mets.

While the onset of the war had prevented the realization of Moses's park in the 1940s, the new Flushing Meadows-Corona Park (as it was officially renamed in 1964) was opened to the public on June 3, 1967, less than two years after the Fair closed. A new attraction was the Queens Zoo (incorporating Buckminster Fuller's geodesic dome that housed a tribute to Winston Churchill during the Fair). The Queens Botanical Garden, which grew out of an exhibit for the first Fair called Gardens on Parade, was relocated just east of the park to make way for the second Fair. Joining the Hall of Science was Theater in the Park, established in the auditorium of the New York State Pavilion, and the Queens Museum, which opened in the New York City Building in 1971. The park promised to become a cultural and recreational mecca.

The timing, however, was hardly auspicious. In 1967, the city, and the nation, still believed that nothing was out of reach, but that faith was being tested. The spirit of the Fair, with its vision of an ever-improving human condition, embodying a faith in progress only somewhat less believable than the 1939 version, still drove urban planners and social engineers. At the same time, of course, the city was facing the reality of shrinking resources and cracks in the social edifice. There were still bold plans but diminishing resources for completion and maintenance.

During the mayoralty of John V. Lindsay (1966–1974), the new park almost immediately began to suffer from neglect. The fountains stopped working, and the Fountain of the Planets became increasingly stagnant, filled with

Tent of Tomorrow, Flushing Meadows–Corona Park, 2008. (David W. Dunlap.)

garbage and weeds. The revolving restaurant atop the towers of the New York State Pavilion never reopened and the machinery was finally removed. The enormous open space under the Tent of Tomorrow was left exposed, and the detailed terrazzo map of the state literally disintegrated over the years, a process speeded up when the surface was used as a roller-skating rink. The Federal Building remained empty, and lacking both funds for maintenance and a purpose, it was demolished in 1976.[28] What explains this seeming contradiction between cultural expansion and deferred maintenance? Ironically, it was Lindsay who as a candidate for mayor in 1965 made an issue of keeping the publicly financed Federal and New York State Pavilions.

The fate of one outsized structure from the Fair clearly demonstrates this problem. The Singer Bowl had been the site of the opening ceremonies, athletic contests, and musical performances during the Fair's two-year run, but only intermittently used in following years. The Metropolitan Opera came in 1968, and rock promoter Bill Graham brought a series of concerts to the venue, but by 1969 it was abandoned to vandals and the elements. Deterioration was so swift and a sustained commitment so lacking that the city announced the stadium would be demolished. As with any decision, particularly one awaiting funding, demolition was delayed; in 1971, the Parks Department proposed a massive soccer stadium (the Cosmos had joined the fledgling North American Soccer league in late 1970), an idea not warmly received by adjacent communities. In 1972, the Singer Bowl was renamed Louis Armstrong Stadium, honoring the jazz musician who lived in Corona, and the rededication on July 4, 1973, brought together Ella Fitzgerald, Count Basie, Earl Hines, Eubie Blake, Gene Krupa, and Dizzy Gillespie. Typically, this was a one-shot event, and the stadium was abandoned again.[29] In 1974, the U.S. Open relocated from the West Side Tennis Club in Forest Hills to Flushing Meadows, and Armstrong Stadium found new life as a venue for championship tennis.

Emblematic of the city's shameful neglect of the park and an indictment of the times was the theft of eight bronze sculptures in Paul Manship's Zodiac series, ripped from its pedestal in front of the Queens Museum for the value of the metal. So low had the city's prospects fallen that when the possibility of a third World's Fair for 1989 was floated in the early 1980s, the idea sank without any public discussion. A third iteration found no champions in or out of government.[30]

Public Housing and the Challenge of Race

While the private sector rushed to build homes for the white middle class, the market did nothing for racial minorities and the poor. This was due in part to the limited profitability of such properties, but also to the prevailing attitude that housing that would welcome Blacks would not be accepted by whites, and white families were far and away the majority of those seeking homes in Queens.

Building housing for low-income New Yorkers was left to the public sector, and the confidence and commitment of the city in the decades after the war is remarkable. By 1950, twenty-eight projects containing approximately 30,000 apartments had been completed or were under construction, and eleven more with an additional 13,000 units would soon start construction. New York State Housing Commissioner Herman Stichman explained that public housing was a necessary government activity because the private sector could not clear slums or build low-income housing. James H. England, executive director of the New York City Housing Authority (NYCHA), pointed out that many of these were being funded entirely by the city, with no federal or state dollars at all.[31] Seventy-five years later, the city would be unable to even properly maintain its stock of public housing, let alone construct new units, without federal dollars.

Across southern Queens, from Richmond Hill and Ozone Park to South Jamaica and the Rockaways, the spaces were "filling up." There may have been a few small truck farms holding out, but they were surrounded by blocks of one- and two-family houses. Here, the question of race came to the fore. As white families moved east into Nassau, "newcomers from Manhattan and the Bronx" moved in, particularly in Jamaica. The South Jamaica Houses opened in 1940, built specifically for Black residents and replacing blocks of dilapidated homes. But when the City Planning Commission announced a proposal for new low-income housing in the Baisley Park-Locust Manor area, it aroused "vociferous protest from civic groups." Most of these homeowners had achieved their suburban dream within the city, but even in the 1950s they saw public housing projects as threats to their hard-earned security. More slum clearance was promised, and with it more controversy.[32]

The projects built for low-income New Yorkers were not particularly distinguished in terms of architecture. Built along the lines of the tower-in-the-park, they incorporated none of the ideas embodied at Sunnyside Gardens and the Phipps Garden Apartments or Fresh Meadows. In western Queens, the Woodside Houses, the Astoria Houses, and the Ravenswood Houses were completed between 1949 and 1951. NYCHA built the Astoria Houses on the site rejected in the late 1930s as being too far from the subway and would therefore tend to become isolated from the rest of the community. That was indeed the result. On the Rockaway Peninsula, the Arverne Houses opened in 1951, the Redfern Houses in 1953, and the Hammels Houses in 1955. The days when Rockaway was the playground of upper- and middle-class New Yorkers were long past, but it remained a popular destination for a day at the beach. Another factor was the changing complexion of public housing residents. When it opened, Queensbridge housed fifty-two Black families and 3,097 white families. In 1955, the manager of Queensbridge pointed out that "there are more Negroes and Puerto Ricans among the 10,500 tenants nowadays." To maintain the desired racial balance, many units were actually kept vacant rather than be rented to minorities.[33]

Racial integration had never been a primary aim of public housing advocates. According to historian Nicholas Dagen Bloom, "NYCHA administrators intuitively understood that should public housing only serve the minority population, public support, in a white majority city, would fade. The authority also sensed that directly challenging racial divisions in the city would prove costly from a political standpoint." In 1940, Mary Simkhovitch, head of the Public Housing Conference, justified this approach, explaining that the "overwhelming population in NYC is white. We don't want to act in such a way and do this thing in such a way that it will deter white people from going into the projects." However much integration might have been a desired end, it could not be forced. "You may say it is up to the white population to receive the colored people in equal numbers everywhere because that is justice," she said. "But you know very well we haven't arrived at that condition of social justice that we should. And though we should do certain things, and the best things we can, we don't want to kick over the whole business of housing. We have to think first of housing."[34]

The shortage of housing for returning veterans, the majority of whom were white, remained a concern for years. Accordingly, many of the proposals were pitched as serving that population. Mayor William O'Dwyer advocated a new program of public housing for middle-income families, those earning too much to qualify for an apartment in public housing and too little to afford market-rate rentals or to purchase a new home. Funded by the sale of municipal bonds, the "No Cash Subsidy" program ultimately funded construction of twenty projects, a total of 17,000 units across the five boroughs. One of those middle-income developments was Pomonok Houses, a 2,071-unit project built on the grounds of the old Pomonok County Club.[35] When opened, these projects were almost entirely white; only gradually over the following decades did the racial makeup change.

The city also encouraged the formation of limited-dividend corporations to build housing, whereby profits above 6 percent would be reinvested in housing. This was the model that built Sunnyside Gardens in the 1920s. The Brotherhood of Electrical Workers formed such a corporation to construct Electchester, a fifty-seven-acre complex built on another section of the

Pomonok golf course. The low-rise buildings contained 2,225 units, with generous open space between.³⁶

In advancing these programs, the city violated the understanding that government housing would not compete with the private sector. First, these new projects involved no slum clearance but went up on vacant sites. Second, the city was targeting families of moderate means, not the low-income population. Homeowners objected that their tax dollars were being used to build such housing. The Bowne Park Civic Association complained to Mayor O'Dwyer "that they should not be required to support public services by public taxation in order to provide low cost housing for families that are in higher income groups than themselves." This wrong would be doubled if places like Electchester were to be granted an exemption from real estate taxes, as was proposed.³⁷

While it was true that few New Yorkers lived in integrated neighborhoods, not all blithely accepted the status quo. The city had been attempting to address the issue of housing segregation since the war. Speaking at the conference of the New York State Committee on Discrimination in Housing in February 1949, Robert F. Wagner Jr., then chairman of the City Planning Commission, stated that in a time of competition on the international stage with global communism, "we cannot overlook the threat to our democratic faith arising from continued prejudice and discrimination on our shores." Restrictive practices in housing persist in the city even though they "have no legal or moral base; no economic justification," he said. "It is time we exploded the pernicious myth that non-discriminatory neighborhoods breed racial tensions; that Negro occupancy results in declining property values."³⁸

At the time of Wagner's remarks, New York City was more than 90 percent white, and Queens was more than 96 percent white. The small Black population was mostly confined to a handful of neighborhoods, or isolated pockets in white communities. Elected mayor in 1953, Wagner supported racial integration, but he also recognized that housing integration would be especially difficult to achieve. A report from the Department of City Planning in 1962 stated that "racial and ethnic considerations are an integral part of any sound planning approach in this city. A color-blind government policy carried out in a color-conscious housing market can only entrench and aggravate the segregation of racial and ethnic groups, with all its enervating and corrosive consequences."³⁹ However much they might have wanted to further racial equity in housing, policy makers were politically astute enough to acknowledge the limitations. Could they have forced the issue, and would such an approach have achieved the goal of integration? Or, was the gradualist approach not only more prudent and realistic politically, but also more likely to succeed?

As early as 1950, Lewis Mumford found much to criticize in the new NYCHA housing. He called them "dull and bleak," and thought them "planned without regard for the human scale and with so little respect for the needs of family and neighborhood life." The city, he wrote, has "treated the shortage of lower-income housing as a disease that can be cured by segregating the sufferers in an isolation ward." This deliberate policy of isolation was not isolation by race, however. "Though the Housing Authority, with admirable zeal, has abolished racial segregation," he added, "the law under which it operates has established segregation by income, a class-distinction all too plainly embodied in the Authority's great building units. Again, under the terms of the law, this housing has been separated from every other normal manifestation of neighborhood life, so although these estates are physically neighborhoods, or even small cities, they lack most of the organs and attributes of a full-fledged domestic community."[40] Whatever racial fears remained unspoken, the fact that public housing brought in people of lower economic standing was why many Queens residents resisted its introduction in their neighborhoods.

Rochdale Village was an exception. The United Housing Foundation (UHF), an organization with roots in the Jewish labor movement, built the complex on the site of the old Jamaica Racetrack, which shut down in 1959. With 5,860 units, it was the largest cooperative housing complex in the world. The name honored the Rochdale Pioneers, artisans who formed a cooperative store in the town of Rochdale in England in 1844. The twenty identical red-brick fourteen-story buildings were clustered in groups of four across a superblock. The complex had its own power plant and featured an enclosed mall designed by Victor Gruen. South Jamaica then was a predominately African American area; still, thousands of white families rushed to move into the new towers. Peter Eisenstadt's family was among the first residents. In his history of the Rochdale Village, he wrote that it "represented the marriage of two ideals; the culmination of a half-century struggle for inexpensive cooperative housing for New York City's workers, and a more recent fight for integrated housing and education."[41]

The UHF claimed that when Rochdale Village was fully occupied in 1965, 80 percent of the residents were white and 20 percent Black, though many doubted that the number of Black families was that high. Two-thirds of the white families were Jewish, many of them leaving changing neighborhoods in the Bronx and Brooklyn. Abraham Kazan, president of the UHF, boasted

Rochdale Village, Jamaica, 2024. (Laura Heim Architect.)

that "white and non-white people will be living next door to each other as neighbors. Never before in private or public or cooperative housing has there been such an opportunity to demonstrate that people can live together." The dream of integration did not hold, however, for the ideal came up against the realities of where the children would go to school. This was also when the crime rate was rising precipitously across the city, and "South Jamaica was no exception to the general rule that predominantly minority areas of the city had high rates of crime." At first, the building entrances were never locked, but that changed in 1968. Crime was "Rochdale Village's soft underbelly," and the divisive teachers' strike in 1968 put additional strains on race relations. According to Eisenstadt, "By the early 1970s whites were moving out in vast numbers, and by the late 1970s there were few white families left."[42] At the end of the decade, the population was almost 85 percent Black. But Rochdale Village was not an exception in that sense; hundreds of thousands of white families fled New York during the 1970s, the only decade when the city actually lost population.

The Battle of Forest Hills

When John V. Lindsay was elected mayor in 1965, he was determined to aggressively pursue the goal of racial equality. Like Wagner, he hoped to further integration, but his was far from the measured approach of his predecessor. In 1967, President Johnson appointed the liberal Republican vice-chairman of the National Advisory Commission on Civil Disorders, commonly known as the Kerner Commission after its chairman, Illinois governor Otto Kerner. The commission's report issued the next year emphasized the damaging impact of racial segregation, particularly in regard to housing, concluding that "federally aided low and moderate-income housing programs must be reoriented so that the major thrust is in nonghetto areas." The report asserted that racism and white flight were responsible for the increasingly intense racial strife in the city, and that conclusion certainly determined Lindsay's attitude toward the white ethnics in the outer boroughs.[43]

The Kerner Commission concluded that the solution to the social pathologies and disorder associated with minority-dominated inner-city neighborhoods was the integration of the suburbs, and if the federal government did not actively seek to build in middle-class white neighborhoods, housing programs would "continue to concentrate the most impoverished and dependent segments of the population into the central city ghettos where there is already a critical gap between the needs of the population and the public resources to deal with them. This can only continue to compound the conditions of failure and hopelessness which lead to crime, civil disorder and social disorganization."[44] Queens residents heard this and concluded that the mayor saw their stable, middle-class neighborhoods as being directly responsible for the city's racial problems, and that he proposed pushing the solution onto their backs.

The new mayor embraced the idea of scatter-site housing, the idea that low-income housing should be built on vacant land in middle-class neighborhoods, neighborhoods that were by definition almost certainly white. According to Jewel Bellush, "This was more than a housing program; it was a deliberate policy aimed at producing a community integrated along racial, as well as economic, lines." Further, it "dovetailed neatly with his plans to project himself as the city's progressive programmer and held out the additional lure of enhancing his national reputation."[45]

Before the 1960s, there was little political will nationally to address racial inequities in housing, but with Johnson's Great Society the question became not whether to remedy the situation, but how to do so. "From the standpoint of the larger society," wrote urban historian Richard C. Wade, "a policy encouraging scatter-site housing would put the burden of accommodation on all communities equally." Such a strategy "would allow low and moderate-income families to take advantage of social services normally denied them without straining these services to the breaking point. Instead of a vicious cycle of social pathologies we would have a beneficial spiral of social betterment—an antipoverty program, in effect—based on sharing and diffusing the burden of accommodation throughout society."[46] The pathologies attributed to inner-city Black neighborhoods—broken families, crime, welfare, poor education—would thus be overcome.

The Great Society was at high tide, its checkbook open. Low-income housing built along these lines would address two social problems—the urban crisis and racial exclusion. Wade saw the problem of the racial ghetto as perhaps the most intractable dimension of the urban crisis. For generations, European immigrants had settled in the urban core and gradually moved upward and outward. This was "the genius of American society," wrote Wade, allowing "millions of people from different lands, people speaking different languages and having different cultures and religions, to enter American life and ultimately join the metropolitan mainstream." This pattern was assumed to be "automatic and inevitable," but with Blacks and Puerto Ricans it proved to be different. "Instead of serving as a staging area for population dispersal, the ghetto simply moved out block by block, overtaking old white neighborhoods and spreading across most of downtown. This was something new."[47]

The youthful Lindsay team "hoped to slow down, and perhaps halt, the expansion of the city's ghettos; by enabling low-income Black and Puerto Rican families to improve their lifestyles, they hoped to end the brutalized impact of those ghettos. Less stigma would be attached, they thought, to inconspicuous public-housing projects, especially when these were located in stable white communities. Lesser numbers of low-income families might find it much easier to be accepted and assimilated in middle-class neighborhoods." The goal was ambitious, idealistic, and ultimately unrealistic. It set out to create a city they believed people ought to live in, rather than engaging the social, economic, and political character of the city as it was. "The creation of racially balanced communities within the city was a concept based on abstract notions about democracy and social justice," wrote Bellush. "Acceptable as a normative position, these notions were unsupported by the perceptive reasoning and empirical data so necessary to effective implementation." The truth of that analysis was evident in Queens. As Walter Goodman wrote in the *New York Times*, Forest Hills was where the battle was engaged between "the ideals and limitations of those who are trying to manage this poor city and the dangerously conflicting needs and emotions of those who are trying to live in it."[48]

Days after his inauguration, Lindsay received a report from his Housing and Urban Renewal Task Force, prepared by Charles Abrams in collaboration with Ed Logue, I. D. Robbins, and others. In his *Forest Hills Diary*, Mario Cuomo wrote that the report clearly suggested that "the mayor's housing policy ought to provide for racial and income diversity throughout the city. In effect it called for 'scatter-site' housing. It also cautioned that the city ought to listen attentively to the community's own ideas. It stated that whatever projects were constructed by way of an attempt at racial dispersal, the buildings should be designed so as to fit in neatly 'as part of existing neighborhoods' and should not 'massively be superimposed on them.'"[49]

Lindsay and his team rushed to embrace the first part of their recommendation and disregarded entirely the second. Historian Nicholas Dagen Bloom concluded that Lindsay "saw little to lose and everything to gain politically in standing up to the city's declining, increasingly defensive, white population. He miscalculated when he discounted the political capital at stake in openly challenging social divisions." Perhaps Lindsay and his advisors believed that the liberal Jews of Forest Hills would respond to the appeals for social justice. If so, he betrayed a willful ignorance of the fear many Jews were feeling, especially in the wake of the divisive school strike of 1968 and the clear evidence of how the experiment at Rochdale Village was unraveling. According to Clarence Taylor, "The racial tension created by the Forest Hills housing controversy exacerbated the animosity across the city that was already growing out of the teachers' strike."[50]

The response from the boroughs to the scatter-site program was immediate and clear. As one resident explained, "We don't object to this low-income project on a racial basis but only on the economic level and the type of people that inhabit these projects regardless of color." Rejecting a project proposed for Kingsbridge, Bronx councilman Bertram R. Gelfand stated, "It is neither unfair nor un-American for middle-income parents to aspire to have their children raised in a community where they come in contact with children of similar economic and cultural level."[51]

Another reason, of course, was fear of crime associated with Black youths. In an essay in the *New York Times Magazine*, Nathan Glazer, coauthor with Daniel Patrick Moynihan of *Beyond the Melting Pot*, emphasized that the Jewish residents of Forest Hills were concerned for their safety. Many had fled declining neighborhoods in Brooklyn and the Bronx, and they did not wish to face those conditions again. In Queens, "the houses were better not only because they were newer, but because there was less regular damage by drug addicts and vandals; the stores were better because the operators had fewer broken windows to repair and did not have to defend themselves against regular robbery; the schools were better because they were safer." The unfortunate conclusion many reached, that "Black equals crime," was simply wrong, wrote Glazer. Still, he noted that poor Blacks "provide a breeding ground for crime—and anyone who values his safety, white or Black, is going to try to distance himself from a tangle of pathology." Carrying the argument further, he asked, "Does not the confusion grow when liberals and Black organizations argue that the people escaping from crime are really trying to escape from the presence of Blacks?" Glazer asserts that "what seems quite unfair is that in their fight for a hard-won security, they should be labeled racists."[52] But that is the level to which the controversy descended.

More than seven hundred Queens residents descended upon a hearing of the City Planning Commission to oppose public housing proposed for Corona, Flushing, Woodside, and Lindenwood. The differences between the outer-borough homeowners and the Manhattan-centric administration were stark. William H. Booth, chairman of the Commission on Human Rights, testified that the scatter-site program was "the only hope for getting people out of the ghetto." Mrs. Theresa Bria received great applause when she said, "We improved our lot by struggle. The Negroes want everything for free. How much can we take? How much can we pay? We'd be better off on relief."[53]

The Lindsay administration backed down. A decision on the Flushing site would be postponed, and the Corona site would be repurposed for a new high school. Two years later, the proposal for scatter-site housing in Fresh Meadows and Flushing returned. The hearing was tense, and, if anything, the battle lines had hardened. Homeowner John Favicchio testified, "Most of the middle-class was not born with a silver spoon in their mouths. We sweated to get where we are—and there were no government agencies waiting in the wings to help us." George E. Foster said, "We homeowners have a right to live where we are, and we want to maintain it the way it is. Anyone—Black or white—who will pay his own way is welcome in Fresh Meadows." Robert Moore of the Urban League dismissed such arguments and insisted that the "primary reason for the opposition is bigotry—outspoken, vulgar bigotry."[54]

Aldean Moore, a Black homeowner, was president of the Flushing Suburban Civic Association. Like his neighbors, white and Black, Moore feared that a low-income project intended for occupancy by Blacks or Puerto Ricans would upset the neighborhood's racial balance and adversely impact the local schools. "Unfortunately, those who support the plan for this new housing may have the best of intentions," he said, but "they do not really know the facts about this particular neighborhood that they are hoping to integrate. Our neighborhood is already integrated." After Moore testified before the Board of Estimate, Manhattan Borough President Percy Sutton responded, "I am always disturbed when one of us who has managed to escape the ghetto turns his back on others."[55] Such a remark reinforced the certainty of the Queens homeowners that the liberal elite was intent on imposing it racial agenda on the homeowning middle class, and revealed how for many pushing these projects race was the real issue.

In a split vote, the Board of Estimate approved the projects. Several three- and seven-story buildings housing 320 families would be built at 71st Avenue and 161st Street, adjacent to Electchester (the original plan called for six 10-story buildings); garden apartments for 330 families would be built at 59th Avenue and Fresh Meadows Lane.[56]

After the Corona neighborhood successfully stopped the construction of affordable housing there with the assistance of an unknown Queens lawyer named Mario Cuomo, the city proposed that the project be located three blocks away on an eight-acre site at 108th Street and 62nd Drive in Forest Hills. A year later, the federal Department of Housing and Urban Development approved the plan, a complex of three 10-story buildings, three 12-story buildings, and one 22-story tower housing 828 low-income families; the plan evolved into three 24-story towers with 840 units. It was a far cry from the recommendation from the Housing and Urban Renewal Task Force that new housing should be designed to fit into the existing neighborhood context. The news immediately elicited angry opposition. Marvin Cohen, the Democratic district leader, remarked, "If we are branded bigots because we're fighting this [project] then reason is dead."[57] But that is indeed how the public debate transpired.

Streetwise columnist Jimmy Breslin, a proud son of Queens, observed this drama and saw through the posturing of both sides. The liberal, Manhattan-centered Lindsay administration simply assumed that the good people of Queens would quietly acquiesce and follow their lead. Breslin knew better:

> The term is "scatter-site housing." The start of the beginning of breaking up the ghettos and having the poor and the blacks desegregated. Wonderful thought! Except that this scatter-site housing was to be placed in the middle of a place in New York City, in the Borough of Queens, in the neighborhood called Forest Hills. And Queens is a place that is across the river from Manhattan and the distance is much more than that. People in Queens, when going to Manhattan, say, "I'm goin' to New York." Queens is white and it votes for Nixon and

Buckley. Bella Abzug is New York? Come over to Queens, population about two million, and see.⁵⁸

Ed Koch, then a congressman from Manhattan, was a supporter of the concept of scatter-site housing, but in one of the earliest expressions of sympathy for the anxieties of middle-class New Yorkers, he rejected the thinking behind this plan. His remarks presaged the core message of his mayoral run in 1977, with an appeal to the, if not forgotten, then ignored, residents of the outer boroughs. "A concentration of this many low-income people within a middle-class neighborhood intensifies the fears and difficulties of economic integration," he explained. "If you have worked hard all your life, as most Forest Hills residents have, to give your family a safe home and a decent education, you rightfully worry about possible deterioration of your neighborhood. And it's an understandable fear that a large infusion of poverty stricken people, many on welfare, will pose a threat to the way of life in a middle-class community." Where other voices reduced opposition to racism, Koch understood what the people were feeling. "Like all New Yorkers," he stated, "the residents of Forest Hills are alarmed about the increase in street crime and school violence. To characterize this concern as 'racism' is an outrageous charge that evades what is really going on and unnecessarily polarizes New Yorkers."⁵⁹

Koch could see what those pushing the plan could not, namely that the opponents were people of goodwill who felt that the Lindsay administration had disregarded their interests. "The waste, ineptitude, and highhandedness of the city administration has destroyed much of the good will the city needs to win acceptance of its scatter site housing program," said Koch. "One cannot expect middle-class New Yorkers to rally to the cause of the city if the city administration scorns them, ignores them or plays favorites at their expense."⁶⁰ Of course, this was also the moment when *All in the Family* debuted on CBS, featuring Carroll O'Connor as Archie Bunker, a white, working-class homeowner in Queens at odds with the changing values of the day. In a sense, Koch was speaking for all the Archie Bunkers in Queens.

Lindsay ran for re-election in 1969, and both the primary and the general brought out divisions among New Yorkers in high relief—between liberals and conservatives, between Manhattan and the outer boroughs, and between Black and white. Troubled by the prolonged and destructive teacher's strike, conservative state senator John Marchi of Staten Island challenged Lindsay for the Republican nomination. Lindsay won decisively in Manhattan but lost in each of the other boroughs. In Queens, Marchi prevailed by 40,469 to 26,658 and won the nomination. Running on the Liberal line in November, Lindsay was re-elected with 42 percent of the vote, as Marchi and Democrat Mario Procaccino split the opposition vote. In Queens, Marchi and Procaccino together garnered nearly 64 percent of the total, a clear indication of the borough's dissatisfaction with Lindsay's liberal agenda.[61]

In June 1972, Lindsay appointed Mario Cuomo to try to work out a compromise. Throughout the summer Cuomo listened to all parties in the controversy: Blacks who saw opposition as simply racism, Jews frightened of crime and neighborhood decline, and government officials from every agency involved. He came to realize that the issue could not be reduced to Black and white. It was "clear that the objection is to crime and deterioration and not color. The coincidence that most of the lower economic class are Black is what produces confusion." Still, he concluded, "There is one thing everyone seems to agree on—the severity of the ghetto problem, and that something must be done about it. Even the Forest Hills community will concede that; common sense, which they have in abundance, makes the conclusion inevitable. Their feeling is not that the problem should not be solved, but rather that this project will not help solve the problem, and will in fact make it worse by simply spreading the blight."[62]

After six tense and exhausting months, Cuomo submitted his report. Instead of three 24-story towers, there would be three 12-story buildings housing 432 low-income families. Further, the units would be cooperative apartments, a far cry from a public housing project; 63 percent of the residents were white, and only 2 percent were on welfare. The episode revealed the limits of top-down social programming and new political fault lines. As Jimmy Breslin pointed out, there was a great distance between urban liberals in Manhattan and middle-class homeowners and renters in Queens.[63]

The Accelerating Pace of Change

For its entire history, Queens grew and changed in the shadow of New York City. Its farms fed the teeming population in the city, and its suburbs welcomed an urban middle class seeking refuge. It accepted industries forced out of the urban core by rising land values and attracted droves of working-class families on weekends. When new mass transit lines connected Queens with Manhattan, the borough experienced a population explosion, and during the Depression it changed again as the site of major public works projects built to serve the needs of the entire city, while simultaneously erecting the infrastructure that would serve the automobile age.

But this chapter in the borough's history has come to a close. Over the quarter century after the war, Queens seemed remarkably stable, even as it experienced a wave of building and population growth. The ethnic neighborhoods settled into comfortable patterns of life and work. Major shopping streets, such as Main Street in Flushing, Steinway Street and Broadway in Astoria, Jamaica Avenue, and Metropolitan Avenue in Glendale and Middle Village, retained businesses for generations. Parents brought their children to the same stores where their parents had taken them. Neighborhood movie theaters continued to attract steady crowds.

By the 1970s, however, such stability appeared tenuous. The Fiscal Crisis brought a retrenchment of municipal services, and crime was rising. During that decade, every borough except Staten Island lost population; Queens saw its population decline by nearly 100,000, as the city lost more than 800,000 people. Despite the dire predictions of pundits, however, the city did not sink into irreversible decline. By 2000, New York City had gained back all the numbers it had lost and more, topping 8 million.

This was not a matter of returning to what had been, however. That city was fading away and a new one was arising, one to be built by a new generation and new immigrants.

The Retail Landscape

Jamaica Avenue remained the borough's primary shopping area, attracting consumers from Brooklyn and Nassau who annually pumped more than $300 million into Jamaica's retail shops. But by the mid-1950s, new rivals arose in the form of shopping centers, new downtowns surrounded by acres of convenient parking.

Macy's opened a branch on 165th Street in Jamaica in 1947. Architect Robert D. Kohn, who had for a time headed the Housing Division of the Public Works Administration during the New Deal, designed the two-story structure in a streamlined modern style. The most innovative feature was rooftop parking, a sign that the store intended to serve customers from the new automobile-centered suburbs. Other department stores, including Lord & Taylor, Bloomingdale's, B. Altman, and Brooklyn-based A & S, followed that pattern, opening branches in Garden City, Manhasset, and Hempstead. The stores were simply following their loyal customers to the suburbs. While investing in Jamaica, Macy's also opened a large branch at Roosevelt Field.

In 1965, Macy's opened another branch on Queens Boulevard in Elmhurst. The corporate firm of Skidmore, Owings and Merrill designed a cylindrical structure, with parking wrapping the exterior. The Jamaica store closed in 1977. That closing presaged another change in the retail landscape, the abandonment of older downtowns and the concentration of department stores in shopping malls. Bloomingdale's opened a branch in Fresh Meadows when that garden apartment community was built in the late 1940s, the company announced in May 1991 that it was closing its store there; later Bloomingdale's abandoned its home in Garden City for Roosevelt Field. At around the same time, A & S announced the closing of its Hempstead store, once the largest suburban department store in the nation, and that it, too, would be relocating to Roosevelt Field. Revenues at the Hempstead store had fallen as the Black population in the surrounding neighborhood increased, but it remained profitable to the end.[64]

13

The Most Diverse Place on the Planet

All in the Family went on the air on January 12, 1971. Produced by Norman Lear, the sitcom starred Carroll O'Connor as Archie Bunker, a white, working-class, cigar smoking, home-owning Queens guy, and Jean Stapleton as his wife, Edith, whom he often referred to as "dingbat." The house in the opening credits was at 89–70 Cooper Avenue in Glendale. *New York Times* critic Fred Ferretti decried the use of insulting ethnic slurs as "not funny" and of the show declared, "What is lacking is taste." The Paper of Record took offense that a blue-collar New Yorker would express sentiments the editorial board found distasteful, if not crude. The top-rated show ran for twelve years.

While Brooklyn certainly possessed a recognizable persona, Queens never did. Until it found its face and voice in Archie Bunker. While there were millions of working men like Archie across the country, they had rarely been presented as a believable character in film or television. The show was set in New York, the nation's most liberal and sophisticated city, but Archie lived in Queens, a place unfamiliar to most Americans and most Manhattanites, whose experience of the borough was that they drove past cemeteries to get to LaGuardia or Kennedy. Viewers could laugh at and look down on Archie for his benighted attitudes, but here, for the first time, we saw an ordinary working man negotiating the changing political, social, economic, racial, and

89–70 Cooper Avenue, Glendale, 2024. (Laura Heim Architect.)

sexual landscape in his family, in his neighborhood, in the city, and in the nation. But while we laughed at what Archie said, we never laughed at him as a person. The character was at heart always a man worthy of our sympathies. Even after the show left the air, Archie seemed to embody Queens, somehow removed from the changing city but always standing for a culture resisting those changes.

Archie Bunker is no more. In a very real sense, his Queens is no more. The world he struggled to hold on to has shrunken to near invisibility. The political context he would find unrecognizable, and the cultural forces he resisted have triumphed. The story can be told in numbers.

Reopening the Golden Door

In 1950, Queens was 96.5 percent white. The borough's residents were Protestant, Catholic, and Jewish, but almost all were white. Archie was a Protestant. When CBS first aired *All in the Family*, the borough was still 85 percent white; by the time it went off the air in the early 1980s, the borough's white population had dropped by 363,638, or 21.4 percent. In 2020, the non-Hispanic white population of the borough was 22.8 percent, a drop of 337,000, or 38 percent over the previous decade. Accounting for that demographic

Table 20
Racial and Ethnic Change in Queens, 1940–2020

	Totals	Percentage of population	Decennial change / percentage change
1940	**1,297,634**		
White	1,270,731	97.9%	
Black	25,890	2.0%	
Asian	3,593	0.28%	
Hispanic	3,367	0.26%	
Native-born (white)	994,143	78.2%	
Foreign-born (white)	276,588	21.8%	
1950	**1,550,849**		**253,215 / 19.51%**
White	1,497,126	96.5%	226,395 / 17.82%
Black	51,526	3.3%	25,636 / 99.02%
Asian	5,148	0.33%	1,555 / 43.23%
Hispanic	5,620	0.36%	2,253 / 66.91%
Native-born	1,262,652	81.5%	268,509 / 27.01%
Foreign-born	288,197	18.6%	11,609 / 4.2%
1960	**1,809,994**		**259,145 / 16.71%**
White	1,654,947	91.5%	157,821 / 10.54%
Black	145,855	8.1%	94,329 / 183.07%
Asian	?	?	
PR/Spanish surname	17,432	0.96%	11,812 / 210.18%
Native-born	1,474,371	81.5%	211,719 / 16.77%
Foreign-born	335,623	18.5%	47,426 / 16.46%
1970	**1,986,473**		**176,479 / 9.75%**
White	1,699,443	85.6%	44,496 / 2.67%
Black	257,873	13%	112,018 / 76.8%
Asian	45,285	2.3%	—
Spanish-origin	33,141	1.7%	15,709 / 90.12%
Native-born	1,581,291	79.6%	106,920 / 7.25%
Foreign-born	405,183	20.4%	69,560 / 20.73%
1980	**1,891,325**		**−95,148 / −4.79%**
White	1,335,805	70.6%	−363,638 / −21.4%
Black	354,129	18.7%	96,256 / 37.33%
Asian	93,780	5%	48,495 / 107.09%
Hispanic	262,422	13.9%	229,281 / 691.83%
Native-born	1,350,507	71.4%	−230,784 / −14.59
Foreign-born	540,818	28.6%	135,635 / 33.47%
1990	**1,951,598**		**60,273 / 3.19%**
White	1,129,192	57.9%	−206,613 / −15.47%
Black	423,211	21.7%	69,082 / 19.51%
Asian	238,336	12.2%	144,556 / 154.14%
Hispanic	381,120	19.5%	118,698 / 45.23%
Native-born	1,244,445	63.8%	−106,062 / −7.85%
Foreign-born	707,153	36.2%	166,335 / 30.76%

(continued)

Table 20 *(Continued)*

	Totals	Percentage of population	Decennial change percentage change
2000	2,229,379		277,781 / 14.23%
White	982,725	44.1%	−146,467 / −12.97%
Black	446,189	20%	22,978 / 5.43%
Asian	391,500	17.6%	153,164 / 64.26%
Hispanic	556,605	25%	175,485 / 46.04%
Native-born	1,201,040	53.9%	−43,405 / −3.49%
Foreign-born	1,028,339	46.1%	321,186 / 45.42%
2010	2,230,722		1,343 / 0.06
White	886,053	39.7%	−96,672 / −9.84%
Black	426,683	19.1%	19,506 / −4.37%
Asian	511,787	22.9%	120,287 / 30.72%
Hispanic	613,750	27.5%	57,145 / 10.27%
2020	2,405,464		174,742 / 7.83%
Non-Hisp. white	549,358	22.8%	−336,695 / −38%
Non-Hisp. Black	381,375	15.9%	−45,308 / −10.62%
Non-Hisp. Asian	656,583	27.3%	144,796 / 28.29%
Hispanic	667,861	27.8%	54,111 / 8.82%

SOURCE: U.S. Census Bureau, *Census of Population, 1940 to 2020*, https://www.census.gov/programs-surveys/decennial-census/decade.html, Vol. 2.

transformation is the central theme in the borough's story from the 1970s forward.

To attribute the drastically changing demographics to "white flight" misreads a complex historical process. As a proportion of the total, the white population of New York City had been declining since 1950, and that gradual trend accelerated after the passage of the Immigration and Nationality Act of 1965, known as the Hart-Celler Act. For economist Louis Winnick, the act "was less a manifesto than an atonement. It rectified the shamelessly skewed quotas of 1924 by establishing equal national quotas, subject to a global ceiling of 290,000, 170,000 for the Eastern Hemisphere and 120,000 for the Western hemisphere." President Johnson stated that it would "repair a very deep and painful flaw in the fabric of American justice. It corrects a cruel and enduring wrong in the conduct of the American nation. . . . It will strengthen us in a hundred unseen ways." The bill was intended to benefit immigrants from Eastern and Southern European countries, nationalities limited by the 1924 act. No one thought that those numbers would ever be reached. A few thousand at most, the experts predicted. In actuality, an estimated 80,000 newcomers arrived in the city each year during the 1970s and

Table 21
Foreign-Born Population, 1960–2000 (%)

	1960	1970	1990	2000
Queens	18.5	20.4	36.2	46.1
Manhattan	22	19.9	25.8	29.4
Brooklyn	20	17.3	29.2	37.8
Bronx	21	15.4	22.8	29.0
Staten Island	11	8.7	11.8	16.4
New York City	20	17.9	28.4	39.9

SOURCE: U.S. Census Bureau, *Census of Population, 1960 to 2000*, https://www.census.gov/programs-surveys/decennial-census/decade.html, Vol. 2.

about 88,000 each year in the 1980s. Almost all of them came not from Europe, as had been expected, but from Asia, the Caribbean, and Central and South America.[1]

Each of the five boroughs attracted its share of the new immigration, but in Queens the demographic transformation was most pronounced. In 1960, fewer than one in five residents of Queens was foreign-born, and that population was aging. Almost all had arrived in the country before the quotas were imposed, with a smaller number arriving after World War II. Census data show how the percentage increased decade by decade until by 2000 nearly half of the borough's population was foreign-born (neither the 2010 nor the 2020 census recorded data about citizenship or nativity). In no other borough did the foreign-born population top 40 percent.

Every older American city reached its peak population in 1950 and then saw its numbers decline. Manufacturing relocated to low-wage, nonunion states or overseas, and thousands of families elected to move to new homes in the suburbs, a process occurring in cities with a sizable Black population and in cities with a negligible number of Black residents. Only New York continued to grow, the population increasing into the 1960s. By 1970, however, the city's problems were impossible to paper over, particularly the rising crime. In 1975, the city nearly fell into bankruptcy, with an unprecedented contraction of municipal services. That decade was the only time in the city's history when the population declined, falling by 820,000. Queens lost nearly 100,000 residents. For many New Yorkers, the city was simply no longer a desirable place to raise a family or invest in a business. This was precisely the moment when the new immigrants arrived.

Writing in 1988, Nathan Glazer observed that "the immigrant flow into New York seemed unaffected, or scarcely affected, by changing economic circumstances, by the phenomenal decline in manufacturing jobs, by the destruction of low-cost housing in the great waves of abandonment of the 1970s. Whatever the changes that were affecting New York for the worse in the 1970s, to the immigrant it was still apparently the city of opportunity. And it remains so." The city provided "the setting—primarily economic, but also social and political—for new groups of very different ethnic and racial origins and different educational and economic backgrounds, to find a satisfying life, or at least take the first steps toward such a life." While older residents saw only decline in the city's economic prospects and livability compared to preceding decades, the new immigrants set their gaze forward and saw only opportunity.[2]

As the older generation of white ethnics died off and the younger generation moved beyond the old neighborhood, a reflection of upward mobility over the generations rather than "white flight," the newcomers promised a "demographic renewal." Winnick saw this influx of new people and new cultures as New York's saving grace. In his 1990 book about the transformation of Sunset Park in Brooklyn, he wrote, "Without its new foreigners New York would be an emptied out city of no more than six million, a doleful fate toward which the demographic trends of the last generation were inexorably dragging it."[3]

From the very beginning of this surge, Queens absorbed a higher percentage of the newcomers than did the other boroughs. Almost every neighborhood was transformed, and even in places that retained their old character many of the local stores gained new owners. In downtown Flushing, Chinese and Korean merchants revitalized the commercial streets, and as they became more established, Asian families moved east to homes in Bayside and Little Neck. Astoria, once home to Germans, Czechs, and Italians, attracted thousands of Greeks, and in turn a stretch of Steinway Street sprouted Egyptian hookah bars and a mosque. South Ozone Park attracted families from Guyana, and Rego Park, a largely Jewish neighborhood, became home to Jews from former Soviet republics. Similar examples of ethnic succession could be found in almost all parts of Queens, excepting perhaps Douglas Manor and Forest Hills Gardens, which remained rather wealthy enclaves.

Perhaps nothing encapsulates the unrivaled diversity better than the 7 train, the subway line running from Times Square (now Hudson Yards) and Flushing. It serves neighborhoods of immigrants from Ireland, Rumania, Turkey, South America, Central America, the Caribbean, China, Korea, South Asia, the Philippines, and, without exaggeration, everyplace

Elmhurst, 2024. (Laura Heim Architect.)

else. In 1999, the White House Millennium Council designated the 7 train a "National Millennium Trail" in honor of its representation of the immigrant experience and "emblematic of American history and culture." Beyond the demographics of the riders, the line was significant in another way. On workdays, it carried 450,000 passengers, making the 7 train the fourth-largest transit line in the nation all by itself.[4]

Elmhurst-Corona

In his aptly titled 1998 book, *The Future of Us All*, Roger Sanjek, an anthropologist at Queens College, documented the borough's dramatic transformation by focusing in on the neighborhoods of Elmhurst and Corona, together comprising Community Board 4. This was roughly the area north of Queen Boulevard and the Long Island Expressway, between the Brooklyn-Queens Expressway and Flushing Meadows-Corona Park (of course, any local would quibble over those boundaries). Sanjek essentially embedded himself in those neighborhoods, attending various public gatherings and meetings of the community board, the school board, and voluntary associations. In this way, he reveals how the residents experienced and coped with, made peace with, and resisted rapid demographic change. Surprisingly, perhaps, he found "little overt conflict."[5]

Given the overwhelming demographic shift, it would be understandable to assume that any conflict would involve the older, diminishing white population and the racially and linguistically diverse newcomers. This would ignore how the newcomers interacted with each other, how Asians in Flushing thought about Hispanics in Corona, for example. They were just as prone to view others as ethnic stereotypes as were older whites, and from such encounters the new character of Queens would emerge.[6]

The changes were indeed dramatic. In 1960, Elmhurst-Corona was 98 percent white. In the following decade the percentage dropped by a third, and by 1980, the white population was down to 34 percent. In 1990, the number fell to only 18 percent, with Asians numbering 26 percent and Hispanics 45 percent.[7]

In the 1960s, Corona was predominately Italian, with many families tracing their neighborhood roots back generations. Nearly all of the families in Elmhurst were of European heritage, with no single ethnicity predominating. A woman born in 1922 explained, "We were the only Germans, but it never occurred to us. We didn't make a distinction. People were all family-oriented and took pride in the neighborhood." With immigration all but closed off until the 1960s, the schools, churches, and public spaces of neighborhoods like Elmhurst proved a fertile ground for assimilation. Individual families retained their customs, of course, but in the public sphere they developed shared characteristics and a common culture. This woman certainly had a rosy view of the city of her youth, the seemingly stable city of the mid-twentieth century, but the deterioration of Elmhurst since troubled her. Many residents, she said, "don't seem to care. People are pulling it down."[8]

Tensions during these years of intense ethnic succession were certainly present, but the situation was always more nuanced than a story of bigotry and flight. On the front stoop of his house in Jackson Heights, an elderly man of Italian descent told me that the newcomers were ruining the block. A moment later, a Hispanic boy ran up for a hug from "Uncle Frankie" and asked if he could use his bathroom, and of course he did. Who was this man, then? An Archie Bunker type resenting neighborhood change, or "Uncle Frankie," the old guy making friends with the children of the new immigrants?

The small Black population was concentrated in East Elmhurst, along Flushing Bay. Free Blacks had lived and worked in Newtown all through the nineteenth century, but their numbers were never great. As in other parts of the county, housing options for African Americans were limited, and there were scarcely any integrated blocks in Elmhurst and Corona. This changed in the 1970s.

Samuel Lefrak owned perhaps the largest portfolio of rental housing in the city. In 1962, he opened Lefrak City, a forty-acre complex of 4,650 units in five sections of four 18-story buildings adjacent to the Long Island Expressway. Even with amenities like swimming pools and doormen, Lefrak had difficulty filling his buildings with his targeted population, young families and white-collar professionals. While Lefrak was accused of refusing to rent to Blacks and other minorities in his other properties, Lefrak City welcomed tenants of diverse backgrounds, to a point. In 1970, it was 70 percent white, including a high proportion of Jewish tenants; 14 percent were Hispanic, mainly Puerto Rican, 8 percent Asian, and 9 percent Black. After complaints were brought to the state and the city, Lefrak City agreed to rent to more Black tenants. By 1976, the proportion of Black residents had risen to 70 percent. Even though these were middle-class renters and not welfare cases, white residents fled. That Lefrak's policy of not accepting welfare tenants was affirmed in court was of no consequence. This was, Sanjek states, clearly white flight. Overall, the Black population of Elmhurst and Corona rose, but few resided beyond Lefrak City.[9]

The uncomfortable truth was that the new wave of immigrants arrived at the moment of the intersection of several long-term factors. First, the white population of the city was already decreasing as a result of the passing of the older generation and the out-migration of young families. Further, the city suffered severe contraction of public services during the fiscal crisis, with the resulting decline in quality of life. No one could remain oblivious to that. A 1980 report by the Twentieth Century Fund, a liberal think tank, was pessimistic about the city's future and suggested that "public policymakers should assume that the decline in households will continue, at least for the immediate future," and in practice, the city "must be willing to close facilities or reduce services if they are in excess of the needs of the remaining population."[10] Endorsing the notion of "planned shrinkage" advanced by Housing and Development Administrator Roger Starr, the report accepted the contraction of municipal services not as a necessary response to a financial crisis but as prudent governance. Whatever the rationale, the budgets made daily life in the neighborhoods more difficult.

While Sanjek found examples of older residents blaming the deterioration on the new immigrants, he concluded that on the whole they worked to assimilate their new neighbors into the city's civic culture. Part of that civic culture, particularly at a time of declining city services, was fighting City Hall for better schools, more policing, and other local needs.[11]

The schools were where the changes were most evident. Between 1960 and 1976, the five primary schools in Elmhurst-Corona dropped from 89 percent white to 28 percent. By then, children from Latin America made up 50 percent of the enrollment, Asians 12 percent, and Blacks 10 percent. Newtown High School, an elegant 1897 building designed by C.B.J. Snyder with dramatic flourishes in the style of the northern Baroque, went from a student body that was 93 percent white to only 38 percent, as the number of Latin Americans rose to 37 percent, Asians 9 percent, and Blacks 16 percent. Within a decade, the schools went from 70 percent of capacity to 114 percent. Newtown High School was at 143 percent. With the city still struggling even as the fiscal crisis eased, construction of new schools was almost impossible. In 1992, the district was "rated sixth worst among the city's thirty-two school districts in physical conditions. By 1994 it was the most crowded, its schools averaging 140 percent of capacity. By 1996, more than half its pupils read below national norms for their grade level."[12]

That Elmhurst and Corona were only part of a much larger school district only complicated the picture. District 24 also included Ridgewood, Glendale, Middle Village, and Maspeth, neighborhoods of predominately white, middle- and working-class homeowners. If any place could be labeled the land of Archie Bunker, it was there. Representatives from those neighborhoods controlled the local school board, and they worked to confine the burgeoning population of immigrants in certain schools, resulting in overcrowding in some and empty seats in others. John Costello of the very active Newtown Civic Association blamed the overcrowding on "illegal aliens." He argued, "if teachers must take time to explain to non-English-speaking children, they are taking time away from English-speaking children." Peter Nefsky, an Argentinian member of the community board, rebutted that line of thinking. "Sometimes I think all this talk is a conspiracy to get rid of Hispanic immigrants," he remarked. "We hear the most bitter charges imaginable being made about Hispanic immigrants. The vast majority of the so-called illegal aliens in Elmhurst and Corona are here legally. The flap is caused by those who simply don't like it."[13]

Changes in the schools highlighted both the friction between old and new residents and the limited resources the city had to deal with overcrowding and English-language instruction for students speaking dozens of languages. Elmhurst and Corona also experienced a palpable decline in the quality of life on the streets of the neighborhood. This was not, however, the inevitable outcome of the influx of immigrants from different cultures. Communities across the city experienced the same as the city cut back on police and sanitation, park maintenance, libraries, and public transit. The impact of the fiscal crisis was felt across the five boroughs. Still, that the decline happened as the population was changing led many to conclude that the newcomers were responsible. Sanjek makes clear that the people of Elmhurst and Corona worked hard to counter those arguments and cooperated to address neighborhood problems.[14]

Residents complained about crowding on the subway, especially the shoulder-to-shoulder conditions on the Queens Boulevard line during rush hour. As in other neighborhoods, they complained about the lack of parking, for an increasing population brought with it an increase in the number of vehicles. Here they also complained about unregulated auto repair businesses operating on residential streets and sidewalks, not to mention chop shops that dismembered stolen cars for parts. But budget cuts had decimated the city offices regulating such businesses. Single-family homes were illegally divided into multifamily residences, but the Department of Buildings had few code enforcement officers to follow up complaints. The Sanitation Department was slow to respond to reports of illegal dumping, and, of course, not even the Police Department was spared cuts in personnel. Repeatedly residents called in information about drug sales, gambling operations, and disturbances by groups of teens, but the police did not have the resources to respond. How many times could observations of drug dealing in the same location by the same people be called in?[15]

The older residents, the assimilated white ethnics, as it were, led the way in confronting the city for better services, especially from the Police and Sanitation Departments, and lobbying for the construction of new schools, but they brought into the effort many law-abiding and equally troubled neighbors from the immigrant communities. By any objective measure, Elmhurst and Corona were in decline. The schools were overcrowded, the streets were dirtier, and crime was pervasive. But that was not for a lack of civic engagement by the citizenry. City Hall simply did not have the resources to address the problems and stem the decline.[16]

The demographic transformation of these neighborhoods continued into the twenty-first century, and conditions on the streets and in the schools gradually stabilized and then improved. A similar change came to the civic organizations, as leadership passed from the white ethnics to the new immigrants. Among the positive changes was a long-sought downzoning of the residential blocks. Across the borough, smaller houses were demolished and

Roosevelt Deli Grocery—95th Street and Roosevelt Avenue, Jackson Heights, Queens, June 2004. (Joel Sternfeld.)

larger multifamily structures rose in their place, increasing pressure on parking, schools, and municipal services. By 1993, half of Queens had been downzoned. As one longtime resident explained, "We are proud of the manner in which we adjusted to the transformation of Elmhurst from a community which was home to only a few ethnic groups to one in which scores—literally scores—of nationalities and cultures are represented. Ours has become a truly rainbow population.... But we feel only anger and distress as a result of losses and hardships suffered by the mis-zoning of 1961 which opened the way for enormous overbuilding ... extremely overcrowded schools, overburdened public transit, and other services."[17]

As an established community faded away, a new one was born.

Children of the Rainbow

In 1985, the Schools Chancellor Richard Green issued a directive intended to develop policies and initiatives that would "bring about elimination of practices which foster attitudes and/or actions leading to discrimination against students, parents, or school personnel on the basis of race, color, religion, national origin, gender, age, sexual orientation and/or handicapped condition." Green had been aggressively working to implement his directive when in 1989 he suddenly died. Joseph Fernandez was appointed his successor and moved his predecessor's initiative forward. The final product was Children of the Rainbow Curriculum, a 443-page guide for first-grade teachers unveiled in September 1991.[18]

Green had intended to introduce the topic of sexual orientation in the sixth grade, not earlier, but under Fernandez the topic was inserted into the first-grade curriculum. In response to lobbying by gay rights groups, a member of the Gay and Lesbian Teachers Association had been brought in to help draft a section on "fostering positive attitudes toward sexuality." The guide advised teachers that "classes should include references to lesbian/gay people in all curricular areas,' and recommended that teachers initiate these discussions because they were "not likely to come up." It suggested activities as well as content, as "children need actual experience, via creative play, books, visitors, etc., in order for them to view lesbians/gays as real people." Schools Chancellor Fernandez informed all districts that they "must be sure to address sexual orientation at the elementary school level."[19]

Hailed by many as a much needed and overdue step toward inclusivity and acceptance, the curriculum engendered strident opposition in District 24 in Queens, the large and diverse district stretching from Glendale to Corona, the same district analyzed by Roger Sanjek. In February 1992, school board president Mary Cummins of Middle Village threw down the gauntlet. She labeled the curriculum "part of the homosexual movement" and "gay and lesbian propaganda." "We will not accept two people of the same sex engaged in deviant sex practices as a 'family,'" she declared. Specifically, she objected to the inclusion of three titles in the list of recommended readings: *Heather Has Two Mommies*, *Daddy's Roommate*, and *Gloria Goes to Gay Pride*. The *Times* described Cummins as "bothered by books," but parents challenged the inclusion of those titles in school libraries across the country.[20]

Cardinal John O'Connor of the Archdiocese of New York voiced his opposition to Children of the Rainbow because homosexuality was anathema to church teaching. Bishop Thomas V. Daily of the Brooklyn Diocese, which included Queens, spoke against the curriculum and also led demonstrations against the distribution of condoms in schools. Parents in Sunset Park in Brooklyn marched in protest and compelled their local school board to suspend the teaching of the section on homosexuality. In response, the

AIDS advocacy group Act-Up staged a demonstration outside St. Patrick's Cathedral to protest the Catholic Church's position.[21]

This was a battle between a political and cultural establishment in Queens and rising political and cultural interests, largely centered in Manhattan. Liberals, of course, notably Mayor David Dinkins and Borough President Ruth Messinger, supported the schools chancellor, in part because gays and lesbians were a growing constituency. The AIDS crisis had radicalized segments of the gay community, and in 1986 the City Council had enacted the first gay rights bill by a vote of 21–14. The *New York Times* described the curriculum as intended "to teach first graders to respect the city's myriad racial and ethnic groups" and explained the opposition as the product of "fear and misunderstanding." The paper marveled at how "a curriculum intended to foster tolerance has deeply divided the city and provoked vicious expressions of intolerance."[22]

Mary Cummins and her entire school board were Catholic, but this was more than a Catholic issue. Also speaking in opposition were leaders of the Orthodox Jewish community, Black Baptist ministers, and Hispanic Pentecostal ministers.[23] Children of the Rainbow had spawned a rainbow coalition in opposition. Even so, the gay rights advocates focused their anger on the Catholic Church.

The issue came down to competing value systems. The issue was "what role moral values should play in the schools, and who should determine what is taught about those values." On one side, parents contended "that they and they alone should decide what their children learn about such sensitive subjects as homosexuality." On the other, gay rights groups "view the gay curriculum as a measure of acceptance, and the Chancellor's related policies on AIDS education and condom availability as a matter of survival." They saw schools "as a way of teaching children to overcome the prejudices of their parents."[24] Framing the issue that way only confirmed for opponents that the curriculum was an assault on their values and an attempt to indoctrinate their children.

As the battle lines hardened, voices on each side became more strident. The opponents refused the inclusion of any positive references to homosexuality, rejecting the very idea of tolerance. Proponents increasing demonized Cardinal O'Connor and fixed on the Catholic Church as an enemy. The leader of a social service agency working with gay youth stated, "Although the Cardinal claims to respect all human life, The Archdiocese has consistently advocated for the right to discriminate against gays and lesbians. Now the Cardinal is engaged in a battle to distort the content and intent of multicultural education that is inclusive of gay and lesbian issues." For their part, Catholic parents in Queens scoffed at the notion that they took orders from the church. "Parents are the ones that have been most vocal and agitated about the condom issue and the Rainbow issue," said one woman. "I think the parents were there well before any statements by the church." For her and many others, the issue came down to parental control over what was taught to their children, and they did not want the schools infusing their children with ideas and practices at odds with their religion or their family values.[25]

When Cummins and her board refused to adopt Children of the Rainbow or any curriculum advocating tolerance for homosexuality, Schools Chancellor Joseph Fernandez suspended the school board. The Board of Education swiftly reversed the chancellor's decision, and then did not renew his contract. In the school board election the following May, Cummins finished first among twenty-four candidates, and Father John Garkowski, another vocal opponent, finished second. Voters in the district clearly supported their aggressive stance against the curriculum. Even so, it would be a mistake to conclude that they would have embraced Children of the Rainbow. Tolerance for gays and lesbians was still far from universal, and the cultures from which they came did not necessarily accept homosexuality.

It is almost impossible to understand how such a seemingly innocuous section—of course there were families headed by same-sex couples then—could have led to such a political crisis. One can scarcely imagine how Mary Cummins and her neighbors would have reacted to the legalization of gay marriage or Drag Queen Story Hour. In 1992, however, the school board's opposition was clearly reflecting the sentiments of a very large proportion of Queens residents, if not a majority. Few in New York City would agree with them today, but they were acting on a deeply held set of traditional beliefs. They were fighting for their children, and for the future of their city. But while they won the battle over Children of the Rainbow, Cummins, Cardinal O'Connor, and Archie Bunker lost the war.

In June 1993, Queens held its first Gay Pride Parade along 37th Avenue from 89th to 75th Streets in Jackson Heights. An estimated ten thousand attended that first year, and attendance rose each year after, with elected officials marching proudly. Daniel Dromm, an elementary school teacher in Queens, was the driving force behind the event, moved to act by the Children of the Rainbow controversy and the July 1990 gay-bashing of Julio Rivera, a twenty-nine-year-old man who had been lured to a playground in Jackson Heights and murdered by teens. In 2009, Dromm was elected to the City Council.[26]

The 7 train, Sunnyside, 2024. (Laura Heim Architect.)

The Shape of a Changing Borough

Development in the first decades of the twentieth century set the pattern for housing, and the New Deal funded transportation and infrastructure projects to accommodate growth. New immigrants simply stepped into a mature cityscape, remaking established places but for the most part leaving neighborhoods intact. A city is never complete, of course, and as New York recovered from the fiscal crisis, changing uses and changing needs brought on a new wave of development. In places, the city sought to guide development, while in others it struggled to keep pace with rapid change.

From the 1970s on, Queens finally recognized its unique assets and began capitalizing on them—the Hunters Point waterfront; Kaufman Astoria Studios and the American Museum of the Moving Image; and Flushing Meadows-Corona Park, with the panorama from the 1964 World's Fair in the Queens Museum and the new home of the U.S. Open tennis tournament. During those years, residents in neighborhoods across the borough recognized that there was much to cherish in its seemingly ordinary places, and the movement to preserve significant structures and historic districts gained momentum.

Still, political leaders viewed much of Queens as a blank slate, as it had been during the previous periods of fevered growth in the 1920s and the 1950s. The question became how to accommodate new development—housing, businesses, entertainment venues—while recognizing that residents had invested in a particular quality of life and sought to preserve it.

The 1961 zoning resolution was designed to accommodate a population of 10 million in the five boroughs, and several areas were zoned for higher density than currently built. A neighborhood of one- and two-family houses might be zoned for apartment buildings, even though there were none at the time.

In 1967, Nathan Silver shocked New Yorkers with *Lost New York*, a collection of photographs showing the architectural gems that had been demolished in recent years. Published two years after Mayor Wagner signed the landmarks law, the book reinforced just why that law was necessary.[27] He included Pennsylvania Station, of course, and the Brokaw Mansion on Fifth Avenue, the demolition of which finally compelled Mayor Wagner to sign the legislation, but also commercial structures, churches, public spaces such as the dignified pedestrian way in the middle of Park Avenue, and even the vanished kiosks at subways entrances. All those grand or overlooked structures had been erased from the streets, and in some cases from memory. "Unlike history, unlike politics or philosophy or even art," wrote Silver, "the environment allows the actual experience of cultural continuity to be felt." It was only through architecture that we can discover and experience the past in the urban environment, and that, he recognized, is why preservation is so vital.[28]

While Silver lamented what had been lost, Elliot Willensky and Norval White celebrated the architectural glories (and ordinaries) that remained. They prepared the first *AIA Guide to New York City* in 1967 for the AIA national convention held in New York that year and expanded it into a book in 1968; tall and narrow, the volume was designed to slide easily into a pocket. The authors intended for readers to use it on the streets, not in their libraries. The indispensable book was updated in 1978, 1988, 2000, and, finally, 2010, with Fran Leadon completing the work. Willensky died in 1990, White in 2009. Expanded with each edition, its girth and heft permit it to fit into very few pockets now.

Ironically, appreciation for the city's architecture and history grew even as the city deteriorated. Parks, libraries, schools, and transit all suffered from a decline in municipal investment, while crime and disorder only increased. During the decade of the 1970s, as the city slid toward bankruptcy, New York's population declined for the first time in its history. This was precisely the moment when individuals in neighborhoods across the city came together not only to protect their quality of life, but also to protect its historic buildings and streetscapes. An entire library of small volumes appeared to highlight historic places and to advocate for designation by the Landmarks Preservation Commission. That the commission neglected Queens in favor of the fine row house neighborhoods of Brooklyn and Manhattan was not surprising.

The nation's Bicentennial in 1976 inspired a renewed interest in history, and many discovered history right outside their doors. Pam Byers wrote *Small Town in the Big City: A History of Sunnyside and Woodside*; Robert A. Hecht, *A History of College Point*; Walter J. Hutter et al., *Our Community, Its History and People: Ridgewood, Glendale, Maspeth, Middle Village, Liberty Park*; William Kroos, *A Peak at Richmond Hill through the Keyhole of Time*; and Barbara W. Stankowski, *Maspeth: Our Town* and *Old Woodhaven: A Victorian Village*.[29]

More than anyone, Vincent Seyfried dedicated his life to documenting the history of Queens. He published a multivolume history of the Long Island Railroad and numerous volumes on specific neighborhoods, including Long Island City, Elmhurst, Corona, Queens Village, and Woodhaven. These self-published books drew heavily upon his earlier labor of love—the indexing of long-gone newspapers like the *Newtown Register* and the *Long Island City Daily Star*. These typewritten manuscripts in the Queens Borough Public Library have proven invaluable to students and local historians.[30]

Taken together, these little books revealed their authors' affection for their city, demonstrated an appreciation of its architecture and history, and made clear that people in every neighborhood contributed to the story of New York. Theirs was far from an elite conception of history and preservation. Historic preservation was not usually a primary concern for local historians, but their research supported the efforts of others seeking the protection of landmark designation. Queens, they could assert, had as much history as Manhattan, and its treasured places merited designation as much as Brooklyn Heights or SoHo. Advocates published volumes on specific neighborhoods to support their campaigns for designation by the Landmarks Preservation Commission. Examples include Margaret Moore and Truman Moore, *End of the Road for Ladies Mile?* (1986), Gary Hermalyn and Robert Kornfeld, *Landmarks of the Bronx* (1989), and Andrew Dolkart, *The Texture of Tribeca* (1989). Preservation advocates in Queens produced several volumes intended to influence the commission and the borough's political leaders, including *Historic Preservation in Queens* (1988) by Jeffrey A. Kroessler and Nina Rappaport, *Jackson Heights: A Garden in the City* (1990) by Daniel Karatzas, Barry Lewis's *Kew Gardens: Urban Village in the Big City* (1999), and Kevin Wolfe's *This*

Salubrious Spot: The First 100 Years at Douglas Manor, 1906–2006 (2006).[31] Jackson Heights and Douglas Manor were designated historic districts; Kew Gardens never was.

During the 1970s and 1980s, the Landmarks Preservation Commission aggressively designated historic districts and individual landmarks. In no small measure, these designations halted the city's descent and anchored its revival. Designation rewarded the investment of neighborhood residents and demonstrated that New York was a desirable place to live. Each designation needed approval from the Board of Estimate, a body including the mayor, the controller, the president of the city council, and the five borough presidents. Until the U.S. Supreme Court ruled this body unconstitutional in 1989 for violating the principle of one person, one vote, the Board of Estimate had final authority over all contracts and land use issues.

Unlike Manhattan and Brooklyn, where the political establishment recognized the value of landmark designation and supported local advocates, the political leaders in Queens were openly hostile to preservation, particularly Borough President Donald Manes. Manes took office in 1971 and vetoed several designations, including the row houses built by the Steinway & Sons Company for their workers and the LaLance and Grosjean factory complex in Woodhaven. In 1974, he denied the Triboro Theatre on Steinway Street, a magnificent movie palace. This was in contrast to the fate of Loew's Kings on Flatbush Avenue in Brooklyn. Shuttered in 1977, the city acquired it two years later and during the administration of Mayor Michael Bloomberg it was completely restored, reopening in 2015. A decade after dooming the Triboro, Manes vetoed the designation of the RKO Keith's on Northern Boulevard in Flushing. Designed by famed theater architect Thomas W. Lamb, it was another atmospheric movie palace, with baroque and gothic flourishes. Manes allowed the designation of the foyer and grand lobby to stand, but a succession of owners left the place a ruin.[32]

Donald Manes was a political boss who knew how to profit from his position. In 1983, he pushed through a plan to hold a Grand Prix race in Flushing Meadows-Corona Park, with his former executive assistant heading the enterprise. He gained support from Mayor Koch and neutralized local opposition. But at 1:50 A.M. on January 10, 1986, police stopped a car driving erratically on Grand Central Parkway. Officers found the borough president bleeding from a self-inflicted knife wound. Four days later, Geoffrey G. Lindenauer, deputy director of the Parking Violations Bureau, was arrested on charges he accepted a $5,000 bribe from a contractor, half of which was for

Manes. Manes had also been implicated in a bribery scheme involving cable television franchises. On March 13, three days after Lindenauer agreed to cooperate with investigators, Manes committed suicide, plunging a knife into his heart in the kitchen of his Jamaica Estates home. The Grand Prix in Flushing Meadows died with him.[33]

Deputy Borough President Clare Shulman succeeded Manes, but she had as little interest in historic preservation as her predecessor. In 1996, over the pleas of Queens preservationists, architects, and celebrities, she approved the demolition of the Aquacade, an eleven-thousand-seat seat amphitheater that was one of the few survivors from the 1939 World's Fair. Built as the New York State Pavilion, it was intended to be a permanent fixture in the park. Repurposed as a public pool and revitalized for the 1964 Fair, it was permanently closed in 1982, and the city allowed it to decay. Even so, she did not block the designation of four new historic districts: Jackson Heights (1993), Douglas Manor (1997), Fort Totten (1999), and Stockholm Street in Ridgewood (2000).[34]

As important as it was to preserve the landmarks and historic neighborhoods of Queens, it was also necessary to build for the future. But what was the borough's future?

Acknowledgments

Jeffrey Kroessler would be the first to acknowledge how much he benefited from advice and assistance of many thoughtful men and women. All those who contributed to this book, you know who you are and, under the circumstances, you cannot all be specifically thanked. He would, though, start with those to whom he had already dedicated the book, Vincent Seyfried, Barry Lewis, and Richard C. Wade, all of whom are deceased and all of whom impacted and shared Jeffrey's approach and appreciation of Queens.

Vincent Seyfried was a historian of Long Island who, from 1950 to 2010, wrote volumes on Queens and Long Island communities as well as the Long Island Railroad. His indexed transcripts of local newspapers and his extensive personal collection were essential to Jeffrey's original dissertation research. His work created a deep resource to begin further study of the urban evolution of Queens. He thoughtfully reviewed Jeff's dissertation. Jeff was indebted to the extent and thoroughness of his research and collection.

Barry Lewis, the New York City architectural historian known for his televised walking tours, including *A Walk through Queens*, shared with Jeff extensive knowledge of Queens as well as a desire to make complex material accessible to everyone. He was a friend who could visit for a BBQ in our backyard in Queens and talk endlessly and enthusiastically about the great borough of Queens. The comradery and respect was apparent between them, as well as their unique appreciation of Queens.

Richard C. Wade was, by Jeff's description, a friend and adviser with whom he studied at the City University of New York (CUNY) Graduate School. He showed by example how to be a historian. He guided Jeff through his PhD process, and they remained in close contact throughout his life. Dick was a pioneer in introducing urban history as an important academic subject. He understood the importance of this type of study of Queens in the historiography of New York City.

Any work completed by Jeff would include thanks to numerous members of the New York City preservation community. Additionally, he would express sincere thanks to his colleagues at Lloyd Sealy Library at John Jay College of Criminal Justice, CUNY, who were supportive and encouraging during the writing and final completion of the book's production. The members of the Seminar on the City at Columbia University were always appreciated for their ongoing discussion on the many strands of urban history, especially New York City. This book was supported, in part, by a grant from the Office for the Advancement of Research at John Jay College.

The images for the book were selected with an emphasis on Queens sources, beginning with the impressive collections at the Archives at the Queens Borough Public Library and the LaGuardia and Wagner Archives (including the New York City Housing Authority collection). Additionally, the Queens Historical Society, the Rego-Forest Preservation Council, and Preserve Long Island contributed. Images also came from greater New York sources, including the New York Public Library, the Brooklyn Public Library, the Brooklyn Museum, the Museum of the City of New York, and the New York City Department of Parks and Recreation. Thanks go to Kristen Nyitray of the State University of New York at Stonybrook, for assisting in locating an illustration from Vincent Seyfried's work which ultimately led to Cornell. Thus, farther afield, Cornell University, the U.S. Geological Survey, and the Library of Congress were image sources. Finally, special thanks go to David W. Dunlap and Joel Sternfeld for generously providing original photographs for this publication.

For the posthumous production work, special thanks go first to Geng H. Lin, Library Systems Manager at John Jay College, for locating Jeffrey's complete dissertation on the John Jay College server. It was open as Jeff was working on the book. To begin the process, Ross Wheeler assisted in the preliminary review of the manuscript and select pre-submission text editing. My role was to complete the selection of illustrations and shepherd the book though the publication process. Special thanks go to Kathleen Collins for detailed follow-up and interface with John Jay College. As mentioned, manuscript readers Joshua B. Freeman and Stephen Petrus; the editor, Peter Mickulas; and Rutgers University Press deserve much thanks and appreciation for their insightful comments and perseverance.

Jeff would be so pleased to see his life's work available to all.

Laura Heim

Notes

Abbreviations

CHC	City Housing Corporation
Encyclopedia of New York City	*The Encyclopedia of New York City*, 2nd ed., ed. Kenneth T. Jackson (New Haven, CT: Yale University Press, 2010)
FRRC	Flushing Railroad Company
LIRR	Long Island Railroad
LIRR	Vincent F. Seyfried, *The Long Island Rail Road: A Comprehensive History*, 7 vols. (Garden City, NY: Vincent F. Seyfried, 1961–1975)
LISI	Long Island Studies Institute
LWA	LaGuardia and Wagner Archives at LaGuardia Community College of the City University of New York
NYCDOP	New York City Department of Parks
NYCHA	New York City Housing Authority
NYFRRC	New York & Flushing Railroad Company
NYPL	New York Public Library
N-YHS	New-York Historical Society
QBPL	Queens Borough Public Library
QHS	Queens Historical Society
SSRRC	South Side Railroad Company

Introduction

1. Queens Borough Public Library (QBPL), *Annual Report*, 1994.
2. Daniel Denton, *A Brief Description of New York, Formerly New Netherlands with the Places thereunto Adjoining. Introduction and Copious Notes by Gabriel Furman* (New York: William Gowans, 1845 [1670]), 20; George H. Peters, *The Trees of Long Island* (Farmingdale, NY: Long Island Horticultural Society, 1952), 11.
3. [Samuel Latham Mitchill], *The Picture of New-York; or The Traveller's Guide, through the Commercial Metropolis of the United States, by a Gentleman Residing in This City* (New York: I. Riley, sold by Brisham and Brannan, City-Hotel, Broadway, 1807), 11; Thomas Bender, *New York Intellect: A History of Intellectual Life in New York City, from 1750 to the Beginnings of Our Own Time* (New York: Alfred A. Knopf, 1987), 29–30, 37, 56. For a geologic history of Long Island, see Paul Bailey, *Physical Long Island: Its Glacial Origin, Historic Storms, Beaches, Prairies and Archaeology* (Amityville, NY: Long Island Forum, 1959), 36–37; Jay T. Fox, "The Geology of Long Island," in *Long Island: A History of Two Great Counties, Nassau and Suffolk*, ed. Paul Bailey, 3 vols. (New York: Lewis Historical Publishing, 1949), 1:1–11.
4. [Mitchill], *Picture of New-York*, 131; Daniel M. Tredwell, *Personal Reminiscences of Men and Things on Long Island*, pt. I (Brooklyn: Charles Andrew Ditmas, 1912), 135–149; *Flushing, College Point, and Vicinity, Their Representative Business Men and Points of Interest* (New York: Mercantile Publishing, 1893), 8–9; F. Scott Fitzgerald, *The Great Gatsby* (New York: Charles Scribner's Son, 1925); Robert Moses, "From Dump to Glory," *Saturday Evening Post*, January 15, 1938.
5. Henry D. Waller, *History of the Town of Flushing, Long Island, New York* (Flushing, NY: J. H. Ridenour, 1899), 172.
6. Henry Onderdonk Jr., *Queens County in Olden Times: Being a Supplement to the Several Histories Thereof* (Jamaica, NY: Welling, 1865), 37; Waller, *History of the Town of Flushing*, 179.
7. Henry Isham Hazelton, *The Boroughs of Brooklyn and Queens, Counties of Nassau and Suffolk, Long Island, New York, 1609–1924*, 5 vols. (New York: Lewis Historical Publishing, 1925), 1:4–5.
8. Onderdonk, *Queens County*, 34; maps in the Fosdick Collection, Queens Historical Society (QHS), ca. 1830s, show property lines in the marsh and along the Rockaway shore. An 1814 scarf in the collection of the Museum of the City of New York shows a street peddler offering "Rockaway sand" in the city, depicted in Jerry E. Patterson, *The City of New York: A History Illustrated from the Collections of the Museum of the City of New York* (New York: Harry N. Abrams, 1978), 98.
9. Onderdonk, *Queens County*, 7, 12; see the ca. 1840 map in the Fosdick Collection, QHS, for a detailed sketch of the mill along the Fosters Meadow Road; E. Belcher Hyde, *Atlas of the Borough of Queens, City of New York*, vol. 4C, *So. East Part of the 4th Ward, Jamaica* (New York: E. Belcher Hyde, 1945), plates 4 and 8; for an illustration of the Springfield mill ca. 1890, see the Charles Henry Miller Collection, QHS.
10. Onderdonk, *Queens County*, 78, 86, 90–93.
11. [Mitchill], *Picture of New-York*, 161, 165.
12. Denton, *Brief Description of New York*, 6; Thomas F. Gordon, *Gazetteer of the State of New York* (Philadelphia, 1836), 636; Winslow C. Watson, *The Plains of Long Island* (Albany, NY, 1860).
13. *An Accurate Description of the British Colonies in North-America* (Salisbury, England: Collins and Johnson, 1777).

14 Walt Whitman, "Paumanok, and My Life on It as a Child and Young Man," in *Complete Poetry and Collected Prose* (New York: Library of America, 1982), 697.
15 [Mitchill], *Picture of New-York*, 165; Richard Stalter and Wayne Seyfert, "The Vegetation History of Hempstead Plains, New York." *Prairie Pioneers: Ecology, History and Culture: Proceedings of the Eleventh North American Prairie Conference* (Lincoln: University of Nebraska, 1989), 41–45.
16 Gabriel Furman, "Introduction & Notes," in Denton, *Brief Description of New York*, 34–36; Gordon, *Gazetteer*, 633–636; Tredwell, *Personal Reminiscences*, pt. I, 86–93; Tredwell also offers a tribute to Mitchill (pt. I, 166–171); Arthur T. McManus, *The Hempstead Plains: A Vanishing Heritage* (Hempstead, NY: Citizens for Hempstead Plains [1967]); *Newsday*, July 29, 1988; Nature Conservancy, *Long Island Chapter News*, Fall 1988.
17 Frank Gray Griswold, *Sport on Land and Water* (Norwood, MA: Plimpton Press, privately printed, 1913), 4–8, 16–20, 32, 44–5; *Queens County Review*, November 15, 1895. For a map of the Meadow Brook Hunt Club, see Chester A. Wolverton, *Atlas of Queens County, Long Island, New York* (New York, 1891). The club grounds were later transformed into a golf course, and the remaining undeveloped portion is part of the Hempstead Plains Preserve.
18 Surprisingly little has been published about these incidents; see Dennis J. Maika, "Commemoration and Context: The Flushing Remonstrance Then and Now," *New York History* 89, no. 1 (2008): 28–42.
19 For colonial Queens, see Jessica Kross, *The Evolution of an American Town: Newtown, New York, 1642–1775* (Philadelphia: Temple University Press, 1983); Jean Peyer, "Jamaica, Long Island, 1656–1776: A Study in the History of American Urbanism" (PhD diss., City University of New York, 1974). There is no recent history of colonial Flushing.
20 Henry Isham Hazelton, *The Boroughs of Brooklyn and Queens, Counties of Nassau and Suffolk, Long Island, New York, 1609–1924*, 3 vols. (New York: Lewis Historical Publishing Company, 1925); Volume II, 1027; Table 19, "Population of Queens and Nassau Counties, 1910–2020."
21 "About," Queens County Farm Museum, accessed November 14, 2024, https://www.queensfarm.org/about/.
22 Jane Cowan, *Addisleigh Park* (New York: Historic Districts Council, 2008), http://hdc.org/wp-content/uploads/2012/08/HDC-Addisleigh-Park-Report.pdf; "About," Louis Armstrong House Museum, accessed November 14, 2024, https://www.louisarmstronghouse.org/about/.
23 Peter Eisenstadt, *Rochdale Village: Robert Moses, 6,000 Families, and New York City's Great Experiment in Integrated Housing* (Ithaca, NY: Cornell University Press, 2010).
24 "Lovable bigot" was first used to describe Archie Bunker in a January 13, 1971, *Variety* review and was commonly used thereafter.
25 U.S. Census Bureau, https://data.census.gov/table?q=Queens%20county%20race%202020&t=Asian.

Chapter 1   Queens under the Dutch and the English

1 Hazelton, *Boroughs of Brooklyn and Queens*, 1:48–54.
2 John Webb Pratt, *Religion, Politics, and Diversity: The Church-State Theme in New York History* (Ithaca, NY: Cornell University Press, 1967), 5, 11.

3   Pratt, *Religion, Politics, and Diversity*, 6–7, 22–24.
4   John Romeyn Brodhead, *History of the State of New York, First Period, 1609–1664* (New York: Harper and Brothers, 1853), 614–618.
5   Brodhead, *History*, 617–618; Henry H. Kessler and Eugene Rachlis, *Peter Stuyvesant and His New York* (New York: Random House, 1959), 170–171.
6   John Cox Jr., *Quakerism in the City of New York, 1657–1930* (New York: privately printed, 1930), 11–13.
7   Cox, *Quakerism*, 14.
8   Haynes Trebor, ed., special issue, *Facts about Flushing* 5, no. 1 (March 1957): 29–31.
9   Haynes Trebor, ed., *The Flushing Remonstrance (The Origin of Religious Freedom in America)* (Flushing, NY: Bowne House Historical Society, 1957), 3–4; Maika, "Commemoration and Context."
10 Trebor, *Flushing Remonstrance*, 18–20. A stuiver was worth one-twentieth of a guilder and was, in effect, the Dutch equivalent of a nickel. Brodhead, *History*, 637–638.
11 Cox, *Quakerism*, 12.
12 Brodhead, *History*, 689; Sanford H. Cobb, *The Rise of Religious Liberty in America: A History* (New York: Burt Franklin, 1970 [1902]), 318–321.
13 Brodhead, *History*, 705–706.
14 Herbert F. Ricard, ed., *The Journal of John Bowne, 1650–1694* (New Orleans: Friends of the Queensborough Community College Library and Polyanthos, 1975); Brodhead, *History*, 706–707.
15 Benjamin F. Thompson (Benjamin Franklin), *History of Long Island; from Its Discovery and Settlement, to the Present Time* (New York: Gould Banks, 1843 [1839]), 387–388.
16 Thompson, *History of Long Island*, 79; George L. Smith, *Religion and Trade in New Netherland: Dutch Origins and American Development* (Ithaca, NY: Cornell University Press, 1973), 220–230.
17 Cobb, *Rise of Religious Liberty*, 32–35.
18 Ann Gidley Lowery, *The Story of the Flushing Meeting House* (Flushing, NY: Flushing Monthly Meeting of the Religious Society of Friends, 1969).
19 Thompson, *History of Long Island*, 71; Brodhead, *History*, 614; Cobb, *Rise of Religious Liberty*, 303–325; Henri Van der Zee and Barbara Van der Zee, *A Sweet and Alien Land: The Story of Dutch New York* (New York: Viking Press, 1978), 6.
20 Lester Leake Riley, *The Pageant of Flushing Town* (Flushing, NY: Flushing Centennial Celebration Committee, 1937).
21 Margaret I. Carman, *The Bowne House Historical Society* (Flushing, NY, 1951[?]), 26–32; "Our History," Bowne House, accessed November 14, 2024, https://www.bownehouse.org/ourhistory.
22 New York State Legislature, *Interim Report of the New York State Joint Legislative Committee for the Celebration of the 300th Anniversary of the Signing of the Flushing Remonstrance*, Legislative Doc. No. 30 (Albany, NY: State of New York, 1957).
23 *Long Island Star-Journal*, October 11, 1957.
24 *Long Island Star-Journal*, October 11, 1957.
25 J. Franklin Jameson and Woodrow Wilson Collection, *Narratives of New Netherland, -1664* (New York: Charles Scribner's Sons, 1909), https://www.loc.gov/item/09024463/.
26 Henry R. Stiles, *History of the City of Brooklyn, NY, Volume 1* (Brooklyn: 1867), 125.

27 Hazelton, *Boroughs of Brooklyn and Queens*, 1:XX, The Charter of Liberties and Privileges Granted by His Royal Highnesse to the Inhabitants of New Yorke, and its Dependencies, https://archive.org/details/boroughsofbrookl01haze/page/134/mode/1up?q=127.
28 Hazelton, *Boroughs of Brooklyn and Queens*, 1:123–127.
29 For colonial Queens, see Kross, *Evolution of an American Town*; Peyer, "Jamaica, Long Island"; Waller, *History of the Town of Flushing*. There is no recent history of colonial Flushing.
30 Hazelton, *Boroughs of Brooklyn and Queens*, 1:123–127, 2:939; Peter Ross, *A History of Long Island, from Its Earliest Settlements to the Present Time*, 3 vols. (New York: Lewis Publishing, 1902), 1:69–70.
31 Nadine Brozan, "Here's to Queen Catherine, Who Gave Queens a Name," *New York Times*, October 11, 1990; Joseph P. Fried, "Catherine of Queens?," *New York Times*, July 26, 1992.
32 Jeffrey A. Kroessler, "A Statue That's Unfit for Queens," *Newsday*, February 10, 1995.
33 Barry Bearak, "The Queen of Ethnic Nightmares: Cultural Politics Mires Statue of Borough's Namesake," *New York Times*, January 9, 1998; David Gold, letter, *New York Times*, October 11, 1998.
34 Audrey Flack, letter, *The East Hampton Star*, February 2, 1998.
35 "Asides: No Queen for Queens?," *Wall Street Journal*, January 8, 1998.
36 Carl Bridenbaugh, *Mitre and Sceptre: Transatlantic Faiths, Ideas, Personalities, and Politics 1689–1775* (New York: Oxford University Press, 1962), 120–121; Hazelton, *Boroughs of Brooklyn and Queens*, 1:165–166.
37 Hazelton, *Boroughs of Brooklyn and Queens*, 1:165–166.
38 Hazelton, *Boroughs of Brooklyn and Queens*, 1:169.
39 Ross, *History of Long Island*, 1:182, 191–192.
40 Myron H. Luke and Robert W. Venables, *Long Island in the American Revolution* (Albany: New York State American Revolution Bicentennial Commission, 1976), 12–13.
41 Ross, *History of Long Island*, 1:183.
42 Hazelton, *Boroughs of Brooklyn and Queens*, 1:167–168, 198.
43 Ross, *History of Long Island*, 1:182, 191–198.
44 Ross, *History of Long Island*, 1:202–204.
45 Michael Hayes, "Nathaniel Woodhull and the Battle of Long Island," *Long Island Historical Journal* 7, no. 2 (Spring 1995): 166–177; Ross, *History of Long Island*, 1:237–244.
46 Thompson, *History of Long Island*, 509; Silas Wood and Alden J. Spooner, *A Sketch of the First Settlement of the Several Towns on Long Island, with Their Political Condition, to the End of the American Revolution* (Brooklyn: printed for the Furman Club, 1865 [1828]), 191–192; Hayes, "Nathaniel Woodhull."
47 Ross, *History of Long Island*, 1:221–225; Wood and Spooner, *Sketch of the First Settlement*, 120–122; Hazelton, *Boroughs of Brooklyn and Queens*, 2:943–946.
48 Wood and Spooner, *Sketch of the First Settlement*, 120–122; Henry Onderdonk Jr. quoted in Ross, *History of Long Island*, 1:221–225; Hazelton, *Boroughs of Brooklyn and Queens*, 2:861.
49 Wood and Spooner, *Sketch of the First Settlement*, 120–122; Hazelton, *Boroughs of Brooklyn and Queens*, 2:861.
50 Hazelton, *Boroughs of Brooklyn and Queens*, 1:231–233.

Chapter 2 The Rural Landscape

1. Evan Cornog, *The Birth of Empire: DeWitt Clinton and the American Experience, 1769–1828* (New York: Oxford University Press, 1998), 116.
2. Barbara A. Chernow, "Robert Morris and Alexander Hamilton: Two Financiers in New York," in *Business Enterprise in Early New York*, ed. Joseph R. Frese and Jacob Judd (Tarrytown, NY: Sleepy Hollow Press, 1979), 92–93.
3. Long-Island Canal Company, *Documents Presented to the Legislature of the State of New-York at Its Last and Present Sessions, Setting Forth the Expediency and Public Importance of Incorporating the Long-Island Canal Company for the Purpose Expressed by the Petitioners* (New York: printed by Joseph C. Spear, Coffee House Slip, 1826).
4. Long-Island Canal Company, *Documents*; New York State Senate, *Reports of the Committees in Relation to the Long-Island Canal Company* (Albany, NY: Croswell and Van Benthuysen, 1827), 6.
5. For a discussion of banking in terms of the relationship between the metropolitan center and the hinterland, see Michael P. Conzen, "The Maturing Urban System in the United States, 1840–1910," *Annals of the Association of American Geographers* 67, no. 1 (March 1977): 88–108; Long-Island Canal Company, *Documents*; New York State Senate, *Reports of the Committees*, p. 6.
6. Long-Island Canal Company, *Documents*.
7. [Long-Island Canal and Navigation Company], *Report on the Project of Uniting the Great Bays of Long-Island by Canals from Coney-Island to Bridgehampton* (Brooklyn: E. B. Spooner, Printer, 1848). Another canal project never realized was a plan to bypass Hell Gate by cutting through what is now Astoria, then Hallett's Cove; see *Hurl Gate and the Proposed Canal* (New York [1832]). For the Erie Canal, see Cornog, *Birth of Empire*, chs. 8 and 12; for an overview of the canal era and the impact of the railroad, see George Rogers Taylor, *The Transportation Revolution, 1815–1860* (New York: Rinehart, 1951), chs. 3 and 5.
8. Hazelton, *Boroughs of Brooklyn and Queens*, 1:231–233.
9. Onderdonk, *Queens County*, 38, 47, 89; Waller, *History of the Town of Flushing*, 165; William Prince, *A Treatise on Fruit and Ornamental Trees and Plants, Cultivated at the Linnëan Botanic Garden, Flushing, Long-Island, near New-York* (New York: T. and J. Swords, 1820).
10. QHS, "Kingland Homestead," accessed November 14, 2024, https://queenshistoricalsociety.org/kingsland-homestead/; Henry Hope Reed and Sophia Duckworth, *Central Park: A History and a Guide*, rev. ed. (New York: Clarkson N. Potter, 1972), 30, 38–39; Laura Wood Roper, *FLO: A Biography of Frederick Law Olmsted* (Baltimore: Johns Hopkins Press, 1973), 65, 147, 403; Brooklyn Botanic Garden, leaflets, series 24, nos. 3–5, December 9, 1936; New York City Department of Parks, *Kissena Park: Botanical Guide to a Historic Grove*, 1981; Peters, *Trees of Long Island*, 18, 22–23.
11. *Flushing Journal*, June 8, 1844.
12. John A. King, *An Address, Delivered October 6th, 1848, at the Seventh Annual Exhibition of the Queens County Agricultural Society, at Jamaica, Long Island.* (Jamaica, NY: printed by Charles S. Watrous, 1849), 9–12.
13. Charles A. King, *An Address, Delivered September 29th, 1852, at the Eleventh Annual Exhibition of the Queens County Agricultural Society, at Flushing, Long Island* (Jamaica, NY: printed at the office of the Long Island Farmer, 1852).

14 Marc Linder and Lawrence S. Zacharias, *Of Cabbages and Kings County: Agriculture and the Formation of Modern Brooklyn* (Iowa City: University of Iowa Press, 1999), 26.
15 Waller, *History of the Town of Flushing*, 172–173.
16 George W. Winans, *Old Roads of Jamaica Township in Colonial Days* (Jamaica, NY, 1935), Long Island Collection, QBPL, 7–8; Vincent F. Seyfried, *300 Years of Long Island City* (Garden City, NY: Edgian Press, 1984), 16–17, 25; Mathew Dripps, *Map of the Cities of New York, Brooklyn, Jersey City, Hudson City, and Hoboken* (New York, 1859).
17 Ira Rosenwaike, *Population History of New York City* (Syracuse, NY: Syracuse University Press, 1972), 16; Jan Peterson and Vincent Seyfried, *A Research Guide to the History of the Borough of Queens* (Flushing, NY: Queens College, 1987), 13. For detailed maps of the villages in Queens County, see F. W. Beers, *Atlas of Long Island, New York* (New York: F. W. Beers, 1873).
18 Linder and Zacharias, *Of Cabbages and Kings County*, 4–6.
19 Jeffrey A. Kroessler, "Brooklyn's Thirst, Long Island's Water: Consolidation, Local Control, and the Aquifer," *Long Island History Journal* 22, no. 1 (2011), https://lihj.cc.stonybrook.edu/2011/articles/brooklyns-thirst-long-islands-water-consolidation-local-control-and-the-aquifer/.
20 Harold Coffin Syrett, *The City of Brooklyn, 1865–1898: A Political History* (New York: Columbia University Press, 1944), 12–13; see also Jacob Judd, "Water for Brooklyn," *New York History* 47, no. 4 (October 1966): 362–371; Ross, *History of Long Island*, 1:350–351; Paul Bailey, ed., *Long Island: A History of Two Great Counties, Nassau and Suffolk*, 3 vols. (New York: Lewis Historical Publishing, 1949), 1:427 (ch. 13); Peterson and Seyfried, *Research Guide*, 13; Rosenwaike, *Population History*, 31–32; Joseph J. Salvo and Arun Peter Lobo, "Population," in *The Encyclopedia of New York City*, 2nd ed., ed. Kenneth T. Jackson (New Haven, CT: Yale University Press, 2010), 1019 (hereafter cited as *Encyclopedia of New York City*).
21 Edward K. Spann, *The New Metropolis: New York City 1840–1857* (New York: Columbia University Press, 1981), 108–109; *Long Island Democrat*, May 20, 1835, and August 14, 1839. Throughout the 1840s and 1850s, the *Flushing Journal* featured many advertisements for steamboats running between New York and communities along the East River and Long Island Sound.
22 1850 Census of the State of New York, https://www2.census.gov/library/publications/decennial/1850/1850a/1850a-22.pdf; Edgar J. McManus, *A History of Negro Slavery in New York* (Syracuse, NY: Syracuse University Press, 1966), 174–179; Linder and Zacharias, *Of Cabbages and Kings County*, 81–82; David Nathaniel Gellman, *Emancipating New York: The Politics of Slavery and Freedom, 1777–1827* (Baton Rouge: Louisiana State University Press, 2006); Ira Berlin and Leslie Harris, eds., *Slavery in New York* (New York: New Press, 2005).
23 Waller, *History of the Town of Flushing*, 175–177. The records of the Flushing Female Association are in the QHS archives.
24 Waller, *History of the Town of Flushing*, 195–196; Census of Queens County, New York, 1850, vol. 1 https://www2.census.gov/library/publications/decennial/1850/1850a/1850a-22.pdf; for an image of Newtown, see *View of Elmhurst*, ca. 1839, an anonymous oil painting in the collection of the Nassau County Museum. The name of the painting is inaccurate, for not until April 1896 did Cord Meyer change the name of the place from Newtown, to eliminate any association with the foul waters of Newtown Creek.

Chapter 3 The Railroad and Long Island

1. State of New York, Laws of 1832, ch. 256: An Act to Incorporate the Brooklyn and Jamaica Rail-Road Company.
2. State of New York, Laws of 1834, ch. 178: An Act to Incorporate the Long Island Rail-Road Company; Elizur B. Hinsdale, *History of the Long Island Railroad Company, 1834–1898* (New York: Evening Post Job Printing House, 1898), 1–2; Hazelton, *Boroughs of Brooklyn and Queens*, 1:386–387.
3. *Long Island Democrat*, April 27, 1836.
4. Seyfried, *300 Years*, 84–85; Mildred H. Smith, *Early History of the Long Island Railroad, 1834–1900* (Uniondale, NY: Salisbury Printers, 1958); Edwin L. Dunbaugh, "New York to Boston via the Long Island Railroad, 1844–1847," in *Evoking a Sense of Place*, ed. Joann P. Krieg (Interlaken: Heart of the Lakes Publishing, 1988), 75–79; *Long Island Democrat*, April 26, 1837; September 18, 1839; June 9, 1840. The most detailed work on the LIRR is Vincent F. Seyfried's *The Long Island Rail Road: A Comprehensive History*, 7 vols. (Garden City, NY: Vincent F. Seyfried, 1961–1975), though he treats each rail line separately and does not tie the story together into a single narrative (hereafter cited as *LIRR* followed by volume and page number).
5. Long Island Railroad (LIRR), *Report of the Board of Directors of the Long Island Railroad Company to the Stockholders, in Relation to the Condition of Its Affairs, and Prospects When Completed to Greenport* ([New York], 1843); Hinsdale, *History*, 4–5. This episode, marking Vanderbilt's entrance into railroading, has received minimal attention from the Commodore's biographers. See Wheaton J. Lane, *Commodore Vanderbilt: An Epic of the Steam Age* (New York: Alfred A. Knopf, 1942), 66, 72–74; John Steele Gordon, *The Scarlet Woman of Wall Street* (New York: Weidenfeld and Nicolson, 1988), ch. 3.
6. Reprinted in the *Flushing Journal*, May 6, 1843.
7. David Robinson George, "A Brief History of the Long Island Rail Road," in Bailey, *Long Island*, 2:397–398; Dunbaugh, "New York to Boston," 75–84; Clarence Ashton Wood, *First Train to Greenport in 1844* (Bayshore, NY: Long Island Forum, 1944).
8. Nathaniel S. Prime, *A History of Long Island, from Its First Settlement by Europeans to the Year 1845, with Special Reference to Its Ecclesiastical Concerns* (New York: Robert Carter, 1845), pt. I, 59–60; Georger, "Brief History," 400.
9. Wood, "First Train to Greenport in 1844," 10–12; *Flushing Journal*, May 2, 1846.
10. George H. Peters, "The Flora of Long Island," in Bailey, *Long Island*, 2:150; "History of the Long Island Pine Barrens," Long Island Pine Barrens Society, accessed November 14, 2024, https://www.pinebarrens.org/history-of-the-pine-barrens/.
11. Dunbaugh, "New York to Boston," 82–83.
12. See Vincent Seyfried, *LIRR*, vol. 2.
13. *Map of the Village of Flushing* (April 1, 1841); *Map of Valuable Property Situated in and Adjoining the Village of Flushing (the Village Line Running thro' the Property) Belonging to Mr. Gansevoort, for Sale by W. Smart, Agent* (New York, July 1850); H. F. Walling, *Topographical Map of the Counties of Kings and Queens* (New York: W. E. and A. A. Baker, 1859).
14. *Flushing Journal*, November 15, 1851; March 12 and 19, 1853.
15. *Flushing Journal*, May 14, 1842.
16. *Flushing Journal*, June 22, 1844.

17 *Flushing Journal*, September 9, 1850.
18 *Flushing Journal*, December 28, 1850.
19 *Flushing Journal*, April 19, 1850; November 7, 1846.
20 *Flushing Journal*, June 21 and 28, 1851.
21 *Flushing Journal*, June 21, 1851.
22 *Flushing Journal*, June 28, 1851.
23 *Flushing Journal*, July 12, 1851.
24 *Flushing Journal*, September 14, 1850; Mathew Dripps, *Map of Kings and Part of Queens Counties* (New York, 1852).
25 *Flushing Journal*, March 6, 1852; Flushing Rail Road Company, Articles of Association, February 24, 1852, in Minutes of the Board of Directors (hereafter cited as "FRRC Minutes").
26 Flushing Rail Road Company, Minutes, March 22, 1852; *Flushing Journal*, March 20 and 27, 1852; Seyfried, *LIRR*, 2:3.
27 Both reprinted in the *Flushing Journal*, May 8, 1852.
28 FRRC Minutes, April 10 and 17, May 22, July 10, September 25, October 1, December 27, 1852; February 22, April 6, 1853; *Flushing Journal*, June 5, 1852, May 14, August 27, September 17, 1853; Seyfried, *LIRR*, 2:4–7; Harry C. Lewis, *Corporate and Financial History of the Following Corporations, All of Which Have Been Merged into or Otherwise Acquired by the Long Island Railroad Company* ([Washington, DC]: Bureau of Valuation, Interstate Commerce Commission, 1919), 53–56.
29 FRRC Minutes, August 22 and 31, September 13 and 23, October 19, November 15, 1853; *Flushing Journal*, September 24, 1853; Seyfried, *LIRR*, 2:6–7.
30 *Astoria Gazette*, October 21, 1852; Seyfried, *300 Years*, 83–85.
31 FRRC Minutes, May 4 and 12, July 2, September 23 and 27, 1853; March 20, August 15, November 13, 1854; *Flushing Journal*, February 19, March 5, December 3, 1853; Seyfried, *LIRR*, 2:6–8.
32 FRRC Minutes, February 13, 16, 20, and 28, March 6, 1854.
33 FRRC Minutes, September 23, October 19, 1853.
34 Seyfried, *LIRR*, 2:9–10; FRRC Minutes, April 25, 1854.
35 *Flushing Journal*, January 22, 1853; Seyfried, *LIRR*, 2:11–13.
36 *Flushing Journal*, May 28, 1853; FRRC Minutes, January 3 and 9, May 22, June 26, 1854.
37 H. C. Lewis, *Corporate and Financial History*, 53–56.
38 FRRC Minutes, September 1, December 22, 1856; January 30, February 21, March 24, 1857; Seyfried, *LIRR*, 2:19–20.
39 Allan Nevins, *Abram S. Hewitt, with Some Account of Peter Cooper* (New York: Harper and Brothers, 1935), 136.
40 Hinsdale, *History*, 9.
41 Seyfried, *LIRR*, 2:22–23.
42 Robert A. Hecht, *A History of College Point* (College Point, NY: Bicentennial Commission of College Point, 1976), ch. 5; Seyfried, *LIRR*, 2:23.
43 *Long Island Democrat*, June 26, 1839.
44 Linder and Zacharias, *Of Cabbages and Kings County*, 25–26.
45 J. A. King, *An Address*, 13–15; see Thomas Schnebly, *The Quality of the "Wild Lands" of Long Island: Examined, and Detailed Evidences Given of Their Value, Together with a Reasonable Conjecture Why They Have Not Been Improved* (New York: The Sun Book and Job Printing Office, 1860); Linder and Zacharias, *Of Cabbages and Kings County*, 49–50.

46 *Flushing Journal*, July 28, 1855.
47 *Jamaica, Hempstead, Richmond Hill, Morris Park and Woodhaven: Their Representative Business Men and Points of Interest* (New York: Mercantile Publishing, 1894), 35–36.
48 City of Brooklyn Common Council, *Reports of the Majority and Minority of the Railroad Committee on the Subject of Steam on Atlantic Street* (Brooklyn: L. Darbee and Son Printers, June 1, 1857).
49 City of Brooklyn Common Council, *Reports of the Majority and Minority*.
50 *Remarks on the Proposed Change of Terminus of the Long Island Railroad from Atlantic Street Brooklyn, to Hunter's Point*, September 30, 1858.
51 H. C. Lewis, *Corporate and Financial History*, 153–154; M. H. Smith, *Early History*, 42; Seyfried, *LIRR*, 1:28–31; 3:133–135.
52 South Side Railroad Company of Long Island, Minutes of the Board of Directors, April 20, 1860 (hereafter cited as "SSRRC Minutes").
53 SSRRC Minutes, March 16 and 28, 1866 (there is no record in the minutes of any meeting between 1860 and 1866); H. C. Lewis, *Corporate and Financial History*, 196–199; Seyfried, *LIRR*, 1:2–3.
54 Seyfried, *LIRR*, 1:4–7; 3:138.
55 SSRRC Minutes, February 8, March 14, May 6, and September 17, 1867; Seyfried, *LIRR*, 1:4–5; Hinsdale, *History*, 12.
56 Seyfried, *LIRR*, 1:10–16, 28–29, 63–67; SSRRC Minutes, December 23, 1867; January 12, 1868; H. C. Lewis, *Corporate and Financial History*, 196–199. See Felix E. Reifschneider, "Historical Notes," typed sheets and hand-drawn map (Electric Railroaders Association, 1952) for summaries of the dates for each line and spur of the LIRR and competing lines.
57 Seyfried, *LIRR*, 1:28–31, 35–36.
58 SSRRC Minutes, August 13, September 11, 1872; January 21 and 22, February 4, June 10, September 4, November 5, 1873; Hinsdale, *History*, 22; Seyfried, *LIRR*, 1:55–57.
59 Seyfried, *LIRR*, 3:3; Hinsdale, *History*, 7–9; Flushing and Woodside Rail Road Company, Minutes of the Board of Directors, February 15 and 18, March 4, April 22, May 16, June 8, 1864; February 11, March 28, 1867; New York & Flushing Railroad Company, Minutes of the Board of Directors, July 13, 1867 (hereafter cited as "NYFRRC Minutes"); Seyfried, *LIRR*, 2:38; Elizur Brace Hinsdale, *Autobiography, with Reports and Documents* (New York: J. J. Little, 1901), 38, 48–49.
60 Hinsdale, *History*, 15.
61 Hinsdale, *History*, 22; Flushing and Woodside Railroad Company, Minutes of the Board of Directors, February 10 and 15, April 27, September 26, 1868; July 5, 1870; NYFRRC Minutes, August 11, 1868; H. C. Lewis, *Corporate and Financial History*, 59–71, 93–97; Seyfried, *LIRR*, 2:52–58, 65.
62 NYFRRC Minutes, October 25, 1869; June 6, 1870; Hunters Point and South Side Railroad Company, Minutes, January 5, June 6, 1870; H. C. Lewis, *Corporate and Financial History*, 109.
63 NYFRRC Minutes, September 15, 1873; Seyfried, *LIRR*, 1:29–31; Hinsdale, *History*, 20–21; Beers, *Atlas of Long Island*, plate 53, shows Furman's trout farm.
64 Hinsdale, *History*, 22.
65 Hinsdale, *History*, 19; H. C. Lewis, *Corporate and Financial History*, 142–143; Seyfried, *LIRR*, 3:71–83.
66 Seyfried, *LIRR*, 3:64–67; vol. 5 covers the history of the railroads in the Rockaways, esp. chs. 1, 2, 4, and 5.

67 Hinsdale, *History*, 13–14; Seyfried, *LIRR*, 1:55–56.
68 *Dictionary of American Biography* (1935), s.v. "Stewart, Alexander Turney"; Seyfried, *LIRR*, 2:81–83.
69 Vincent F. Seyfried, *The Founding of Garden City, 1869–1893* (Uniondale, NY: Salisbury Printers, 1969); Mildred H. Smith, *History of Garden City* (Garden City, NY: Garden City Historical Society, 1980); Kenneth T. Jackson, *Crabgrass Frontier: The Suburbanization of the United States* (New York: Oxford University Press, 1985), 81–84.
70 Flushing and North Side Rail Road Company, Minutes of the Board of Directors, January 24 and February 3, 1871; January 7, 1873; Central Rail Road of Long Island Company, Minutes of the Board of Directors, March 3, 1871; February 20 and October 16, 1872; January 6 and 7, 1873; H. C. Lewis, *Corporate and Financial History*, 1–2, 18–25; Seyfried, *LIRR*, 2:83–85.
71 Hinsdale, *History*, 18; Seyfried, *LIRR*, 3:90; Beers, *Atlas of Long Island*, shows the three depots serving the Village of Hempstead.
72 Flushing, North Shore & Central Railroad Company, Minutes of the Board of Directors, June 19, 1874; H. C. Lewis, *Corporate and Financial History*, 27–30, 74–91 167–173, 210–213.
73 Hinsdale, *History*, 23; Seyfried, *LIRR*, 3:114–116.
74 Southern Railroad Company of Long Island, Minutes of the Board of Directors, May 3, 1876, August 22, 1877; Flushing, North Shore & Central Rail Road Company, Minutes, May 3, 1876, August 18, 1877; Hinsdale, *History*, 23–24.
75 LIRR, *Long Island & Where to Go!! A Descriptive Work Compiled for the Long Island R. R. Co. for the Use and Benefit of Its Patrons* (New York: LIRR, 1877); *LIRR*, 3:118–125.
76 Flushing, North Shore & Central Railroad Company, Minutes, August 18, 1877; January 30, 1879; Seyfried, *LIRR*, 3:129, 174–175; Hinsdale, *History*, 25.
77 Seyfried, *LIRR*, 3:150–160.
78 Seyfried, *LIRR*, 3:160–163.
79 H. C. Lewis, *Corporate and Financial History*, 27; Seyfried, *LIRR*, 3:174; Hinsdale, *History*, 27.
80 *Dictionary of American Biography* (1935), s.v. Corbin, Austin; Glendale and East River Railroad Company, Minutes of the Board of Directors, December 22, 1876; January 12, 1877; Hinsdale, *History*, 27–31; H. C. Lewis, *Corporate and Financial History*, 5–14, 122–130, 186–192.
81 Austin Corbin, "Quick Transit between New York and London," *North American Review* 159, no. 468 (November 1892): 513–527; see also, Austin Corbin, *Extracts from the Press* [New York, 1896].
82 Will H. Lyford, *Report on a Proposed Development of Transatlantic Steamship Terminal as Montauk, on Fort Pond Bay, Long Island* (New York, August 1923).
83 *New York Times*, June 5, 1896.

Chapter 4   The Verdant Suburbs

1 C. King, *An Address*, 11–15.
2 For Brooklyn Heights, see Jackson, *Crabgrass Frontier*, 25–32; Seyfried, *300 Years*, 16–19.
3 Seyfried, *300 Years*, 16–19; Dripps, *Map*.
4 Edith Wharton, *A Backward Glance* (New York: Charles Scribners and Sons, 1985 [1933]), 13.

5. Walling, *Topographical Map*; Seyfried, *300 Years*, 56–61. The Currier and Ives print is in the New-York Historical Society (N-YHS) Collection. See Gwendolyn Wright, *Moralism and the Modern Home* (Chicago: University of Chicago Press, 1980), 10–11, for a discussion of Downing's advocacy of the Gothic Revival cottage.
6. Lydia Maria Childs, *Letters from New-York* (New York, 1852 [1844]), 61–68.
7. *New York World*, November 24, 1895; Beers, *Atlas of Long Island*, plate 53; Wolverton, *Atlas of Queens County*, plate 4.
8. George von Skal, *Illustrated History of the Borough of Queens, New York City* (New York: F. T. Smiley Publishing, for the Flushing Journal, 1908), 44, 48.
9. Anonymous, "Fair Bayside" (1873); Bloodgood Haviland Cutter, *The Long Island Farmer's Poems, Lines Written on the "Quaker City" Excursion to Palestine and Other Poems* (New York: N. Tibbals and Sons, 1886); Mark Twain, *The Innocents Abroad* (New York: Signet Classics, 1966 [1869]), 54, 68; Jeffrey A. Kroessler, "Cutter, Bloodgood H(aviland)," in *Encyclopedia of New York City*, 338.
10. *Long Island Democrat*, August 14, 1839.
11. LIRR, *Long Island & Where to Go!!*, 6, 132.
12. Vincent F. Seyfried, "Garden City," in *The Encyclopedia of New York State*, ed. Peter Eisenstadt (Syracuse, NY: Syracuse University Press), 619; Jackson, *Crabgrass Frontier*, 81–84.
13. Kate Matson Post, *The Story of Richmond Hill* (Richmond Hill, NY: Richmond Hill Record, 1905), 3; Barry Lewis, *Kew Gardens: Urban Village in the Big City* (Kew Gardens, NY: Kew Gardens Council for Recreation and the Arts, 1999), 10.
14. LIRR, *Long Island & Where to Go!!*, 157–161; *Jamaica, Hempstead*, 38; for a general discussion of railroad suburbs, see Jackson, *Crabgrass Frontier*, ch. 5.
15. [H. F. Gunnison], *The Beauties of Long Island* (New York: LIRR, 1895), 52–53.
16. B. Lewis, *Kew Gardens*, 13.
17. B. Lewis, *Kew Gardens*, 10–15.
18. LIRR, *Long Island & Where to Go!!*, 157–161; Beers, *Atlas of Long Island*; City of Brooklyn, Department of Parks, *Annual Report*, 1896; B. Lewis, *Kew Gardens*, 10–15.
19. [Gunnison,] *Beauties of Long Island*, 52–53; *Jamaica, Hempstead*, 36–38; see also [Julian Ralph], *Long Island of To-Day* (New York: [American Bank Note Company], 1884), 25; "Borough of Queens: A Review of Its Progress because of Excellent Location, Remarkable Resources & Superior Natural Advantages," *American Journal of Commerce* 14, no. 15 (1900), 21.
20. Jacob Riis, *The Making of an American* (New York, 1920 [1901]), 284–290, 437. The Riis house was demolished in 1973, despite its listing on the National Register of Historic Places.
21. Riis, *Making of an American*, 284–290, 437.
22. M. H. Smith, *Early History*, p. 34; LIRR, *Long Island & Where to Go!!*, 105–109.
23. LIRR, *Long Island & Where to Go!!*, 114.
24. LIRR, *Long Island & Where to Go!!*, 155–157; see also Beers, *Atlas of Long Island*, for the actual state of suburban development.
25. George W. Bromley and Walter S. Bromley, *Atlas of the City of New York, Borough of Queens* (Philadelphia: G. W. Bromley, 1909), plates 32, 33, 40, 41; E. Belcher Hyde, *Atlas of the Borough of Queens* (Brooklyn: E. Belcher Hyde, 1901), vol. 1, plates 4 and 5.
26. William Kroos, *A Peek at Richmond Hill through the Keyhole of Time* (Richmond Hill, NY: Richmond Hill Savings Bank, 1983), 13–20.

27 *Jamaica, Hempstead,* 41–42; Wolverton, *Atlas of Queens County,* plate 18; Hyde, *Atlas of the Borough of Queens* (1901), vol. 1, plates 4 and 5.
28 [Gunnison,] *Beauties of Long Island,* 55.
29 von Skal, *Illustrated History,* 59; Bromley and Bromley, *Atlas of the City of New York, Borough of Queens,* plate 39; Daniel Czitrom, "Big Tim Sullivan," in *Encyclopedia of New York City,* 1264. Tammany Hall was an American political organization formed in 1788 in New York City. Over time, it became the local political machine of the Democratic Party, controlling New York City and New York state politics.
30 Advertisement in the *Long Island Magazine,* September 1903; Bromley and Bromley, *Atlas of the City of New York, Borough of Queens,* plate 28.
31 *Queensborough,* January 1923.
32 von Skal, *Illustrated History,* 36.

Chapter 5 The Noxious Industries

1 For Newtown, Flushing, and Jamaica, see Wolverton, *Atlas of Queens County,* plates 8, 9, 17, and 21; for industries in East Williamsburgh, see Beers, *Atlas of Long Island,* plates 48 and 103; Hecht, *History of College Point,* ch. 5; Seyfried, *300 Years,* ch. 9; Vincent F. Seyfried, *The Story of Woodhaven and Ozone Park* (Woodhaven, NY: Leader Observer, 1985), ch. 4.
2 Beers, *Atlas of Long Island,* plate 66; Wolverton, *Atlas of Queens County,* plate 22; Hecht, *History,* 35–40.
3 Richard K. Lieberman, *Steinway & Sons* (New Haven, CT: Yale University Press, 1995), 17–21.
4 Lieberman, *Steinway & Sons,* 77–80.
5 Lieberman, *Steinway & Sons,* 77–85.
6 *Newtown Register,* July 22, 1880; Seyfried, *300 Years,* 69–74; Lieberman, *Steinway & Sons,* 77–80. The Steinway family's papers and the records of the piano company are in the Steinway & Sons Collection, LaGuardia and Wagner Archives at the LaGuardia Community College of the City University of New York (hereafter cited as LWA). For documents relating to the German community in Astoria, see the Geipel Collection, QHS.
7 *Long Island City Star,* March 12, April 6 and 16, November 5, 1886; May 6, July 15, 1887. The Sohmer Piano Company abandoned Queens in 1982; the factory building was designated a city landmark in 2007. See Landmarks Preservation Commission, *Sohmer & Company Piano Factory Building,* Designation List Report, February 27, 2007, https://www.nyc.gov/html/records/pdf/govpub/2867sohmer.final.pdf.
8 *Long Island City Star,* February 26, April 2 and 9, July 16, 1886; April 8, March 2, 1888; Wolverton, *Atlas of Queens County,* plate 4; Seyfried, *300 Years,* 89, 95–98.
9 *Long Island City Star,* August 24, 1888; January 31, July 18, 1890; *Newtown Register,* October 28, August 12 and 26, 1880; September 21, 1881; Beers, *Atlas of Long Island,* plates 40, 43, and 46; Wolverton, *Atlas of Queens County,* plates 4 and 5; Seyfried, *300 Years,* 89, 95–98; Curtis Cravens, *Copper on the Creek: Reclaiming an Industrial History* (Brooklyn: Place in History, 2000). Charles Pratt was a pioneer of the U.S. petroleum industry who established his kerosene refinery, Astral Oil Works, in Brooklyn in the 1860s.
10 *Newtown Register,* October 28, August 12 and 26, 1880; September 21, 1881.

11. John C. Philip and Henry H. Browne, *Insurance Surveys of the Petroleum Depots in New York and Vicinity* (New York: Perris and Browne, 1863); *Newtown Register*, August 12 and 26, 1880; September 21, 1881; *Long Island City Star*, January 31, July 18, 1890; Seyfried, *300 Years*, 111–113.
12. *Newtown Register*, July 28, 1881; January 12, March 2, and April 13, 1882; August 2, 1883; Beers, *Atlas of Long Island*, plate 48; Seyfried, *300 Years*, 109.
13. *Flushing Journal*, January 14, March 25, and May 27, 1893.
14. James Dao, "Label It Made in Queens," *New York Daily News* (Queens edition), January 28, 1990.
15. Hazelton, *Boroughs of Brooklyn and Queens*, 2:1027.
16. Martin V. Melosi, *Fresh Kills: A History of Consuming and Discarding in New York City* (New York: Columbia University Press, 2020), 60, 91–94; Thomas J. Campanella, *Brooklyn: The Once and Future City* (Princeton, NJ: Princeton University Press, 2019), ch. 6.
17. Jeffrey A. Kroessler, "Jamaica Bay and Marine Park" and "Rockaway Improvement," in *Robert Moses and the Modern City: The Transformation of New York*, ed. Hillary Ballon and Kenneth T. Jackson (New York: W. W. Norton, 2007), 166–168, 171–172.
18. Melosi, *Fresh Kills*, 48–51, 92.
19. George A. Soper, "Court's Decision Forces City to Solve Its Refuse Problems," *New York Times*, May 24, 1931; Melosi, *Fresh Kills*, 150–155.
20. Soper, "Court's Decision."
21. Soper, "Court's Decision"; Melosi, *Fresh Kills*, 127–128, 138.
22. Soper, "Court's Decision"; Daniel C. Walsh, "The Evolution of Refuse Incineration: What Led to the Rise and Fall of Incineration in New York City?," *Environmental Science & Technology* 36, no. 15 (2002): 316–322.
23. Melosi, *Fresh Kills*, 95–96, 146.
24. Melosi, *Fresh Kills*, 146–149.
25. Vincent F. Seyfried, *Corona: From Farmland to City Suburb, 1650–1935* (Garden City, NY: Edgian Press, 1986), 67–68; Jeffrey A. Kroessler, "Flushing Meadows-Corona Park," in Ballon and Jackson, *Robert Moses*, 197–200; Melosi, *Fresh Kills*, 92.

Chapter 6   The Leisure Landscape

1. Hazelton, *Boroughs of Brooklyn and Queens*, 3:1647.
2. Hazelton, *Boroughs of Brooklyn and Queens*, 3:1647–1650. For a history of early horse racing in Queens County, see Melvin L. Adelman, *A Sporting Time: New York City and the Rise of Modern Athletics, 1820–1870* (Urbana: University of Illinois, 1986), chs. 2–4, esp. 43–45; and John Eisenberg, *The Great Match Race: When North Met South in America's First Sports Spectacle* (Boston: Houghton Mifflin, 2006).
3. Daniel M. Tredwell, *Personal Reminiscences of Men and Things on Long Island*, pt. II (Brooklyn: Charles Andrew Ditmas, 1917), 197; Vincent F. Seyfried, *Queens: A Pictorial History* (Norfolk, VA: Donning, 1982), 129; Russel Crouse, *Mr. Currier and Mr. Ives: A Note on Their Lives and Times* (Garden City, NY: Garden City Publishing, 1937), 46, and plate following 44; Hazelton, *Boroughs of Brooklyn and Queens*, 3:1647–1650.
4. "Base Ball: Brooklyn Nine vs. New-York Nine—New-York Victorious," *New York Times*, September 11, 1858.

5   Hazelton, *Boroughs of Brooklyn and Queens*, 3:1648–1650; "Sporting Intelligence: Grand Fox-Chase at Union Course, L.I.," *New York Times*, January 12, 1866; "A Pack of Bipedal Brutes," *New York Times*, January 13, 1866.
6   Hazelton, *Boroughs of Brooklyn and Queens*, 3:1653–1654.
7   Alfred H. Bellot, *History of the Rockaways, from the Year 1685 to 1917* (Far Rockaway, NY: Bellot's Histories, 1917), 84.
8   *Album of the Rockaways and Long Beach* (New York: Wittemann Bros., 1881); Cromwell Childe, *Water Exploring: A Guide to Pleasant Steamboat Trips Everywhere* (Brooklyn: Brooklyn Daily Eagle, 1902); Beers, *Atlas of Long Island*, plates 35 and 39, shows the railroad line from Canarsie to East New York.
9   *Newtown Register*, August 5, 1880.
10 Bellot, *History of the Rockaways*, 25, 99, 104–105. Bellot actually relates the story of the Rockaway Beach Hotel twice, once with the date 1879 and once dated 1881; for an engraving of the hotel, see *Album of the Rockaways and Long Beach*.
11 *Long Island City Star*, April 26, 1889; *LIRR*, 5:23–35; John F. Kasson, *Amusing the Million: Coney Island at the Turn of the Century* (New York: Hill and Wang, 1978), 30–31.
12 *Newtown Register*, July 13, November 2, 1882; June 7, 1883; *Long Island City Star*, September 6, 1889; *Far Rockaway, Rockaway Beach, Rockaway Park, Long Island* (New York: American Photograph Company, 1910), 3, 42–43; Willam M. Laffan, *The New Long Island: A Hand Book of Summer Travel Designed for the Use and Information of Visitors to Long Island and Its Watering Places* (New York: Rogers and Sherwood, 1879), 63–65; LIRR, *Hotels and Boarding Cottages on Long Island, N. Y.* (New York: LIRR, 1892); Wolverton, *Atlas of Queens County*, plates 11–13; Cromwell Childe, *Trolley Exploring* (Brooklyn: Brooklyn Daily Eagle, 1902), 29; for photographs of the "cottages," including the home of Lillian Russell, see William Soper Pettit, *History & Views of the Rockaways* (Far Rockaway, NY, 1901).
13 Jeffrey A. Kroessler, "Breezy Point," in *Encyclopedia of New York City*, 152; Jennifer Callahan, dir., *The Bungalows of Rockaway* (New York: Kino Lorber, 2016), https://www.thebungalowsofrockaway.com/. See also Beachside Bungalow Preservation Association, "Some Bungalow Exteriors," accessed November 14, 2024, https://preserve.org/bungalow/exteriors.htm.
14 Corey Kilgannon, "A Man's Beach Bungalow Is His Castle, under Siege by Developers," *New York Times*, August 11, 2006; Kroessler, "Breezy Point," 152.
15 *Flushing Journal*, July 25, 1874.
16 Childe, *Trolley Exploring*, 7–8.
17 John Rousmaniere, "Cemeteries," in *Encyclopedia of New York City*, 220–221; "History," Green-Wood Cemetery, accessed November 14, 2024, https://www.green-wood.com/history/.
18 *Long Island City Weekly Star*, January 25, 1889; John W. Reps, *The Making of Urban America: A History of City Planning in the United States* (Princeton, NJ: Princeton University Press, 1965), 325–331; Joy M. Giguere, "'Too Mean to Live, and Certainly in No Fit Condition to Die': Vandalism, Public Misbehavior, and the Rural Cemetery Movement," *Journal of the Early Republic* 38, no. 2 (2018): 293–324.
19 Dorothy Speer, "History of Niederstein's," Juniper Park Civic Association, September 29, 2006, https://junipercivic.com/history/history-of-niedersteins.
20 *Flushing Journal*, August 1, 1891.
21 *Newtown Register*, June 15 and 29, 1882; May 10, 1883; June 25, 1885.
22 *Newtown Register*, June 15 and 29, 1882.

23 *Newtown Register*, August 17, 1882; *Long Island City Star*, July 18, 23, and 30, 1886; April 22 and July 22, 1887.
24 *New York Times*, May 31, 1891.
25 Roy Rosenzweig and Elizabeth Blackmar, *The Park and the People: A History of Central Park* (Ithaca, NY: Cornell University Press, 1992), 248–249, 312.
26 *Long Island City Star*, April 15, 22, 29, May 6, 20, and June 17, 1887; Seyfried, *330 Years*, 122.
27 *Long Island City Star*, April 15, 22, 29, May 6, 20, and June 17, 1887; Seyfried, *300 Years*, 122; George Walsh, *Gentleman Jimmy Walker, Mayor of the Jazz Age* (New York: Praeger, 1979), 33.
28 Hecht, *History of College Point*, 63–68; *Flushing Journal*, April 10, 1875; *Long Island City Star*, July 1, 1887.
29 "Chat with Mr. Steinway," *New York Times*, November 24, 1895.
30 *Newtown Register*, July 8, 1880; March 6, 1884; Seyfried, *300 Years*, 120.
31 *Flushing Journal*, May 13, 1893.
32 *Newtown Register*, June 25, 1885.
33 Jackson, *Crabgrass Frontier*, 112–113; for Coney Island, see Kasson, *Amusing the Million*; for descriptions of these resorts, see contemporary guidebooks, including *Appleton's Dictionary of New York* (New York: D. Appleton, 1898); L. H. Glazier, *Easy Guide to Points of Interest & Business Sections in Greater New York* (New York, 1901); *Kenny's Guide* (New York: F. H. Kenny, 1889); Gustav Heerbrandt, *Illustrirter Führer durch New York* (New York, 1893); and Jaroslav Vojan, *Velky New York (Greater New York)* (New York: New-Yorkských List, 1908).
34 William Miller, *Bowery Bay Road*, 1877, N-YHS. The house was designated an official landmark by the city's Landmark Preservation Commission in 1966 and remains a private residence.
35 *Long Island City Star*, July 21, 1882; July 24, 1885; *Newtown Register*, June 28, 1883.
36 *Long Island City Star*, August 7, 1885.
37 *Long Island City Star*, April 9 and May 14, 1886.
38 *Long Island City Star*, June 25, 1886.
39 *Long Island City Star*, January 21, 1887; August 16, 1889.
40 *Long Island City Star*, June 11 and July 16, 1886.
41 Bowery Bay Beach Building and Improvement Company, *A Day's Outing at Bowery Bay Beach* (New York, 1889).
42 For a discussion of the relationship between working-class leisure patterns and the rise of trolley parks, see Roy Rosenzweig, *Eight Hours for What We Will: Workers and Leisure in an Industrial City, 1870–1920* (New York: Cambridge University Press, 1983), ch. 7; see also Kasson, *Amusing the Million*; Richard W. Flint, "Meet Me in Dreamland: The Early Development of Amusement Parks in America," *Nineteenth Century* 8, nos. 1–2 (1982): 99–107.
43 *Long Island City Star*, July 9, 1886.
44 *Long Island City Star*, June 11, 1886; Bowery Bay Beach Building and Improvement Company, *A Day's Outing*.
45 *New York Times*, August 5, 1887.
46 *New York Times*, July 12, 1896.
47 *Flushing Times*, May 1905.
48 *Long Island Farmer*, August 2, 1907.
49 Kathy Peiss, *Cheap Amusements: Working Women and Leisure in Turn-of-the-Century New York* (Philadelphia: Temple University Press, 1986), 121.

50 Tickets to events held at North Beach are in the Dora Geipel Collection, QHS; Rosenzweig, *Eight Hours*, 181.
51 Geipel Collection, QHS.
52 William Kells, oral history interview with the author, January 8, 1982, LWA.
53 *Appleton's Dictionary of New York*.
54 *New York Times*, August 2, 3, and 9, 1897. The same game was found at Coney Island: "Loudly was the passer-by incited to hit the colored man whose face decorated the center of the curtain, and to get thereby a good cigar." Lindsay Denison, "The Biggest Playground in the World," *Munsey's Magazine* 33, no. 5 (August 1905): 557–566. For another example, see Fatty Arbuckle's 1915 comedy short, *Fatty and Mabel at the San Diego Exposition*.
55 Vincent F. Seyfried, *The New York and Queens County Railway and the Steinway Lines, 1867–1930* (Hollis, NY: Vincent F. Seyfried, 1950), 39.

Chapter 7   The Politics of Consolidation

1 Gary D. Hermalyn and Lloyd Ultan, "Bronx," in *Encyclopedia of New York City*, 162.
2 David C. Hammack, *Power and Society: Greater New York at the Turn of the Century* (New York: Russell Sage Foundation, 1982), 185. For a history of annexation, see Jackson, *Crabgrass Frontier*, ch. 8.
3 Edward A. Bradford, *"Great York": An Inquiry into the Relation of Rapid Transit and Consolidation to Past and Present Poverty, Disease, Crime, and Mortality and Their Remedy* (Brooklyn: Consolidation League of Brooklyn, 1894).
4 *Long Island City Star*, July 9, 1886.
5 Hazelton, *Boroughs of Brooklyn and Queens*, 3:1534.
6 Reprinted in the *Flushing Journal*, April 18, 1891.
7 State of New York, Laws of 1869, ch. 670; Linder and Zacharias, *Of Cabbages and Kings County*, 133, 139.
8 State of New York, Laws of 1873, ch. 861, secs. 1, 7–12; Linder and Zacharias, *Of Cabbages and Kings County*, 157, 162, 177.
9 Linder and Zacharias, *Of Cabbages and Kings County*, 196–197, 306–307.
10 Argument of Edward C. Graves of Brooklyn before the Consolidation Inquiry Commission, April 2, 1891; Addenda, January 18, 1892; In.re. consolidation of New York & Brooklyn, 1892 https://discover.bklynlibrary.org/item?b=12425273; Hazelton, *Boroughs of Brooklyn and Queens*, 3:1534; *36th Annual Report of the Department of Parks of the City of Brooklyn, 1896* (Brooklyn: Brooklyn Eagle Press, 1897), 83–89.
11 *Long Island City Star*, April 5, 1889.
12 Hammack, *Power and Society*, 187–195.
13 *Flushing Journal*, January 11, March 22, April 12, 1890.
14 *Long Island City Star*, May 9, 1890; *Flushing Journal*, May 17 and June 7, 1890.
15 *Long Island City Star*, December 10, 1886.
16 *Flushing Journal*, April 11 and December 19, 1891.
17 *Flushing Journal*, March 19, 1892.
18 *Flushing Journal*, April 12, 1890.
19 *Flushing Journal*, January 25 and March 5, 12, 19, 1892; September 16, 1893.
20 *Brooklyn Daily Eagle Almanac 1899* (Brooklyn: Brooklyn Daily Eagle, 1899), 135; *Flushing Journal*, March 4, 1893; Hammack, *Power and Society*, 204.
21 *Newtown Register*, October 11, October 25, 1894.

22 Waller, *History of the Town of Flushing*, 220–224; *Brooklyn Daily Eagle Almanac 1899*, 135; *Newtown Register*, February 27, March 5, 12, 26, April 23, 30, and May 14, 1896.
23 Hammack, *Power and Society*, 214–223; Richard L. McCormick, *From Realignment to Reform: Political Change in New York State, 1893–1910* (Ithaca, NY: Cornell University Press, 1981), 90–94.
24 *Newtown Register*, March 26 and May 14, 1896; unfortunately, no copies of the *Flushing Journal* exist for the years after 1893.
25 *Brooklyn Daily Eagle Almanac 1899*, 135.
26 Tredwell, *Personal Reminiscences*, pt. II, 324.
27 Benjamin Franklin Hough, *Census of the State of New York for 1865* (Albany, NY: C. Van Benthuysen and Sons, 1867), xxxi.
28 Queens County Board of Supervisors, 1869, 4–5; Edward J. Smits, "The Creation of Nassau County," *Long Island Historical Journal* 1, no. 2 (Spring 1989): 171–173.
29 See Seyfried, *300 Years*, 111; Smits, "Creation of Nassau County," 173–174.
30 Charles J. McDermott, "Mark Twain's L. I. Poet 'Lariat,'" *Long Island Forum*, December 1958, 229–233.
31 *Long Island Democrat*, May 22, 1877; "Early Bill for Nassau," *Long Island Sunday Press*, November 11, 1937; Bailey, *Long Island*, 2:215 (ch. 30).
32 *New York Times*, March 16, 1877; *Flushing Journal*, January 16, 1875.
33 Clarence F. Birdseye, *The Greater New York Charter [...] Constituting Chapter 378 of the Laws of 1897* (New York: Baker, Voorhis, 1897), xxvi; *Newtown Register*, February 4, 1897.
34 *Flushing Journal*, January 30, 1892.
35 Mark Ash, *The Greater New York Charter as Enacted in 1897* (Albany, NY: Weed-Parsons, 1897), ch. 1, sec. 8; *Long Island Democrat*, December 7, 1897; *Flushing Journal*, November 13, 1897; *Queens County Review*, May 7, 1897; September 23, 1898; Bellot, *History of the Rockaways*, 106; Paul E. Kerson, "Union of Queens with New York City: What Was Gained and What Was Lost," unpublished manuscript, 1988, QBPL Archives.
36 *Newtown Register*, July 15, 1897.
37 *Queens County Review*, November 8, 1895; January 1, 1897.
38 *Queens County Review*, January 28, February 11, 1898; Smits, "Creation of Nassau County," 177–178; Bailey, *Long Island*, 2:216–217.
39 State of New York, Laws of 1898, ch. 588; *Queens County Review*, April 15, 1898.
40 See Kroessler, "Brooklyn's Thirst."
41 Brooklyn Department of City Works, *Report on Future Extensions of Water Supply for the City of Brooklyn* (Brooklyn, 1896), 8; Jacob Judd, "Water for Brooklyn," *New York History* 47, no. 4 (October 1966); Bailey, *Long Island*, 1:427 (ch. 13); 2:274–278 (ch. 32); *Queens County Review*, May 28, 1897.
42 *Queens County Review*, November 8, 1895; May 15 and 29, 1896; February 12, September 17 and 24, 1897.
43 Brooklyn Department of City Works, *Report on Future Extension*, 8, 23–31.
44 *Queens County Review*, March 13, May 1, and June 6, 1896; John R. Freeman, *Report upon New York's Water Supply, with Particular Reference to the Need of Procuring Additional Sources and Their Probable Cost* (New York: Martin B. Brown, 1900), 7–17, 31–32, 100, appxs. 15 and 16.
45 *Flushing Journal*, June 4 and 18, 1892; March 25, 1893; Freeman, *Report*, 32.
46 *Queens Borough, Its Growth and Prosperity; Some Statistical Information That Will Surprise and Instruct the Citizens; Lower Tax Rate for 1905; Expenditures for*

Improvements and Where the Money Comes From; The Borough's Splendid Roads, anonymous pamphlet (New York, 1905); Joseph Cassidy, "The Borough of Queens, Past, Present and Future," *Long Island Magazine* 1, no. 1 (June 1903).

Chapter 8   The Queensboro Bridge

1. David B. Steinman and Sara Ruth Watson, *Bridges and Their Builders* (New York: Dover Publications, 1957 [1941]), ch. 12; Joseph Gies, *Bridges and Men* (Garden City, NY: Doubleday, 1963), ch. 19.
2. *Long Island Democrat,* October 26, 1836.
3. *Long Island Democrat,* August 16, 1837; "Suspension-Bridge," in *The Family Magazine, or Monthly Abstract of General Knowledge,* vol. 5, *1837–1838* (New York: J. S. Redfield, 1838), 41–43.
4. David G. McCullough, *The Great Bridge: The Epic Story of the Building of the Brooklyn Bridge* (New York: Simon and Schuster, 1972), 64, 75–82.
5. Roebling, Letters 1850–1857, Folder 4, Box 2, Series III, Roebling Collection, Rensselaer Polytechnic Institute.
6. State of New York, Laws of 1867, ch. 395: An Act to Incorporate the New York and Long Island Bridge Company, and ch. 399: An Act to Incorporate the New York Bridge Company ((hereafter cited as "Laws of" followed by year and chapter). McCullough makes no mention of the charter for the Blackwell's Island bridge, leaving the impression that Roebling's bridge was unique; see McCullough, *Great Bridge,* 24–25.
7. Laws of 1867, ch. 395.
8. Laws of 1867, ch. 395.
9. Laws of 1871, ch. 437; the charter was extended again in 1879, granting the company until 1885 to complete the span (Laws of 1879, ch. 426); again in 1885, granting an extension for the start of construction to 1888 (Laws of 1885, ch. 392); and again in 1892, mandating completion by 1900 (Laws of 1885, ch. 411).
10. *Newtown Register,* December 9, 1880. The officers at that time were George F. Harsell, president, Blaize L. Harsell, treasurer, and Benjamin W. Hitchcock, one of the most active real estate developers in Queens, secretary; see J. S. Kelsey, *History of Long Island City, New York. A Record of Its Early Settlement and Corporate Progress* (Long Island City, NY: Long Island Star, 1896), 79–81. Kelsey's account is inaccurate in several particulars, but the bridge company's records have not survived.
11. Kelsey, *History of Long Island City,* 79–81.
12. New York and Long Island Bridge Company, *Report of Board of Consulting Engineers, Appointed to Recommend a Plan for the New and Long Island Bridge across the East River at Blackwell's Island* (New York: Graphic Company, 1877); *Watson's New Map of New York and Adjacent Cities* (New York: Gaylord Watson, 1876) shows the line of the proposed bridge across the northern part of Blackwell's Island; see McCullough, *Great Bridge,* chs. 16 and 17.
13. New York and Long Island Bridge Company, *Report.* The Cincinnati Bridge Company submitted a rebuttal to the committee's findings, contending that their plan "was of a well known and established system for long spans, to which we had designed improvements for rigidity"; see Cincinnati Bridge Company, *Statement by the Cincinnati Bridge Co. in Reference to the New York & Long Island Bridge* (New York: Graphic Company, 1877).
14. Kelsey, *History of Long Island City,* 81–82; *Newtown Register,* May 12, 1881.

15 Kelsey, *History of Long Island City*, 80–81. Ironically, the tunnel bringing the LIRR into Grand Central Terminal crosses the East River at roughly the location envisioned by Dr. Rainey.
16 *Newtown Register*, May 12, 1881; *New York Sun*, April 10, 1887, reprinted in Jere Johnson, *Village of Flushing* (New York, 1887); Laws of 1885, ch. 392.
17 *Long Island City Star*, July 9 and 16, 1886.
18 *Long Island City Star*, December 10, 1886.
19 *Long Island City Star*, March 4, 1887; June 13, 1890.
20 Kelsey, *History of Long Island City*, 82.
21 The New York and Long Island Railroad Company, promotional booklet (n.d.); "Statement," 1892, [New York and] Long Island Railroad Records, Boxes 4 and 5, Steinway& Sons Collection, Miscellaneous, Box 2, LWA; *Flushing Journal*, February 1 and December 13, 1890.
22 Malcolm W. Niven to William Steinway, April 8, 1896, Box 5, Steinway & Sons Collection, LWA; Clifton Hood, *722 Miles: The Building of the Subways and How They Transformed New York* (New York: Simon and Schuster, 1993), 162–168.
23 Hinsdale, *Autobiography*, 292–298.
24 *Long Island City Weekly Star*, August 24, 1894.
25 *Newtown Register*, October 27, 1898; June 8, 1899.
26 *Newtown Register*, December 1, 1898; January 12 and 19, 1899.
27 *Newtown Register*, June 1, November 16, and December 14, 1899; March 8, April 19 and 26, 1900.
28 *Newtown Register*, May 3, August 2, and November 8, 1900. Joseph Cassidy went on to become Queens Borough president and was ultimately convicted of corruption and sent to prison.
29 Steinman and Watson, *Bridges and Their Builders*, 310–312; Gies, *Bridges and Men*, 220–227; *Engineering Record* 51, no. 21 (May 27, 1905): 587–588.
30 *Engineering Record* 51, no. 9 (March 4, 1905): 239–240.
31 Gies, *Bridges and Men*, 224.
32 *Engineering Record* 51, no. 9 (March 4, 1905): 239–240; 51, no. 11 (March 18, 1905): 314–315; 54, no. 11 (September 15, 1906): 289–291.
33 *Engineering Record* 54, no. 11 (September 15, 1906): 289–291.
34 *Engineering Record* 55, no. 9 (March 2, 1907): 284–285.
35 *Engineering Record* 55, no. 23 (June 8, 1907): 670.
36 *Engineering Record* 54, no. 11 (September 15, 1906): 282–283; 54, no. 22 (December 1, 1906): 594–596; 55, no. 7 (February 16, 1907): 170.
37 Gies, *Bridges and Men*, 225.
38 *Report of the Royal Commission on the Cause of the Collapse of the Quebec Bridge*, app. 1. The Royal Commission's report, dated February 20, 1908, was reprinted in *Engineering Record* 57, no. 11 (March 14, 1908): 309–320.
39 *Engineering News* 56, no. 10 (September 7, 1907): 71–72 (Current News suppl.); *New York Times*, August 30, 1907.
40 Gies, *Bridges and Men*, 222–227.
41 *Engineering Record* 56, no. 21 (November 23, 1907): 567; no. 23 (December 7, 1907): 623–625; no. 25 (December 21, 1907): 670; no. 26 (December 28, 1907): 705–706; 57, no. 2 (January 11, 1908): 38; no. 21 (May 23, 1908); no. 22 (May 30, 1908): 681–682.
42 William H. Burr, *The Safe Live Loads for the Blackwell's Island Bridge*, a report prepared for Commissioner of Bridges J. W. Stevenson; and Alfred P. Boller and Henry Wilson Hodge, *The Carrying Capacity of the Blackwell's Island Bridge*, a

report prepared for the Hon. James W. Stevenson—both published in *Engineering Record* 58, no. 20 (November 14, 1908): 535, 558–566.
43 *Engineering Record* 58, no. 19 (November 7, 1908): 505; no. 20 (November 14, 1908): 535; *Long Island City Star*, November 12, 13, and 14, 1908.
44 *Long Island City Star*, October 16 and 30, 1908; *Engineering Record* 58, no. 14 (October 3, 1908): 367. In March 2011, much to the dismay of Queens residents, the City Council, at the behest of Mayor Michael Bloomberg, voted to rename the span the Ed Koch Queensboro Bridge.
45 *Long Island City Star*, October 3 and 10, 1908; *Bloomingdale's Diary, 1909 and Souvenir Commemorative of the Opening of the Queensboro Bridge, 1901–1909* (New York: Bloomingdale Bros., 1909), 33–35, 47.
46 *Long Island City Star*, October 16, 1908.
47 *Bloomingdale's Diary*, 23–27.
48 *Newtown Register*, April 1, 1909.
49 *Long Island City Star*, October 27 and 29, 1908.
50 *New York Times*, February 4 and May 20, 1909.
51 *New York Times*, June 12, 1909; *Queensboro Bridge Celebration: Official Program* (New York: Queensboro Bridge Celebration Committee, 1909).
52 *New York Times*, June 13, 1909.
53 *Queensboro Bridge Celebration*; *New York Times*, June 13, 1909; Community History Program, *Transportation; Work; Housing; and Leisure* (New York: LaGuardia Community College; City University of New York, 1981), 22–24; *New York Times*, June 20, 1909.
54 Sharon Reier, *The Bridges of New York* (New York: Quadrant Press, 1977), 41, 47; Steinman and Watson, *Bridges and Their Builders*, 312.
55 Edward Hopper, *Blackwell's Island* (1911) and *Queensboro Bridge* (1913), both in the Whitney Museum of American Art; Woody Allen, dir., *Manhattan* (Los Angeles: United Artists, 1979); Fitzgerald, *Great Gatsby*, 69.

Chapter 9   The Booming Borough

1 Olivier Zunz and David Ward, eds., *Landscape of Modernity: Essays on New York City, 1900–1940* (New York: Russell Sage Foundation, 1992).
2 One of the best views of the Williamsburg Bridge promenade comes at the end of the 1948 film noir classic *Naked City*; the scene shows pedestrians strolling and mothers sitting on benches, tending baby carriages and watching their children play as the detective chases down the suspect.
3 Matthew Dripps, *Map of Brooklyn and Vicinity* (New York, 1868); G. W. Bromley, *Atlas of the City of Brooklyn*; Hyde, *Atlas of the Borough of Queens* (1903), vol. 2, plates 22–24; see also the 1908 edition (corrected to 1910), plates 34–35; and the 1929 edition (corrected to 1947); *Guide Map of the Borough of Brooklyn, Brooklyn Daily Eagle Almanac*, 1900, 1907, 1911, and 1913; Wolverton, *Atlas of Queens County*; Bromley and Bromley, *Atlas of the City of New York, Borough of Queens*; "Mathews Model Flats, Solving the Housing Problem," in *Mathews Bulletin for 1928* (New York: G. X. Mathews, 1928). The bulletin was "issued for the benefit of the customers and prospective buyers of the G. X. Mathews Co., Lincoln Avenue Subway Station, Queens, published every now and then by the G. X. Mathews Co."
4 For an illustration of the changes in Long Island City, cf. Wolverton, *Atlas of Queens County*, plates 4 and 5; Hyde, *Atlas of the Borough of Queens* (1908), vol. 1,

plates 2 and 3; Hyde, *Atlas of the Borough of Queens* (1928), vol. 1; and *Newtown Register,* February 10 and November 24, 1910.

5 Lorraine B. Diehl, *The Late, Great Pennsylvania Station* (New York: American Heritage Press, 1985). For the electrification of the Long Island and the construction of Penn Station, see *Engineering Record* 52, no. 19 (November 4, 1905): 504; 54, no. 1 (July 7, 1906): 11–12, no. 2 (July 14 1906): 29–34, and no. 4 (July 28, 1906): 100–101; 57, no. 14 (April 4, 1908): 468–470; 61, no. 15 (April 9, 1910): 489; and no. 16 (April 16, 1910): 509–510, 521–524.

6 Franklin J. Sherman, *Building Up Greater Queensboro: An Estimate of Its Development and the Outlook* (New York: Brooklyn Biographical Society, 1929), 55–60.

7 "The Largest Arch Bridge in the World," *Scientific American* 46, no. 23 (June 8, 1907): 468; Reier, *Bridges of New York,* 58–65.

8 Listing Statements, New York Stock Exchange, Vol. 12, A-4356, The New York Connecting Rail Road Company; Diehl, *Late, Great Pennsylvania Station,* 49; H. W. Schotter, *The Growth and Development of the Pennsylvania Railroad Company* (Philadelphia: Pennsylvania Railroad, 1927), 271–280, 323–324, 350; George H. Burgess and Miles C. Kennedy, *Centennial History of the Pennsylvania Railroad Company* (Philadelphia: Pennsylvania Railroad, 1949), 536–537; Reier, *Bridges of New York,* 58–65; Bromley and Bromley, *Atlas of the City of New York, Borough of Queens,* plates 1, 2, 4, 8, 11, 12, and 13 show the center line of the New York Connecting Rail Road, linking up with the LIRR's Manhattan Beach Branch in Ridgewood.

9 *New York Times,* August 18, 1984; January 15, 1997.

10 New York City Department of Docks and Ferries, *Report on the Proposed Plan of Operation for Jamaica Bay Improvement* (New York, 1911); Harry Chase Brearley, *The Problem of Greater New York and Its Solution* (New York: Brooklyn League, 1914); N. B. Killmer, *The Authorized Freight and Passenger Tunnel under the Narrows between Brooklyn and Staten Island* [. . .] (New York: Jamaica Bay Improvement Association, 1925); Committee on the Regional Plan of New York and Its Environs, *Regional Survey of New York and Its Environs,* vol. 4, *Transit and Transportation* (New York: Regional Plan of New York and Its Environs, 1928), 130–147 (hereafter cited as *Transit and Transportation*). Jeffrey A. Kroessler, "Jamaica Bay: The Greatest Port That Never Was," *Seaport Magazine,* Fall 1994; *Transit and Transportation,* 160.

11 Queens Planning Commission, *Initial Report of the Queens Planning Commission,* ed. H. J. Haarmeyer (New York: H. J. Haarmeyer, 1929), 90–91; Eugene L. Armbruster, *Long Island, Its Early Days and Development* (Brooklyn: Brooklyn Daily Eagle, 1914), 6–7; *Queensborough,* September 1929, 432; January 1930, 14; November, 574; *Transit and Transportation,* 137–138, 147–149; Committee on the Regional Plan of New York and Its Environs, *Regional Survey of New York and Its Environs,* vol. 1, *The Graphic Regional Plan* (New York: Regional Plan of New York and Its Environs, 1929), 329, 394; vol. 2, *The Building of the City* (New York: Regional Plan of New York and Its Environs, 1931), 493–497. For the history of the Dual Subway System, see Hood, *722 Miles,* ch. 7; Peter Derrick, *Tunneling to the Future: The Story of the Great Subway Expansion That Saved New York* (New York: New York University Press, 2001); Hazelton, *Boroughs of Brooklyn and Queens,* 1:371–377; Stan Fischler, *Uptown Downtown* (New York: Hawthorne Books, 1976), 235–246; Peterson and Seyfried, *Research Guide,* 28–30; and Seyfried, *300 Years,* 170–173. The Dual Subway System, also known as The Dual Contracts, were

contracts signed between the city and two separate, private companies, the IRT and the BRT, to build and upgrade several NYC subway lines.

12 E. Belcher Hyde, *Rapid Transit & Development Map of the Boroughs of Manhattan, Bronx, Brooklyn and Queens, City of New York, Including a Portion of Nassau County, L. I., Showing Valuable Suburban Localities Connected with Manhattan* (New York, 1910); Dwight-Murray Realty Company, *Little Neck Hills*, brochure, 1910.
13 Kevin Wolfe, *This Salubrious Spot: The First 100 Years at Douglas Manor, 1906–2006* (Douglaston, NY: Douglas Manor Association, 2006), 11–15, 19–22.
14 Wolfe, *This Salubrious Spot*, 26–37, 46–55.
15 Linder and Zacharias, *Of Cabbages and Kings County*, 37–38, 73–74, 306–307.
16 LIRR, *The Home Builder on Long Island* (New York: LIRR, 1907); see also Seyfried, *LIRR*, vol. 7, *The Age of Electrification, 1901–1916*.
17 *Queensborough*, October 1914, 41–42; *Newtown Register*, January 12, 1899.
18 *Queensborough*, March 1914, 16; August 1915, 66; September 1915, 69.
19 *Queensborough*, February 1925, 104.
20 *New York Times*, April 23, 1922; *Newsday*, May 19, 2002.
21 Robert A. M. Stern, *The Anglo-American Suburb* (London: Architectural Design, 1981), 42–43; Robert A. M. Stern, *Pride of Place* (Boston: Houghton Mifflin, 1986), ch. 4; Susan L. Klaus, *A Modern Arcadia: Frederick Law Olmsted, Jr. and the Plan for Forest Hills Gardens* (Amherst: University of Massachusetts Press, 2002); Daniel Karatzas, *Jackson Heights: A Garden in the City* (Jackson Heights Beautification Group, 1990); Clarence Stein, *Toward New Towns for America* (Cambridge, MA: MIT Press, 1978 [1957]); Jeffrey A. Kroessler, *Sunnyside Gardens: Planning and Preservation in a Historic Garden Suburb* (New York: Fordham University Press, 2021).
22 Sage Foundation Homes, *Forest Hills Gardens, the Suburban Land Development of the Russell Sage Foundation* (New York: Sage Foundation Homes, 1911), 8.
23 Sage Foundation Homes, *Forest Hills Gardens*, 7; F. A. Austin, "Development of Forest Hills Gardens," in *The Real Estate Magazine* 2, no. 4 (April 1913): 12–18; Russell Sage Foundation, press release, September 4, 1911.
24 Russell Sage Foundation, press release, September 4, 1911.
25 Sage Foundation Homes, *Forest Hills Gardens*, pamphlet no. 1 (February 1911); *Forest Hills Gardens, Preliminary Information for Buyers*, pamphlet no. 3 (April 1913); *Declaration of Restrictions, etc., Affecting Property Known as Forest Hills Gardens* (April 1913). Even Lewis Mumford repeats this mistaken view of the intentions of the Sage Foundation, in his introduction to Clarence Stein's *Toward New Towns*: "[Stein and Wright's] excessive economy here was reinforced, probably, by their memory of Forest Hills; meant to serve as a working-class community, but designed by the very generosity of its housing to become an entirely middle class, indeed upper middle class community."
26 "Our History," West Side Tennis Club, accessed November 14, 2024, https://thewestsidetennisclub.com/About_Us/Our_History.
27 Philip Benjamin, "Color Line Bars Bunche and Son from Forest Hills Tennis Club," *New York Times*, July 9, 1959.
28 Stern, *Pride of Place*, 142–143.
29 B. Lewis, *Kew Gardens*, 3.
30 Karatzas, *Jackson Heights*, 12–13.
31 *Newtown Register*, July 22, 1920; Karatzas, *Jackson Heights*, chs. 3 and 4.

358 • Notes to Pages 233–243

32. "Plans Block of $9 a Month Rooms," *New York Times*, February 23, 1922; "Metropolitan Life Insurance Company Finances Huge Building Operations in Queens Borough," *New York Times*, March 12, 1922.
33. Seyfried, *300 Years*, 146–156; Roy Lubove, *Community Planning in the 1920's: The Contribution of the Regional Planning Association of America* (Pittsburgh: University of Pittsburgh Press, 1963), 50–53; Karatzas, *Jackson Heights*, 48–49; *New York Times*, February 5 and 23, and March 12, 1922.
34. *Queensborough*, August 1922, 392.
35. Stein, *Toward New Towns*, 15; Lubove, *Community Planning*, ch. 3.
36. Stein, *Toward New Towns*, 16–19.
37. *Queensborough*, July 1926, 442; Stein, *Toward New Towns*, 34; Lewis Mumford, *Green Memories: The Story of Geddes Mumford* (New York: Harcourt Brace, 1947), 26–31. For a presentation of City Housing Corporation (CHC) ideals, see *The City*, a forty-minute film produced for the 1939 World's Fair and directed by Willard Van Dyke, with text by Lewis Mumford and music by Aaron Copland. The film can be viewed on YouTube; see Travel Film Archive, "The City (1939)," YouTube video, 41:34, August 19, 2015, https://www.youtube.com/watch?v=OaTn36YjLf8.
38. *Sunnyside Gardens: A Home Community* (New York, CHC, ca. 1925); *Queensborough*, July–August 1924, 388; March 1924, 148; July 1926, 442; January 1929, 53.
39. Stein, *Toward New Towns*, 21; *Sunnyside Gardens*.
40. Fraklin Havelick and Michael Kwartler, "Sunnyside Gardens: Whose Land Is It Anyway?," *New York Affairs* 7, no. 2 (1982): 70; Abraham Goldfield, *Toward Fuller Living through Public Housing and Leisure Time Activities* (New York: National Public Housing Conference, 1934), 23.
41. *Sunnyside Gardens*; Lewis Mumford, *The Urban Prospect* (New York: Harcourt, Brace and World, 1968), 67–77.
42. *Queensborough*, February 1925, 86, 94; April 1925, 222–224.
43. "Mathews Model Flats."
44. *Long Island Daily Star*, April 25, 1925.
45. Jeffrey A. Kroessler, *Lighting the Way: The Centennial History of the Queens Borough Public Library, 1896–1996* (New York: QBPL, 1996).
46. *Queensborough*, October 1929, 439; Sherman, *Building Up Greater Queensboro*, 38–41.
47. "Mathews Model Flats."
48. Sherman, *Building Up Greater Queensboro*, 18–20; *Queensborough*, July 1929, 350.
49. Old Law Tenements were constructed in New York City between 1879 and 1901 and required fire escapes and that the habitable rooms have a window opening to fresh air resulting the dumbbell shape associated with this building type.
50. *Queensborough*, September 1929, 404.

Chapter 10 The Crisis of the Great Depression

1. Nathaniel S. Keith, *Politics and the Housing Crisis since 1930* (New York: Universe Books, 1973), 13–19.
2. Hoovervilles were makeshift shanty settlements primarily for victims of the Great Depression from 1929 to 1941. Named for President Herbert Hoover, they were set up, in varying sizes, across the nation.
3. *Queensborough*, January 1931; November 1932; March 1933, 63.
4. Lieberman, *Steinway & Sons*, 184–186.

5 Albert H. Amend, "Diary," typed copy in QHS.
6 *Queensborough*, February 1933, 96.
7 *Queensborough*, July 1933, 202–203; December 1934, 293, 300.
8 *Queensborough*, October 1933, 280; November 1933; December 1933, 315.
9 *Queensborough*, February 1933, 39–47; *New York Times*, January 26, 1933; Kenneth S. Davis, *FDR: The New York Years, 1928–1933* (New York: Random House, 1979), 367–371.
10 *Queensborough*, January 1934, 12.
11 *Queensborough*, May 1934, 128.
12 *Queensborough*, July 1934, 184.
13 *Queensborough*, July 1934, 184.
14 *Queensborough*, December 1933, 333; Keith, *Politics and the Housing Crisis*, 25.
15 *Architectural Forum*, February 1934: 91; *Queensborough*, December 1933, 333.
16 *Queensborough*, September 1932; January 1935; Keith, *Politics and the Housing Crisis*, 24.
17 Kroessler, *Sunnyside Gardens*, ch. 6; Daniel Pearlstein, "Sweeping Six Percent Philanthropy Away: The New Deal in Sunnyside Gardens," *Journal of Planning History* 9, no. 3 (2010): 170; *Newsday*, March 18, 1979; Havelick and Kwartler, "Sunnyside Gardens," 70–71; Stein, *Toward New Towns for America*, 35.
18 *Queensborough*, June 1934, 167; August 1934, 205; September 1934, 223, 227.
19 *Queensborough*, June 1934, 167; August 1934, 205; September 1934, 223, 227.
20 *Queensborough*, March 1936, 50.
21 F. L. Ackerman, "Controlling Factors in Slum Clearance and Housing," *Architectural Forum*, February 1934, 94; Harold Ickes, "The Housing Policy of the PWA," *Architectural Forum*, February 1934, 92; Robert D. Kohn, "The Government Housing Program," *Architectural Forum*, February 1934, 88–91.
22 *Queensborough*, February 1934, 50.
23 William E. Leuchtenburg, *Franklin D. Roosevelt and the New Deal* (New York: Harper and Row, 1963), 134.
24 *New York Times*, November 4, 1935; *Queensborough*, June 1934, 158; December 1936; Jeffrey A. Kroessler, "Boulevard Gardens," in *Affordable Housing in New York*, ed. Nicholas Dagen Bloom and Matthew Gordon Lasner (Princeton, NJ: Princeton University Press, 2016), 67–70; "Historical Overview," Boulevard Gardens, accessed November 14, 2024, https://boulevardgardens.nyc/history.
25 *Queensborough*, September 1933, 259; *United States v. Certain Lands in the City of Louisville*, 78 F. (2d) 684 (C.C.A. 6th, 1935), in Leuchtenburg, *Franklin D. Roosevelt*, 134; J. Joseph Huthmacher, *Senator Robert F. Wagner and the Rise of Urban Liberalism* (New York: Atheneum, 1971), 205–216, 224–228, 254.
26 LaGuardia to Ickes, July 14, 1936, Box 9020, New York City Housing Authority (NYCHA) Papers, LWA. Box 9020 also contains information about the process of selecting the Queensbridge site over Hallett's Cove.
27 *Long Island Press*, April 23, 1938; August Heckscher, *When LaGuardia Was Mayor: New York's Legendary Years* (New York: W. W. Norton, 1978), 249.
28 *Long Island Press*, November 26, 1938.
29 NYCHA, *Facts about Queensbridge* (1940); NYCHA, *The Preferential Rating System* (January 1, 1940).
30 *New York Times*, February 3, 1939; Catherine Bauer, *Modern Housing* (New York: Houghton Mifflin, 1934), 146.
31 *Long Island Press*, March 21, 1939.

32 *Long Island Star-Journal*, March 4, 1940.
33 *Long Island Star-Journal*, November 18, 1940.
34 NYCHA, *Facts about South Jamaica* (March 15, 1940); NYCHA photographs of the South Jamaica Houses, 1939–1940, NYCHA Papers, LaGuardia and Wagner Archives; Ted Stone Collection, Museum of the City of New York; Nicholas Dagen Bloom, *Public Housing That Worked: New York in the Twentieth Century* (Philadelphia: University of Pennsylvania Press, 2008), 87–89.

Chapter 11 Building the World of Tomorrow

1 Thomas Kessner, *Fiorello H. La Guardia and the Making of Modern New York* (New York: McGraw-Hill, 1989), 292–299; *Queensborough*, October 1936, 212.
2 Robert Moses, *The Triborough Bridge: A Modern Metropolitan Traffic Artery* (New York: Triborough Bridge Authority, 1936); see also photographs in the Triborough Bridge Authority files and in the Parks Photo Archive, Parks Historian's Office, New York City Department of Parks (NYCDOP). See Ballon and Jackson, *Robert Moses*, for a description of each Moses project.
3 Moses, *Triborough Bridge*; Laura Rosen, "Triborough Bridge," in Ballon and Jackson, *Robert Moses*, 229–231.
4 *Long Island Press*, July 26, 1937.
5 Robert Caro, *The Power Broker: Robert Moses and the Fall of New York* (New York: Vintage Books, 1974), 391; New York City Department of Plants and Structures, *Triborough Bridge, Connecting the Boroughs of Manhattan, the Bronx, and Queens* (1930).
6 Moses, *Triborough Bridge*.
7 Moses, *Triborough Bridge*; Rosen, "Triborough Bridge," 229–231.
8 Caro, *Power Broker*, 448–451. For a contrary view of Moses, see Kenneth T. Jackson, "Robert Moses and the Rise of New York: The Power Broker in Perspective," in Ballon and Jackson, *Robert Moses*, 67–71.
9 *Queensborough*, January 1935, 10–11. For the relationship of LaGuardia and Moses, see Kessner, *Fiorello H. La Guardia*, 306–319.
10 NYCDOP, *The Rockaway Improvement* (1939). For Moses's plans for Coney Island, see NYCDOP, *The Improvement of Coney Island, Rockaway and South Beaches* (1937); NYCDOP, *The Improvement of Coney Island* (1939); Jeffrey A. Kroessler, "Long Island State Parks Commission and Jones Beach," in Ballon and Jackson, *Robert Moses*, 158–160; and Jeffrey A. Kroessler, "Coney Island," in Ballon and Jackson, *Robert Moses*, 165.
11 NYCDOP, *The Future of Jamaica Bay* (1938); Kroessler, "Jamaica Bay and Marine Park," 166–168; Kroessler, "Rockaway Improvement," 171–172.
12 See Killmer, *Authorized Freight and Passenger Tunnel*; see also maps in the QBPL Archives, esp. New York City Department of Docks and Ferries, *Plan for Development of Jamaica Bay* (n.d.) and *Map of Jamaica Bay* (February 10, 1930); NYCDOP, *Future of Jamaica Bay*.
13 NYCDOP, *Future of Jamaica Bay*.
14 NYCDOP, *Future of Jamaica Bay*; NYCDOP, *Rockaway Improvement*; NYCDOP, *Circumferential Parkway* (1938); Marine Parkway Authority, *Published on the Occasion of the Opening of the Marine Parkway, July 3rd, 1937*, brochure (New York, 1937). Photographs of the Rockaway Beach Improvement are in the QBPL Archives, and the Parks Photo Archive. See also Kroessler, "Jamaica Bay and Marine Park."

Caro mentions neither the controversy over the garbage dump and incinerator nor the NYCDOP's *Future of Jamaica Bay*.
15. Robert Moses, "From Dump to Glory," *Saturday Evening Post*, January 15, 1938; Triborough Bridge Authority, *The Bronx-Whitestone Bridge* (New York, 1939); Triborough Bridge Authority, *Completion of Francis Lewis Boulevard, Queens, Mixed Traffic Approach to the Bronx-Whitestone Bridge* (New York, 1940); *Circumferential Parkway*.
16. Grover Whalen, *Mr. New York: The Autobiography of Grover Whalen* (New York: G. P. Putnam's Sons, 1955), 26–27; Moses, "From Dump to Glory"; Caro, *Power Broker*, 1082–1085; Seyfried, *Corona*, 67–68.
17. *New York Times*, April 20, March 12, and May 19, 1913; Seyfried, *Corona*, 68.
18. Jeffrey A. Kroessler, "Jamaica Bay: The Greatest Port That Never Was," *Seaport Magazine*, Fall 1994.
19. *Queensborough*, May 1916; Seyfried, *Corona*, 68–70.
20. Fitzgerald, *Great Gatsby*, 23–24.
21. Whalen, *Mr. New York*, 199; *Long Island Press*, June 11, 1937.
22. Seyfried, *Corona*, 90.
23. Committee on the Regional Plan of New York and Its Environs, *Regional Survey of New York and Its Environs*, vol. 5, *Public Recreation* (New York: Regional Plan of New York and Its Environs, 1928), 25; Moses, "From Dump to Glory"; *Jackson Heights News*, March 3, 1937; Board of Public Improvements, Topographical Bureau, *Map or Plan Showing a General Design for a System of Streets, Avenues, Public Squares and Places, Parks, Bridges, etc. in That Part of the 2nd Ward (Formerly Town of Newtown) in the Borough of Queens* (New York, August 1, 1899), supplement to the *Newtown Register*, October 5, 1899; Caro, *Power Broker*, 654, 1082–1085.
24. Whalen, *Mr. New York*, 176; *Official Guide Book, New York World's Fair, 1939* (New York: Exposition Publications, 1939), 26–27.
25. Hazel Evans, ed., *New Towns: The British Experience* (New York: Wiley, 1972); Kroessler, *Sunnyside Gardens*, ch. 5.
26. *Official Guide Book*, 27–30; *Your World of Tomorrow*, souvenir booklet of Democracity (New York: Rogers-Kellogg-Stillson, 1939); Stein, *Toward New Towns*, 37–72; Caro, *Power Broker*, 904–911, 918.
27. Whalen, *Mr. New York*, 203–204; see also Richard Sherman, "The Life of Riley" (1943), reprinted in Esther Morgan McCullough, *As I Pass, O Manhattan* (New York: Coley Taylor, 1956).
28. *The City* can be viewed on YouTube; see Travel Film Archive, "The City (1939)," YouTube video, 41:34, August 19, 2015, https://www.youtube.com/watch?v=OaTn36YjLf8. See also Howard Gilette Jr., "Film as Artifact: The City," *American Studies* 18 (Fall 1977): 71–85. For a description of the greenbelt suburbs, see Stein, *Toward New Towns*; and Kroessler, *Sunnyside Gardens*, ch. 7.
29. *Official Guide Book*, 167–169; General Motors Corporation, *Futurama*, souvenir brochure (1940); Ford Motor Company, *The Ford Exposition, New York's World Fair*, souvenir brochure (1939–1940); Benjamin Appel, *The People Talk: American Voices from the Great Depression* (New York: Touchstone, 1982 [1940]), 48–52; Jackson, *Crabgrass Frontier*, 248; Mark H. Rose, *Interstate: Express Highway Politics, 1939–1989* (Knoxville: University of Tennessee Press, 1990), 1–2; E. L. Doctorow, *World's Fair* (New York: Random House, 1985), 250–257.
30. *New York Times*, March 25, 1938; *New York Journal-American*, March 25, 1938; New York World's Fair 1939, Department of Exhibits and Concessions, *Plans of the Home*

Building Center (including "The Town of Tomorrow"), Boxes 835, 836, and 837, New York World's Fair 1939 and 1940 Incorporated Records, Archives and Manuscripts Division, New York Public Library; Federal Writers' Project of the Works Progress Administration, *New York Panorama* (New York: Pantheon, 1984 [1938]), 494; Warren Sussman, *Culture as History: The Transformation of American Society in the Twentieth Century* (New York: Pantheon, 1984), ch. 11.

31 *Long Island Press*, May 15, 1939; *Long Island Star-Journal*, August 15, 1940; *New York Times Magazine*, October 27, 1940.

Chapter 12   Prosperity and Stability in Postwar Queens

1 New York State Department of Transportation, *A Comprehensive Study of Proposed Bridge Crossings of Long Island Sound, Summary* (Albany, NY, 1972); Peter Bales, "Rockefeller, Moses, and the Bridge That Never Was," in *Robert Moses, Single Minded Genius*, ed. Joann P. Krieg (Interlaken, NY: Heart of the Lakes Publishing, 1989), 79–88; Jeffrey A. Kroessler, "Bridges and the Urban Landscape," in *Long Island Historical Journal* 2, no. 1 (Fall 1989): 104–117.

2 Carol Taylor, "Queens Has a Street Named Utopia," *World-Telegram*, October 14, 1948; Edith J. Cahill and Thomas Furey, "The Move Is to the Suburbia within the City—Queens," *World-Telegram and The Sun*, July 11, 1963. Both quoted in Sylvie Murray, *The Progressive Housewife: Community Activism in Suburban Queens, 1945–1965* (Philadelphia: University of Pennsylvania Press, 2003), 19.

3 George Barrett, "Our Changing City: North Shore-Central Queens," *New York Times*, August 5, 1955.

4 "School Expansion Held Inadequate," *New York Times*, June 17, 1955; Murray, *Progressive Housewife*, 111–112.

5 Murray, *Progressive Housewife*, ch. 4.

6 *New York Times*, August 1, 1955.

7 Jesse Kling, "Solid Brick Homes: The Continuing Row House Tradition of Brooklyn and Queens" (Master's thesis, Columbia University, 2022).

8 Murray, *Progressive Housewife*, 26.

9 Murray, *Progressive Housewife*, 71–74.

10 Jeffrey A. Kroessler, "Glen Oaks," in *Encyclopedia of New York City*, 513.

11 Murray, *Progressive Housewife*, 144.

12 Kroessler, *Lighting the Way*, 35–45, 121, 124.

13 Patricia A. Doyal, "Fresh Meadows," in *Encyclopedia of New York City*, 483; Lewis Mumford, *From the Ground Up: Observations on Contemporary Architecture, Housing, Highway Building, and Civic Design* (New York: Harcourt, Brace and World, 1956), 3–19.

14 Mumford, *From the Ground Up*, 3–19.

15 Murray, *Progressive Housewife*, 25–26.

16 "Helmsley-Spear Accused of Bias," *New York Times*, November 4, 1983; George W. Goodman, "Housing Bias Pervasive, Yet Difficult to Prosecute," *New York Times*, May 20, 1984. Founded in 1866, Helmsley-Spear is America's oldest continuously operating real estate company.

17 "Landlords Settle in Race Bias Suit," *New York Times*, October 25, 1984.

18 Robert Moses, "From Dump to Glory," *Saturday Evening Post*, January 15, 1938.

19 Robert A. M. Stern, Gregory Gilmartin, and Thomas Mellins, *New York 1930: Architecture and Urbanism between Two World Wars* (New York: Rizzoli, 1987), 723.

20 *Long Island Star Journal*, October 18 and 19, 1946; *New York Times*, October 19, 1946.
21 Robert Moses, "Natural and Proper Home of the United Nations," *New York Times Magazine*, October 20, 1946.
22 Caro, *Power Broker*, 771–774.
23 Jeffrey A. Kroessler, "World's Fairs," in *Encyclopedia of New York City*, 1414–1415; Jeffrey A. Kroessler, "Parkways and Expressways in Brooklyn and Queens," in Ballon and Jackson, *Robert Moses*, 220–224.
24 Robert A. M. Stern, Thomas Mellins, and David Fishman, *New York 1960: Architecture and Urbanism between the Second World War and the Bicentennial* (New York: Monacelli Press, 1995), ch. 14. Harrison and Abramovitz's first significant project was the United Nations headquarters.
25 Robert Moses, "Robert Moses on the Battle of Brooklyn," *Sports Illustrated*, July 22, 1957.
26 Moses, "Robert Moses"; Matthew Kachur, "A Stadium for Flushing Meadows," *Long Island Historical Journal* 5, no. 2 (Spring 1993): 181–183.
27 Kachur, "Stadium," 185–188, 190.
28 David Oats, "The World in a Park," *Queens Tribune*, October 16–22, 1980.
29 David Oats, "The World in a Park," *Queens Tribune*, October 23–29, 1980.
30 David Oats, "The World in a Park," *Queens Tribune*, October 30–November 5, 1980.
31 "Housing Plans Described," *New York Times*, February 19, 1949.
32 Milton Bracker, "Our Changing City: Gaps in Queens Are Filling Up," *New York Times*, August 8, 1955; Tony Hiss, *The Experience of Place* (New York: Alfred A. Knopf, 1990), 120–125.
33 Bloom, *Public Housing That Worked*, 86–89; *New York Times*, August 1, 1955.
34 Bloom, *Public Housing That Worked*, 86–89.
35 Murray, *Progressive Housewife*, 30, 45–49, 52.
36 Murray, *Progressive Housewife*, 30, 45–49.
37 Murray, *Progressive Housewife*, 47–49, 53–57.
38 "Segregation Held Breeder of Evils," *New York Times*, February 19, 1949.
39 Jewel Bellush, "Housing: The Scattered-Site Controversy," in *Race and Politics in New York City: Five Studies in Policy-Making*, ed. Jewel Bellush and Stephen M. David (New York: Praeger, 1971), 99.
40 Mumford, *From the Ground Up*, 123–128.
41 Eisenstadt, *Rochdale Village*, 4–6.
42 Eisenstadt, *Rochdale Village*, 4–5, 17, 228; chs. 9–11.
43 David K. Shipler, "The Changing City: Housing Paralysis," *New York Times*, June 5, 1969; David K. Shipler, "Housing for the Poor: A Typical Reaction," *New York Times*, November 19, 1971; Clarence Taylor, "Race, Rights, Empowerment," in *Summer in the City: John Lindsay, New York, and the American Dream*, ed. Joseph P. Viteritti (Baltimore: Johns Hopkins University Press, 2014), 66–69.
44 Shipler, "Changing City"; Shipler, "Housing for the Poor."
45 Bellush, "Housing," 98–99, 114.
46 Richard C. Wade, "Housing: A Comparative View," in *Urban Professionals and the Future of the Metropolis*, ed. Paula Dubeck and Zane Miler (Port Washington, NY: Kennikat Press, 1980), 72–77.
47 Wade, "Housing," 72–77.
48 Bellush, "Housing," 115–116; Walter Goodman, "The Battle of Forest Hills—Who's Ahead?," *New York Times*, February 20, 1972.

49 Mario Cuomo, *Forest Hills Diary: The Crisis of Low-Income Housing* (New York: Random House, 1974), 66.
50 Bloom, *Public Housing That Worked*; Taylor, "Race, Rights, Empowerment," 66–69.
51 Bellush, "Housing," 124; Steven V. Roberts, "2 Housing Plans Draw Protests," *New York Times*, May 12, 1966; Goodman, "Battle of Forest Hills."
52 Nathan Glazer, "When the Melting Pot Doesn't Melt," *New York Times*, January 2, 1972.
53 Steven V. Roberts, "Housing Projects in Queens Scored," *New York Times*, June 16, 1966.
54 "Badillo Scores Mayor on Housing Projects," *New York Times*, June 24, 1966; Steven V. Roberts, "Mayor Defeated by Borough Heads," *New York Times*, October 28, 1966; Steven V. Roberts, "Estimate Board Approves 5 Low Rent Housing Projects over Middle-Class Neighborhood Protests," *New York Times*, January 17, 1968.
55 Murray, *Progressive Housewife*, 163; Roberts, "Estimate Board."
56 Roberts, "Estimate Board."
57 *Long Island Daily Press*, November 30, 1966; November 14, 1967.
58 Jimmy Breslin, preface to Cuomo, *Forest Hills Diary*, vi.
59 U.S. Congress, *Congressional Record*, Vol. 117, no. 190, December 7, 1971.
60 U.S. Congress, *Congressional Record*, Vol. 117, no. 190, December 7, 1971.
61 Charles Brecher, "Mayoralty," in *Encyclopedia of New York City*, 813.
62 Cuomo, *Forest Hills Diary*, 49, 113, 117–118.
63 Bloom, *Public Housing That Worked*, 203–207.
64 *Western Queens Tribune*, May 3–9, 1991; *New York Times*, May 4, 1991.

Chapter 13   The Most Diverse Place on the Planet

1 David M. Reimers, "Immigration, 1900–Present," in *Encyclopedia of New York City*, 639–643; Nathan Glazer, "The New New Yorkers," in *New York Unbound*, ed. Peter D. Salins (New York: Basil Blackwell, 1988), 54–72; Louis Winnick, *New People in Old Neighborhoods: The Role of New Immigrants in Rejuvenating New York's Communities* (New York: Russell Sage Foundation, 1990), xv–xvi; Tyler Anbinder, *City of Ambition: The 400-Year Epic History of Immigrant New York* (New York: Houghton Mifflin Harcourt, 2016), 512–514.
2 Glazer, "New New Yorkers."
3 Winnick, *New People*, xvii, 7.
4 Stephane Tonnelat and William Kornblum, *International Express: New Yorkers on the 7 Train* (New York: Columbia University Press, 2017), 4, 19, 33.
5 Roger Sanjek, *The Future of Us All: Race and Neighborhoods Politics in New York City* (Ithaca, NY: Cornell University Press, 1998), 1–2.
6 Tonnelat and Kornblum, *International Express*, ch. 2.
7 Sanjek, *Future of Us All*, 1.
8 Sanjek, *Future of Us All*, 231.
9 Sanjek, *Future of Us All*, 53–60.
10 Masha Sinnreich, *New York—World City: Report of the Twentieth Century Fund Task Force on the Future of New York City: Background Paper* (Cambridge, MA: Oelgeschlager, Gunn and Hain, 1980), 22–28.
11 Sanjek, *Future of Us All*, chs. 12–14.
12 Sanjek, *Future of Us All*, 250–253.

13. Sanjek, *Future of Us All*, 68–74.
14. Sanjek, *Future of Us All*, ch. 9.
15. Sanjek, *Future of Us All*, ch. 9.
16. Sanjek, *Future of Us All*, chs. 12–14.
17. Sanjek, *Future of Us All*, 326–329.
18. Sanjek, *Future of Us All*, 250–253; "First Grade Culture Wars: The Children of the Rainbow Curriculum Controversy of 1992," LWA, accessed November 14, 2024, https://www.laguardiawagnerarchive.lagcc.cuny.edu/EdPrograms/LGBTQ_Exhibits.aspx?Exhibit=Children-Of-The-Rainbow.
19. Josh Barbanel, "Under 'Rainbow,' a War: When Politics, Morals and Learning Mix," *New York Times*, December 27, 1992; lagarchivist (LWA), "Ron Madson Adding References to Same Sex Headed Households to the Children of the Rainbow Curriculum," YouTube video, 3:58, June 4, 2022, https://www.youtube.com/watch?v=bG357HYoBfw&t=.
20. Barbanel, "Under 'Rainbow.'"
21. "Protest Outside Cathedral," *New York Times*, December 14, 1992; Sam Roberts, "Politics and the Curriculum Fight," *New York Times*, December 15, 1992.
22. Steven Lee Myers, "Ideas & Trends; How a 'Rainbow Curriculum' Turned into Fighting Words," *New York Times*, December 13, 1992.
23. Roberts, "Politics and the Curriculum Fight."
24. Barbanel, "Under 'Rainbow.'"
25. Joseph Berger, "A Mix of Earlier Skirmishes Converges in the Rainbow Curriculum Battle," *New York Times*, December 3, 1992; Roberts, "Politics and the Curriculum Fight."
26. "About," New Queens Pride, accessed November 14, 2024, https://newqueenspride.org/about/; "First Grade Culture Wars."
27. The New York City Landmarks Law was enacted in 1965 to protect historic landmarks and neighborhoods from being inappropriately altered or demolished. The law also established the creation of the New York City Landmarks Preservation Commission.
28. Nathan Silver, *Lost New York* (Boston: Houghton Mifflin, 1967), 20–21.
29. Pam Byers, *Small Town in the Big City: A History of Sunnyside and Woodside* (Sunnyside, NY: Sunnyside Community Service Center, 1976); Hecht, *History of College*; Walter J. Hutter et al., *Our Community, Its History and People: Ridgewood, Glendale, Maspeth, Middle Village, Liberty Park* (Ridgewood, NY: Greater Ridgewood Historical Society, 1976); Kroos, *Peek at Richmond Hill*; Barbara W. Stankowski, *Maspeth: Our Town* (Maspeth, NY: Maspeth Federal Savings and Loan, 1978), and her *Old Woodhaven: A Victorian Village* (Flushing, NY: QHS, 1978).
30. Vincent F. Seyfried, *The Story of Queens Village* (Queens Village, NY: Centennial Association, 1974); Seyfried, *300 Years*; Seyfried, *Story of Woodhaven and Ozone*. See Jeffrey A. Kroessler, "Who Has Done More? Vincent Seyfried and the Discovery of Queens History," *Long Island Historical Journal* 10, no. 1 (Fall 1997): 79–85.
31. Karatzas, *Jackson Heights*; Jeffrey A. Kroessler and Nina S. Rappaport, *Historic Preservation in Queens* (Sunnyside, NY: Queensborough Preservation League, 1990); B. Lewis, *Kew Gardens*; Wolfe, *This Salubrious Spot*.
32. Kroessler and Rappaport, *Historic Preservation in Queens*.
33. Deirdre Carmody, "Queens Board Supports Grand Prix Plan," *New York Times*, April 8, 1983; Wayne Barrett and Rick Hornung, "A Profile in Corruption: The Double Life of Donald Manes," *Village Voice*, September 22, 1987.
34. Lynette Holloway, "Love in the Ruins," *New York Times*, June 6, 1995.

Bibliography

Archives

Archives at the Queens Borough Public Library
Brooklyn Historical Society
Brooklyn Public Library
Collection of Vincent Seyfried
Department of Manuscripts and University Archives, Cornell University Library
Greater Astoria Historical Society
LaGuardia and Wagner Archives at the LaGuardia Community College of the City University of New York
Long Island Studies Institute, Hofstra University
New-York Historical Society
New York Public Library
Queens Historical Society
Roebling Collection, Rensselaer Polytechnic Institute
Triborough Bridge and Tunnel Authority

Websites

Beachside Bungalow Preservation Association: https://preserve.org/bungalow/
Boulevard Gardens: https://boulevardgardens.nyc/
Bowne House: https://www.bownehouse.org/
Green-Wood Cemetery: https://www.green-wood.com/
Juniper Park Civic Association: https://junipercivic.com/
Long Island Pine Barrens Society: https://www.pinebarrens.org/
Louis Armstrong House Museum: https://www.louisarmstronghouse.org/
New Queens Pride: https://newqueenspride.org/
Queens County Farm Museum: https://www.queensfarm.org/
Queens Historical Society: https://queenshistoricalsociety.org/
West Side Tennis Club: https://thewestsidetennisclub.com/

Local Histories

Armbruster, Eugene L. *Brooklyn's Eastern District*. Brooklyn, 1942.
———. *Long Island, Its Early Days and Development*. Brooklyn: Brooklyn Daily Eagle, 1914.
Bellot, Alfred Henry. *History of the Rockaways from the Year 1685 to 1917*. Far Rockaway, NY: Bellot's Histories, 1918.
Byers, Pam. *Small Town in the Big City: A History of Sunnyside and Woodside*. NY: Sunnyside Community Service Center, 1976.
Community History Program. *Transportation; Work; Housing; and Leisure*. New York: LaGuardia Community College of the City University of New York, 1981.
Comstock, Sarah. *Old Roads from the Heart of New York: Journeys Today by Ways of Yesterday within Thirty Miles around the Battery*. New York: Knickerbocker Press, 1915.
Connell, Joseph, comp. *The Hallett's of Hallett's Point, Newtown, L.I.* n.p., 1981.
Doggett, Marguerite V. *Ravenswood. The Gothic Revival and Alexander Jackson Davis*. n.p., n.d. (QBPL)
Edwards, Richard. *A Descriptive Review of the Manufacturing and Mercantile Industries of the City of Brooklyn and the Towns of Long Island and Staten Island*. New York: Historical Publishing, 1883. (N-YHS)
———. *An Historical and Descriptive Review of the City of Brooklyn and Her Manufacturing and Mercantile Industries, Including Many Sketches of Leading Public and Private Citizens*. New York: Historical Publishing, 1883.
Flushing, College Point, and Vicinity: Their Representative Business Men and Points of Interest. New York: Mercantile Publishing, 1893. (QBPL)
Flux, James A., and Irving Levine. *Bayside: Its Yesterdays and Tomorrows*. Bayside, NY: Bayside Times Publishing, 1957.
Fowler, George C., and Ernestine H. Fowler. *Through the Years in Little Neck and Douglaston*. Printed by Angle Offset, 1963.
Hazelton, Henry Isham. *The Boroughs of Brooklyn and Queens, Counties of Nassau and Suffolk, Long Island, New York, 1609–1924*. 5 vols. New York: Lewis Historical Publishing, 1925.
Hecht, Robert A. *A History of College Point*. College Point, NY: Bicentennial Commission of College Point, 1976.
Hutter, Walter J., et al. *Our Community, Its History and People: Ridgewood, Glendale, Maspeth, Middle Village, Liberty Park*. Ridgewood, NY: Greater Ridgewood Historical Society, 1976.
Jamaica, Hempstead, Richmond Hill, Morris Park and Woodhaven: Their Representative Business Men and Points of Interest. New York: Mercantile Publishing, 1894. (QBPL)
Karatzas, Daniel. *Jackson Heights: A Garden in the City*. New York: Jackson Heights Beautification Group, 1990.
Kelsey, J. S. *History of Long Island City, New York: A Record of Its Early Settlement and Corporate Progress*. Long Island City, NY: Long Island Star, 1896.
Kroos, William. *A Peek at Richmond Hill through the Keyhole of Time*. Richmond Hill, NY: Richmond Hill Savings Bank, 1983.
Lawson, Harriet Dondero. *Olde Flushing*. Flushing, NY: Dondero Lawson, 1952.
Lieberman, Janet E., and Richard K. Lieberman. *City Limits: A Social History of Queens*. Dubuque, IA: Kendall Hunt, 1983.
Little Neck Community Association. *The History of Little Neck*. Little Neck, NY: Little Neck Community Association; William James [1952].

Lovely, Thomas J. *The History of Jamaica Estates, 1929–1969.* Jamaica, NY: Jamaica Estates Association, 1969.
Onderdonk Jr., Henry. "Notes on the History of Queens County (Part 2: 1784–1852)." *Journal of Long Island History* 7, no. 2 (Summer–Fall 1967): 36–56.
———. *Queens County in Olden Times: Being a Supplement to the Several Histories Thereof.* Jamaica, NY: Charles Welling, 1865.
Peters, George H. *The Trees of Long Island.* Farmingdale, NY: Long Island Horticultural Society, 1952.
Pettit, William Soper. *History & Views of the Rockaways.* Far Rockaway, NY, 1901.
Post, Kate Matson. *The Story of Richmond Hill.* Richmond Hill, NY: Richmond Hill Record, 1905.
Prime, Nathaniel S. *A History of Long Island, from Its Earliest Settlement by Europeans to the Year 1845, with Special Reference to Its Ecclesiastical Concerns.* New York: Robert Carter, 1845.
Reifschneider, Felix E. "Historical Notes." Typed pages and hand-drawn map. Electric Railroaders Association, 1951.
Riley, Lester Leake. *The Chronicle of Little Neck and Douglaston, Long Island.* Little Neck, NY: Little Neck Division of the Long Island Tercentenary Commemoration of Queens, 1936.
———. *The Pageant of Flushing Town.* Flushing, NY: Flushing Centennial Celebration Committee, 1937.
Ross, Peter. *A History of Long Island: From Its Earliest Settlements to the Present Time.* 3 vols. New York: Lewis Publishing, 1903.
Seyfried, Vincent F. *Corona: From Farmland to City Suburb, 1650–1935.* Garden City, NY: Edgian Press, 1986.
———. *The Founding of Garden City, 1869–1893.* Uniondale, NY: Salisbury Printers, 1969.
———. *Queens: A Pictorial History.* Norfolk, VA: Donning, 1982.
———. *The Story of Queens Village.* Queens Village, NY: Centennial Association, 1974. (QBPL)
———. *The Story of Woodhaven and Ozone Park.* Woodhaven, NY: Leader Observer, 1985. (QBPL)
———. *300 Years of Long Island City, 1630–1930.* Garden City, NY: Edgian Press, 1984.
Sharp, John Kean. *History of the Diocese of Brooklyn, 1853–1953.* New York: Fordham University Press, 1954. (N-YHS)
Stankowski, Barbara W. *Maspeth: Our Town.* Masbeth, NY: Maspeth Federal Savings and Loan, 1978.
———. *Old Woodhaven: A Victorian Village.* Flushing, NY: Queens Historical Society, 1978.
Steinway, Theodore. *People and Pianos: A Century of Service to Music, Steinway & Sons, New York, 1853–1953.* New York: Steinway and Sons, 1953.
von Skal, George. *Illustrated History of the Borough of Queens, New York City.* New York: compiled by the F.T. Smiley Publishing for the Flushing Journal, 1908.
Waller, Henry D. *History of the Town of Flushing, Long Island, New York.* Flushing, NY: J. H. Ridenour, 1899.
Winans, George W. *Old Roads of Jamaica Township in Colonial Days.* Jamaica, NY, 1935. (QBPL)
Wood, Silas, and Alden J. Spooner. *A Sketch of the First Settlement of the Several Towns on Long Island, with Their Political Condition, to the End of the American Revolution.* Brooklyn: printed for the Furman Club, 1865 [1828].

Atlases and Maps

ATLASES
Beers, F. W. *Atlas of Long Island, New York*. New York: F. W. Beers, 1873.
Bromley, G. W. *Atlas of the City of Brooklyn*. New York: G. W. Bromley, 1880.
Bromley, George W., and Walter S. Bromley. *Atlas of the City of New York, Borough of Queens*. Philadelphia: G. W. Bromley, 1909.
Hyde, E. Belcher. *Atlas of the Borough of Queens, City of New York*. Brooklyn: E. Belcher Hyde, 1901, 1908, 1928 (various volumes, some corrected to later dates).
Wolverton, Charles. *Atlas of Queens County, Long Island, New York*. New York, 1891.

MAPS
American Homes Company. *Map of Jamaica Fells*. Jersey City, 1905.
Beers, F. W. *The Flushing and North Side Rail Road, with Its Leased Branches*. New York: Beers, Comstock and Cline, 1873.
Bellaire Estates Company. *Bellaire Estates*. New York, 1908.
Bird's Eye View of Richmond Hill Arcade #3 and Lott Manor. [New York, ca. 1910].
Brooks and Brooks Corp. *Rosedale Square*. New York [1910].
Burr, David H. *Map of the Counties of New York, Queens, Kings, and Richmond*. New York: David H. Burr, 1829.
Committee on the Regional Plan of New York and Its Environs. *Regional Survey of New York and Its Environs*. 8 vols. New York: Regional Plan of New York and Its Environs, 1927–1931.
Cord Meyer Development Company. *Map Showing Location of Forest Hills*. New York: August R. Ohman, 1908.
Degnon Realty and Terminal Improvement Company. *Map of Property, Long Island City, Borough of Queens, N.Y.C.* July 1910.
Department of Public Works, Borough of Queens. *Plan of Proposed Boulevard Connecting Highland Boulevard in Kings County with the Myrtle Avenue and Metropolitan Avenue Entrances of Forest Park, Hoffman Blvd., and Other Boulevards of Queens: Also Showing Park Lands Connected and Cemetery Lands Adjoining Course. Suggested by Alfred Denton, Ass't. Commissioner of Public Works* [1920s].
Dripps, Mathew. *Map of Kings and Part of Queens Counties*. New York, 1852.
———. *Map of the Cities of New York, Brooklyn, Jersey City, Hudson City and Hoboken, Prepared by M. Dripps of New York for Valentines Manual*. New York, 1859.
———. *Map of Long Island City, Queens Co. N.Y., Showing Farm Lines &c. &c.* New York, 1874.
Englehardt Construction Company. *Map of Brooklyn Manor*. Woodhaven, NY [1905].
Flushing United Association. *Map of Flushing*. Flushing, NY, 1920.
Fosdick Collection. (QHS)
Guide Map of the Borough of Brooklyn. In *Brooklyn Daily Eagle Almanac*. Brooklyn: Brooklyn Daily Eagle, 1900, 1907, 1911, and 1913.
H. C. Bennett and Company. *New York City Lots $200, Springfield Section*. [1910].
Hyde, E. Belcher. *Map of the Borough of Queens*. New York, 1910.
———. *Rapid Transit & Development Map of the Boroughs of Manhattan, Bronx, Brooklyn and Queens, City of New York, Including a Portion of Nassau County, L.I., Showing Valuable Suburban Localities Connected with Manhattan*. New York, 1910.
Jamaica Hillcrest Company. *Map of Jamaica Hillcrest*. [1910].
Map of Elmhurst Square. July 1905.

Map of Hempstead Plains, Long Island, Recently Purchased by Mr. A.T. Stewart. Brooklyn Historical Society [1869].

Map of Jamaica Bay. February 10, 1930. (QBPL)

Map of the Village of Flushing. April 1, 1841.

Map of Valuable Property Situated in and Adjoining the Village of Flushing (the Village Line Running thro' the Property) Belonging to Mr. Gansevoort, for Sale by W. Smart, Agent. New York, July 1850.

Map Showing the Limits of Greater New York. Queens, NY: Queens Chamber of Commerce, 1896.

Map Showing the Route & Connections of the Central Rail Road Extension Company of Long Island. New York, 1873.

Meynen, Booth, and Eno Long Island Real Estate. *Map of Jamaica.* Jamaica, NY, 1907.

New Map of Kings and Queens Counties, New York: From Actual Surveys. New York: J. B. Beers, 1886.

New York City Board of Public Improvements, Topographical Bureau. *Map or Plan Showing a General Design for a System of Streets, Avenues, Public Squares and Places, Parks, Bridges, etc. in That Part of the 2nd Ward (Formerly Town of Newtown) in the Borough of Queens.* New York, August 1, 1899, supplement to the *Newtown Register*, October 5, 1899.

———. *Record of Searches in Relation to the Legal Status of Avenues and Streets in the 1st Ward of the Borough of Queens, Formerly Long Island City.* New York, December 31, 1900.

New York City Department of Docks and Ferries. *Plan for Development of Jamaica Bay.* New York, n.d. (QBPL)

New York Land and Warehouse Company. *Reference Map . . . Showing Desirable Factory, Water Front and Building Sites, First Ward, Borough of Queens, City of New York.* 1900.

North Shore Realty Company. *Bayside Park.* New York [1907].

Office of the Borough President of the Borough of Queens, Topographical Bureau. *Tentative Map Showing Proposed Street System for the Territory Bounded by Flushing River, Flushing Bay, Boundary line of Fort Totten, Little Neck Bay, Bayside Ave., Bell Ave., Crocheron Ave., Lonsdale Ave., Wainscott Ave., Beechurst Ave., and Jackson Ave.* New York, March 15, 1912.

———. *Topographical Map Showing Street System and Grades of That Portion of the Second Ward (Town of Newtown) Bounded by Metropolitan Ave., Trotting Course Lane, Satterlee Ave., Dry Harbor Road, Trotting Course Lane, Hoffman Blvd., Omega St., Water Edge Ave. and Union Turnpike, Borough of Queens.* December 1, 1905 (approved by the mayor January 4, 1906).

Ohman Map Company. *New Quick Reference Street Indexed Map of the Borough of Queens, Showing Assembly Districts, Aldermanic Districts, and Municipal Courts Districts.* New York, 1916.

Paris-MacDougall Company. *Map of Kissena Park.* New York, 1908.

Powell, Charles Underhill, and Shore Acres Realty Company. *Map of Beechhurst (Whitestone Landing), Situated in the Third Ward, Borough of Queens, City of New York.* [1915].

Quilitch, E. T. *Astoria.* 1852.

Rand McNally. *Standard Map of the Borough of Queens.* New York, 1903.

Rickert-Finlay Realty Company. *East River Heights.* New York, March 1907.

Sage Foundation Homes Company. *Forest Hills Gardens.* New York, April 1911 and October 1912.

Sauthier, Claude Joseph. *A Chorographical Map of the Province of New York in North America: Divided into Counties, Manors, Patents, and Townships: Exhibiting Likewise All the Private Grants of Land Made and Located in That Province.* [Albany, NY, 1849].
South Jamaica Place. 1910.
Terminal Heights. April 1906.
van der Donck, Adriaen. *Map of New Netherlands, with a View of New Amsterdam, (Now New-York) A.D. 1656.* Nineteenth-century engraving of the original.
Wallace, Franklin R. *Map Showing Real Estate Developments along the LIRR and Jamaica Ave.–Jericho Turnpike from Hollis to Mineola.* 1907.
Walling, Henry Francis. *Topographical Map of the Counties of Kings and Queens, New York.* New York: W. E. and A. A. Baker, 1859.
Watson's New Map of New York and Adjacent Cites. New York: Gaylord Watson, 1876.
Williams Map and Guide Company. *Map of the Borough of Queens.* 1911, rev. April 15, 1917.

Newspapers

Bayside Times, 1935–present (QBPL)
Courier (Richmond Hill), 1919-? 1927–1928 (QBPL)
Daily Star (Long Island City), 1881–1933 (QBPL)
Flushing Daily Times, 1855–1925 (QBPL)
Flushing Evening Journal, begun 1879; became *North Shore Daily Journal* in January 1931; merged with *Daily Star* in 1938 to form *Long Island Star Journal*, 1938-1968 (QBPL)
Flushing Journal, May 1842–June 1907 (QBPL)
Frank Leslie's Illustrated Newspaper, 1855–1922 (QBPL)
Harper's Weekly, 1857–1916 (Internet Archive)
Jackson Heights News, 1918–1970 (QBPL)
Jamaica Herald, 1922-1928 (QBPL)
Leader-Observer (Woodhaven), 1912–present (QBPL)
Long Island Democrat, 1835–1912 (QBPL)
Long Island Farmer, 1821–1920; became the *Long Island Press*, 1922–1977 (QBPL)
Long Island Star Journal, 1938-1968 (QBPL)
Newtown Register, 1873–1935 (QBPL)
New York Daily News, 1919–present
New York Sun, 2002–2008, online since 2022
New York Times, 1851–present
New York World, 1860–1931
Queens Evening News (Jamaica), 1929–1939 (QBPL)
Queens County Review (Freeport), 1895–1898, became *Nassau County Review*, 1899–1921 (LISI)
Rockaway Journal, 1934–present (QBPL)
Rockaway News, 1900–present (QBPL)
Wall Street Journal, 1889–present
Wave of Long Island (Rockaway), 1893–1979; became *Wave* (Rockaway), 1979- present (QBPL)
Whitestone Herald, 1871–1949 (QBPL)

Periodicals

Architectural Forum, 1892-1974 (NYPL)
The Family Magazine, 8 volumes, 1833-1841 (NYPL)
Interborough Bulletin (Interborough Rapid Transit Company), January 1912–December 1918; June 1921–October 1922; April 1923; January 1935–February 1938 (N-YHS)
Long Island Chapter News (Nature Conservancy) (LISI)
The Long Island Magazine, 1893-present (QBPL, N-YHS)
Long Island Today (1884); *Out on Long Island* (1890–1893); *The Beauties of Long Island* (1895–1896); *Long Island Illustrated* (1898–1904, 1907) (all LIRR) (N-YHS)
QueensBorough (Queens Chamber of Commerce)1913-present, (QBPL)
The Real Estate Magazine, vols. 1–6, 1912–1915 (Internet Archive)
Scientific American

Primary Sources

An Accurate Description of the British Colonies in North-America. Salisbury, England: Collins and Johnson, 1777.
Ahmend, Albert H. "Diary." Typed copy in QHS.
Album of the Rockaways and Long Beach. New York: Wittemann Bros., 1881.
Anonymous. "Fair Bayside." 1873.
Appel, Benjamin. *The People Talk: American Voices from the Great Depression*. New York: Touchstone, 1982 [1940].
Appleton's Dictionary of New York. New York: D. Appleton, 1898.
Ash, Mark. *The Greater New York Charter as Enacted in 1897*. Albany, NY: Weed-Parsons, 1897.
Bauer, Catherine. *Modern Housing*. New York: Houghton Mifflin, 1934.
Birdseye, Clarence F. *The Greater New York Charter [...] Constituting Chapter 378 of the Laws of 1897*. New York: Baker, Voorhis, 1897.
Bloomingdale's Diary, 1909 and Souvenir Commemorative of the Opening of the Queensboro Bridge, 1901–1909. New York: Bloomingdale Bros., 1909.
"Borough of Queens: A Review of Its Progress because of Excellent Location, Remarkable Resources & Superior Natural Advantages, with Illustrations." *American Journal of Commerce* 14, no. 15 [1900].
Bowery Bay Beach Building and Improvement Company. *A Day's Outing at Bowery Bay Beach*. New York, 1889.
Bradford, Edward A. *"Great York": An Inquiry into the Relation of Rapid Transit and Consolidation to Past and Present Poverty, Disease, Crime, and Mortality and Their Remedy*. Brooklyn: Consolidation League of Brooklyn, 1894.
Brearley, Harry Chase. *The Problem of Greater New York and Its Solution*. New York: Brooklyn League, 1914.
Brodhead, John Romeyn. *History of the State of New York, First Period, 1609–1664*. New York: Harper and Brothers, 1853.
Brooklyn and Manhattan Transit Company. *Rush Hour Relief for Passengers on Williamsburgh Bridge and Other East New York Lines*. Brooklyn: B.M.T. Lines [1924].
Brooklyn Blue Book and Long Island Society Register. Brooklyn: Brooklyn Life Publishing, 1896–1898, 1899–1919.

Brooklyn Botanic Garden. Leaflets. Series 24, nos. 3–5. December 9, 1936.
The Brooklyn Bridge, Its History and Romance. New York: A. F. W. Leslie, 1883.
Brooklyn Daily Eagle Almanac. Brooklyn: Brooklyn Daily Eagle, 1899.
Brooklyn Department of City Works. *Report on Future Extensions of Water Supply for the City of Brooklyn*. Brooklyn, 1896.
The Candidates for Election in Brooklyn and Long Island, November 5th, 1895. Brooklyn, NY: Brooklyn Eagle Library, November 1895.
Carman, Margaret I. *The Bowne House Historical Society*. Flushing, NY, 1951[?].
Cassidy, Joseph. "The Borough of Queens, Past, Present and Future." *Long Island Magazine* 1, no. 1 (June 1903).
Childe, Cromwell. *Trolley Exploring*. Brooklyn: Brooklyn Daily Eagle, 1902.
———. *Water Exploring: A Guide to Pleasant Steamboat Trips Everywhere*. Brooklyn: Brooklyn Daily Eagle, 1902.
Childs, L. Maria. *Letters from New-York*. New York, 1852 [ca. 1844].
Cincinnati Bridge Company. *Statement by the Cincinnati Bridge Co. in Reference to the New York & Long Island Bridge*. New York: Graphic Company, 1877.
The Citizen Guide to Brooklyn and Long Island: The City's Resources and Residences, the Island's Retreats and Resorts, a Regal City in a Rich Country. Brooklyn, 1893.
City of Brooklyn Common Council. *Reports of the Majority and Minority of the Railroad Committee on the Subject of Steam on Atlantic Street*. Brooklyn: L. Darbee and Son Printers, June 1, 1857.
Clinton, George W. *An Address Delivered September 20th, 1855, at the Fourteenth Annual Exhibition of the Queens Co. Agricultural Society, at Flushing, Long Island*. Flushing, NY: printed at the office of the Flushing Journal, 1855.
Conger, A. B. *Address [...] delivered before the Queens County Agricultural Society, October 5, 1864*. Jamaica, NY: printed at the office of the Long Island Democrat, 1864.
Corbin, Austin. *Extracts from the Press*. [New York, 1896].
———. "Quick Transit between New York and London." *North American Review* 159, no. 468 (November 1892): 513–527.
Cox Jr., John. *Quakerism in the City of New York, 1657–1930*. New York: privately printed, 1930.
Cutter, Bloodgood Haviland. *The Long Island Farmer's Poems, Lines Written on the "Quaker City" Excursion to Palestine and Other Poems*. New York: N. Tibbals and Sons, 1886.
Denison, Lindsay. "The Biggest Playground in the World." *Munsey's Magazine*, August 1905.
Denton, Daniel. *A Brief Description of New York, Formerly Called New Netherlands, with the Places thereunto Adjoining. Introduction and Copious Notes by Gabriel Furman*. New York: William Gowans, 1845 [1670].
Dix, John A. *Address, Delivered October 2D, 1851, at the Tenth Annual Exhibition, of the Queens County Agricultural Society, at Jamaica, L. I.* Hempstead, NY: Hempstead Inquirer, 1852.
"Existing and Proposed Trolley Lines around New York." *Harper's Weekly*, August 1, 1896.
Far Rockaway, Rockaway Beach, Rockaway Park, Long Island. New York: American Photograph Company, 1910.
Federal Writers' Project of the Works Progress Administration. *New York Panorama*. New York: Pantheon, 1984 [1938].

Fifth Ave. Coach Company. *Motor Bus Relief for New York's Transit Needs*. New York: Fifth Ave. Coach, 1917.
Fitzgerald, F. Scott, *The Great Gatsby*. New York: Charles Scribner's Sons, 1925.
Ford Motor Company. *The Ford Exposition, New York's World Fair*. Souvenir brochure. 1939–1940.
Freeman, John R. *Report upon New York's Water Supply, with Particular Reference to the Need of Procuring Additional Sources and Their Probable Cost*. New York: Martin B. Brown, 1900.
General Motors Corporation. *Futurama*. Souvenir brochure. 1940.
Goldfield, Abraham. *Toward Fuller Living through Public Housing and Leisure Time Activities*. New York: National Public Housing Conference, 1934.
Gordon, Thomas F. *Gazetteer of the State of New York*. Philadelphia, 1836.
Gotham. New York: Hall and Ruckel, 1870.
Griswold, Frank Gray. *Sport on Land and Water*. Norwood, MA: Plimpton Press, 1913.
Grout, Edward M. *Improvement and Development of Jamaica Bay and the Water Front of the City of New York Other Than That of Manhattan Island*. New York: Martin B. Brown Press, 1905.
[Gunnison, Herbert Foster]. *The Beauties of Long Island*. New York: Long Island Railroad, 1895.
G. X. Mathews Company. "Mathews Model Flats, Solving the Housing Problem." *Mathews Bulletin*, January 1928.
Heerbrandt, Gustav. *Illustrirter Führer durch New York*. New York, 1893.
Hinsdale, Elizur B. *Autobiography, with Reports and Documents*. New York: J. J. Little, 1901.
———. *History of the Long Island Railroad Company, 1834–1898*. New York: Evening Post Job Printing House, 1898. (N-YHS)
Hough, Benjamin Franklin. *Census of the State of New York for 1865*. Albany, NY: C. Van Benthuysen and Sons, 1867.
"How People Come and Go in New York." *Harper's Weekly*, February 26, 1898.
Ickes, Harold. "The Housing Policy of the PWA." *Architectural Forum*, February 1934.
Interborough Rapid Transit Company. "Twenty-Fifth Anniversary of the Subway." *The I.R.T News*, October 27, 1929.
———. *The New York Subway*. New York: Arno Press, 1904.
Jamaica Board of Trade. *Survey of Jamaica, the Heart of Queensboro*. Jamaica, NY, 1920.
Johnson, Jere. *Village of Flushing*. New York, 1887.
Johnson, Jesse. *Against Consolidation. Should Brooklyn Be Annexed to New York?* Brooklyn: League of Loyal Citizens, 1895.
Kenny's Guide. New York: F. H. Kenny, 1889.
Killmer, N. B. *The Authorized Freight and Passenger Tunnel under the Narrows between Brooklyn and Staten Island* [...]. New York: Jamaica Bay Improvement Association, 1925.
King, Charles. *An Address, Delivered September 29th, 1852, at the Eleventh Annual Exhibition of the Queens County Agricultural Society, at Flushing, Long Island*. Jamaica, NY: printed at the office of the Long Island Farmer, 1852.
King, John A. *An Address, Delivered October 6th, 1848, at the Seventh Annual Exhibition of the Queens County Agricultural Society, at Jamaica, Long Island*. Jamaica, NY: printed by Charles S. Watrous, 1849.
Kohn, Robert D. "The Government Housing Program." *Architectural Forum*, February 1934.

Laffan, Willam M. *The New Long Island: A Hand Book of Summer Travel Designed for the Use and Information of Visitors to Long Island and Its Watering Places*. New York: Rogers and Sherwood, 1879.

Landmarks Preservation Commission. *Sohmer & Company Piano Factory Building*. Designation List Report, February 27, 2007. https://www.nyc.gov/html/records/pdf/govpub/2867sohmer.final.pdf.

League of American Wheelmen. *Road-Book of Long Island*. Published under the auspices of the Brooklyn Bicycle Club. Philadelphia: Franklin Printing House, 1886.

Lewis, Harry C. *Corporate and Financial History of the Following Corporations, All of Which Have Been Merged into or Otherwise Acquired by the Long Island Railroad Company*. [Washington, DC]: Bureau of Valuation, Interstate Commerce Commission, 1919.

[Long-Island Canal and Navigation Company]. *Report on the Project of Uniting the Great Bays of Long-Island by Canals, from Coney-Island to Bridgehampton*. Brooklyn: E. B. Spooner, Printer, 1848.

Long Island City Board of Education records. City Charter Relative to the Department of Public Instruction of Long Island City, 1871.

Long Island Railroad. *The Home Builder on Long Island*. New York: LIRR, 1907

———. *Hotels and Boarding Cottages on Long Island, N.Y.* New York: LIRR, 1892.

———. *Long Island & Where to Go!! A Descriptive Work Compiled for the Long Island R. R. Co. for the Use and Benefit of Its Patrons*. New York: Lovibond and Jackson, 1877.

———. *Long Island, 1905*. New York: LIRR, 1905.

———. *Long Island, the Sunrise Homeland*. New York: LIRR, 1924.

———. *Report of the Board of Directors of the Long Island Railroad Company to the Stockholders, in Relation to the Condition of Its Affairs and Prospects When Completed to Greenport*. [New York], 1843.

———. *Suburban Long Island, the Sunrise Homeland*. New York: LIRR, 1922.

Lyford, Will H. *Report on a Proposed Development of Transatlantic Steamship Terminal at Montauk, on Fort Pond Bay, Long Island*. New York, August 1923.

McCullough, Esther Morgan. *As I Pass, O Manhattan*. New York: Coley Taylor, 1956.

Mapes, James J. *An Address Delivered October 6th, 1853, at the Twelfth Annual Exhibition of the Queen's County Agricultural Society, at Hempstead, Long Island*. n.p., 1854.

Marine Parkway Authority. *Published on the Occasion of the Opening of the Marine Parkway, July 3rd, 1937*. Brochure. New York, 1937.

[Mitchill, Samuel Latham]. *The Picture of New-York; or The Traveller's Guide, through the Commercial Metropolis of the United States, by a Gentleman Residing in This City*. New York: I. Riley; sold by Brisban and Brannan, City-Hotel, Broadway, 1807.

Moses, Robert. "From Dump to Glory." *Saturday Evening Post*, January 15, 1938.

———. *The Triborough Bridge: A Modern Metropolitan Traffic Artery*. New York: Triborough Bridge Authority, 1936.

Nevins, Allan. *Abram S. Hewitt, with Some Account of Peter Cooper*. New York: Harper and Brothers, 1935.

New York and Long Island Bridge Company. *Charter, Amendments and By-Laws*. New York: New York Saturday Review, 1873.

———. *Report of Board of Consulting Engineers, Appointed to Recommend a Plan for the New York & Long Island Bridge across the East River at Blackwell's Island*. New York: Graphic Company, 1877.

New York and Long Island Railroad Company. Promotional booklet. n.d.

New York City Board of Rapid Transit. *Railroad Commissioner's Reports.* 1901–1906.
New York City Department of Docks and Ferries. *Report on the Proposed Plan of Operation for Jamaica Bay Improvement.* New York, 1911.
New York City Department of Parks. *Circumferential Parkway.* 1938.
———. *The Future of Jamaica Bay.* 1938.
———. *The Improvement of Coney Island.* 1939.
———. *The Improvement of Coney Island, Rockaway and South Beaches.* 1937.
———. *Kissena Park: Botanical Guide to a Historic Grove.* 1981.
———.*The Rockaway Improvement.* 1939.
New York City Department of Plants and Structures. *Triborough Bridge, Connecting the Boroughs of Manhattan, the Bronx, and Queens.* 1930.
New York City Housing Authority. *Facts about Queensbridge.* New York, 1940.
New York, New Haven and Hartford Rail Road Company. *Homes on the Sound for New York Business Men.* New York: George L. Catlin, 1875.
New York State Department of Transportation. *A Comprehensive Study of Proposed Bridge Crossings of Long Island Sound, Summary.* Albany, NY, 1972.
New York State Legislature. *Interim Report of the New York State Joint Legislative Committee for the Celebration of the 300th Anniversary of the Signing of the Flushing Remonstrance.* Legislative Doc. No. 30. Albany, NY: State of New York, 1957.
New York State Senate. *Reports of the Committees in Relation to the Long-Island Canal Company.* Albany, NY: Croswell and Van Benthuysen, 1827.
New York State World's Fair Commission, Regional Division No. 1. *Long Island, the Sunrise Homeland: Brooklyn, Queens, Nassau, and Suffolk Counties.* 1939.
Official Guide Book, New York World's Fair, 1939. New York: Exposition Publications, 1939.
Onderdonk, William H. *An Address, Delivered September 15th, 1859, at the Eighteenth Annual Exhibition of the Queens Co. Agricultural Society, at Hempstead, Long Island.* Hempstead, NY: Printed at the office of the Hempstead Inquirer, 1859.
Philip, John C., and Browne, Henry H. *Insurance Surveys of the Petroleum Depots in New York and Vicinity.* New York: Perris and Browne, 1863.
Prince, William. *A Treatise on Fruit and Ornamental Trees and Plants, Cultivated at the Linnaean Botanic Garden, Flushing, Long-Island, near New-York.* New York: T. and J. Swords, 1820.
Queensboro Bridge Celebration: Official Program. New York: Queensboro Bridge Celebration Committee, 1909.
Queens Borough, Its Growth and Prosperity; Some Statistical Information That Will Surprise and Instruct the Citizens; Lower Tax Rate for 1905; Expenditures for Improvements and Where the Money Comes From; The Borough's Splendid Highways. Anonymous pamphlet. New York, 1905.
Queens County, New York State. *Official Canvass of Queens County.* 1897.
Queens Planning Commission. *Report of the Queens Planning Commission.* Edited by Henry J. Haarmeyer. New York: H. J. Haarmeyer, 1929.
[Ralph, Julian]. *Long Island of To-Day.* New York: [American Bank Note Company], 1884.
Real Estate Record and Builders Guide, 1868–1894. Anniversary number, supplement to edition of May 12, 1894.
Regional Plan Association. *From Plan to Reality.* 3 vols. New York: Arno Press, 1974 [1933].
———. *Regional Plan of New York and Its Environs.* Vol. 1, *The Graphic Regional Plan* [1929]; vol. 2, *The Building of the City* [1931]. New York: Arno Press, 1974.

———. *Regional Survey of New York and Its Environs*. 8 vols. New York: Arno Press, 1974 [1928].
Ricard, Herbert F., ed. *The Journal of John Bowne, 1650–1694*. New Orleans: Friends of the Queensborough Community College Library and Polyanthos, 1975.
Richardson, Darby. *Illustrated Flushing and Vicinity*. Flushing, NY, 1917.
Riis, Jacob. *The Making of an American*. New York, 1920 [1901].
Sage Foundation Homes Company. *Declaration of Restrictions, etc., Affecting Property Known as Forest Hills Gardens*. New York, April 18, 1913.
———. *Forest Hills Gardens*. New York, December 1913.
———. *Forest Hills Gardens: Preliminary Information for Buyers*. Pamphlet no. 3. New York, April 1913.
———. *Forest Hills Gardens: The Suburban Land Development of the Russell Sage Foundation*. Pamphlet no. 1. New York, February 1911.
Schnebly, Thomas. *The Quality of the "Wild Lands" of Long Island: Examined, and Detailed Evidences Given of Their Value, Together with a Reasonable Conjecture Why They Have Not Been Improved*. New York: The Sun Book and Job Printing Office, 1860.
Seaton, C. W. *Census of the State of New York for 1875*. Albany, NY: Weed, Parsons, 1877.
Sherman, Franklin J. *Building Up Greater Queens Borough: An Estimate of Its Development and the Outlook*. New York: Brooklyn Biographical Society, 1929.
Schotter, H. W. *The Growth and Development of the Pennsylvania Railroad Company*. Philadelphia: Pennsylvania Rail Road, 1927.
Silver, Nathan. *Lost New York*. Boston: Houghton Mifflin, 1967.
Sinnreich, Masha. *New York—World City: Report of the Twentieth Century Fund Task Force on the Future of New York City: Background Paper*. Cambridge, MA: Oelgeschlager, Gunn and Hain, 1980.
Skinner, John S., *Address Delivered before the Queens County Agricultural Society at Its Fourth Anniversary, at Hempstead, Thursday, October 9th, 1845*. Jamaica, NY: James J. Brenton, Printer, 1846. (QBPL)
Smith, R. A. C., Commissioner of Docks of New York City, *Hell Gate*. New York, July 1, 1917.
Souvenir Improvement Celebration. Jamaica, NY, April 20, 1898. [Jamaica, NY: Bertram Blackwell, printer?], 1898.
Sunnyside Gardens Community Association, Consolidated Home Owners' Mortgage Committee. *Valuation Brief with Reference to Mortgage Payments*. Sunnyside Gardens, NY, April 1935.
36th Annual Report of the Department of Parks of the City of Brooklyn, 1896. Brooklyn: Brooklyn Eagle Press, 1897.
Thompson, Benjamin F. (Benjamin Franklin). *History of Long Island; from Its Discovery and Settlement to the Present Time*. New York: Gould Banks, 1843 [1839].
Treat's Illustrated New York, Brooklyn and Surroundings. New York, 1874.
Tredwell, Daniel M. *Personal Reminiscences of Men and Things on Long Island*. Pt. I. Brooklyn: Charles Andrew Ditmas, 1912.
———. *Personal Reminiscences of Men and Things on Long Island*. Pt. II. Brooklyn: Charles Andrew Ditmas, 1917.
Triborough Bridge Authority. *The Bronx-Whitestone Bridge*. New York, 1939.
———. *Completion of Francis Lewis Boulevard, Queens, Mixed Traffic Approach to the Bronx-Whitestone Bridge*. New York, 1940.
Twain, Mark. *The Innocents Abroad*. New York: Signet Classics, 1966 [1869].

Vojan, Jaroslav. *Velky New York (Greater New York)*. New York: New-Yorkských List, 1908.
Watson, Winslow C. *The Plains of Long Island*. Albany, NY, 1860.
Whalen, Grover. *Mr. New York: The Autobiography of Grover Whalen*. New York: G. P. Putnam's Sons, 1955.
Wharton, Edith. *A Backward Glance*. New York: Charles Scribner's Sons, 1985 [1933].
Whitman, Walt. *Complete Poetry and Collected Prose*. New York: Library of America, 1982.
Wood, Clarence Ashton. *First Train to Greenport in 1844*. Bayshore, NY: Long Island Forum, 1944.
Woodside Heights Land Corporation. *Present and Future Transportation: Its Effect on Real Estate in the Borough of Queens, and Resulting Benefits through the Construction of the Numerous Bridges and Tunnels Now Rapidly Progressing toward Completion [. . .]*. New York, 1906.
Woodward, Arthur. *Spokes in the Wheels to Long Island*. Issued under the direction of the Transportation Committee of the Real Estate Exchange of Long Island. New York: Windsor Land and Improvement, 1910.
Your World of Tomorrow. Souvenir booklet of Democracity, World's Fair 1939–1940. New York: Rogers-Kellogg-Stillson, 1939.

CORPORATE RECORDS

Flushing, North Shore, & Central Railroad Company. Minutes of the Board of Directors.
Flushing and North Side Railroad Company. Minutes of the Board of Directors.
Flushing Rail Road Company. Minutes of the Board of Directors.
Flushing and Woodside Railroad Company. Minutes of the Board of Directors.
Hunters Point and South Side Railroad Company. Minutes of the Board of Directors.
Long-Island Canal Company. *Documents Presented to the Legislature of the State of New-York at Its Last and Present Sessions, Setting Forth the Expediency and Public Importance of Incorporating the Long-Island Canal Company for the Purpose Expressed by the Petitioners*. New York: printed by Joseph C. Spear, Coffee House Slip, 1826.
New York & Flushing Railroad Company. Minutes of the Board of Directors.
Southern Railroad Company of Long Island. Minutes of the Board of Directors.
South Side Railroad Company of Long Island. Minutes of the Board of Directors.

Secondary Sources

BOOKS

Adelman, Melvin L. *A Sporting Time: New York City and the Rise of Modern Athletics, 1820–1870*. Urbana: University of Illinois Press, 1986.
Anbinder, Tyler. *City of Ambition: The 400-Year Epic History of Immigrant New York*. New York: Houghton Mifflin Harcourt, 2016.
Anderson, Will. *The Breweries of Brooklyn*. Croton Falls, NY: Will Anderson, 1976.
Arend, Geoffrey. *Air World's Great Airports: LaGuardia, 1939–1979*. New York: Air Cargo News, 1979.
Bailey, Paul. *Physical Long Island: Its Glacial Origins, Historic Storms, Beaches, Prairies and Archaeology*. Amityville, NY: Long Island Forum, 1959. (N-YHS)
———, ed. *Long Island: A History of Two Great Counties, Nassau and Suffolk*. 3 vols. New York: Lewis Historical Publishing, 1949. (N-YHS)

Ballon, Hilary, and Kenneth T. Jackson. *Robert Moses and the Modern City: The Transformation of New York*. New York: W. W. Norton, 2007.
Bard, Erwin Wilde. *The Port of New York Authority*. New York, 1939.
Barlow, Elizabeth. *The Forests and Wetlands of New York City*. Boston: Little, Brown, 1971. (QBPL)
Bellush, Jewel, and Stephen M. David, eds. *Race and Politics in New York City: Five Studies in Policy-Making*. New York: Praeger, 1971.
Bender, Thomas. *New York Intellect: A History of Intellectual Life in New York City, from 1750 to the Beginnings of Our Own Time*. New York: Alfred A. Knopf, 1987.
Berlin, Ira, and Leslie Harris, eds. *Slavery in New York*. New York: New Press, 2005.
Black, Frederick R. *Jamaica Bay, a History: Gateway National Recreation Area, New York-New Jersey*. Cultural Resources Management Study No. 3. Washington, DC: Division of Cultural Resources, North Atlantic Regional Office, National Park Service, U.S. Department of the Interior, National Park Service, 1981. (QBPL)
Bloom, Nicholas Dagen. *Public Housing That Worked: New York in the Twentieth Century*. Philadelphia: University of Pennsylvania Press, 2008.
Bridenbaugh, Carl. *Mitre and Sceptre: Transatlantic Faiths, Ideas, Personalities, and Politics 1689–1775*. New York: Oxford University Press, 1962.
Boyer, Christine. *Dreaming the Rational City*. Cambridge, MA: MIT Press, 1983.
Burgess, George H., and Miles C. Kennedy. *Centennial History of the Pennsylvania Railroad Company*. Philadelphia: Pennsylvania Railroad, 1949.
Campanella, Thomas J. *Brooklyn: The Once and Future City*. Princeton, NJ: Princeton University Press, 2019.
Carman, Harry James. *The Street Surface Railway Franchises of New York City*. New York: Columbia University Studies in History, Economics, and Public Law No. 88, 1919.
Caro, Robert. *The Power Broker: Robert Moses and the Fall of New York*. New York: Alfred A. Knopf, 1974.
Cobb, Sanford H. *The Rise of Religious Liberty in America: A History*. New York: Burt Franklin, 1970 [1902].
Colean, Miles L. *American Housing: Problems and Prospects*. New York: Twentieth Century Fund, 1944.
Condit, Carl W. *The Port of New York: A History of the Rail and Terminal Pennsylvania Station*. Chicago: Chicago University Press, 1980.
Cornog, Evan. *The Birth of Empire: DeWitt Clinton and the American Experience, 1769–1828*. New York: Oxford University Press, 1998.
Cowan, Jane. *Addisleigh Park*. New York: Historic Districts Council, 2008, http://hdc.org/wp-content/uploads/2012/08/HDC-Addisleigh-Park-Report.pdf.
Cravens, Curtis. *Copper on the Creek: Reclaiming an Industrial History*. Brooklyn: Place in History, 2000.
Crouse, Russel. *Mr. Currier and Mr. Ives: A Note on Their Lives and Times*. Garden City, NY: Garden City Publishing, 1937. (QBPL)
Cunningham, Joseph, and Lemond DeHart. *A History of the New York Subway System*. 3 vols. New York, 1976.
Cuomo, Mario. *Forest Hills Diary: The Crisis of Low-Income Housing*. New York: Random House, 1974.
Davis, Kenneth S. *FDR, The New York Years, 1928–1933*. New York: Random House, 1979.
Derrick, Peter. *Tunneling to the Future: The Story of the Great Subway Expansion That Saved New York*. New York: New York University Press, 2001.

Diehl, Lorraine B. *The Late, Great Pennsylvania Station*. New York: American Heritage Press, 1985.
Doctorow, E. L. *World's Fair*. New York: Random House, 1985.
Doig, Jameson W. *Metropolitan Transportation Politics and the New York Region*. New York: Columbia University Press, 1966.
Eisenberg, John. *The Great Match Race: When North Met South in America's First Sports Spectacle*. Boston: Houghton Mifflin, 2006.
Eisenstadt, Peter. *Rochdale Village: Robert Moses, 6,000 Families, and New York City's Great Experiment in Integrated Housing*. Ithaca, NY: Cornell University Press, 2010.
———, ed. *The Encyclopedia of New York State*. Syracuse, NY: Syracuse University Press, 2005.
Evans, Hazel, ed. *New Towns: The British Experience*. New York: Wiley, 1972.
Fischler, Stan. *Uptown, Downtown: A Trip through Time on the New York Subways*. New York: Hawthorne Books, 1976.
Ford, James. *Slums and Housing: With Special Reference to New York City: History-Conditions-Policy*. Cambridge, MA: Harvard University Press, 1936.
Frese, Joseph R., and Jacob Judd, eds. *Business Enterprise in Early New York*. Tarrytown, NY: Sleepy Hollow Press, 1979.
Gellman, David Nathaniel. *Emancipating New York: The Politics of Slavery and Freedom, 1777–1827*. Baton Rouge: Louisiana State University Press, 2006.
Gies, Joseph. *Bridges and Men*. Garden City, NY: Doubleday, 1963.
Gordon, John Steele. *The Scarlet Woman of Wall Street*. New York: Weidenfeld and Nicolson, 1988.
Gottmann, Jean. *Megalopolis: The Urbanized Northeastern Seaboard of the United States*. Cambridge, MA: MIT Press, 1964 [1961].
Hammack, David C. *Power and Society: Greater New York at the Turn of the Century*. New York: Russell Sage Foundation, 1982.
Haskell, Gilbert. *The Subways and Tunnels of New York*. New York: Wiley and Sons, 1912.
Heckscher, August. *When LaGuardia Was Mayor: New York's Legendary Years*. New York: W. W. Norton, 1978.
Hiss, Tony. *The Experience of Place*. New York: Alfred A. Knopf, 1990.
Hobbs, E. H. *A History of Transit on Atlantic Avenue*. Brooklyn, 1897.
Hood, Clifton. *722 Miles: The Building of the Subways and How They Transformed New York*. New York: Simon and Schuster, 1993.
Huthmacher, J. Joseph. *Senator Robert F. Wagner and the Rise of Urban Liberalism*. New York: Atheneum, 1971.
Jackson, Kenneth T. *Crabgrass Frontier: The Suburbanization of the United States*. New York: Oxford University Press, 1985.
———, ed. *The Encyclopedia of New York City*. 2nd ed. New Haven, CT: Yale University Press, 2010.
Judd, Jacob, and Irwin H. Polishook. *Aspects of Early New York Society and Politics*. Tarrytown, NY: Sleepy Hollow Restorations, 1974.
Kasson, John F. *Amusing the Million: Coney Island at the Turn of the Century*. New York: Hill and Wang, 1978.
Keith, Nathaniel S. *Politics and the Housing Crisis since 1930*. New York: Universe Books, 1973.
Kessler, Henry H., and Eugene Rachlis. *Peter Stuyvesant and His New York*. New York: Random House, 1959.

Kessner, Thomas. *Fiorello H. La Guardia and the Making of Modern New York*. New York: McGraw-Hill, 1989.
Klaus, Susan. *A Modern Arcadia: Frederick Law Olmsted Jr. and the Plan for Forest Hills Gardens*. Amherst: University of Massachusetts Press, 2002.
Krieg, Joann P., ed. *Robert Moses, Single Minded Genius*. Interlaken, NY: Heart of the Lakes Publishing, 1989.
Kroessler, Jeffrey A. *The Greater New York Sports Chronology*. New York: Columbia University Press, 2010.
———. *Lighting the Way: A Centennial History of the Queens Borough Public Library, 1896–1996*. Virginia Beach, VA: Donning, 1996.
———. *New York, Year by Year: A Chronology of the Great Metropolis*. New York: New York University Press, 2002.
———. *Sunnyside Gardens: Planning and Preservation in a Historic Garden Suburb*. New York: Fordham University Press, 2021.
Kroessler, Jeffrey A., and Nina S. Rappaport. *Historic Preservation in Queens*. Sunnyside, NY: Queensborough Preservation League, 1990.
Kross, Jessica. *The Evolution of an American Town: Newtown, New York, 1642–1775*. Philadelphia: Temple University Press, 1983.
Laidlaw, Walter, ed. *Population History of the City of New York*. New York: Cities Census Committee, 1932.
———. *Statistical Sources for Demographic Studies of Greater New York, 1920*. New York, 1922.
Lane, Wheaton J. *Commodore Vanderbilt: An Epic of the Steam Age*. New York: Alfred A. Knopf, 1942.
Leuchtenburg, William E. *Franklin D. Roosevelt and the New Deal*. New York: Harper and Row, 1963.
Lewis, Barry. *Kew Gardens: Urban Village in the Big City*. Kew Gardens, NY: Kew Gardens Council for Recreation and the Arts, 1999.
Lieberman, Richard K. *Steinway & Sons*. New Haven, CT: Yale University Press, 1995.
Linder, Marc, and Lawrence S. Zacharias. *Of Cabbages and Kings County: Agriculture and the Formation of Modern Brooklyn*. Iowa City: University of Iowa Press, 1999.
Lockwood, Charles. *Bricks and Brownstones: The New York Row House, 1783–1929: An Architectural and Social History*. New York: McGraw-Hill, 1972.
Lowery, Ann Gidley. *The Story of the Flushing Meeting House*. Flushing, NY: Flushing Monthly Meeting of the Religious Society of Friends, 1969.
Lubove, Roy. *Community Planning in the 1920's: The Contribution of the Regional Planning Association of America*. Pittsburgh: University of Pittsburgh Press, 1963.
Luke, Myron H., and Robert W. Venables. *Long Island in the American Revolution*. Albany: New York State American Revolution Bicentennial Commission, 1976.
McCormick, Richard L. *From Realignment to Reform: Political Change in New York State, 1893–1910*. Ithaca, NY: Cornell University Press, 1981.
McCullough, David G. *The Great Bridge: The Epic Story of the Building of the Brooklyn Bridge*. New York: Simon and Schuster, 1972.
McManus, Arthur T. *The Hempstead Plains: A Vanishing Heritage*. Hempstead, NY: Citizens for Hempstead Plains [1967].
McManus, Edgar J. *A History of Negro Slavery in New York*. Syracuse, NY: Syracuse University Press, 1966.
Melosi, Martin V. *Fresh Kills: A History of Consuming and Discarding in New York City*. New York: Columbia University Press, 2020.

Moody, John. *The Railroad Builders: A Chronicle of the Welding of the States*. New Haven, CT: Yale University Press, 1919.

Mumford, Lewis. *From the Ground Up: Observations on Contemporary Architecture, Housing, Highway Building, and Civic Design*. New York: Harcourt, Brace and World, 1956.

———. *Green Memories: The Story of Geddes Mumford*. New York: Harcourt Brace, 1947.

———, ed. *Roots of Contemporary American Advertising*. New York: Dover, 1972 [1952].

Murray, Sylvie. *The Progressive Housewife: Community Activism in Suburban Queens, 1945–1965*. Philadelphia: University of Pennsylvania Press, 2003.

Patterson, Jerry E. *The City of New York: A History Illustrated from the Collections of the Museum of the City of New York*. New York: Harry N. Abrams, 1978.

Peiss, Kathy. *Cheap Amusements: Working Women and Leisure in Turn-of-the-Century New York*. Philadelphia: Temple University Press, 1986.

Peterson, Jon, and Vincent F. Seyfried. *A Research Guide to the History of the Borough of Queens*. Flushing, NY: Queens College, 1987.

Pratt, Edward E. *Industrial Causes of Congestion of Population in New York City*. New York, 1911.

Pratt, Frederick B. *Development and Present Status of City Planning in New York City*. New York, 1914.

Pratt, John Webb. *Religion, Politics, and Diversity: The Church-State Theme in New York History*. Ithaca, NY: Cornell University Press, 1967.

Radford, Gail. *Modern Housing for America: Policy Struggles in the New Deal Era*. Chicago: University of Chicago Press, 1996.

Reed, Henry Hope, and Sophia Duckworth. *Central Park: A History and a Guide*. Rev. ed. New York: Clarkson N. Potter, 1972.

Reier, Sharon. *The Bridges of New York*. New York: Quadrant Press, 1977.

Reps, John W. *The Making of Urban America: A History of City Planning in the United States*. Princeton, NJ: Princeton University Press, 1965.

Roper, Laura Wood. *FLO: A Biography of Frederick Law Olmsted*. Baltimore: Johns Hopkins Press, 1973.

Rose, Mark H. *Interstate: Express Highway Politics, 1939–1989*. Knoxville: University of Tennessee Press, 1990.

Rosenwaike, Ira. *Population History of New York City*. Syracuse, NY: Syracuse University Press, 1972.

Rosenzweig, Roy. *Eight Hours for What We Will: Workers and Leisure in an Industrial City, 1870–1920*. New York: Cambridge University Press, 1983.

Rosenzweig, Roy, and Elizabeth Blackmar. *The Park and the People: A History of Central Park* Ithaca, NY: Cornell University Press, 1992.

Sanjek, Roger. *The Future of Us All: Race and Neighborhoods Politics in New York City*. Ithaca, NY: Cornell University Press, 1998.

Schotter, H. W. *The Growth and Development of the Pennsylvania Railroad Company*. Philadelphia, 1927.

Seyfried, Vincent F. *BRT Trolley Lines in Queens County*. 1959.

———. *Jamaica Trolleys: The Story of the Jamaica Turnpike and Trolley Line*. 1953.

———. *The Long Island Rail Road: A Comprehensive History*. 7 vols. Garden City, NY: Vincent F. Seyfried, 1961–1975.

———. *New York & Long Island Traction Company*. 1952.

———. *New York & North Shore Traction Company*. 1956.

———. *The New York and Queens County Railway and the Steinway Lines, 1867–1939.* Hollis, NY: Vincent F. Seyfried, 1950.

———. *The Story of the Long Island Electric Railway and the Jamaica Central Railways, 1892–1933.* 1951.

Smith, George L. *Religion and Trade in New Netherland: Dutch Origins and American Development.* Ithaca, NY: Cornell University Press, 1973.

Smith, Mildred H. *Early History of the Long Island Railroad, 1834–1900.* Uniondale, NY: Salisbury Printers, 1958.

———. *History of Garden City.* Garden City, NY: Garden City Historical Society, 1980.

Spann, Edward. *The New Metropolis: New York City, 1840–1857.* New York: Columbia University Press, 1981.

Spengler, Edwin H. *Land Values in New York in Relation to Transit Facilities.* New York: Columbia University Press, 1930. [reprint, New York: AMS Press, 1968]

Stein, Clarence, *Toward New Towns for America.* Cambridge, MA: MIT Press, 1978 [1957].

Steinman, David B., and Sara Ruth Watson. *Bridges and Their Builders.* New York: Dover, 1957 [1941].

Stern, Robert A. M. *The Anglo-American Suburb.* London: Architectural Design, 1981.

———. *Pride of Place.* Boston: Houghton Mifflin, 1986.

Stern, Robert A. M., David Fishman, and Jacob Tilove. *New York 2000: Architecture and Urbanism between the Bicentennial and the Millennium.* New York: Monacelli Press, 2006.

Stern, Robert A. M., Gregory Gilmartin, and John Montague Massengale. *New York 1900: Metropolitan Architecture and Urbanism, 1890–1915.* New York: Rizzoli, 1983.

Stern, Robert A. M., Gregory Gilmartin, and Thomas Mellins. *New York 1930: Architecture and Urbanism between Two World Wars.* New York: Rizzoli, 1987.

Stern, Robert A. M., Thomas Mellins, and David Fishman. *New York 1880: Architecture and Urbanism in the Gilded Age.* New York: Monacelli Press, 1999.

Stern, Robert A.M., Thomas Mellins, and David Fishman, *New York 1960: Architecture and Urbanism between the Second World War and the Bicentennial.* New York: Monacelli Press, 1995.

Strickland, Roy, and James Sanders. *At Home in the City: Housing in New York, 1810–1983.* New York, 1983.

Sussman, Warren. *Culture as History: The Transformation of American Society in the Twentieth Century.* New York: Pantheon, 1984.

Swan, Herbert S. *The Housing Market in New York City.* New York: Reinhold Publishing, 1944.

Syrett, Harold Coffin. *The City of Brooklyn, 1865–1898: A Political History.* New York: Columbia University Press, 1944.

Tarr, Joel A., *The Search for the Ultimate Sink: Urban Pollution in Historical Perspective.* Akron, OH: University of Akron Press, 1996.

Taylor, George Rogers. *The Transportation Revolution, 1815–1860.* New York: Holt, Rinehart and Winston, 1951.

Tonnelat, Stephane, and William Kornblum. *International Express: New Yorkers on the 7 Train.* New York: Columbia University Press, 2017.

Trebor, Haynes, ed. *The Flushing Remonstrance (The Origin of Religious Freedom in America).* Flushing, NY: Bowne House Historical Society, 1957.

Van der Zee, Henri, and Barbara Van der Zee. *A Sweet and Alien Land: The Story of Dutch New York.* New York: Viking Press, 1978.

Viteritti, Joseph P., ed. *Summer in the City: John Lindsay, New York, and the American Dream*. Baltimore: Johns Hopkins University Press, 2014.
Walker, James B. *Fifty Years of Rapid Transit, 1864–1917*. New York: Arno Press, 1970.
Walsh, George. *Gentleman Jimmy Walker, Mayor of the Jazz Age*. New York: Praeger, 1979.
Ward, David, and Olivier Zunz, eds. *The Landscape of Modernity: Essays on New York City, 1900–1940*. New York: Russell Sage Foundation, 1992.
Warner, Sam Bass. *Streetcar Suburbs: The Process of Growth in Boston, 1870–1900*. Cambridge, MA: Harvard University Press; MIT Press, 1962.
Willensky, Elliot, and Norval White. *AIA Guide to New York City*. 4th ed. New York: Three Rivers Press, 2000.
Winnick, Louis *New People in Old Neighborhoods: The Role of New Immigrants in Rejuvenating New York's Communities*. New York: Russell Sage Foundation, 1990.
Wolfe, Kevin. *This Salubrious Spot: The First 100 Years at Douglas Manor, 1906–2006*. Douglaston, NY: Douglas Manor Association, 2006.
Wood, Edith Elmer. *Recent Trends in American Housing*. New York, 1931.
Wright, Gwendolyn. *Building the Dream: A Social History of Housing in America*. New York: Pantheon, 1981.
——— . *Moralism and the Modern Home*. Chicago: University of Chicago Press, 1980.

ARTICLES AND BOOK CHAPTERS

Bellush, Jewel. "Housing: The Scattered-Site Controversy." In *Race and Politics in New York City: Five Studies in Policy-Making*, edited by Jewel Bellush and Stephen M. David, 98–134. New York: Praeger, 1971.
Chernow, Barbara A. "Robert Morris and Alexander Hamilton: Two Financiers in New York." In *Business Enterprise in Early New York*, edited by Joseph R. Frese and Jacob Judd, 77–98. Tarrytown, NY: Sleepy Hollow Press, 1979.
Conzen, Michael P. "The Maturing Urban System in the United States, 1840–1910." *Annals of the Association of American Geographers* 67, no. 1 (March 1977): 88–108.
Dunbaugh, Edwin L. "New York to Boston via the Long Island Railroad, 1844–1847." In *Evoking a Sense of Place*, edited by Joann P. Krieg, 75–79. Interlaken, NY: Heart of the Lakes Publishing, 1988.
Flint, Richard W. "Meet Me in Dreamland: The Early Development of Amusement Parks in America." *Nineteenth Century* 8, nos. 1–2 (1982): 99–107.
George, David Robinson. "A Brief History of the Long Island Railroad." In *Long Island: A History of Two Great Counties, Nassau and Suffolk*, vol. 2., edited by Paul Bailey, 397–404. New York: Lewis Historical Publishing, 1949.
Giguere, Joy M. "'Too Mean to Live, and Certainly in No Fit Condition to Die': Vandalism, Public Misbehavior, and the Rural Cemetery Movement." *Journal of the Early Republic* 38, no. 2 (2018): 293–324.
Gilette Jr., Howard. "Film as Artifact: The City." *American Studies* 18 (Fall 1977): 71–85.
Glazer, Nathan. "The New New Yorkers." In *New York Unbound*, edited by Peter D. Salins, 54–72. New York: Basil Blackwell, 1988.
Harris, Richard. "Industry and Residence: The Decentralization of New York City, 1900–1940." *Journal of Historical Geography* 19, no. 2 (1993): 169–190.
Havelick, Franklin, and Michael Kwartler. "Sunnyside Gardens: Whose Land Is It Anyway?," *New York Affairs* 7, no. 2 (1982): 66–86.
Hayes, Michael. "Nathaniel Woodhull and the Battle of Long Island." *Long Island Historical Journal* 7, no. 2 (Spring 1995): 166–177.

Jackson, Kenneth T. "Robert Moses and the Rise of New York: The Power Broker in Perspective." In *Robert Moses and the Modern City: The Transformation of New York*, edited by Hilary Ballon and Kenneth T. Jackson, 67–71. New York: W. W. Norton, 2007.

Judd, Jacob. "Water for Brooklyn." *New York History* 47, no. 4 (October 1966): 362–371.

Kachur, Matthew. "A Stadium for Flushing Meadows." *Long Island Historical Journal* 5, no. 2 (Spring 1993): 178–194.

Kroessler, Jeffrey A. "Boulevard Gardens." In *Affordable Housing in New York*, edited by Nicholas Dagen Bloom and Matthew Gordon Lasner, 67–70. Princeton, NJ: Princeton University Press, 2016.

———. "Bridges and the Urban Landscape." *Long Island Historical Journal* 2, no. 1 (Fall 1989): 104–117.

———. "Brooklyn's Thirst, Long Island's Water: Consolidation, Local Control, and the Aquifer." *Long Island History Journal* 22, no. 1 (2011), https://lihj.cc.stonybrook.edu/2011/articles/brooklyns-thirst-long-islands-water-consolidation-local-control-and-the-aquifer/.

———. "Coney Island." In *Robert Moses and the Modern City: The Transformation of New York*, edited by Hilary Ballon and Kenneth T. Jackson, 165. New York: W. W. Norton, 2007.

———. "Flushing Meadows-Corona Park." In *Robert Moses and the Modern City: The Transformation of New York*, edited by Hilary Ballon and Kenneth T. Jackson, 197–200. New York: W. W. Norton, 2007.

———. "Jamaica Bay and Marine Park." In *Robert Moses and the Modern City: The Transformation of New York*, edited by Hilary Ballon and Kenneth T. Jackson, 166–168. New York: W. W. Norton, 2007.

———. "Long Island State Parks Commission and Jones Beach." In *Robert Moses and the Modern City: The Transformation of New York*, edited by Hilary Ballon and Kenneth T. Jackson, 158–160. New York: W. W. Norton, 2007.

———. "Parkways and Expressways in Brooklyn and Queens." In *Robert Moses and the Modern City: The Transformation of New York*, edited by Hilary Ballon and Kenneth T. Jackson, 220–224. New York: W. W. Norton, 2007.

———. "Rockaway Improvement." In *Robert Moses and the Modern City: The Transformation of New York*, edited by Hilary Ballon and Kenneth T. Jackson, 171–172. New York: W. W. Norton, 2007.

———. "Who Has Done More? Vincent Seyfried and the Discovery of Queens History." *Long Island Historical Journal* 10, no. 1 (Fall 1997): 79–85.

Landman, David. "Montauk, Phantom Rival to New York Port." *New York History* 33, no. 2 (April 1952): 115–137.

Maika, Dennis J. "Commemoration and Context: The Flushing Remonstrance Then and Now." *New York History* 89, no. 1 (2008): 28–42.

Pearlstein, Daniel. "Sweeping Six Percent Philanthropy Away: The New Deal in Sunnyside Gardens." *Journal of Planning History* 9, no. 3 (2010): 170–182.

Peters, George H. "The Flora of Long Island." In *Long Island: A History of Two Great Counties, Nassau and Suffolk*, vol. 2., edited by Paul Bailey, 137–150. New York: Lewis Historical Publishing, 1949.

Rosen, Laura. "Triborough Bridge." In *Robert Moses and the Modern City: The Transformation of New York*, edited by Hilary Ballon and Kenneth T. Jackson, 229–231. New York: W. W. Norton, 2007.

Smits, Edward J. "The Creation of Nassau County." *Long Island Historical Journal* 1, no. 2 (Spring 1989): 171–173.
Stalter, Richard, and Wayne Seyfert. "The Vegetation History of Hempstead Plains, New York." *Prairie Pioneers: Ecology, History and Culture: Proceedings of the Eleventh North American Prairie Conference*, 41–45. Lincoln, Nebraska. Lincoln: University of Nebraska, 1989.
Swan, Herbert S. "Home Ownership in New York City." *Journal of the American Institute of Architects* 6, no. 1 (January 1918): 28–29.
———. "How Zoning Works in New York." *National Municipal Review* 7, no. 3 (May 1918): 244–254.
Tabor, George. "The Saga of the Triborough Bridge." *Bronx County Historical Journal* 9, no. 2 (July 1972): 53–55.
Taylor, Clarence. "Race, Rights, Empowerment." In *Summer in the City: John Lindsay, New York, and the American Dream*, edited by Joseph P. Viteritti, 61–80 (Baltimore: Johns Hopkins University Press, 2014.
Trough, Rosalind. "Building Costs and Total Costs at Sunnyside Gardens, L. I." *Journal of Land & Public Utilities* 8, no. 2 (May 1932): 164–174.
———. "Production Costs of Urban Land in Sunnyside, Long Island." *Journal of Land & Public Utilities* 8, no. 1 (February 1932): 43–54.
Wade, Richard C. "Housing: A Comparative View." In *Urban Professionals and the Future of the Metropolis*, edited by Paula Dubeck and Zane Miler, 69–78. Port Washington, NY: Kennikat Press, 1980.
Walsh, Daniel C. "The Evolution of Refuse Incineration: What Led to the Rise and Fall of Incineration in New York City?" *Environmental Science & Technology* 36, no. 15 (2002): 316–322.
Wood, Edith Elmer. "Slums and the City Plan: A Plea to Make Slum Clearance and Replotting an Integral Part of Every City Plan Which Deals with an Already Existing Community." *American City* 41 (August 1929): 95–96.

DISSERTATIONS AND THESES

Kling, Jesse. "Solid Brick Homes: The Continuing Row House Tradition of Brooklyn and Queens." Master's thesis, Columbia University, 2022.
Levine, Steven A. "In Gotham's Shadow: Brooklyn and the Consolidation of Greater New York." PhD diss., City University of New York, 2002.
Peyer, Jean. "Jamaica, Long Island, 1656–1776: A Study in the History of American Urbanism." PhD diss., City University of New York, 1974.
Valles, Madeline B. "History of Flushing." Master's thesis, Columbia University, 1938.

Index

Page numbers in italics refer to illustrations.

A & S (department store), 308–309
Abdoh, Djakal, 286
abolition, 56–58
Abrams, Charles, 303
Ackerman, Frederick L., 234, 257
Addisleigh Park, 14
Agricultural Adjustment Administration (AAA), 269
agriculture: and canal development, 45–48; and consolidation of New York, 166–167; and early twentieth-century land values, 225; and the manure industry, 80–85; nursery industry, 48–53, 69, 76, 244; Queens County Farm Museum, 13, 287
AIA Guide to New York City (Willensky and White), 327
AIDS advocacy and education, 324
airports, 128, 159, 262, 264, 268, 271
Albany, 34
alcohol: public intoxication, 57, 71, 141, 144–145, 150–151, 154, 156, 158; Sunday restrictions on, 145–149, 155; temperance movement, 69, 71, 147, 155
Aldrich, Winthrop W., 290
Allen, Woody, 216
All in the Family (television show), 14, 15, 306, 311–312

American Dream, 14, 16, 273
American Institute of Planners, 275
American Museum of the Moving Image, 326
American Revolution, 38–43
Amersfoort (Flatlands), 20, 33, 54
Ammann, Othmar H., 208, 264
amusement parks, 11, 140, 149–150, 153–159, *154*
Anabaptists, 20
Annexed District, 163, 182
Appleton's Dictionary of New York, 158
Aqueduct Racetrack, 136
Arbitration Rock, 3
Ariel (LIRR), 65
Armstrong, Louis, 14, 142, 295
Articles of Capitulation, 29, 33
Arverne Hotel, 138, 139, *139*
Arverne Houses, 296
Asians, 15, 315, 316, 318, 320
Astor, John Jacob, 102
Astoria: Astoria Houses, 296; development of, 75, 102–104; ferry served by, 56; immigrants in, 197, 316; Park and Pool, 262, 265; Schuetzen Park, 142, 211; Steinway and Sohmer piano factories, 120–124, *124*, 347n7; Steinway Street, *12*, 316, 329; as a wealthy retreat, 102

389

Astoria & Williamsburgh Turnpike Co., 74
Astoria Gazette, 75
Atlas of Long Island (Beers), 124
Atterbury, Grosvenor, 228
Auburndale, 116
Augenti, Elizabeth, 216
automobile age, 116, 217–218, 269, 276–277

Babylon, 85–86, 178
Backward Glance, A (Wharton), 102
Baker, George W., 127
ballparks: "Picked Nines" teams, 135; rowdiness of Sunday games, 144–146, 149; Shea Stadium, 191–193
Baltimore and Ohio Railroad, 96
Bank of Manhattan, 226
Bank of New-York, 48
banks and banking: in Bridge Plaza, 226–227; and canal development, 46, 48; foreclosures by, 241–242
Barclay, James, 192
Barnard, J. G., 193
Barren Island, 128
Baruch, Bernard, 142
Basie, Count, 14, 295
Bauer, Catherine, 256, 257
Bayside, 105, 113, 116, 224, 284, 316
Beebe, George W., 103
Beebe estate, 125
Beers, F. W., 124; *The Flushing and North Side Railroad, with Its Leased Branches, 88; New Map of Kings and Queens Counties, New York: From Actual Surveys, 114*
Bel Geddes, Norman, 275–276
Bellerose, 42, 287
Bell Park Manor, 287
Bell Park Terrace, 287
Bellush, Jewel, 301
Belmont, August, 136, 211, 212
Belmont Park, 136
Belmont Tunnel, 227
Belt Parkway, 262, 266, 268, 291
Bergen, 33
Bethpage, 92
Bing, Alexander M., 234
Black, Frank S., 174, 183
Blacks, 13–15; Baptist ministers, 324; demographics, 56–58, *60,* 286, 289, 299, *313–314,* 314–322; in East Elmhurst, 318–319; Forest Hills Tennis Club closed to, 230; ghettos of, 302–304, 307; housing discrimination, 286, 289, 297–300, 319; integration, 14, 31–32, 258–259, 297–307; New Deal public housing, 257–258, *258;* opposition to proposed statue, 36, 37; postwar public housing, 295–307
Blackwell's Island Bridge (*renamed* Queensboro Bridge). *See* Queensboro Bridge
Bliss, Archibald M., 192, 193
Bloom, Nicholas Dagen, 297, 303
Bloomberg, Michael, 329
Bloomingdale, Samuel J., 211
Bloomingdale's (department store), 211, 308, 309
Bloomingdale's Diary, 213
blue laws. *See* Sunday restrictions
Board of Education, 69, 284, 325
Board of Estimate, 201, 209, 244, 254, 263, 271, 305, 329
Bodine, John A., 103
Bodine Castle, 103
Bogart, James H., 183
Bohemian Hall, Astoria, 142
Boller, Alfred, 209, 210
Booth, William H., 304
Borden Avenue, Long Island City, as it Appeared in an Earlier Day, Looking from the Roof of the Long Island Railroad Station, 75
Borough Development Company, 270
Boston, 37, 63, 64, 68, 238
Boston & Providence Railroad, 64
Boston Tea Party, 39
Boulevard Gardens, 252, *253,* 262
Bowery Bay (North Beach), 149–159
Bowery Bay Beach Improvement Company, 151–152
Bowne, John, 27–30, 32
Bowne House, *28,* 29–31, *42*
Bowne House Historical Society, 30
Bowne Park Civic Association, 298
Bradford, Edward A., 164
Breezy Point, 140
Breslin, Jimmy, 305, 307
Breukelen (Brooklyn), 20, 32–33
breweries, 10, 120, 126, 158, 219
Bria, Theresa, 304

Bridenbaugh, Carl, 37
Bridge Plaza, 214, 220, 226, 227
bridges: Bronx-Whitestone Bridge, 244, 247, 262, 263, 268; Brooklyn Bridge, 165, 194, 196, 211–212, 216, 217; cantilever design, 195, 203–209; Firth of Forth, 189, *190*, 203; Manhattan Bridge, 202, 203, 216; Marine Parkway Bridge, 128; Quebec Bridge collapse, 206–209; Queensboro Bridge, 165, 187, 189–216; Williamsburg Bridge, 116, 200, 227
Brokaw Mansion, 327
Bronx, 150, 164, 217, 222, 264, 303
Bronx-Whitestone Bridge, 244, 247, 262, 263, 268
Brookhaven, Long Island, 40, 48, 68
Brooklyn: annexation and consolidation, 164, 165–167, 171, 173, 184; Atlantic Avenue, trains on, 83–85, 96, 112; and the Brooklyn and Jamaica Railroad Company, 52, 64; Colonia Era (Breukelen), 20, 32–33; demographics, nineteenth century, 54–56, *57*, 64, 165; incorporation and charter of, 54, 64; as a Kings County township, 64–65 (*see also* Kings County); and railroads, 63–67, 74, 81–85, 112, 200; Revolutionary forces in, 40, 41; street grid, 54; urbanization, 102; water resources, 54–56, 184–186
Brooklyn and Jamaica Railroad Company, 52, 64
Brooklyn Ash Removal Company, 270, 272
Brooklyn Bridge, 114, 165, 192, 194, 196, 211–212, 216, 217
Brooklyn Common Council, 83–84, 86–87
Brooklyn Dodgers, 291–293
Brooklyn Eagle, 171
Brooklyn Forest Park (now Forest Park), 109, 166
Brooklyn Heights, 102, 328
Brooklyn Historical Society, 175
Brooklyn Manhattan Transit (BMT), 227
Brooklyn Rapid Transit (BRT), 158, 219, 227, 270
Brooklyn Star, 66–67, 175
Brooklyn Times, 185–186
Brooks mansion, 124
Brotherhood of Electrical Workers, 297
Brushville (Queens Village), 39

Bryant, William Cullen, 178, 183
Bunche, Ralph, 230, 286
Bunker, Archie, 14, 306, 311–312, 318, 320
Burke, James A., 290
Burr, Aaron, 46, 134
Burr, David H., *Map of the counties of New York, Queens, Kings, and Richmond*, 46
Burr, William H., 209, 210
Bushwick, 3, 33, 54, 74, 87, 138, 166
Byers, Pam, 328

Calvary Cemetery, 56, 72, 96, 142
Calvinists, 19–20, 21
Campbell, Edward, 129
canals, 45–48, 52, 63, 222, 270–271
Caribbean, 315, 316
Caro, Robert, 262, 263, 265
Cassatt, Alexander, 99
Cassidy, George W., 245–246
Cassidy, Joseph, 186–187, 203
Catherine, of Braganza, Queen, 34, 36–37
Catholics, 20, 69, 72, 139, 141, 312, 323–325
Cautley, Marjorie Sewell, 234
Celtic Park, 142
cemeteries, 11, 56, 72, 96, 141–42, 227, 311
Central Park, 49–50, 146
Central Railroad Company of Long Island, 91–93, *93*
Centreville, 135–136
Chanute, Oliver, 193
Charles II, King of England, 32–34
Charlick, Oliver, 78–80, 85, 86, 88, 89, 90, 92, 94, 192, 193
Charlick, Willett, 85
Chicago, 164, 165, 190, 238
Child, Lydia Maria, 103
Children of the Rainbow Curriculum, 322–325
Chinese, 316
Church of England, 37–38
Church of the Resurrection, 109
City, The (film), 275–276
City Housing Corporation (CHC), 234, 235, *236*, 237, 248, 274, 358n37
City Planning Commission, 296, 298, 304
Civilian Conservation Corps (CCC), 269
Civil War, U.S., 68, 80, 86, 91, 95–97, 104, 120, 192
Civil Works Administration, 261

Clarenceville, 107, 114
Clarke, Gilmore D., 289
Clarke, Reeves and Company, 194, 195
Classis of Amsterdam, 23, 26, 33
Clement, Henry, 170
Clinton, DeWitt, 48
Cock, Townsend D., 178
Coe, Benj., 6
Cohen, Marvin, 305
Colden, Charles S., 31
College Point, 56, 79–80, 89, 92, 106, 112, 119–120, *121*, 147–149, 169, 193
Committee of Forty, 201–203, 211, 214
Committee of Twenty on Street and Outdoor Cleanliness, 129
Coney Island, 96–97, 137, 138–140, 150, 157, 196, 211, 265
Coney Island Jockey Club, 136
Conover, John T., 193
Consolidation League of Brooklyn, 164
consolidation of New York: Brooklyn and Kings County, 164, 165–167, 173; commercial interests of, 163–164; Greater New York Commission and Bill, 168–174; map, *175*; and municipal improvements, 189, 191, 201; and Nassau County, 174–183; and Queens, 164, 168–174; voting results, *173*; and water resources, 184–187
Cooper, James Fennimore, 41
Cooper, Peter, 78, 87
Cooper, Theodore, 207, 208
cooperative housing, 299–300
Copland, Aaron, 275
Corbin, Austin, 96–98, 137, 198–200
Corbin Banking Co, 97
Cormier, Francis, 289
Cornbury, Viscount (Edward Hyde, 3rd Earl of Clarendon), 37–38
Corn Exchange Bank, 226
Corona: Armstrong in, 14, 295; ethnic changes documented, 317–322; Flushing Rail Road depot in, 77, 78; public housing in, 304, 305
Corona Dumps, 4, 13, 131, 262, 266, 271
Costello, John, 320
covenants (planning), 109, 231–232
Cox, Benjamin, 147
Crane, Ely and Company, 74–75
Crane, Jonathan, 75

Creedmoor, 96, 113
crime, 14, 151, 300, 303–304, 306–308
Crimmins, John D., 214
Croker, Richard, 203
Cross Island Parkway, 268
Cummins, Mary, 323–325
Cuomo, Mario, 303, 305, 307
Currier, Nathaniel: *Peytona and Fashion*, *135*; *Ravenswood, Long Island, Near Hallet's Cove*, *104*
Cutter, Bloodgood Haviland, 105, 178
Cypress Hills Cemetery, 96, 142
Czechs, 142–143, 316

Daily, Thomas V., 323
Daufkirch, Henry, 156
Davis, Alexander Jackson, 103
Dead Horse Bay, 128
Deans, John Stirling, 207
DeForest, Robert W., 228, 230
Degnon, Michael, 130, 269–271
Degnon Realty and Terminal Improvement Company, 270
De Hart, William, 40
De Lancy, Oliver, 41
Delaware & Hudson Coal Company, 78
Delaware Bridge Company, 194, 195
Democratic Party, 147, 176, 290
demolition: of historic buildings, 327, 329, 330, 346n20; slum clearance programs, 251, 252, 254, 257–258, 296
Denton, Daniel, 2, 7, 8
Denton, Nathaniel, 27
Depew, Chauncey M., 202
Deutschmann, Frederick, 157
Dickinson, Jacob M., 214
Dick-Meyer Corporation, 252
Dinkins, David, 324
Diogenes Brewing Company, 219
Ditmars, Abram D., 193
diversity: in Community Board 4, 317–322; demographic changes in, 56–58, *60*, 286, 289, 299, 312–317, *313–315*, 318; educational curriculum on, 322–325; and immigration after 1965, *313–315*, 314–317; Lindsay's approach to increasing, 301–307; of New Netherland, 19–20; Queens as an exemplar of, 1; of Sunnyside Gardens, 235–236
Dobson, Betty, 36

Dodgers, 291–293
Dognan, Thomas, 34
Donck, Adriaen van der, *Map of New Netherlands, with a view of New Amsterdam*, 20
Dongan Charter, 167
Donnelly's Grove, 147
Doudney, Richard, 23
Doughty, Francis, 21
Douglas, William Proctor, 224
Douglas Manor, 224, 232, 316, 329, 330
Drexel, Morgan & Co, 95–97, 138, 195
Dreyfuss, Henry, 273
Drisius, Samuel, 33
Dromm, Daniel, 325
Dudley, E. T., 76
Dutchess (County), 34
Dutch Kills Creek, 76, 125
Dutch Reformed Church, 21, 22, 23, 26, 27
Dutch settlers and settlements, 2, 10, 19–20
Dutch West India Company, 19, 21, 22, 27–29

Eads, James B., 194–195, 207
Eastchester, 163, 179
East Elmhurst, 318–319
East New York, 85, 112, 119, 137, 227
East River: boats and ferries on, 56, 64, 69–70; Colonial settlements and travel along, 5, 10; geography, 2, 3, 4–5; industrialization along (*see* industrialization); railroad terminals on, 67, 72, 73, 86, 87, 89; Shore Road's demise, 104; wealthy suburban development along, 102–103. *See also* bridges
East River Drive, 264
East River Light Company, 103
East Williamsburgh (Ridgewood), 120, 126–127, 218–219. *See also* Ridgewood
economic development: building boom of the 1920s, 217–240, 251; and consolidation of New York, 163–164, 170; and the Fiscal Crisis of the 1970s, 308, 315–316, 327–328; and historic preservation, 326–330; and the New Deal (*see* New Deal); postwar prosperity, 281–284; Queensboro Bridge's effect on, 189–190, 217; and railroads, 65–66, 220–223
Ehret, George, 151, 152, 155, 157
Eisenhower, Dwight D., 31
Eisenhower Park, 9

Eisenstadt, Peter, 299, 300
Electchester, 297–298
Elevated Railway Company, 195
elevated railway lines, 116, 163, 227
Elias (ship), 33
Elmhurst, *317*; ethnic changes documented, 317–322; name change, 341n24; Newtown High School, 1, 320; Queens Boulevard, 309; suburban development in, 227. *See also* Newtown
Ely, Charles, 75
Embury, Aymar, II, 289
Emergency Housing Corporation, 247, 251
Emergency Public Works Commission, 262
Engelhardt, Theodore H., 252
Engineering Record, 203–204, 207, 208, 209, 210, 220
England, James H., 296
Enoch Dean (ferry), 76
Enterprise Hard Rubber Works, 120
Equitable Life Assurance Company, 248
Erie Canal, 10, 45–48, 51, 55
Everett, Richard, 27
Evergood, Philip: *The Story of Richmond Hill*, 109
evictions, housing, 241, 248–249, *249*, 254
E. W. Serrell and Son, 194
expressways, 274, 276–277, 281, 291. *See also* parkways

Family Welfare Society of Queens, 243
Farley, James A., 290
Farmingdale, 92
Farrington, Edward, 25
Far Rockaway, 137, *138*, 139
Far Rockaway Branch Railroad Company, 90
Fashion Race Course (National Race Course), 135
Faubus, Orval, 31
Favicchio, John, 304
Feake, Tobias, 24–25
Federal Housing Administration (FHA), 247, 254
Fernandez, Joseph, 323, 325
Ferretti, Fred, 311
ferries: and the Dongan Charter, 167; and the Flushing Rail Road, 69–72, 76, 77, 79–80; and the LIRR, 64, 65, 66, 68; and suburban development, 102, 105–106

Ferriss, Hugh, 291
fertilizer industry, 80–87, 127, 128
Fire Island, 5, 95
fires: from industrial sites, 125–126; and railroad construction, 67–68
First Mortgage Guarantee Company, 226
Firth of Forth (bridge), 189, *190*, 203
fishing industry, 125
Fisk, George B., 67
Fiske, Haley, 234
Fitch, Ashbel P., 182
Fitzgerald, Ella, 14, 295
Fitzgerald, F. Scott, 4, 216, 271
Flack, Audrey, 34, 36
Flatbush (Mitwout), 20, 33, 54, 166
Flatlands, 166–167
Flatlands (originally Amersfoort), 20, 33, 54
Flower, Roswell P., 171
Floyd Bennett Field (airport), 128
Floyd-Jones, Elbert, 178
Flushing: abolition in, 56–58; and consolidation of New York, 170, 173, 174, 180, 181; demographics, 61, 69, 316; historic buildings, 329; home construction in, 227; as a new Queens township, 34; New York and Flushing Railroad, 78–80; nursery industry, 48–53, 69, 76; *The Pageant of Flushing Town*, 30; public housing in, 304; Quakers in, 10, 23–32, 56–58; steamboats serving, 69–70; Sunday closings in, 147; as Vlissingen, 21, 24; wealth in, 69
Flushing, North Shore & Central Railroad Company, *94*, 94–95
Flushing and North Side Railroad, *88*, 89–90, 92, 93
Flushing Bay, 4, 269–271
Flushing Bay Improvement Company, 270
Flushing Cemetery, 142
Flushing Creek, 4–5, 270, 271
Flushing Female Association, 56
Flushing Horticultural Society, 50
Flushing Journal: on consolidation of New York, 168, 170, 174, 178–179; on industrial pollution, 127; on leisure activities, 141, 143; on railroads, 68, 69, 70, 71, 72–73, 75–76, 77, 81, 83; on suburbs in Queens, 117
Flushing Meadows: industrial park development plans, 130–131, 269–271; as a landfill ("Corona Dumps"), 4, 13, 262, 271; as UN site, 285, 290–291; as World's Fairs site, 4, 272
Flushing Meadows-Corona Park: Grand Prix race planned for, 329–330; Moses's plans for, 285, 289–291; neglect of, 293–295; opening and attractions, 293; preservation and development, 326; topography, 4; U.S. Open in, 230, 287, 295, 326
Flushing Meeting House, 29, *30*, 42, *42*
Flushing Rail Road Company, 68–69, 72–78, *79*, 85, 86, 135
Flushing Remonstrance, 25–26, 30–32
Flushing River Park, 271–272
Flushing Suburban Civic Association, 304
foreclosures, 241, 248–249
Forest Hills: Forest Hills Gardens, 228–231, *229*, 238; Forest Hills-Kew Gardens Apartment Owners Association, 250; low-income housing, 307; scatter-site housing in, 303, 305–307; West Side Tennis Club, 230, 295
Forest Hills Diary, 303
Forest Park, 109
Forth Bridge, Scotland, 189, *190*, 203
Fort James, 33
Fort Orange, 33
Fort Pond Bay, 97, 99
Fort Totten, 330
Foster, George E., 304
Fowler, Oliver, 107
Fox, Charles, 85
Fox, George, 29
fox chases, 136
Fox Oaks, 29
Francis Lewis Boulevard, 268
freedom of conscience, 21–25, 37–38. *See also* religious freedom
Freeman, Pliny, 103, 193
Fresh Kills landfill, 131
Fresh Meadows, 14, 285, 287–289, *288*, 304
Fresh Meadows Country Club, 287
Fresh Pond, 89, 96, 113
Friedan, Betty, 286, 287
Frugal Housewife, The (Child), 103
fruit tree nurseries, 49–52
Fuller, Buckminster, 293
Fulton Ferry, 54, 74, 135
Fulton Market Slip, 56
Fulton Street, 74, 77, 116
Funke, Herman, 149, 193

Funke, Hugo, 149
Furman, William E., 89
Furman's Island, 89
Future of Jamaica Bay, The (Parks Department), 266, 268
Future of Us All, The (Sanjek), 317–322

Gale, Cyrus B., 183
gambling, 158, 159
garbage disposal and dumping, 128–131, 266, 268–271
garden apartments, postwar, 284–289
garden cities, 227–236
Garden City, 9, 91–92, 107
Garden City Cathedral, 107
Garkowski, John, 325
Garvin, Alex, 231
Gateway National Park, 268
Gateway National Recreation Area, 140
Gay and Lesbian Teachers Association, 323
gay rights, 323–325
Gazetteer of the State of New York (Gordon), 8
Geipel, August, 157
Geipel, Wilhelmina, 157
Gelfand, Bertram R., 303
George, Henry, 114
George III, King of England, 39
Georger, David Robinson, 67
German American Citizens Association, 196–197
Germans: contributions and influence, 89, 120, 121, 127, 193, 196–197, 219; leisure activities, 96, 142, 147, 148, 157; neighborhoods, 79, 235, 316, 318
Gibbons, Sarah, 23
Gilded Fox (ship), 27
Gil Hodges Bridge, 128, 266
Gillespie, Dizzie, 142
Gillette, George L., 147
Gilmore, Quincy A., 193
Glazer, Nathan, 303, 315
Gleason, Patrick Jerome, 142, 146–147, 174, 186
Glendale, 113, 311, *312*, 320
Glenn, Alberta, 234
Glenn, John M., 229, 230
Glen Oaks Village, *285*, 285, 287
Gold, David, 36
Goode, John, 124

Goodman, Walter, 302
Goodyear, Charles, 79, 120
Gordon, Thomas, 8
Gowanus, 20
Graham, Elizabeth Jennings, 142
grain and grain mills, 8, 43, 45, 51, 52, 53
Grand Central Parkway, 264, 272, 291
Grand Street Park, 144–145
Grauer (J. Geo.) Brewery, 219
Graves, Roswell, 190
Gravesend, 23, 40, 54, 167
Great Britain: Colonial era English settlements, 10, 19–23, 29, 32–34, 133; English garden cities movement, 228, 232, 234, 238, 274; Revolutionary occupation, battles and plunder, 37–41
Great Depression, 241–259; and the business community, 243–247; impact of, 241–243, *242*; New Deal and the housing crisis, 247–253; Queensbridge Houses project, 253–259; taxation on houses during, 228
Greater New York: Commission and Bill, 168–174; map, *175*. See also consolidation of New York
Greater New York Union Terminal Railroad, 199
Great Gatsby, The (Fitzgerald), 4, 216, 271
Great Lakes, 47
Great Migration, 13
Great Society, 15, 301–302
Greeks, 316
Green, Andrew Haswell, 2, 168–169
Green, Richard, 322–323
Green Memories (Mumford), 234–235
Greenport, 64, 66, 67, 95
Green-Wood Cemetery, 141
Gresser, Lawrence, 210, 211
Griswold, Frank Gray, 9
Grosjean, Florian, 120, 329
Gross and Lemmerman (firm), 236
Gross-Morton Company, 287
Gruen, Victor, 299
Guinea (ship), 33
Gutwasser, Johannes, 22
Guyanans, 316
G. X. Mathews Company, 219, 237, 239

Hale, Nathan, 41
Halletts Cove, 102

Hallett's Cove Gardens, 252
Halsey, B. S., 192
Halsey, Stephen A., 102
Hammack, David C., 163
Hammel, Louis, 137
Hammels Houses, 296
Hamptons, 95
Harlem, 263
Harlem River Houses, 253
Harriman, Averell, 31–32
Harrison, William Henry, 176
Harrison and Abramovitz, 291
Harris White Lead & Zinc Company, 125
Harris Zinc and Lead Company, 103
Hart, Edward, 24–26
Hart-Cellar Act, 15, 314
Harvey, George U., 244, 245, 254, 256
Havemeyer, Henry, 94
Head of the Fly (Meadow Lake), 4
Heard, Nathaniel, 40
Hecht, Robert A., 328
Hell Gate Bridge, *221*, 221–222, *264*
Helmsley-Spear, 289
Hempstead: English settlement of, 10, 21, 23; and Nassau County formation, 172, 178, 179–180, 183; as a new Queens township, 34; Patriots break away from, 39; railroads in, 91, 92
Hempstead and Rockaway Railroad, 91
Hempstead Harbor, 4
Hempstead Lake, 184
Hempstead Plains, *7*, 7–9, 64, 91–92
Henry Flad and Company, 194
Hewitt, Abram S., 167
Hicks, Valentine, 64
Hicksville, 64, 65, 66
highways. *See* expressways; parkways
Hill, David B., 168
Hinsdale, Elizur Brace, 78–79, 86, 88–89, 90, 92, 94, 199–200
Hirschman, Stuart, 254
Hispanics, 15, 315, 318, 319, 320, 324
historic district designations, 329, 330
historic preservation, *42*, 103, 120, 326–330
Historic Preservation in Queens (Kroessler and Rappaport), 328
History of Brooklyn (Stiles), 54
History of College Point, A (Hecht), 328
History of Long Island (Prime), 134

History of the Town of Flushing (Waller), 56–57
Hochul, Kathy, 222
Hodge, Henry W., 209, 210
Hodgson, Robert, 23–24
Holland, Michael P., 137
Hollis, 115
Home Builder on Long Island (LIRR), 223
homeownership, 15, 248
Home Owners' Loan Corporation (HOLC), 249
Homeyer, Richard, 225
Hone, Philip, 136
Hoover, Herbert, 240, 242
Hoovervilles, 241, 358n2
Hopper, Edward, 216
Horn, A. E., 250
Hornbostel, Henry, 203, 216
Horne, Lena, 14
horse racing, 11, 116, 133–136, *135*
horses, 81, 84, 127, 128
horticulture, 48–53, 69, 76
hotels and resorts: in Averne by the Sea, 138–39, *139*; in College Point, 147; in North Beach, 150–159; Rail Road Hotel, 65; in the Rockaways, 6, 136–140; Sohmerville Hotel, 124
Houdini, Harry, 142
Housatonic River, 185
houses: row houses, 79, 109, 116, 219, 227, 230, 237, 283, 287, 329; single-family, 115–116, 227, 230, 232, 233, 236, 256, 273, 278, 281, 283, 321; semi-detached two-family, *219*; wood-frame, 12, 110, 113, 114, 219
housing: cooperative, 299–300; Depression's impact on, 241–259, *242*; evictions, 241, 248–249, *249*; garden apartments, 284–289; garden cities, 228–236; Garden City, 9, 91–92, 107; Lefrak City, 319; low-income, 219, 223, 233–240, 251, 295–296 (*see also* public housing; tenements); New Deal public housing programs, 14, 247–259; postwar, 281–289; racial discrimination in, 14, 286, 289, 298–300, 319; racial integration, 258–259, 297–307; railroad flats, 219; scatter-site, 301–307; surplus, 241, 250–251; tax and investment incentives, 227–228

Housing and Urban Renewal Task Force, 303, 305
Howard, Ebenezer, 234
Howe, Frank Ray, 244–246
Howe, William, 40
Huber, Otto, 138
Hudson Railroad, 70
Hudson River, 198–199
Hughes, Charles Evans, 214
Hunters Point: industrialization in, 120, 125; Queensboro Bridge's effect on, 220; railroad terminals, 68, 74–75, 77, 79, 85, 86, 89, 95, 113, 176; waterfront development, 326
Huntington, 178
Hutter, Walter J., 328

Ickes, Harold L., 251, 252, 253, 265
immigration: and Community Board 4, 317–322; increases in, after 1965, 15, 314–317; nineteenth and early twentieth centuries, 13, 58, 60–61. *See also specific nationalities and ethnic groups*
Immigration and Nationality Act of 1965 (Hart-Cellar Act), 15, 314
imperialism, 36–37
incineration, 130
indebtedness, 180–182, *181*
Independent Press, 74
India Rubber Comb Company, 120
industrialization, 101, 103–104, 119–120; and consolidation, 164; industrial villages, 120–124; and pollution, 125–131; and waste disposal, 128–131
infrastructure. *See* public works
Inglis, John, 103
Innocents Abroad (Twain), 105
insurance companies, 228, 233
Interboro Parkway, 264
Interborough Rapid Transit (IRT), 199, 227
International Declaration of Human Rights, 290
International Town, City and Regional Planning Conference, 238
Irish, 36, 60, 91, 142, 235
Irving, Washington, 137
Island City (ferry), 71, 76, 78
Italians, 316, 318

Jackson, Andrew, 134
Jackson Heights, 228, 232–233, 238, *322,* 325, 329, 330
Jackson Heights (Karatzas), 328
Jamaica: and the Brooklyn and Jamaica Railroad Company, 52, 64; Colonial era, 2, 21, 23, 27, 34; and consolidation of New York, 172, 179, 180, 181; economic growth, 83; home construction in, 227; Jamaica Avenue, 308–309; Liberty Avenue, *15;* and LIRR, 61, 63–67, 83; Revolutionary era occupation, 37–38, 39, 40, 41
Jamaica: Rochdale Village, 14, 299–300, *300;* South Jamaica Houses, 257–259, *258,* 262, 296
Jamaica Avenue, 14
Jamaica Bay: annexation of, 164; commercial interests, 270; harbor development plan, 222–223; Moses's plans for, 266, 268; topographical history, 5–6; waste disposal in, 128–131
Jamaica Race Course, 136, 299
Jamaica South Realty Corporation, 222–223
James II, King of England. *See* York, Duke of
James Slip, 79
Javits, Jacob, 32
Jay Cook & Company, 94
jazz musicians, 14, 142, 295
Jerome, Leonard W., 136
Jews: Fort Hills Tennis Club closed to, 230; neighborhoods of, 235, 289, 303–304, 307, 316, 319; opposed to proposed statue, 36; Orthodox community, 324; and Rochdale Village, 299–300, 303; tolerance of, in New Netherlands, 21–22
Jogues, Isaac, 19
John L. Franklin (ship), 69
Johnson, Lyndon, 15, 301, 314
Johnson, Philip, 291
Jones Beach, 265
Jones Inlet, 5
J. P. Morgan Chase, 46
Juniper Valley Park, 262

Kalbfleisch family, 87
Karatzas, Daniel, 328
Kaufman Astoria Studios, 326
Kazan, Abraham, 299–300
Kells, William, 157–158

Kennedy, Alfred J., 270
Kerner Commission, 301
Kew Gardens, 109, 231–232, 238, 329
Kew Gardens (Lewis), 328
Kew Gardens Interchange, 264
Kieft, Willem, 21
King, Charles, 52
King, John A., 51–52, 65, 77, 80–81, 101, 136
Kingsbridge, 163, 303
Kings County: agricultural development and production, 52, 54, 166–167; Brooklyn as a township of, 64–65; and consolidation of New York, 164, 165–167, 173; Loyalist support in, 39, 43; maps, *46, 55, 114*; newly named, 34; population, 54, 55, *57, 58, 60,* 64–65
Kingsland Homestead, 49
Kissena Park, 50, *50*
Klaus, Susan, 231
Kneeland, Henry, 191
Koch, Ed, 306, 329
Koehler, Theodore, 179
Kohn, Robert D., 234, 251, 308
Koreans, 316
Kraemer, Henry, 147
Kremer, George W., 156
Kroessler, Jeffrey A., 328
Kroos, William, 328

LaGuardia, Fiorello, 30, 248, 249, 253, 257, 261, 265
LaGuardia Airport, 159, 262, 268
Lalance, Charles, 119–120, 329
Lamb, Thomas W., 329
landfills, 4, 13, 128–131, 262, 266, 271
landmark buildings, *42,* 103, 120, 326–330, 347n7
Landmarks Preservation Commission, 328, 329
Law and Order Societies, 149
Lawrence, Edward A., 177
Leadon, Fran, 327
Lee, Charles, 40
Lefrak, Samuel, 319
Lefrak City, 14, 319
Lehman, Herbert H., 251, 252
Lent Homestead, 150
Lewis, Barry, 232, 328
Lewis, William, 183

Liberty Avenue Line, 227
libraries, 238, 287, 323
limited dividend corporations, 249, 251–253, 274, 297–298
Lindenauer, Geoffrey G., 329–330
Lindenthal, Gustav, 203, 216, 221, 222
Lindenwood, 304
Lindsay, John V., 293, 295, 300–307
Linnaean Botanic Garden, 49, 69
LIRR. *See* Long Island Railroad
Litchfield, Electus B., 80
Little Neck, 316
Little Neck Bay, 4, 164, 224
Little Neck Hills, 223
Little Rock high school desegregation, 31
Littleton, Martin W., 211–212
Locke, John, 89
Lockwood, Benjamin A., 90
Logue, Ed, 303
Longfellow, Henry Wadsworth, 137
Long Island: agricultural industry, 80–81; canals and development, 45–48; Colonial era, Dutch and English settlements, 2, 20, 21, 32–34; Colonial era, self-government in, 32–34, 36–39; and consolidation of New York, 164–165, 174–187; geography, 2–9, *7*; North Shore, 4, 56, 105–106; promotional booklet, 95, 106–107, 108, 109; and Queens, 1–2; and railroads (*see under* railroads); Revolutionary era, 39–43; roads, 53, 56, 92, 262; South Shore, 5, 47–48, 63, 184, 187; suburbs (*see* suburbanization); water resources, 54–56, 184–187. *See also specific counties and towns*
Long Island & Where to Go!! (LIRR), 95, 106–107, 108, 109
Long-Island Canal Company, 46–47
Long Island City: blue laws in, 146; and consolidation of New York, 168–169, 172–180, 186; county courthouse built in, 178; development of, 85; German immigrants in, 197; housing, 233, 237; indebtedness in, 180; industrialization in, 123, 125, 127; postwar description of, 284; and Queensboro Bridge, 193, 194, 197, 199, 212, 217, 220
Long Island City Savings Bank, 226
Long Island City Star: on consolidation, 165, 168–169; index, 328; on industrialization,

123–124; on Queensboro Bridge, 197, 210, 211; on weekend visitors, 146, 150–151
Long Island Democrat, 65–66, 106, 190–191
Long Island Historical Society, 175
Long Island Press, 254
Long Island Railroad (LIRR), 11, 61, 63–68; agricultural products carried by, 80–85; bankruptcy and consolidation, 93–99, *97,* 113; bridge connection to Manhattan, 196, 198–200; challenges to, 86, 88–91; economic growth from, 61, 63–67, 220–223; fires caused by, 67–68; *Home Builder on Long Island,* 223; *Long Island & Where to Go!!,* 95, 106–107, 108, 109; *Old Jamaica LIRR Station, 98;* Pennsylvania Station and modernization, 220–221, 223; state assistance of, 66; suburban growth along, 11, 112–113; "White Line," 90
Long Island Star-Journal, 32
Long Island State Parks Commission, 262
Lord, Samuel, 61, 76
Lord & Taylor (department store), 61, 308
Lost New York (Silver), 327
Lott Manor, *108*
Louis Armstrong Stadium, 295
Lovelace, Francis, 39, 133
Lowery, Archibald H., 191
Luckman, Charles, 291
Ludlam, James H., 183
lumber industry, 68
Lundy, James A., 31
Lutheran Cemetery, 96, 142
Lutherans, 20, 22
Lyons, James A., 290

MacDougall, Edward Archibald, 210, 232
Machpelah cemetery, 142
MacKaye, Benton, 234
Macy's (department store), 308, 309
Making of an American, The (Riis), 111
Man, Albon Platt, 107–108, 231–232
Manes, Donald, 329–330
Manhasset, 106–107
Manhasset Bay, 4
Manhattan: as Colonial-era New York County, 34, *46;* and consolidation of New York, 165–169; demographics, 164, 217; and the Queensboro Bridge, 196, 198–200, 212–213; real estate in the 1920s,
238–239, *239;* and the Triborough Bridge, 263, 264
Manhattan (film), 216
Manhattan and Queens Traction Company, 225
Manhattan Avenue Bridge, 75
Manhattan Bridge, 202, 203, 216
Manhattan Company, 46
Mann, Frank, 237
Manship, Paul, 295
manure industry, 80–87, 127, 128
Marchi, John, 306–307
Marine Park Authority, 128, 262
Marine Parkway Bridge (Gil Hodges Bridge), 128, 262
Marine Pavilion, 136–137
Martin (ship), 33
Maspeth, 21, 77, 320
Maspeth (Stankowski), 328
mass transit, 117, 227, 232, 307. *See also* subways
Mather, Cotton, 37–38
Mathews, A. F., 239
Mathews, Gustave Xavier, 219
Mathews (G. X.) Company, 219, 237, 239, 240
Mathews Model Flats, 219, 233
Matinecock County, 183
McAloney, J., 124
McAneny, George, 272
McCarthy, John A. ("Fishhooks"), 270
McClellan, George, 213
McCormick, Richard C., 169
McGowan, Patrick F., 211
McKim, Mead & White, 107, 220
McMahon, Father, 69
Meadow Lake, 4
Megapolensis, Dominie Johannes, 22
Menai Strait Bridge, 191
Mespat (Maspeth), 21
Messenger, Andrew, 27
Messinger, Ruth, 324
Metropolitan Jockey Club, 116, 136
Metropolitan Life Houses, 228, 233–235
Metropolitan Sewerage Commission, 129
middle class: integration of neighborhoods of, 301–307; nineteenth-century railroad suburbs, 104–117; postwar public housing for, 297; twentieth-century suburbs and garden cities, 223–240

Middle Village, 142, *143*, 227, 308, 320
Midwout, 33
Miller, William, 150
Miller, William G., 183
Milner, Michael, 24
Mineola, 91
Ministry Act of 1693, 37
Mitchill, Samuel L., 3, 6, 8
model tenements, 233–234, 236–238
Montauk, 97–98
Monteverde, William, 144, 145
Moore, Aldean, 304
Moore, Robert, 304–305
moraine, terminal, 2–5, *4*, 108, 113, 115, 166, 184
Morgan, J. Pierpont, 138
Morris, F. P., 170
Morris, Gouverneur, Jr., 76
Morrisania, 163
Morris Grove, 96
Morris Park, 113–114, *114*
mortgage foreclosures, 241, 242, 248–249
mortgage relief, 249–250
Moses, Robert, 261–279; career and achievements, 13, 261–262; criticism of, 264–265; Jacob Riis Park, 267, 268; New Deal projects, 262–265; postwar projects, 281, 285, 289–295; on public housing, 254; Rockaway Improvement, 262, 265–268; Shea Stadium, 291–293; Triborough Bridge, 245, 246–247, 262–265, *264*; World's Fair (1939), 13, 262, 265, 272–279; World's Fair (1964), 291–295
Mr. New York (Whalen), 274–275
Muistes, 20
Mumford, Lewis, 234–235, 236, 275, 288, 289, 299, 357n25, 358n37
municipal services: and consolidation, 169; postwar shortages, 284, 287, 308, 319–322
Museum of Science and Technology, 291

NAACP (National Association for the Advancement of Colored People), 289
Nadler, Jerrold, 222
Nassau County: formation of, 174–183; naming of, 183; postwar growth, 281–282, *282*; suburban development in, 117
Nast, Thomas: *Something That Did Blow Over—November 7, 1871*, 172

National Advisory Commission on Civil Disorders, 301
National Association of Real Estate Boards, 247
National Association of Retail Lumber Dealers, 247
National Housing Act (NHA), 247, 250
"National Millennium Trail," 317
National Race Course, 77, 135
National Recovery Administration (NRA), 246
Native Americans, 20
Nature Conservancy, 9
Nefsky, Peter, 320
Netherlands, 21–22
New Amsterdam, 2, 10, 19, 20; Dutch settlement of, 19, 20, 21; English takeover and renaming, 29, 32–34; map, *20*; Quakers in, 24, 26, 29, 32–33. *See also* New York (City)
New Deal: business community's resistance to, 244–253; public housing, 247–259; public works programs, 12–13, 244–247, 261–279
New England: Hell Gate Bridge's connection to, 222; Puritans, 10, 23; Quakers in, 23, 26; religious toleration and growth in, 19, 20
New Haarlem, 33
New Haven Railroad, 70
New Jersey, 125, 129, 130, 198, 222
New Lots, 54, 167
Newmarket, 133
New Netherland, 7, 10, 19, 133; economic pattern of growth, 19–20; English control of, 21, 30, 32; map, *20*; religions in (*see* religious freedom). *See also* New Amsterdam
Newtown: Astoria as a village within, 102; and consolidation of New York, 171, 172, 179–181, 186; demographics, nineteenth century, 61, 318; and the Flushing Rail Road, 73, 76, 77; German immigrants in, 197; *Landscape*, *58*; name change, 341n24; as a new Queens township, 34; Revolutionary soldiers quartered in, 41. *See also* Elmhurst
Newtown Creek: canals through, 222, 270; ferries along, 72; geographical features,

3–4; industrialization along, 101, 120, 125–127, 341n24; railroads along, 73–76, 85, 86, 89, 113, 142; settlement near, 21
Newtown Register, 125, 137, 171, 181, 201, 202, 220, 225
New Utrecht, 33, 54
New York (City): access of agricultural markets to, 46–48; annexation to, 163–165; compared to other cities, 1890, 164, *164*; consolidation (*see* consolidation of New York); Department of City Planning, 298; Department of Docks and Ferries, 130; Department of Sanitation, 130; population, nineteenth century, 53–54, *57, 58, 60, 164,* 164–165; population, twentieth century, 170, 217, *218, 225, 226,* 308, *315,* 315–316; Queens relationship, 1–2, 10, 51–53, 61; real estate valuation (1920s), 238–239, *239*; suburbs (*see* suburbanization; *specific towns and regions*)
New York (County), 34, *46. See also* Manhattan
New York (Province of): county divisions, 10, 34, *35*; English possession and name change, 29, 32–34; maps, *35, 46*; self-government in, 37–39
New York (State): Chamber of Commerce, 167–168; Committee on Discrimination in Housing, 298; Erie Canal's effect on farms in, 45, 46; New Deal social reforms in, 246
New York & Flushing Railroad, 78–80, 89
New York and Long Island Bridge Company, 192–195, 198, 200
New York and Long Island Railroad Company, 198–199
New York and Queens County Bridge Company, 193, 353n110
New York & Queens County Railway, 212
New York and Queens County Railway Company, 220
New York and Rockaway Railroad, 90
New York Architectural Terra Cotta Works, 103, 125
New York Association for the Improvement of the Breed of Horses, 133–134
New York City Housing Authority (NYCHA): New Deal public housing,

251–259, *255, 258*; postwar public housing, 296–297, 299
New York City Landmarks Law, 327, 365n27
New York City Parks Commissioner, 262. *See also* Moses, Robert
New York Connecting Railroad, 221
New Yorker, 288
New York harbor, 163–164
New York Herald, 106
New York Iron & Chemical Company, 125
New York Jockey Club, 136
New York Life Insurance Company, 287, 288, 289
New York Panorama (WPA), 277
New York Post, 37, 165–166
New York Sumac Extract Company, 103
New York Times: on curriculum for diversity, 324; on Forest Hills, 302; on fox chases, 136; on postwar Queens, 283, 284, 311; on public behavior, 145–146, 154–155, 158; on Queensboro Bridge opening, 213, 214; on Rikers Island, 129; Steinway interview, 148
New York Times Magazine, 291, 303
New York Tribune, 198
New York World, 103
New York World's Fairs. *See* World's Fair (1939); World's Fair (1964)
Nicolls, Richard, 33–34, 133
Niederstein's Restaurant, 142, *143*
Niven, Malcolm W., 199
Noble, William, 25
Noble estate, 125
Norfolk County, 183
North American Review, 97
North Beach, 148, 149–159, *154*
North Hempstead, 177, 178, 179, 183
North Richmond Hill (Kew Gardens), 109
North Shore, Long Island, 4, 56, 105–106
North Side Railroad, 105
Norwich & Worcester Railroad, 64
nursery industry, 48–53, 69, 76
NYCHA. *See* New York City Housing Authority

Ocean County, 178
ocean dumping, 129–130
O'Connor, John, 323–325
O'Dwyer, William, 290, 297, 298

Ogden, Samuel Gouverneur, 103
Olmsted, Frederick Law, 50, 109, 231
Olmsted Brothers (firm), 228
O'Malley, Walter, 292
Onderdonk, Henry, Jr., 42
Onderdonk House, 4, *42*
Open Housing Center of New York, 289
Orange County, 34
Orchard Beach, 265
Ottendorfer, Oswald, 193
Our Community, Its History and People (Hutter et al*)*, 328
Oyster Bay, 4, 34, 178, 179, 183

Pageant of Flushing Town, The, 30
Palmer, Francis, 103
Panic of 1837, 66
Panic of 1873, 94
Parents Magazine, 287
parks: ball playing and drinking in, 142–149; Central Park, 49–50, 146; Flushing Meadows-Corona Park (*see* Flushing Meadows-Corona Park); Marine Park, 128; picnic grounds, 11, 96, 124, 141–144, 147–153, 219
parkways: of the New Deal, 6, *82,* 262, 266, 268, 272; postwar, 281, 291; Pretzel interchange, 264, 285, 291. *See also* expressways
Parkway Village, 285–286, *286,* 287
Parkway Village Community Association, 286
Parshall, Charles, 103
Parsons, Anna, 30
Parsons, Bertha, 30
Parsons, Robert E., 49
Parsons, Samuel Bowne, 49, 69, 71
Parsons, Samuel Bowne, Jr., 49
Parsons and Sons Company nursery, 49–50, *50,* 76
Patchogue, 87
Peak at Richmond Hill through the Keyhole of Time, A (Kroos), 328
Pearsall, James B., 178, 183
Peck, Curtis, widow of, 77
Pelham, 163
Penn, William, 10, 29
Pennsylvania Railroad, 98–99, 220–221
Pennsylvania Station, 116, 220–221, 327

Penny Bridge, 77
People's Recreation Grounds, 146–147
petroleum industry, 125–126
Petry, George, 146
Phenix Bank, 48
Phillips, Wendell, 178
Phoenix Bridge Company, 207, 208
piano industry, 120–124, *124,* 347n7
picnic grounds, 11, 96, 124, 141–144, 147–153, 219
Picture of New-York, The (Mitchill), 3, 6, 8
Pierson, H. R., 84
Pike, Benjamin, 122
planned communities. *See* garden apartments, postwar; garden cities; Garden City
Platt, Thomas C., 147, 174, 202, 203
Plunkitt, George Washington, 202
police, 321
political corruption, 146–147, 180, 182, 186, 202–203, 329–330
pollution, industrial, 125–131
Pomonok Houses, 297
Poppenhusen, Adolph, 149
Poppenhusen, Alfred, 94, 149
Poppenhusen, Conrad: College Point development, 79–80, 119, 120; railroad ventures, 89, 90, 92–95, 97, 112
Poppenhusen, Herman C., 94, 193
Poppenhusen Institute, 80, 120
population tables: 1790–1860 (Queens County), *59*; 1790–1860 (New York, Kings, and Queens) by race, *60*; 1790–1860 (New York, Kings, and Queens) growth, *58*; 1850–1892 (Queens County), *177*; 1890–1930 (New York City), *218*; 1910–1915 (New York City), *226*; 1910–2020 (Queens and Nassau Counties), *282*; 1940–2020 (Queens) racial and ethnic change, *313–314*; 1960–2000 (New York City) foreign-born population, *315*
Port Authority of New York and New Jersey, 223
Portugal, 34, 36
Power Broker, The (Caro), 262, 263, 265
Powers, William, 154
Pratt, Charles, 125
Presbyterians, 37–38

Pretzel interchange, 264, 285, 291
Prime, Nathaniel S., 134
Prince, William, 5, 49, 50–51, 76
prisons, 128–130
private sector: beach development, 152; as major builders of Queens homes, 248; public housing in violation of competition with, 298; public housing opposed by, 244–253, 256; road construction, 53
Procaccino, Mario, 307
Professional Golfers Association Championship, 287
Prohibition era, 155
Prospect Park, 146
Protestants, 19
public art, 34, 36–37
public housing, 14; business community's resistance to, 247–252; middle-income, 297; in middle-income neighborhoods, 301–307; postwar, 295–307; Queensbridge Houses, *215*, 253–259, *255*; South Jamaica Houses, 257–259, *258*
public rowdiness and intoxication, 57, 71, 141, 144–145, 150–151, 154, 156, 158
Public Voice, 77
public works: expressways and parkways, *82*, 262, 266, 268, 272, 274, 276–277, 291; of the New Deal, 12–13, 244–247, 261–279; Rockaway Improvement, 262, 265–268; Triborough Bridge, 245, 246–247, 262–265, *264*. *See also* bridges; parks; roads
Public Works Administration (PWA), 247, 263, 269
Public Works Emergency Housing Corporation (division of PWA), 247, 251, 253
Puerto Ricans, 297, 302, 319
Puritans, 10, 19, 20

Quakers: and abolition, 56–58; and the Flushing Remonstrance, 25–26, 30–32; persecution of, 23–29; tolerance and Bowne's legacy, 27–32
Quebec Bridge, 206–209
Queen Anne style houses, 109, 115
Queens: agricultural production, 48–53, 80–81, 101–102, 167; Colonial era settlements, 10, 19, 20–21, 34, *35*, 133; Committee of Forty, 201–203, 211, 214; Community Board 4, 317–322; and consolidation of New York, 1–2, 164, 168–174, 179–182, *181*; county division, 176–183; first skyscraper in, 226; geography, 2–9, *55*, 115; historic preservation and landmarks, *42*, 103, 120, 326–330, 347n7; industrialization in, 101, 103–104, 119–131; maps, *46*, *55*, *114*; namesake of, and controversial statue, 34, 36–37; New York City relationship, 1–2, 10, 51–53, 61; population, nineteenth century, 54, 55–56, *58*, *59*, *60*, 64–65, 169, *177*, *218*; population, twentieth century, 1, *218*, *226*, *282*, 308, 312–317, *313–314*, *315*; Queensboro Bridge's impact on growth, 189–190; railroad's importance to (*see* railroads); Revolutionary era, 39–43; rural-urban divisions within, 176, 179–180; thematic history, 10–16; tricentennial, 34; urbanization, 10–11, 186–187; water resources, 186–187
Queensboro Bridge, 187, 189–216, 262; aesthetics, 216, 217; Blackwell's Island Bridge name changed to, 210; design and construction, 203–210; opening, 211–216; photos, *205*, *206*, *212*, *215*; plans and proposals, 190–200; political delays, 201–203; safety concerns, 209–210; trains on, 227
Queensboro Corporation, 232–233
Queensboro Plaza, 227
Queensborough (magazine), 225–226, 244, 246
Queens Borough Hall and Court House, 262
Queensborough Line, 227
Queens Borough Public Library, 238, 287, 328
Queens Botanical Garden, 293
Queens Boulevard, 264
Queensbridge Houses, *215*, 253–259, *255*, 297
Queens Chamber of Commerce, 223, 243–247, 249, 250, 252, 265
Queens Council of Social Welfare, 255
Queens County Agricultural Fair, 51
Queens County Agricultural Society, 52, 80, 101
Queens County Board of Supervisors, 171, 179, 180
Queens County Court House, 177–178
Queens County Farm Museum, 13, *82*, 287
Queens County Hounds, 9

Queens County Review, 182, 184
Queens Historical Society, 49
Queens Jockey Club, 136
Queens-Midtown Tunnel, 244, 247, 262
Queens Museum, 293, 326
Queens Share the Work Committee, 243
Queens Village, 39, 115–116, 328
Queens Zoo, 293
Quinn, Hugh, 256

race: demographic changes, 15, 56–58, *60*, 286, 289, 299, 312–318, *313–314*, *315*; housing discrimination, 286, 289, 297–301, 319; integration, 14, 31–32, 258–259, 297–307; and postwar public housing, 295–307; white flight of the 1970s, 300, 301, 303, 314, 316, 319
racetracks, 11, 116, 133–136, *135*
railroad companies: Baltimore and Ohio Railroad, 96; Brooklyn and Jamaica Railroad Company, 52, 64; Central Railroad of Long Island, 91–93; Far Rockaway Branch Railroad Company, 90; Flushing, North Shore & Central Railroad Company, *94*, 94–95; Flushing and North Side Railroad, 89–90, 92, 93; Flushing Rail Road Company, 68–69, 72–78, *79*, 85, 86, 135; Hempstead and Rockaway Railroad, 91; Long Island Railroad (*see* Long Island Railroad (LIRR)); New York & Flushing Railroad, 78–80, 89; New York and Queens County Railway Company, 220; New York and Rockaway Railroad, 90; New York Connecting Railroad, 221; North Side Railroad, 105; Norwich & Worcester Railroad, 64; Pennsylvania Railroad, 98–99, 220–221; Rockaway Railroad, 90–91; Southern Railroad Company of Long Island, 94–95; South Side Railroad (SSRR), 85–91, *87*, 94
railroads, 63–99; agricultural freight, 80–81; bankruptcy and consolidation, 80, 93–99, 112; commercial importance, 51, 52, 61, 63; competition among, 88–93; and economic development, 65–66, 70, 73, 83; elevated railway lines, 227; finances, 73, 76–80, *79*, 86, 87, 89–99, *94*; leisure business, 96, 137, 139; manure and fertilizer transport, 80–85, 87; modernization and electrification, 92, 99, 105, 220–223; newspaper trains, 95; and suburbanization, 101–102, 112–113 (*see also* suburbanization); Sunday service, 67, 68, 71–72, 79, 96; theater trains, 112–113
Rainey, Thomas, 195, 196–203, 214
Ramapo River, 185
Randalls Island, 262, 263
Rappaport, Nina, 328
Ravenswood, 103, *104*, 124–125
Ravenswood Bridge, 195, 201, 210
Ravenswood Houses, 296
Raynor, Preston, 67
real estate: Depression's impact on, 241–259; limited dividend corporations, 249, 251–253, 274, 297–298; rising land values in the 1920s, 225–228, 230, 238–240, *239*
Redfern Houses, 296
Red Hook Houses, 253, 254, 255
Regional Plan Association, 272
Regional Planning Association of America, 234
Register, 144
Rego Park, 316
religious freedom, 10, 19–32; of Catholics, 69; in the Charter of Liberties and Privileges, 34; and the Flushing Remonstrance, 25–26, 30–32; and Jews, 21–22; and Lutherans, 22; prayer in schools, 69; Quakers' struggle for, 23–32; and Sabbath travel, 67, 68, 71–72, 79
Remsen, James S., 137
Rensselaerwyck, 33
Republican Party, 174, 176
resorts. *See* hotels and resorts
retail stores, 308–309
Revolution, American, 38–43
Rheinstein, Alfred, 254, 255, 256
Rhode Island, Quakers in, 23, 24, 26
Richards, Edward A., 250
Richmond, 34, *46*, 164
Richmond, Edward, 107, 108
Richmond Hill, 107–112, *108*, *111*, 113, 227
Richmond Hill Country Club, 109
Richmond Hill South, 116–117
Rickert-Finley Realty Company, 224
Ridgewood, 120, 126–127, 218, 219, 320, 330
Ridgewood Grove, 219

Ridgewood Reservoir, 55, 136, 184, 186
Riis, Jacob: *Our House in Winter, 111*; in Richmond Hill, 110–112, 346n20
Riis Park, 262, *267,* 268
Rikers Island, 128–130, 269
Rivera, Julio, 325
roads: after consolidation, 11, 189; early development of, 5, 53, 92; of Forest Hills, 231; New Deal funding of, 244, 245, 264, 268. *See also* expressways; parkways
Robbins, I. D., 303
Robinson, Jackie, 142
Rochdale Pioneers, 299
Rochdale Village, 14, 299–300, *300*
Rochester, NY, 46
Rockaway Railroad, 90–91
Rockaways: bungalow colonies, 139–140, *140*; Far Rockaway, 137, *138,* 139; Moses's Rockaway Improvement, 262, 265–268; postwar public housing, 296–297; railroads in, 90–91, 95; resorts and hotels, 6, 136–140, 150; Rockaway Beach, 180; Rockaway Beach Amusement Park / Playland, 140; Rockaway Beach Hotel, 137–138; Rockaway Improvement, 262, 265–268; topographical history, 5, 6
Rockefeller, Nelson, 281, 285, 290
Roe, Charles, 214
Roebling, John A., 191–192, 194, 196
Roebling, Washington, 194
Roosevelt, Franklin Delano, 12, 241, 257, 262, 265
Roslyn, 178
Rural Cemeteries Act, 141
Russell Sage Foundation, 228–230, 248, 357n25
Rustdorp (Jamaica), 21, 23, 27. *See also* Jamaica
Ruyven, Cornelis van, 33
Ryan and Parker, 204
Rye-Oyster Bay Bridge, 281

Sabbath. *See* Sunday restrictions
Sage Foundation Homes Company, 228–230, 248, 357n25
Sands, Tredwell, 69–70
Sanitary Commission, 91
Sanjek, Roger, 317–322
Saturday Evening Post, 289
Sauthier, Claude Joseph: *A chorographical map of the province of New York in North America,* 35
Schlesinger, A. P., 149
Schmittberger, Max, 213–214
schools: Children of the Rainbow Curriculum, 322–325; demand for, 284; in Elmhurst-Corona, 320; prayer in, 69; segregation in, 300
Schuetzen Park, 142, 211
Scott, John, 32
Scudder, P. Halsted, 183
Seaside Park, 137
Second Avenue Elevated, 227
seed trade, 83
self-governance, 32–34, 37–39
sexual orientation, 323–325
Seyfried, Vincent F., 67–68, 127, 328
Shannon, Joseph B., 245
Sharp, Thomas R., 95–96
Shea, John L., 202
Shea, William, 292
Shea Stadium, 291–293
Shelter Island, 95
Shinnecock Inlet, 5
Shulman, Claire, 37, 330
Silberman, Israel, 242–243
Silver, Nathan, 327
Simkhovitch, Mary Kingsbury, 257, 297
Skidmore, Owings and Merrill, 309
slavery: demographics (1790–1860), *60*; in Flushing, 56–58; proposed statue associated with, 36, 37
slum clearance programs, 251, 252, 254, 257–258, 296
Small Town in the Big City (Byers), 328
Smart, William, 78
Smith, Al, 142, 233
Smith, J. Lee, 103
Smits, Edward, 176
Snyder, C.B.J., 320
social services, 302
Society of Friends, 23, 24, 29, 56. *See also* Quakers
Sohmer Piano Company, 123–124, *124*
Soper, George A., 129
Southern Railroad Company of Long Island, 94–95
South Ferry, 80, 85

South Ozone Park, 316
South Shore, Long Island, 5, 47–48, 63, 184, 187
South Side Pavilion, 90
South Side Railroad (SSRR), 85–91, *87,* 94
Speedy, Kearny, 213
Sperr, Percy L.: *Queens: Little Neck Parkway—74th Avenue 1922-1927* (Queens County Farm Museum), *82*
Spooner, Alden, 175, 176–177
Standard Oil Company, 125
Stankowski, Barbara W., 328
Starr, Roger, 319
Staten Island, 33, 131, 265, 308
steamboats. *See* ferries
Stein, Clarence, 234, 275
Steinway, Henry Englehardt, 119
Steinway, William, 121–123, 148, 151, 193, 195, 199
Steinway and Sons Factory, 123
Steinway & Sons Piano Company, 120–123, 243, 329
Steinway Street, view of (1923), *12*
Steinway Village (lithograph), *122*
Steinweg family, 121
Stern, Robert A. M., 231
Stevens, Ebenezer, 102
Stevenson, James W., 209, 210
Stewart, Alexander Turney, 9, 91–92, 107
Stewart, Cornelia, 107
Stichman, Herman, 296
Stiles, Henry, 54, 81
Straus, Nathan, 254, 257
streetcars. *See* trolleys
street grid: of Brooklyn, 54; of Jackson Heights, 232–233; in Newtown, 77; Queens's lack of, 54, 61
Strong, James, 74–75
Strong, William L., 173
Stuyvesant, Peter: persecution of Quakers, 21–29; surrender to English, 32–33
suburbanization, 101–117; early twentieth century, 116–117, 223–240; East River wealthy retreats, 102–103; garden cities, 228–236; postwar, 281–284; railroad suburbs, 91–92, 104–116, 228–231, *229*; and subway lines, 228, 232; and transportation improvements, 101–102, 104–105, 116, 223–227, 232; wealthy suburbs, 69, 102–103; working-class suburbs, 113, 115, 116, 120; World's Fair's vision of, 272–279, 281, 283

subways: crowding on, 321; diversity on the 7 train, 316–317, *326*; Dual Subway System, 223, 227, 232; Queens Boulevard subway line, 244, 246; suburban development along, 228, 232

Suffolk County: canal company petitioned by, 47; and consolidation of New York, 178, 184; fires in, from LIRR, 67–68; formation, 34; Patriot support of, 39; water resources, 185

Sullivan, Tim ("Big Tim"), 116, 143–144, 147
Sulzberger, Arthur H., 290
Sulzer, William, 271
Sunday restrictions: on alcohol and ball playing, 141–149, 155, 159; and rail service, 67, 68, 71–72, 79, 96
Sunnyside Gardens, 228, 234–238, *236, 248–249, 249,* 250
Surf Pavilion, 137
Sutton, Percy, 305

Tammany Hall, 116, 143, 170, 171–172, 174, 182
taxation: during the 1920s building boom, 227–228, 233, 237, 239; and consolidation of New York, 166–167, 170, 171, 186; Depression-era, 246; and farming, 225
Taylor, Clarence, 303
temperance movement, 69, 71, 147, 155
tenements: construction of, and annexation, 163, 164; escape from, 13, 109, 121, 141; model tenements, 217, 219, 233–234, 236–238; "old law," 240, 358n49; slum clearance programs, 251, 252, 254, 257–258
Ten Mile River, 185
This Salubrious Spot (Wolfe), 328–329
Thomas, Andrew J., 233
Thompson, Abraham G., 47
Thorburn, Grant, 103
Throgs Neck Bridge, 281
Tillinghast, A. W., 287
tolls, turnpike, 53
Tompkins, Daniel, 134
Townsend, Henry, 27
Tredwell, Daniel M., 134, 175
Triboro Theatre, 329

Triborough Bridge, 245, 246–247, 262–265, *264*
Triborough Bridge Authority (TBA), 262, 263, 265
trolleys: and Queensboro Bridge, 220; service expansion, early 1900s, 225–226, *226*; trolley parties, 156–157
Trowbridge, Charles A., 193
Trumbull, John, 137
Tryon, William, 38
tunnels, 105, 113, 116, 166, 198–199
Twain, Mark, 105
Twentieth Century Fund, 319

Ulster County, 34
Umlie family, 257
unemployment: Depression-era, 241–243, 248, 251; New Deal job creation, 269
Union Course, 134
Union News Service, 95
Union Turnpike, 264
United Housing Foundation (UHF), 299–300
United Nations (UN), 285–286, 290–291
Unwin, Raymond, 234, 238
urbanization, 10–11, 102, 186–187
urban liberalism, 14, 15
Urquhart, William, 37
U.S. Bill of Rights, 31
U.S. census. *See* population tables
U.S. Department of Agriculture, 224
U.S. Department of Housing and Urban Development, 305
U.S. Open, 230, 287, 295, 326
U.S. Savings and Loan League, 247
U.S. Supreme Court, 129–130

Valley Stream, 184, 911
Vanderbilt, Cornelius, 64, 66, 68, 91, 195, 214
Vanderbilt, Jeremiah, Jr., 6
Vanderbilt, William K., 136
Van de Water, Lott, 183
Van Wyck, Robert, 201–202
Van Wyck Expressway, 274, 291
Van Zandt, Wyant, 224
Vaux, Calvert, 49
veterans, housing for, 297
Vlissingen, 21, 24. *See also* Flushing
Voorhees, Walker, Foley and Smith, 287
Vreeland, V. H., 240

Wade, Richard C., 301, 302
Wagner, Robert F., 142
Wagner, Robert F., Jr., 32, 142, 293, 298, 300, 327
Wagner-Steagall Housing Act, 253
Wainwright, William, 137
Wakefield, 163
Walker, James J., 263
Wallabout Bay, 20
Wallace, George, 183
Waller, Henry, 56–57
Walling, Henry Francis: *Topographical map of the counties of Kings and Queens, New York,* 55
Wall Street Journal, 37
Wards Island, 263
Washington, George, 40, 43, 49
water resources, 54–56, 184–187
Watson, Thomas J., 290
Waugh, Dorothy, 23
Weatherhead, Mary, 23
Weeping Beech Park, 49
Westchester, 34, 163, 164
West Farms, 163
West Flushing Land Company, 78
West Side Tennis Club, 230, *231,* 295
wetlands, 4, 120, 130–131, 269–271
Whalen, Grover, 270, 273, 274–275, 290
Wharton, Edith, 102, 104
White, Alfred T., 185
White, Norval, 327
White, Stanford, 107
White House Millennium Council, 317
Whitman, Walt, 7–8
Wilkins, Roy, 286
Willensky, Elliot, 327
William and Nicholas (ship), 33
Williams, William H., 210, 211
Williamsburg: annexation and name change, 54–55, 166; and mass transit, 158, 196
Williamsburg Bridge, 116, 200, 217–219, 227, 355n2
Williamsburgh, City of, 54–55, 56; railroad from Flushing to, 70–71, 74, 77; as terminal for SSRR, 86–87
Williamsburgh Times, 74
Williamsburgh Water Company, 54
Wiltwyck, 33

Winans, Anthony W., 103, 192
Winfield, 76, 77, 85
Winnick, Louis, 314
Winter, Gabriel, 69
Witzel's Point View Island resort, 147
Wolfe, Kevin, 328–329
women: delegates, 211; Flushing Female Association, 56; and statue of Queen Catherine controversy, 36–37
Wood, Silas, 41–42, 43
Woodhaven, 96, 119–120, 134
Woodhouse (ship), 23
Woodhull, Nathaniel, 40–41
Woodside: Boulevard Gardens, 252, *253*; public housing in, 304; Woodside Houses, 296; Woodside Water Company, 186
working class: affordable housing for, 219, 223, 233–240 (*see also* public housing; tenements); bridge's benefits to, 196–197; leisure spaces of, 11, 141–149; in North Beach, 148, 150–159; in the Rockaways, 138–140; suburban developments of, 113, 115, 116, 120, 122–124
Works Progress Administration (WPA), 109, 159, 257, 269

"World of Tomorrow." *See* World's Fair (1939)
World's Fair (1939), 13, 262, 265; anti-urban theme, 272–279; Democracity, 272, 273–275, 276; demolition of Aquacade, 330; Futurama (General Motors), 275–276, *276*, 281, 283; Road of Tomorrow (Ford), *277,* 277; site selection, 272; Town of Tomorrow, *278*, 278
World's Fair (1964), 291, 326; neglect of, 293–295; Tent of Tomorrow, 291, 294, *294*
World's Fair Corporation, 270
World-Telegram, 283
World War I, 271
World War II, 29, 116, 281, 315
Wright, Henry, 234
Wurster, Frederick W., 173
Wyckoff, William F., 232

Yonkers, 163
York, Duke of, 32, 33, 34

Zeckendorf, William, 291
Zetlin, Lev, 291
Ziegler, William, 113
zoning, 124, 321–322, 327

About the Author

JEFFREY A. KROESSLER (1952-2023) was a professor at the Lloyd Sealy Library of the John Jay College of Criminal Justice, City University of New York, and author of *Sunnyside Gardens: Planning and Preservation in a Historic Garden Suburb*; *The Greater New York Sports Chronology*; *New York, Year by Year: A Chronology of the Great Metropolis*; *Historic Preservation in Queens*; and other works.